Daily Devotionals for Women

Sitting at His Feet

Daily Devotionals for Women

Sitting at His Feet

Evaline Gore Echols

Wanda Gore Griffith

Mary Ruth Stone

Oleda Glenn Atkinson

Rebecca J. Jenkins

Shelby Aycock Harvell

Beverly Simmons Richardson

Pat Bradbury

Pat Delk Daugherty

Jackie Touchstone Walker

Kathy Sanders

Saundra Jennings Rose

Pathway
P·R·E·S·S

Second Printing

Scripture quotations marked *NIV* are from the Holy Bible, *New International Version* ®. *NIV* ®. Copyright © 1973, 1978, 1984 by International Bible Society. Used by permission of Zondervan Publishing House. All rights reserved.

Scripture quotations marked *NKJV* are from *The New King James Version*. Copyright © 1979,1980, 1982, Thomas Nelson Inc., Publishers.

Scripture quotations marked *RSV* are from the *Revised Standard Version* of the Bible. Copyright © 1946, 1952, 1971 by the Division of the National Council of the Churches of Christ in the U.S.A. Used by permission.

Scripture quotations marked *NASB* are from the *New American Standard Bible* ®. Copyright © The Lockman Foundation 1960, 1962, 1963, 1968, 1971, 1972, 1973, 1975, 1977. Used by permission.

Scripture quotations marked *Amp.* are from *The Amplified Bible*. Old Testament copyright © 1958, 1987 by The Zondervan Corporation. *The Amplified New Testament* copyright © 1958, 1987 by The Lockman Foundation. Used by permission.

Scripture quotations marked *TLB* are from *The Living Bible* ©1971. Used by permission of Tyndale House Publishers, Inc., Wheaton, IL 60189. All rights reserved.

Photos by Miles and Associates. John Miles, photographer.

Library of Congress Catalog Card Number: 96-068516

ISBN: 0871489732

Copyright © 1996 by Pathway Press

Cleveland, Tennessee 37311

All Rights Reserved

Printed in the United States of America

CONTENTS

Foreword

When I became a minister's wife 39 years ago, not much had been written for women by women. Women were simply to read the works of men, which certainly often contain great wisdom but which many times neglect women's experiences. And, frankly, not all the great writers and thinkers are men. It was even more difficult for a preacher's wife, for it seemed to me that it was simply believed that we were supplied everything we needed to be great helpmeets to our husbands and marvelous ministers in our own right when we said the words "I do"!

Somehow, all the qualifications of the woman described in Proverbs 31 automatically were to fall upon us: She has value far greater than jewels; she is trustworthy; she does her husband good; she works with her hands; she provides food and clothing to her family; she has great financial acumen; she is physically strong; she is charitable and altruistic; she is dressed in fine clothes; she is dignified, hopeful, and wise; she teaches kindness; she is industrious; she is praised by her husband and blessed by her children; she fears the Lord. It did not seem to me that I lived up to all of these expectations merely because I married a preacher. I was young, inexperienced, fearful, and I didn't have books like this one to provide insights and encouragement.

But women today have greater resources than we did back then. We have writers and wise counselors like Wanda Griffith, whom God has burdened to address our spiritual lives, to provide encouragement in distressing times, to plant seeds within us to become the women who are truly comfortable *Sitting at His Feet*. Wanda is a Christian first, beautiful in her spirituality and love of God. She is also a wife, mother, and conference and retreat speaker, but she is not these as an afterthought. No, her roles as wife, mother, and minister are part of her relationship with God—as she extends Christ to all those around her and as she touches lives out of her devotion to God. She is an absolute joy to know and spend time with! She emits through her writings the charisma and natural zest for life which are her hallmark.

After reading the first few pages of this book, my soul began to soar as I was moved to new heights in God. Although inspirational, it has a single golden thread that creates wonderful balance. You will be uplifted by reading these chapters through personal tragedy on to triumph. Each daily writing stands as a lone sentinel which provides hope and courage for that day in your life.

As you read, let your eyes drink in the scenes, your imagination play with the words, and your mind begin contemplating the important thoughts expressed. You will recall incidents half-buried under the busyness of your life. Your thoughts will take you to pleasant places that leave you refreshed and ready to begin your day.

God wants you to live more happily in Him, to live each day to the fullest in the victory He has provided through His Son Jesus Christ and the power of His Holy Spirit, and to rest in His holy presence. God, you see, is more precious than gold, more wonderful than any earthly experience, more thrilling than anything your imagination can summon, more tender than the most delicate of children, more beautiful than the most colorful expanse of sky or ocean or mountain range, more giving and loving and helping and encouraging and edifying . . . and any other ebullient adjective you can think of. God is more. And this is what Wanda wants you to see, to seek, to experience.

This book ministers to many needs. Let this book minister to *your* needs. Whether they concern "daily challenges" or "seasons of change," they will be dealt with here. You will learn about "giving thanks," about "new beginnings," and you will be encouraged to "stay strong." You will read words which instruct you to have "visions of hope," a "hearing heart," and "listening ears." "Remembering" how it feels to be wrapped in His arms of "unconditional love," you will become aware of your strong "heritage of faith."

So, let me invite you to "unwrap your gifts," to use them, and to thank God because He rewards those who diligently seek Him. And I pray that you will seek Him, letting this book be a tool He uses to bring you closer to Himself and to teach you His heart.

Thank you, Evaline Echols, Wanda Griffith, Mary Ruth Stone, Oleda Atkinson, Rebecca Jenkins, Shelby Harvell, Beverly Richardson, Pat Bradbury, Pat Daugherty, Jackie Walker, Kathy Sanders, and Saundra Rose for this book. For women . . . for men . . . for teenagers . . . for the elderly . . . for the strong and for the weak . . . for me . . . for anyone who wants to sit at Jesus' feet.

Kathryn Shires White

Acknowledgments

This challenging project would have been impossible without the hard work, artful skills, and invaluable assistance of many people. Special thanks are due the following:

The writers

Evaline Echols, Mary Ruth Stone, Oleda Atkinson, Rebecca Jenkins, Shelby Harvell, Beverly Richardson, Pat Bradbury, Pat Daugherty, Jackie Walker, Kathy Sanders, and Saundra Rose, who sat at His feet and poured their hearts and lives into a computer for hours on end for a month's devotions.

The Pathway family

Kenneth T. Harvell, general director, who permitted me to edit and supervise photo shoots on some of his time; Homer G. Rhea, editor in chief, for accepting the project, offering wise counsel, and keeping me in line (a BIG job); Harold and Noretta Medford for allowing us to invade their lovely home with cameras, bright lights, and props; Wilma Amison, editorial assistant, my friend and right arm throughout the yearlong process; Nellie Keasling, Esther Metaxas, and Becky Wayne for their copyediting skills and generous comments; Barry Eaton, computer designer, for his expertise and patience through many changes; Pat Bradbury, whose middle name is "Marketing." Their combined skills and giftedness are surpassed only by their genuine love for God.

My family

Debbie Claudio, my beautiful daughter-in-law—and granddaughter, Emily—whose excellent modeling skills added the finishing touch to the cover and title pages.

My husband, Bob, for his listening ear, untiring patience, and expert advice.

Introduction

When Barbara Walters was asked the question, "If you could select any person throughout history to interview, who would you select?" she responded without hesitation, "Jesus Christ. He is the most interesting person who has ever lived. If I could spend just one hour with Him, I would have the greatest interview of my life."

When I read that Ms. Walters made this statement, I wanted to assure her that she could have greater access to Him than a one-hour interview. All believers can "approach the throne of grace with confidence, so that we may receive mercy and find grace to help us in our time of need" (Hebrews 4:16, *NIV*).

Time, our most treasured gift, can never be recalled, recycled, or replenished. To those who invest a portion of each day in His presence, He gives a portion of Himself. Sitting at His feet

- Molds character
- Builds faith
- Empowers believers for greater service.

Three of Jesus' closest friends were Mary and Martha and their brother, Lazarus. When Jesus came through their village, He stopped at the home of these special friends who loved Him and made Him feel comfortable.

Luke describes one of these occasions in the 10th chapter of his Gospel. Martha was running in overdrive, slinging pots and pans, making sure everything was perfect for her special guest. Meanwhile out in the living room, her guests were laughing, talking, and listening to Jesus. Mary was closest to Him—sitting at His feet, clinging to every word He said.

Martha boiled inside with a mixture of frustration, envy, and self-pity. Finally, she could stand it no longer! "Lord, don't you care that my sister has left me to do the work by myself? Tell her to help me!"

"Martha, Martha," the Lord answered, "you are worried and upset about many things, but only one thing is needed. Mary has chosen what is better, and it will not be taken away from her" (vv. 40-42, *NIV*).

Jesus was not belittling Martha's service. Her warm hospitality was one reason He came to her home. But in the heat of the kitchen, Martha lost her perspective. She became so focused on the cooking that she forgot the One she was cooking for. She became so caught up with her table setting that she forgot *who* would sit there. While she scurried in the kitchen preparing food, Jesus Christ himself was in the front parlor. Jesus' answer to Martha was a gentle reminder that she had forgotten the importance of the One she was serving.

Like Martha, sometimes I get caught up in doing good things—Bible study, prayer meeting, choir rehearsals, preparing food for a sick family, and on and on. Then I remember my personal time sitting at His feet. Suddenly everything becomes clear. It is then I understand why Mary sat at His feet.

An old hymn from the 19th century, titled "Sitting at the Feet of Jesus," expresses the themes of these devotionals.

> Sitting at the feet of Jesus,
> O, what words I hear Him say!
> Happy place! So near, so precious!
> May it find me there each day!
> Sitting at the feet of Jesus,
> I would look upon the past;
> For His love has been so gracious,
> It has won my heart at last.
>
> Bless me, O my Savior, bless me,
> As I sit low at Thy feet;
> O look down in love upon me,
> Let me see Thy face so sweet;
> Give me, Lord, the mind of Jesus,
> Make me holy as He is;
> May I prove I've been with Jesus,
> Who is all my righteousness.
>
> —Asa Hall

The writers of these devotions have all sat at the feet of Jesus during times of heartbreak, disappointment, disillusionment, and personal struggles. Straight from their hearts flow words of wisdom, moments of self-disclosure, nuggets of truth-filled insight learned from time spent with the Master. Like Mary, let us choose what is better. Let us snuggle up in His presence in the special place He reserved for us at His feet. Let us reflect how others have sat and learned. When, like Mary of Bethany, we spend time at the feet of Jesus, we are choosing that good part that can never be taken from us. Then we, too, will understand why Jesus says, "This is the most important thing."

Wanda Gore Griffith

January
New Beginnings
Evaline Gore Echols

Evaline Gore Echols is a writer of growing influence whose byline appears in religious and professional journals. She is a frequent speaker at seminars and professional meetings. The first edition of *Climb Up Through Your Valleys* was published in 1980 by Pathway Press. In 1994 a new edition was printed.

After completion of her master's degree at the University of Tennessee and her doctor's degree at Louisiana State University, she now serves as professor and chair of the Business Department at Lee College, a post she has held since 1984.

Evaline has two children, Eddie and Sharon, and two grandsons, Darren and Drew.

January 1

Scripture: "I form the light and create darkness, I bring prosperity and create disaster; I, the Lord, do all these things" (Isaiah 45:7, *NIV*).

As you turn the page of your calendar, is it hard to believe that another year has passed? January 1 signifies the first day of the first month of a new year—a new beginning.

During these next 31 days, I would like to invite you to join me on a treasure hunt. Most of the treasures I have found were discovered in the dark against a backdrop of physical and emotional pain, then carefully concealed in my personal journal. Some of the newest gems were discovered quite recently while recuperating from a physical illness.

Some of the journal entries I will share date back to May 1981, when I found myself in what seemed to be total darkness—when I experienced the loss of my husband of 25 years through divorce and the loss of my daddy through death during the same week. During the subsequent 15 years Isaiah 45:3 has become a reality: "I will give you the treasures of darkness, riches stored in secret places" (*NIV*).

So take your Bible and your journal (or notebook) and join me as we sit at His feet. Step into the water and watch as God parts your Red Sea and enables you to cross your Jordan—to experience a new beginning. Allow God to break the fetters of the past that have bound you for too long and to release the prison chains which have imprisoned you. Jack Hayford once said that we can never embrace the future as long as our wrists are chained to the past (*Taking Hold of Tomorrow*, 1989).

As you allow God to use the dark threads, as well as the bright threads, which He has woven into your life, you will see the beginning of a new pattern—a kaleidoscope of beautiful colors. Through the study of His Word and the personal application to your circumstances, hopefully you will begin to see a beautiful rainbow—even while it is still raining.

Father, thank You for giving us the courage to trust You in the dark, as well as in the light. Help us to realize that even in our dark moments we are walking toward the light of a new day.

January 2

Scripture: "For I the Lord thy God will hold thy right hand, saying unto thee, Fear not; I will help thee" (Isaiah 41:13).

In my 8 o'clock business communications class at Lee College, each Monday morning I remind my students, "Mondays are new beginnings." That early in the morning that early in the week, they don't seem to comprehend the profoundness of this statement; in fact, they don't even find any humor in it.

Nevertheless, Mondays are new beginnings on a weekly basis; and so is the first day of each year a new beginning for the new year. My journal chronicles New Year's resolutions (some of them the same for the past 10 years, which I am still trying to keep), as well as reflections on the previous year. Here is one excerpt:

> My resolution for this New Year is to first of all keep my hand in the nail-scarred hand. When I do this, I avoid the danger of going astray, of keeping the wrong company, of visiting the wrong places, and of failing to hear His voice when He speaks to me.

This reminds me of a dream I had a few years ago—in fact, a few months after my daddy went to be with the Lord. I had been asked to speak at North Cleveland Church of God on "How to Deal With Loss Through Death and Divorce." At that time I did not feel I was dealing with either very well, so what did I have to say? In my dream, the morning before I was scheduled to speak that evening, my daddy visited me, and this is all he said: "Honey, don't be afraid to reach out to others as long as you keep one hand in the nail-scarred hand." When I awoke, I knew what to say to the group, and God gave me boldness to proclaim what I believed from the Word—not what I felt in my emotions. This was truly a new beginning of emotional healing.

Shortly after I had written this resolution in my journal, I read the following from Frances Roberts' book *Come Away My Beloved*:

> Clasp thy hand in Mine, and loose not thine hold. For thou canst not tell what great thing I may do for thee through some smallest happening. . . . Look not back, but look ahead, for I have glory prepared for thee. . . .

> Be as a young child and step out in confidence knowing that with thy hand in Mine ye shall be always safe and blessings shall attend thee.

Remember, with your hand in His you can have a new beginning, even on Monday mornings.

Father, give me the courage to drop those things which I have in my hand and commit them into Your hand, knowing that You will guide me safely into the future.

January 3

Scripture: "Each one should use whatever gift he has received to serve others, faithfully administering God's grace in its various forms" (1 Peter 4:10, *NIV*).

In 1974, when I was working in the president's office at Lee College as administrative assistant to Dr. Charles W. Conn, I developed the habit of keeping a personal journal (not because I wanted to but because Dr. Conn was insistent, even persistent, in his encouragement for me to develop this habit). I recognize, over 20 years later, that this was truly a new beginning in my personal and spiritual growth.

I agree with Ronald Klug, who said in his book *How to Keep a Spiritual Journal*, that a journal is a tool for self-discovery, a place to generate and capture ideas, a safety valve for the emotions, a training ground as a writer, a good friend and confidant, and a mirror for the soul. To understand where God is leading me, it is often important to see where I have been.

My journal writing has become an important part of my devotional time—a time when I reflect on His Word, search for His will, and record insights I receive.

This past summer during a time of soul-searching and seeking direction for my future, I took some time out to read from my journal of the past 15 years. This was a painful but rewarding experience.

What benefits did I derive from reading my personal journal?

1. It reminded me of the goals I had achieved and those that were yet to be reached.
2. It helped me to sort out my strengths and weaknesses.
3. It reminded me that life is not lived on a plateau—it is a combination of mountain and valley experiences.
4. It provided favorite scriptures, specific devotionals of encouragement, and prayers of thanksgiving and petition.
5. It helped me to sort out some things in my life and restore some internal order.
6. It was a reminder that I am human with the ability to experience a variety of emotions: anger, happiness, joy, thankfulness, fear—even depression at times.
7. I was able to see an improvement in my ability to express myself and become more creative—slowly but still with great caution (I have a long way to go in that area).
8. I recognized that my journal had forced me to clarify my beliefs on certain issues—some spiritual and some political.
9. It was obvious that my journal had become what Ronald Klug had said it could—my friend and confidant, especially during those times when I needed someone to hear me out.
10. Last, but not least, it reminded me that God's grace is sufficient in the bad times as well as the good times.

David is an excellent example of one who developed his journaling skills. Thanks to him we have the Book of Psalms, which provides songs of praise and thanksgiving, as well as pleas for help and refuge in the time of trouble.

I encourage you to get a notebook and start writing today. I promise you, you will be glad you did.

Thank You, Lord, for friends who encourage us to develop and cultivate the gifts which come from You.

January 4

Scripture: "Search me, O God, and know my heart: try me, and know my thoughts: and see if there be any wicked way in me, and lead me in the way everlasting" (Psalm 139:23, 24).

How many times have you said, "I need to make some changes in my life. I am ready for a new beginning." The month of January seems to be the ideal time for such declarations.

During the past few months a group of faculty and staff at Lee College met during lunch to study Mark Rutland's book, *Hanging by a Thread*. This study forced me to ask myself an important question: Do I possess the virtues of courage, loyalty, diligence, modesty, frugality, honesty, meekness, reverence, and gratitude?

In his book *Inside Out*, Larry Crabb talks about the promise of *real* change in our lives when we are willing to start from the inside out. He contends that most of us spend our lives trying to pretend things are better than they are. Then when reality breaks through (we recognize how imperfect we are), we are strongly inclined to do whatever restores our feigned sense of well-being. For example, we may count our blessings, cut the lawn, eat something sweet, consult a counselor, join the church choir, read a favorite psalm, turn on the TV, resurrender ourself to God, or just go get a pizza. We will do anything to get away from the nagging sense that something is missing, something is wrong.

In this book, Crabb used the analogy of a friend who was forced to travel in his work and be away from home much of the time. To pretend he was home, he would go into the motel room and rearrange the furniture, hoping it would feel like home.

How many times have we simply rearranged the furniture in our lives, pretending we made a genuine change?

A few weeks ago I had new carpet laid in my apartment. When I came home from work, I realized the carpet layers had rearranged my furniture (by mistake). It dawned on me there were corners of the kitchen I had not seen for a while. Also, with the new carpet there was no longer a need to arrange the furniture so the dirty spots would be less obvious. Rearranging the furniture was no longer necessary; real change had taken place.

Ask yourself these questions:

- Am I experiencing real change in my life, or am I guilty of just rearranging the furniture to cover the dirty spots?
- Are there corners of my heart filled with resentment, hurt, greed, pride, lust, or . . . (you fill in the blank) that need to be uncovered?
- Am I willing to start from the inside out and allow God to effect genuine change?

When we allow the Master Carpenter to rip away the old and replace it with the new, real change is possible. In this process we must remember He will also discover those things we have quietly swept under the rug.

It's time to clean house!

Lord, help me to be honest with You and with myself. Turn Your spotlight on areas in my life that need cleansing.

January 5

Scripture: "The steps of a good man are ordered by the Lord: and he delighteth in his way. Though he fall, he shall not be utterly cast down: for the Lord upholdeth him with his hand" (Psalm 37:23, 24).

One morning while driving to work, shortly after the major storm of divorce had hit in our family, the Lord spoke to me in my spirit and said, "Through every wind of adversity blows a gentle breeze of grace." This word from the Lord was truly a new beginning at that turn in the road in my life.

Through this experience I have learned that God is always in control, waiting for us to get beyond our control so He can order our steps. This is all the hope we need.

God sometimes allows the winds of adversity to beat upon us, not to defeat us but to drive us to Him (Psalm 3:6, 7). I am convinced that God uses a world of trouble and sorrow as His classroom to teach us the art of waiting on Him. (I have also learned that this course is not a one-year curriculum.)

During this process of waiting on God, we learn to drop our crutches, remove our masks, and develop our wings of trust—to trust Him as well as those around us. These times of waiting on God are necessary to discover our weaknesses and frailties, and they also help us learn to commit them to Him. We must then allow Him, in His own way and in His own time frame, to fill the void, to replace our weakness with His strength, to remove fear and give faith, and to strengthen any weakened fiber of our lives to prepare us for a new beginning.

Catherine Marshall once said that when life hands us situations we cannot understand, we have one of two choices: We can wallow in misery, separated from God. Or we can say, "God, I need You and Your presence in my life more than I need understanding. I trust You to give me understanding and an answer to my 'Why?' if and when You choose."

May I remind you that we can soar above the turbulence of life's seas. You may discover that the storm that shakes your nest is the storm that teaches you to fly.

Thank You, Father God, that You direct our steps, and even when we stumble You are there to pick us up.

January 6

Scripture: "Like an eagle that stirs up its nest, that hovers over its young, He spread His wings and caught them, He carried them on His pinions. The Lord alone guided him" (Deuteronomy 32:11, 12, *NASB*).

This morning I am trying again to draw the curtains on the past—to not allow the past to cloud my future. I have visualized a large arena with the stage behind the curtains. The space outside the curtains is larger, more expansive, has doors which lead to other arenas, and represents openness—openness to those around me, openness in mind and spirit, and openness to what God has to say.

If I try to remain behind the curtains in the corridors of my past, my view is limited, my opportunities are narrowed, and the doors are closed.

The first 40 years of my life could be classified as the "stage era"—a time when I was in the mainstream of influence at home, school, and church; however, my scope and boundaries were limited. At times I felt as though I was in confinement, imprisoned by walls of insecurity, fear, and dependency.

All of a sudden, about 14 years ago the curtains lifted and suddenly I was thrust from the relatively narrow stage area to a larger arena in my life. True, those "stage years" influence the "arena years," but they should not limit them.

At times even today, it is easy to long to be on stage (or backstage) again with a full cast of players (a family—a husband, two children who still live at home, a mother and father who live in the same town, and in-laws who loved me as their own).

Yes, it is all right to remember, but the curtains have lifted. Now it is time to step forward to the next passage in life—to broader opportunities and responsibilities. It is time to let the crutches fall; it is time to develop wings. I admit my cozy nest of security has been destroyed, but hopefully this next stage in my life will be a part of my greater development.

Lloyd Ogilvie, in his book *Ask Him Anything*, reminds us of three crucial things about God (Deuteronomy 32:11, 12):

1. He is a disturber.
2. He is a developer.
3. He is a deliverer.

God sometimes uses the process of disturbance, His brooding love, and His perfecting strength to lead us to hitherto unknown heights.

Thank You, Lord, that when our circumstances force us to leap from the edge of our nest of security and comfort, we soon discover that Your everlasting arms do more than catch us. They are like the wind lifting us (Deuteronomy 33:26, 27).

January 7

Scripture: "But they that wait upon the Lord shall renew their strength; they shall mount up with wings as eagles; they shall run, and not be weary; and they shall walk, and not faint" (Isaiah 40:31).

We all face times in our lives when our courage fails and our strength needs to be renewed—when the wind is high and the waves are threatening. During these times even the youths and young men need renewal (see Isaiah 40:30).

What happens to our spirits also happens to the wing feathers of eagles. They become battered by the winds and storms. Then the eagle has to wait on his Creator for a miracle of renewal. His ruffled feathers fall out and he grows new ones. Through the molting process, he sheds his old feathers and God replaces them with fresh ones.

What God does for eagles, He also does for His children. He exchanges our old feathers of fear, failures, and frustrations for the new feathers of His strength and new life. He repatterns our whole way of thinking—"bringing into captivity every thought to the obedience of Christ" (2 Corinthians 10:5). He transforms the old thoughts that defeat us into new thoughts that encourage us.

My journal reflects my prayer on one of those days when my spirits needed to be renewed:

Lord, I give You my burdens of discouragement, doubt, and fear. Let this be the day I leave the launching pad and soar with You. Guide me through the clouds of uncertainty, the winds of change, the fog of doubt, and the thundering voices of those around me. Help me to rise above the circumstances of life and to learn to live on a higher place spiritually, physically, emotionally, and intellectually. Make me a scholar of truth and an example of excellence for the furtherance of Your kingdom. Bless my children and keep them under the umbrella of Your love when the storms come.

Perhaps this is your day of renewal—a renewed mind and spirit (Psalm 51:10) and renewed strength (Isaiah 40:31). Allow God to strip you of anything that has become a weight. Make a decision—exchange your weakness for His strength. Allow God to strengthen your spiritual fiber today!

Thank You, Father, for breaking the chains of the past and setting me free to soar like an eagle.

January 8

Scripture: "I want to know Christ and the power of his resurrection and the fellowship of sharing in his sufferings, becoming like him in his death" (Philippians 3:10, *NIV*).

Are you aware that the number 8 is associated with new beginnings? Neither was I until today. It seemed fitting to share this discovery on this eighth day of January. According to E.W. Bullinger, in his book *Numbers in Scripture*, the number 8 is associated with resurrection and regeneration and the beginning of a new era or order.

Charles Spurgeon once said that the Resurrection is the cornerstone of the entire building of Christianity and the keystone of the arch of our salvation. Though we cannot see Him visibly as the disciples did on the day of His resurrection, nor touch Him as did Mary Magdalene, yet we can see Him through eyes of faith. We can get to know Him, as our scripture today says, not only in "the power of his resurrection" but also through "the fellowship of sharing in his sufferings, becoming like him in his death."

In 1978, a few months before the death of my mother, I read Hannah Hurnard's book *Hinds' Feet on High Places*. This book taught me that when we experience sorrow and suffering or loss or humiliation or grief, we become eager to know the Shepherd and to seek His help. It is amazing how much better we get to know Him when suffering and sorrow become our companions.

Perhaps you have lost a loved one through death or divorce, or a child through rebellion. Submit your will to His will as Jesus did when He was hanging on the cross. Can you honestly say, "Father . . . not my will, but thine, be done"? (Luke 22:42). This is not easy.

Noah is an example of one who developed a relationship with Christ that stood when those around him failed to understand. I am convinced Noah learned what it meant to know Him in the power of His resurrection, and in the fellowship of His sufferings.

When the earth was covered with the flood, it was Noah, "the eighth person" (2 Peter 2:5), who stepped out onto a new earth to commence a new order of things. "Eight souls" (1 Peter 3:20) passed through the Flood to the new world.

That sounds like a new beginning to me.

Father, thank You for Your promise that if we suffer with You, we shall also reign with You.

January 9

Scripture: "You are to move out from your positions and follow. . . . Then you will know which way to go, since you have never been this way before" (Joshua 3:3, 4, *NIV*).

One morning, about a week before I was scheduled to speak at a seminar on "New Beginnings," while I was praying and reading in the Book of Joshua, I felt impressed to gather about 100 small stones and heap them on the altar as my visual aid. (My business communication students would be proud of me for practicing what I preach about the importance of using visual aids).

When the day of the seminar arrived, I boldly gathered my bag of stones along with my Bible and speech. After reminding the seminar participants of how God used Joshua to prepare the people to cross the Jordan, I urged those in the audience to move out from their "present positions," come to the altar, and take a stone to symbolize a new beginning.

After God parted the waters for the Israelites, Joshua instructed the people to build a memorial by placing 12 stones in the middle of the Jordan as a reminder of how God delivered them. We must remember that the Israelites would have never crossed the Jordan had they not been willing to move out from their positions and follow the ark. Neither can we.

It is a frightening experience to embark on uncharted waters. Just as Joshua reminded the people of Israel, I believe God is reminding this generation that we have never passed this way before. Only when we are willing to step into the waters by faith will we know which way to go.

My journal reflects how I felt after building a memorial at the seminar:

> I am convinced that God will dry up the waters of despair, disappointment, hurt, or loneliness in our lives and allow us to cross our Jordan on dry land. When this happens, we will be unharmed by the surrounding enemies which try to defeat us— enemies of doubt, fear, insecurity, and poor self-esteem. We will then begin to see the walls of Jericho tumble and victory will be ours.

Make a conscious decision today to step out of your present position of doubt, uncertainty, or despair; step into the water of His grace and watch the waters part. Remember, "you have never been this way before."

Father God, thank You for leading us through the uncharted areas of our lives. Give us courage to move out of our present position and follow You.

January 10

Scripture: "These things happened to them as an example, and they were written for our instruction" (1 Corinthians 10:11, *NASB*).

Have you ever felt like you were at a turning point in your life? You may be asking, "What is a turning point?" In simple terms, it is where two ways meet—one goes one way and one goes the other.

The week before I was scheduled to speak on "Life's Turning Points: God's Meeting Places," I turned the radio on and this is what Charles Swindoll said. He noted that turning points have four common characteristics:

1. They occur in the normal routine of our lives.
2. They are usually sudden and unexpected.
3. They impact the lives of others as well.
4. They prompt changes in us that surprise others.

It was July 26, 1978, one week before the General Assembly, when I found myself lying flat of my back in Bradley Memorial Hospital as a result of an automobile accident. With a broken leg and hip and internal bleeding, I recognized during these next few months that I had reached a major turning point in my life. I had to make a decision; I must go one way or the other—the path of faith or fear. I learned that turning points *are* God's meeting places—fertile soil for new beginnings.

One morning God spoke to me through the Twenty-third Psalm and assured me that He had made me to lie down in green pastures; He was leading me beside the still waters; He was restoring my soul! Through this "rhema" (a personal revelation from God to the individual through His Word), I rested in His peace and love. Even though I did not walk for nine months, I recognized I was enrolled in a new course of study which not only resulted in a book (*Climb Up Through Your Valleys*) but also helped prepare me for some rocky steeps ahead.

When God spoke to Moses through the burning bush, he was going through the normal routine of tending his father-in-law's sheep. Suddenly and unexpectedly, God spoke to Moses; and the impact of the message would affect the lives of others for generations to come.

When God parted the waters at the Red Sea, Moses encountered another major turning point in his life. The Red Sea became God's meeting place with Moses, enabling him to lead God's people out of Egyptian bondage.

Ask yourself these questions: What was the major turning point in my life? Did it occur in my normal routine? Was it sudden and unexpected? Did it impact the lives of others as well? Did it prompt changes in me that surprised others?

The passage in 1 Corinthians 10:11 reminds us: "These things happened to them as an example, and they were written for our instruction" (*NASB*).

Take the time to write how God met you at *your* Red Sea, how He parted *your* waters, how *you* walked across on dry land. Remind the Enemy that life's turning points *are* God's meeting places—even new beginnings.

Thank You, Lord, for meeting us at every turn in the road. Help us to preserve Your blessings by sharing them with others—our children, our grandchildren, and our friends.

January 11

Scripture: "And it came to pass, when the people removed from their tents, to pass over Jordan, and the priests bearing the ark of the covenant before the people; and as they that bare the ark were come unto Jordan, and the feet of the priests that bare the ark were dipped in the brim of the water . . . that the waters which came down from above stood and rose up upon an heap very far from the city Adam . . . and the people passed over right against Jericho. . . . And all the Israelites passed over on dry ground, until all the people were passed clean over Jordan" (Joshua 3:14-17).

I titled a Sunday school lesson I was preparing to teach from the Book of Joshua "Fold Your Tent in the Wilderness for the Last Time."

Long before dawn while others were still sleeping, Joshua arose in his tent. This was an important day—the day to cross over Jordan. This was the day over 2 million Israelites would fold their tents for the last time in the wilderness. Under the leadership of Joshua, they would follow the specific instructions God had given.

Joshua made it clear to the people that this was a brand-new maneuver—a new beginning. He emphasized that there would be times to move when the ark moved, and there would be times to stand still when the ark stood still.

Just as Joshua and the Israelites faced a raging river that overflowed its banks, so will we. Phillip Keller (*Joshua: Man of Fearless Faith*) reminds us that God does not ask us to retreat or withdraw from the threat which would seem to engulf us. Neither does He urge us to find some way around the apparently impossible barriers. Keller says God asks us to remember three things:

1. It is He who brought us here.
2. It is He who will keep and preserve us here.
3. It is He who will take us on from here.

After encouraging the Sunday school class to "fold [their] tents in the wilderness for the last time," my journal reflects how I felt:

> After teaching the class, it seems that God is saying to me: My child, it is time for you to fold your tent for the last time in the wilderness of loneliness and fear. Follow Me closely. When My presence directs you to move, go forward. When My presence directs or impresses you to be still, wait on Me. Do not move ahead unless My presence goes before you. Know that I am your guide and your shepherd. I go before you and My goodness and mercy follow you. There are unexplored territories to be discovered in your life. Remember— when the floods come, I will give you the courage to step into the water with full trust that I will part the waters or that I will walk through the waters with you. You are My child, and I love you. Don't be content to remain in the wilderness—Canaan is just ahead! Trust Me.

Father, help me to no longer be content to remain in the wilderness. Give me courage to listen to Your instructions and then to step into the water unafraid.

January 12

Scripture: "Who, O God is like you? Though you have made me see troubles, many and bitter, you will restore my life again; from the depths of the earth you will again bring me up. You will increase my honor and comfort me once again" (Psalm 71:19-21, *NIV*).

Today I received a letter from a friend, reminding me of what our pastor said in church yesterday about the wilderness experiences in our lives. After reading it several times, I decided this letter was inspired, so I wrote it in my journal. Here are some excerpts:

> God's purpose sometimes allows us to experience trials and troubles. . . . No doubt, you have been in a wilderness. But you have forgotten that the wilderness is but a prelude to your Promised Land, your destiny. . . . In the wilderness process, everything Satan can bring against you can be taken out of your life so you can stand in victory. . . . The time you've spent in the wilderness is comparable to the size of the promise for you. (Seems to me, you're about to receive a mighty big promise.) . . . Though I can't say I have a "word from the Lord," I believe in my spirit that your season is about to change. (Read Psalm 71:19-21.) Be encouraged that rather than functioning in an earthly realm, He is positioning you in His kingdom so He can rule and reign through you.

This letter from my friend Nancy encouraged me to look up—to focus on Canaan rather than Egypt, to step into the water of my Jordan knowing that God will not only part the waters but lead me safely to shore.

Today I set my Ebenezer; I will not look back. I will remind myself that God has been with me in the past and He will protect me from my enemies in the future.

"Then Samuel took a stone, and set it between Mizpeh and Shen, and called the name of it Ebenezer, saying, Hitherto hath the Lord helped us. So the Philistines were subdued, and they came no more into the coast of Israel: and the hand of the Lord was against the Philistines all the days of Samuel" (1 Samuel 7:12, 13).

Father, thank You that You speak through Your children to bring words of hope and restoration. Thank You for this rhema from Your Word—Your personal revelation to one of Your children. As I set my Ebenezer against my enemies of fear and doubt, let today be a new beginning.

January 13

Scripture: "Greater is he that is in you, than he that is in the world" (1 John 4:4).

Do you sometimes feel that you are facing your "Red Sea"? You refuse to return to Egypt and you cannot turn to the left nor to the right. The only way to go is forward; but this great gulf that separates you from where you need to be makes your move forward seem impossible. When this happens, it is time to sit at His feet and experience a new beginning.

A few years ago when I was at Louisiana State University working on my doctoral degree (taking 14 graduate hours and teaching six hours), I faced my Red Sea experience. The Lord assured me through prayer and His Word that He would part the waters (even the waters of advanced statistics) and that I would not even get wet—that I would move forward with confidence in Him.

The day I walked across the stage to receive my Ph.D. and my grandson, Darren, yelled, "Go, Dr. MeeMaw," I knew the waters had parted. In retrospect, six years later, I realize that it is the Red Sea experiences in our lives that prepare us to later cross our Jordan.

After Moses died, Joshua entered a new stage in His life. For Moses the crossing of the Red Sea was an exodus from Egyptian slavery; for Joshua the crossing of the Jordan was a new beginning—an entrance into new territory.

Do you feel that God is leading you into unfamiliar territory? Are you ready to cross your Jordan, knowing that God will dry up the waters of despair, disappointment, hurt, or loneliness, and allow you to walk on dry land? When this happens, I am convinced we will begin to see the walls of Jericho that have held us captive begin to crumble. We can step into the future with courage, knowing "greater is he that is in [us], than he that is in the world."

Thank You, Lord, for parting the waters just in time. Help me to "be strong and courageous" like Joshua and to follow You one step at a time—even when the waters are deep.

January 14

Scripture: "Remember your word to your servant, for you have given me hope. . . . I rise before dawn and cry for help; I have put my hope in your word" (Psalm 119:49, 147, *NIV*).

In July I had the opportunity to retreat for a few days in "sunny Florida," which incidentally, a few days after my arrival, became "stormy Florida." We had storm warnings flashing on the television screen, urging vacationers to evacuate and head north. With my unusual fear of storms (thanks to Daddy Gore and Grandmother Davis for this emotional implant early in life), I was ready to pack the car and head for home. With some reluctance on the part of my friend who accompanied me, we left our place of retreat and arrived home before Hurricane Erin hit near Vero Beach (very close to where we were staying).

My journal reflects what I wrote on Wednesday, July 26, just a few days before the storm hit:

> This week is a time of restoration, refreshment, and renewal. I have made a deliberate effort to leave my cares at home and to learn to leave them at the Cross. During these next few days, I want to sit at His feet, like Mary, and experience newness in body, mind, and spirit. Again, I am reminded of the importance of stepping aside from the hustle and bustle of daily life and being renewed and restored. This is my prayer for today:

> Father, let me experience a new beginning spiritually during these next few days of vacation. Strengthen my body, quicken my mind, and anoint my pen to write. Lord, I want to sit at Your feet and get to know You better, learn how to listen to Your voice, and then obey Your instructions. Help me not to be afraid to face the future, because I know You are with me. You are my hope! Psalm 119:147 reminds me that each day should begin with my cry for help from You.

As the storm clouds of life gather (and they will), it is comforting to know that God uses His radar (His Word) to warn us of impending danger and then gives us wisdom to avoid the storms or to see us through the turbulence.

Thank You, Lord, for giving us Your wisdom to avoid the storms of life or to ride the waves safely to the shore.

January 15

Scripture: "Old things are passed away; behold, all things are become new" (2 Corinthians 5:17).

Today reminds me of a very important day in the history of the Gore family. On January 15, 1912, W.C. Gore, Sr., was born in Georgia into what we would classify today as a dysfunctional family. When he was a young child, his mother was left with two boys to raise but without the means to make a proper living. Therefore, these two boys were forced to make it on their own at an early age. Both boys chose the road that led to sin and destruction—at least for a while.

Eventually the boys faced a crossroads in their lives; one chose to follow Christ and the other chose the pleasures of sin.

When my daddy made his decision to follow Christ (one month before I was conceived), it was truly a new beginning for our family. Later Mother told the children (all six of us—five girls and one boy) how dramatic the transformation in Daddy's life had been. One day he was outside fighting while she was in church; the next day he was a new creature in Christ. Indeed, "old things [had] passed away; [and] all things [had] become new."

For the next 43 years (from 1938 until his death in 1981), W.C. Gore would spread the gospel in churches he pastored in Alabama and after his retirement in revivals in Tennessee and Alabama.

When Daddy chose to make the right turn and follow Christ, his decision was far-reaching. He not only impacted the lives of his six children, 11 grandchildren, and 13 great-grandchildren, but he also impacted the lives of hundreds during his 38 years as pastor.

Since today would have been Daddy's birthday, please allow me to offer this prayer of thanks for godly parents. Perhaps you may want to join me:

Father, thank You for directing the steps of my parents. Thank You for a praying mother who refused to give up on her husband when at times the circumstances seemed impossible. Thank You for the prayers for their children and grandchildren, which I am convinced live on today. Lord, help me as a parent to provide footprints for my children and grandchildren which will lead them "in the paths of righteousness for [Your] name's sake" (Psalm 23:3). Father, if there is one child, grandchild, or great-grandchild who has not experienced this new beginning, let it be so today, in the name of Jesus.

January 16

Scripture: "'For I know the plans I have for you,' declares the Lord, 'plans to prosper you and not to harm you, plans to give you hope and a future'" (Jeremiah 29:11, *NIV*).

This morning during my time of devotion, God gave me this gem: "As we walk through the dark times in our lives, God provides a lantern of hope."

When I was growing up in Alabama, we often visited homes of members of the church where Daddy pastored. On one occasion a severe thunderstorm caused a power outage; all the lights were out and we were in total darkness. My friend's mother assured us that there was no reason to be afraid; she would light the old kerosene lantern and we could find our way through the darkness—which is what she did.

In his book *God Works the Night Shift*, Ron Mehl reminds us that when the darkness comes into our lives, when the light vanishes and we begin to feel as though the sun will never again break the heaviness of night, that is the time to trust in the name of the Lord. That is the time to rely on God and wait for Him. Mehl reminds us that those who scramble around trying to manufacture their own light and comfort apart from God will instead find only hurt and sorrow.

Mehl goes on to say that the problem with providing your own fire and protection (according to Isaiah 50:11) is that the very blaze you kindle may end up burning you.

Have you ever been tempted to light your own fire in the darkness? Are you tempted at times to pretend the darkness does not exist, only to find yourself stumbling helplessly in the darkness?

I have. In fact, this is where I have been during the past few weeks. The thunder of physical and emotional pain has been rolling and the lightning flashes of fear and hopelessness have been the only illumination in my darkness. What do you do? This is what I did. I scrambled in the darkness until I could find my lantern of hope, and this is what the light reflected: "'For I know the plans I have for you,' declares the Lord, 'plans to prosper you and not to harm you, plans to give you hope and a future.'"

Pick up your lantern (His Word) and allow the fire of His Holy Spirit to furnish your path with light. He will lead the way into the full light of marvelous love. What a new beginning!

Thank You, Father, that Your Word is a lamp to my feet and a light to my path. Lead me gently through the dark days with the light of Your Word and guide my steps with the fire of Your Holy Spirit.

January 17

Scripture: "Brace yourself like a man; I will question you, and you shall answer me. . . ." (Job 40:7, *NIV*). "Then Job replied to the Lord: 'I know that you can do all things; no plan of yours can be thwarted.' . . . The Lord blessed the latter part of Job's life more than the first" (Job 42:1, 2, 12, *NIV*).

This morning after I read several chapters in the Book of Job (which is not where I usually find my inspiration), I felt like God was saying to me: "Brace yourself like a woman. I will question you, and you will answer Me." Like Job, my reply was "I know that You can do all things; and no plans of Yours can be thwarted."

The story of Job is one of new beginnings. After losing his family, his health, his possessions, and his friends, God not only gave restoration; but He also "blessed the latter part of Job's life more than the first" (42:12).

The significance of verse 10 resonated in my mind: "*After* [italics mine] Job had prayed for his friends, the Lord made him prosperous again and gave him twice as much as he had before."

Could this be a prerequisite to my restoration? Is this scripture saying that I must pray for my friends (even those who have falsely accused me and judged me wrongly)? I did *not* want to. But I prayed anyway.

Perhaps Job did not want to pray for his friends, but He braced himself like a man and prayed anyway. The result? A new beginning.

Have you been hurt, falsely accused, misunderstood, misjudged, or betrayed by those you love the most? Brace yourself and close that chapter in your life. The best days of your life are ahead. Step into the future with courage.

Thank You, Lord, that no plans of Yours can be thwarted by man. Help us to love our enemies and pray for those who spitefully use us (Luke 6:28).

January 18

Scripture: "Forget the former things; do not dwell on the past. See, I am doing a new thing! Now it springs up; do you not perceive it?" (Isaiah 43:18, 19, *NIV*).

Have you ever felt that you were stuck between the pain of the past and the promise of the future? In her book *Unstuck*, Carolyn Koons uses the analogy of a river and how we often get stuck on the bank. She explains how at times in our lives we hit one set of rapids after another. Not only do we get knocked around, but we also get cold and eventually numb. She points out that numbness is not only dangerous, but it's also an unnatural state—because real people feel.

After I read this book, my journal reflects how I felt. Perhaps you can identify too:

> During the past few months, actually the last two years, I have felt the blows of the rapids of life—some that have actually caused me to feel numb and almost paralyzed. My lack of interest in writing in my journal and for other professional and religious publications has been an indication that I have been stuck on the riverbank. My numbness has included fear of getting back into the water—fear that the waves will overwhelm me and I may go under for the third time. Many boats have come by to urge me to dive back in (opportunities to write for publications, opportunities in my profession, and nudgings by friends and family members), but I felt paralyzed by fear and numb from the blows of the raging rapids in my life.
>
> When my son, Eddie, went through a divorce two years ago, this blow almost paralyzed me. In my numbness, I retreated to the riverside for safety. This was like the tidal wave I had gone through personally 14 years ago when I experienced the dissolution of my

own marriage of 25 years. Only this time it left me numb—without feeling, or with an unwillingness to even admit I had been hit severely with these cruel rapids of divorce—this time with my son and grandsons. I was left wounded and hurt with no will to dive back into the mainstream. I went through the motions—reading my Bible, praying, encouraging others who were fighting similar waves—but I felt numb and paralyzed. I could not muster the courage to dive back in.

Reading this book has urged me to the edge of the water. With God's help, I am ready for a new beginning. I am believing that going through these deep waters will give me the courage to plunge back into the mainstream.

Perhaps you find yourself stuck on the riverbank. I believe Isaiah 43:18, 19 is urging us to forget the past and get ready for the "new thing" God will do when we make the plunge with Him.

Thank You, Lord, for providing Your tributaries to help us get back in the mainstream of Your will. Help us to cling to Your raft (Your Word) to keep us on course.

January 19

Scripture: "In the Lord put I my trust" (Psalm 11:1).

When David wrote this psalm, the environment was stormy. The sun had gone down, the stars were hidden, the waters were out, and the roads were broken up. But in the midst of the darkness and desolation, David cried out triumphantly: "In the Lord put I my trust." This was David's song in the night.

J.H. Jowett (*Springs in the Valley*, p. 202) tells the story of the little birds whose nest had been ruined. As the poet walked among the trees in his garden after the storm, he found the torn nest lying on the ground. He began to brood sadly, pitying the birds whose home had been wrecked. But as he stood and mused, he heard a twittering and chattering over his head; looking up, he saw the birds busy building again their ruined nest.

I believe God is saying to you and me, "Begin to build anew." Don't waste time brooding over your nest that has been destroyed. Focus on what you have left.

Again my journal reflects how I felt recently right after I read Marion Bond West's book *The Nevertheless Principle*:

> After I read this book, I could imagine God smiling and saying, "Evaline, you are at a crucial moment now. You have been shipwrecked and nearly drowned in icy waters of fear. But you have kept swimming and you are within reach of an island." In

Marion's words, "Right now you can crawl upon the shore and be safe there. It is called the Island of Trust."

During the past five weeks I have again been forced to crawl upon this "Island of Trust." Because of a physical illness which left me weak physically and emotionally, during my first day back in the classroom after several weeks, I felt I was treading icy waters of fear. But I was reminded of Psalm 18:16, "He sent from above, he took me, he drew me out of many waters."

Perhaps your nest of security has been destroyed. Join in the choir with David and sing, "In the Lord put I my trust."

Thank You, Father God, for leading me gently when I can only crawl—for picking me up when I grow weak and for giving me courage to trust in You when the waves are high.

January 20

Scripture: "What I tell you in the darkness, speak in the light" (Matthew 10:27, *NASB*).

When I think of a new beginning, I immediately think of one of my favorite Bible characters—Joseph. From the time Joseph was sold by his brothers and placed in confinement at age 17 until he was promoted from the prison to the palace at age 30, the Scripture says, "God was with him" (Genesis 39:21, *NIV*).

As we walk through dark times in our lives, we must remind ourselves that just as God was with Joseph, so will He be with us. Even though Joseph did not understand the reasons for the dark days, God had a purpose—not only to save a whole nation from famine but also to save his own family. Joseph was walking through this tunnel of darkness by divine appointment.

Recently I turned on the radio and heard this statement: "Our dark moments will last only as long as is necessary for God to accomplish His purpose." You may be saying, as I did, "Lord, please don't let it take 13 years."

According to Charles Stanley, Joseph learned some valuable lessons:
1. He learned more about himself.
2. He learned that his faith in God could be tested.
3. He learned personal contentment in spite of the circumstances.
4. He discovered that God had given him a gift (to interpret dreams).
5. He learned to use this gift.

We must remember that even in our dark moments we are walking through the darkness toward the light of a new day. Our pastor, Dr. David Bishop, recently reminded the congregation, "There is an end to 'the through.'" Just as Joseph was quick to tell in the light what he had learned in the dark, so must we. Genesis 41:16, says: "And Joseph answered Pharaoh, saying, It is not in me: God shall give Pharaoh an answer of peace. "

Joseph provided one of the greatest lessons we can learn—forgiveness—when he said to his brothers: "But as for you, ye thought evil against me; but God meant it unto good, to bring to pass, as it is this day, to save much people alive" (Genesis 50:20).

Father, thank You for the lessons we learn in the dark. Give us courage to share with others what You have accomplished in our lives.

January 21

Scripture: "Nay, in all these things we are more than conquerors through him that loved us. For I am persuaded that neither death, nor life, nor angels, nor principalities, nor powers, nor things present, nor things to come, nor height, nor depth, nor any other creature, shall be able to separate us from the love of God, which is in Christ Jesus our Lord" (Romans 8:37-39).

As chaplain of the sanctuary choir at our church, I have been preparing a devotional for Wednesday night. My topic is "When Life Pressures You at the Seams, How Do You Not Become Unraveled?"

At times we all feel that we are being stretched at the seams—that we will surely unravel. When this happens, it is time for a new beginning.

The Word reminds us that we are made of the finest fabric—in the image of God. In the words of David, we are "fearfully and wonderfully made" (Psalm 139:14)—made to endure intense pressure. Like Daniel, God may not deliver us *from* the lions' den, but He will be with us and deliver us *in* the lions' den. With Paul, we can say, "For I know whom I have believed, and am persuaded that he is able to keep that which I have committed unto him against that day" (2 Timothy 1:12).

A few months ago I was talking with a friend who is at a point in her life where it would be easy for her to feel that she is being stretched at the seams (emotionally and physically) and will surely come unraveled. To be left as a single parent in your early 40s with the responsibility of raising three children would make most of us feel like we were coming unraveled. The Lord impressed me to share this scripture with her:

"Enlarge the place of your tent, stretch your tent curtains wide, do not hold back; lengthen your cords, strengthen your stakes. For you will spread out to the right and to the left. . . . Do not be afraid; you will not suffer shame. Do not fear disgrace; you will not be humiliated. You will forget the shame of your youth and remember no more the reproach of your widowhood. For your Maker is your husband" (Isaiah 54:2-5, *NIV*).

When we feel stretched at the seams (whether it is physical, financial, emotional, or spiritual), I believe God is encouraging us to enlarge our vision, broaden our horizons, and strengthen our stakes in His Word.

What a rewarding experience when you watch a friend do just that—when her ministry becomes worldwide rather than local, when her horizons include other cultures and other denominations, and when her stakes become deeper in the Word of God. What a confirmation that "we are more than conquerors"—even when we are stretched at the seams.

Thank You, Lord, for those times when You allow us to be stretched in order that we may grow and become mature in You. Help me to enlarge the place of my tent and broaden my horizons.

January 22

Scripture: "I will give you the treasures of darkness, riches stored in secret places" (Isaiah 45:3, *NIV*).

A few years ago I had the opportunity to pray the invocation at summer commencement at Lee College. My journal records excerpts from my prayer:

> Father, we thank You for guidance and strength for those who teach and for those who learn as we endeavor to pass our rich heritage to each new generation. We pray that this commencement will be a new beginning for each of us. Grant us admittance to the School of Prayer, for it is here that we gain understanding to know You better, diligence to seek You earnestly, and wisdom to discover Your will for our lives daily. Father, give us intelligence to understand You, patience to wait for You, eyes to behold You, and a heart to hear You. In Jesus' name.

When something is ending, we can rest assured that something else is beginning. Endings remind us that we are closing certain chapters in our lives, but they also remind us that it is time to begin a new chapter.

The Book of Genesis reminds us that Joseph's dungeon was the road to the palace. During those dark days when Joseph was betrayed, forgotten, and forsaken, he discovered hidden treasures. Had Joseph not been Egypt's prisoner, he would not have been Egypt's governor. His commencement day was when the iron chains about his feet ushered in the golden chain about his neck. Joseph obviously had closed the chapter on rejection and hurt; his new chapter was titled "Forgiveness." "You meant evil against me; but God meant it for good" (Genesis 50:20, *NKJV*).

Whether you are graduating from college or adjusting to being a single parent, you are commencing a new chapter in your life. Remember, "a man's heart deviseth his way: but the Lord directeth his steps" (Proverbs 16:9)—even during the dark times. Learn from Joseph—discover some hidden treasures.

Father, help us to discover the treasures You have reserved for us. Help us to remember that You will be with us just as You were with Joseph.

January 23

Scripture: "The Lord my God will enlighten my darkness. . . . Weeping may endure for a night, but joy cometh in the morning" (Psalm 18:28; 30:5).

Have you ever felt that you were suddenly thrust into the darkness without a warning signal?

David felt this. He went from a shepherd tending his father's sheep to the anointed king of Israel. However, his mountaintop experience was short-lived. He was soon charged with treason and a death sentence and was pursued from one end of Israel to the other. In other words, he was actually running for his life. He finally took refuge in a limestone cave in the Judean wilderness.

Ron Mehl, in his book *God Works the Night Shift*, said David took a sudden fall from the limelight to a limestone hall. It can happen to any of us.

How do we handle the sudden darkness that comes into our lives? First of all, we take courage in the fact that David's dark days did not last forever. David wrote in his prayer journal, "The Lord my God will enlighten my darkness. . . . Weeping may endure for a night, but joy cometh in the morning." Daniel was also one who could write about darkness. While he was just a boy, he was dragged from his home and placed in captivity. Daniel 2:22 records what he learned in the dark: "He reveals deep and secret things; He knows what is in the darkness, and light dwells with Him" (*NKJV*). What treasures have you discovered in the dark? What will *you* write in *your* prayer journal? This is what I wrote a few years ago during a time in my life when I felt the sun would never shine again:

> Today I read what Charles H. Spurgeon once said during a dark season in his life. "Am I in the dark? Then Thou, O Lord, will lighten my darkness. Before long, things will change. Affairs may grow worse and more dreary, and cloud upon cloud be piled upon cloud; but if it grows so dark that I cannot see my own hand, still I shall see the Hand of the Lord."

Thank You, Lord, that You illuminate our path so that we may follow You one step at a time—even during the dark seasons.

January 24

Scripture: "And I, behold, I establish my covenant with you, and with your seed after you; and with every living creature that is with you. . . . And I will establish my covenant with you; neither shall all flesh be cut off any more by the waters of a flood; neither shall there any more be a flood to destroy the earth. And God said, This is the token of the covenant which I make between me and you and every living creature that is with you, for perpetual generations: I do set my bow in the cloud, and it shall be for a token of a covenant between me and the earth" (Genesis 9:9-13).

Recently I received a card from a friend with this inscription: "The paths of the Lord are lined with rainbows." God has provided a rainbow for every cloud of life.

In his book *Climbing the Rainbow,* Lloyd Ogilvie tells of a little boy in Missouri who loved to watch with his dad the magnificent display of nature in an Ozark rainstorm. One day when the boy saw a storm approaching, he ran to get his dad and led him outside. Hand in hand they watched the approaching storm—they beheld the lightning, heard the thunder, and felt the spray from the earth-replenishing rain.

After the rain subsided while the clouds still hung dense in the sky, the little boy squeezed his dad's hand. He said, "Dad, I think I smell a rainbow cookin'! I believe God is cookin' up a rainbow."

God is constantly "cookin' up rainbows" for His children. These rainbows are assurances of His faithfulness of His covenant with us. But there are times when our trust in His faithfulness is sorely tested by the circumstances of life. Too often our lives are filled with thunderclouds of doubt and fear. We must remember that through these clouds God sends His rainbows to us—promises from His Word.

Many times God cooks up a rainbow while it is still raining, and during those times it is difficult for us to see the long-range purpose of His direction.

When God gives us a rainbow promise in the midst of cloudy indecision, showing us a step we are to take, it is difficult for us to respond unless we remember that He can take the worst that may happen and use it for His good.

It is during these times that we need to grasp this promise that splashes the rainbow on our fearful hearts: "And we know that all things work together for good to them that love God, to them who are the called according to his purpose" (Romans 8:28).

Father God, help me to remember that without the storm, there would be no rainbow.

January 25

Scripture: "And, behold, the angel of the Lord came upon him, and a light shined in the prison: and he smote Peter on the side, and raised him up, saying, Arise up quickly. And his chains fell off from his hands" (Acts 12:7).

When I was growing up in Alabama, we frequently sang this chorus:

> Jesus breaks every fetter,
> Jesus breaks every fetter,
> Jesus breaks every fetter,
> And He sets me free.

Years later I must admit that as a child I was not sure what I was singing. "What is a fetter?" *Webster's New Collegiate Dictionary* defines a *fetter* as "a chain or shackle for the feet; something that confines."

One morning in 1987 (when I was living in Baton Rouge, Louisiana, going to Louisiana State University), I attended a local church where this chorus was sung frequently. My journal reflects the day I learned the meaning of this song—the day I experienced a new beginning emotionally:

> I believe the bonds of the past have held me captive; they have hampered my progress in every way—physically, mentally, emotionally, and spiritually. I believe when the chains of the past are broken, the fetters will begin to fall, the obstacles will be removed, and the powers of darkness will fade away in the light of God's love.
>
> I believe God has broken these chains that held me—just like He broke the chains of Paul and Silas when they were imprisoned, just like he released the chains from Peter's hands when he was in jail (Acts 12:6, 7).

When you are in prison, you are restrained by chains and walls and locked doors. I believe God has released the chains of hurts, removed the walls of fear and rejection, and opened the doors of opportunity and ministry.

When God sent an angel to visit Peter in that prison and admonished him to "arise up quickly," the chains that bound him were released. Perhaps God is saying to you, "Arise up quickly and allow Me to loose the chains that have bound you for too long." Let today be your new beginning. Walk out of your prison and be set free.

Thank God for freedom from emotional bondage. Lord, help me to be sensitive to Your angels You send to minister to me.

January 26

Scripture: "But one thing I do: Forgetting what is behind and straining toward what is ahead, I press on toward the goal to win the prize for which God has called me heavenward in Christ Jesus" (Philippians 3:13, 14, *NIV*).

Have you ever left home for a trip when the sun was shining, not a cloud in sight, only to find yourself suddenly engulfed in dark clouds and stormy weather?

On July 17, 1980, my 14-year-old daughter, Sharon, and I were driving to Alabama to visit her Grandmother Brooks. Suddenly we were engulfed in black clouds, loud thunder, streaking lightning, and hail the size of marbles. Trying to be a brave mother (which is not my nature during storms), I assured her that the storm would soon subside and that we would look for the first exit and wait until the storm passed over—which is what we did.

Continuing our trip on Interstate 59 about 10 minutes later, as we looked forward we began to see rays of sunlight shining through the clouds; as we looked backward, we could still see the dark clouds.

That evening after arriving at Mama Brooks' home, I missed Sharon for about an hour. When she returned to the living room where Mama Brooks and I were, she was eager to share what she had written—the lesson she had learned from the storm that day:

> This afternoon when Mom and I were on our way to Alabama to see Mama Brooks, I had a funny feeling (I guess like a burden) when we got on the interstate. I prayed and asked the Lord to take care of us, but I was still carrying the burden. About an hour later we saw some dark clouds, and Mom was getting worried that we were heading right into the storm. All of a sudden it started hailing, lightning, and thundering; and I was scared. Mother said, "Sharon, don't worry; the Lord will take care of us."
>
> After about 10 minutes we were out of the storm. I looked back and the clouds were real dark and you could still see the lightning. But when I looked ahead, there were beautiful clouds, and the sun was shining through. And I thought, *I don't have to worry about what was behind me because the Lord's already brought me through it. But just think about the beautiful things ahead.* And my burden was lifted.

In retrospect, Sharon and I are amazed how God used a storm to teach us a valuable lesson that would sustain us when the storms of life hit—some unexpectedly without any warning. We learned that when we are battered with the winds of rejection, the hailstones of disappointment, the thunder of fear, or the threatening lightning of bitterness, as Paul said, we must "[forget] those things which are behind and [reach] forward to those things which are ahead" (Philippians 3:13, *NKJV*).

Just as surely as the dark clouds gather, so will the sun shine again. As Jack Hayford once said, "We must not allow the shadows of yesterday to block the sunlight of tomorrow."

One morning in my devotions during a time in my life when it was tempting to look back, God impressed this thought on my mind: "Don't waste your time looking back; you could miss the next turn in the road."

Father, thank You for the storms You have brought me through. Help me to draw the curtains on the past and step forward into the future with courage and faith.

January 27

Scripture: "For if you forgive men when they sin against you, your heavenly Father will also forgive you. But if you do not forgive men their sins, your Father will not forgive your sins" (Matthew 6:14, *NIV*).

A few months ago we had a time of Solemn Assembly at our church—a weekend spent in fasting, praying, and repenting of our sins (Joel 2:15-17). As Pastor David Bishop put it, "I felt like I had heart surgery spiritually." As we examined ourselves and searched the deep recesses of every room, every corner of our hearts, I was in pain—severe pain. What I discovered did not agree with what I always wanted to believe about myself—that I am a *very forgiving person* who harbors no hurt.

In my time of prayer and asking God to turn His spotlight on my heart, I discovered some clogged arteries of unforgiveness—not unforgiveness for how others had hurt me but for how they had hurt my children. I realized that this obstruction in my spiritual heart was hurting me more than the offender.

So I had a choice—to continue to mask my unforgiveness (which I really had not known was there) or allow the Master Surgeon to do His work. I chose surgery.

What I discovered was not only that the surgery was painful but also that recovery required some time in intensive care with the Great Physician. I also discovered that in order to remove all traces of hurt and unforgiveness, I must pick up the telephone and make an effort to ask forgiveness from the person whom I had refused to forgive for hurting my children—which is what I did.

This lesson taught me that forgiveness is not passive; it involves action. Forgiveness was a part of Jesus' lifestyle. He forgave the paralytic (Matthew 9:2); He forgave the woman caught in adultery (John 8:10, 11); and He forgave the men who nailed Him to the cross: "Father, forgive them; for they know not what they do" (Luke 23:34). How can we, then, not forgive?

Father, thank You for the healing power of forgiveness. Help me to forgive others as You forgive me.

January 28

Scripture: "Fear not, for I am with you; be not dismayed, for I am your God. I will strengthen you, yes, I will help you, I will uphold you with My righteous right hand" (Isaiah 41:10, *NKJV*).

Have you ever felt paralyzed by fear? Most of us (if we are honest) have been infected by this contagious disease called fear, which saps our energy and robs us of joy in life.

Fear cripples many Christians and often pervades our families, even our churches. I must admit that fear invaded my world during the past few months of recuperation from a physical illness.

To fight the invasion of this unwelcome guest in my home, I discovered that God's Word constantly reminds me to "fear not." There are 366 "fear not" verses in the Bible (one for each day), most of which are followed by an assurance of the Lord's presence or a reminder of an aspect of His nature—His faithfulness, goodness, or loving-kindness. These scriptures reminded me that He was ready to take me by the hand and lift me above the shadows of fear—which is what He did.

Lloyd Ogilvie once said that when the Lord takes hold of our right hand with His grace-filled right hand, that puts us eye to eye with Him. It is then that He can get through to the deep inner place in us where our fears fester. When this happens, we are reminded that He is Jehovah-Shammah, which means "The Lord is there."

Where are you today? Are you trying to find your way out of a dark tunnel of fear? Do you feel as though the sun will never shine again? Most of us can identify with these tunnel experiences.

It amazes me how God provides a light of faith to lead us through the dark, fearful tunnel experiences. One morning I turned the radio on; what I heard Charles Stanley say provided light for me on this particular day. Perhaps it is for you today:

No child of God ever steps into the darkness. We walk through the darkness, but we never step into it because God is always going to light the way at least one step at a time. . . . Even in our dark moments we are walking toward the light of day. . . . God sometimes puts us in the dark that we may see the light. Take heart. He is Jehovah-Shammah. Fear not. The Lord is there.

What a new beginning!

Thank You, Lord, for leading me through the dark tunnel of fear. Help me to never turn loose of Your hand.

January 29

Scripture: "Which hope we have as an anchor of the soul, both sure and stedfast" (Hebrews 6:19).

In his book *Stress Fractures*, Charles Swindoll reminds us that our bodies have been constructed to withstand an enormous amount of stress and pressure. We can go through seasons of illness, financial reversals, domestic disappointments, or even the death of a loved one, if we don't lose one ingredient—*hope*.

The Scriptures call *hope* the "anchor of the soul." Hope is the opposite of despair. God provides for each of us a refuge of hope. When we accept the fact that sometimes seasons are dry and times are hard—but that God is in control of both circumstances—we discover a sense of divine refuge.

The word *anchor* is used often in ancient literature, but the anchor metaphor is used only once in the New Testament (Hebrews 6:19): "Which hope we have as an anchor of the soul, both sure and stedfast." There are many hymns and gospel songs that make use of the anchor metaphor. Their inspiration owes credit to this verse that refers to the "anchor of the soul."

One writer, Walter Henrichsen, painted a word picture. An ancient vessel was finding its way through a narrow entrance to a harbor. As the ship moved through the opening, the captain had to guard against a gust of wind running it onto a sandbar. Skeletons of many ships could be seen on the rocks, giving testimony to the fact that in some instances the captain had failed the navigation test. To minimize the risk, the olden-day skipper would lower the ship's anchor into a smaller boat, which would then be rowed through the narrow entrance of the harbor. The anchor would then be dropped and this ship, with sails down, would be pulled past the obstacles, through the narrow opening, and into the safety of the harbor.

The point of this story is not anchors, skippers, ships, or harbors. The point is this: That is exactly what Jesus Christ does when the bottom of life drops out.

When I read this story, I thought, *How many times has God sent a small boat in the form of a friend, a relative, or a colleague to help me through a narrow entrance into a safe harbor?* How many times has God used you to help someone to avoid shipwreck? Probably more than you realize.

This week I listened to my son, Eddie, sing Ray Boltz's song "The Anchor Holds." As Eddie sang the song, it was obvious that this was his testimony: The anchor *does* hold though the ship's been battered. The anchor *does* hold though the sails are torn. The anchor *does* hold in spite of the storm. Eddie has learned some lessons through the storms in his life that I could never teach him: that Jesus Christ is the anchor of his soul—both sure and steadfast.

Father, thank You for providing hope in the midst of despair. Thank You for family members and friends who are there when the storms hit.

January 30

Scripture: "Have not I commanded thee? Be strong and of a good courage; be not afraid, neither be thou dismayed: for the Lord thy God is with thee whithersoever thou goest" (Joshua 1:9).

January is usually the month when businesses take inventory. Most of us spend some time during the month of January taking personal inventory—reviewing our goals for the previous year and setting new goals for the new year.

My method for taking personal inventory involves reading my journal for the past year, reviewing some of the same goals I have set for several years, and facing the fact that some of the same shelves in my life remain empty.

According to Ron Mehl, in his book *God Works the Night Shift*, God takes inventory of our lives during the dark seasons. He said God does what any good manager does when he locks the store for the night. He restocks the shelves. He stated that God does five things:

1. He takes inventory.
2. He notes what you're missing.
3. He takes stock of what you're low on and observes what you have to spare.
4. He checks out what's fresh and what's about to go stale.
5. He runs His eye across every shelf in your life.

Ron Mehl suggests that during the trying times of our lives when we hear bumps and thumps in the darkness, these are God's workmen stocking the shelves from heaven's infinite storehouse.

Do you ever feel as though your shelves are empty? Do you feel as if your energy is depleted and you are running on fumes? It is time to take inventory and allow God to do a new thing.

The first chapter of Joshua is a constant reminder to "be strong and courageous." God was saying to Joshua, "My Word does not change, but the nature of My miracle working will take new forms." God still wants to display His mighty acts in creative ways. In order for Him to do this, we must be willing to take the first step—lay hold of His promises. Allow God to run His eye across every shelf in your life.

His grace is sufficient, even when our shelves are empty.

Thank You, Father, for teaching me the lesson that stocking some shelves in our lives take time. Help me to be "strong and courageous" and remain in partnership with You and Your Word.

January 31

Scripture: "Now thanks be unto God, which always causeth us to triumph in Christ, and maketh manifest the savour of his knowledge by us in every place" (2 Corinthians 2:14).

Thanks for joining me on this treasure hunt during January. While we have shared in these periods of sitting at His feet, I hope your journal reflects some golden nuggets you have collected, which will give you the courage to step into the water of your Red Sea, watch the waters part, cross your Jordan, and claim your promise.

Let me remind you that we do not possess new territory or a "new beginning" without a battle. The battle begins when we make an effort to bury the prohibitions and glories of the past to conquer and take what God has for us. But the good news is, conquest is always attended by the presence of the miraculous. Moses needed the miraculous, Joshua needed the miraculous, and so do we.

When Paul and Silas were released from jail, it took the miraculous. When Daniel was delivered from the lions' den, it took the miraculous. When Jesus was raised from the dead, it took the miraculous. When you and I are released from the fetters of the past, it will take the miraculous.

Last night I reread *Sand in My Shoes*, which is written by my sister and my best friend, Wanda Griffith. In this book she recounts the miraculous healings we witnessed in our family when we were growing up in small parsonages in Alabama. She also gives us glimpses of valleys which she has walked through—valleys of physical pain, financial difficulties, and emotional distress which comes with raising children. But her admonition is to "keep walking—even when we have sand in our shoes."

I join with Wanda in inviting you to follow the example of the oyster:

> What does the oyster do when a grain of sand invades its shell? Complain and make all the other oysters on the beach miserable? Deny that anything is wrong? Question God with "Why me?" Rebel?

> No. No. No. The oyster recognizes the sand. Slowly and patiently it wraps the grain of sand with a God-given milky substance called nacre. Then it covers each sharp corner and coats every cutting edge, thereby turning misfortune into blessing, pain and distress into beauty—transforming the grain of sand into a luxurious pearl.

Let's join Wanda in her strategy for walking in the sand: Let's walk in His commandments, and remember that He makes pearls.

As we turn the page of this devotional book into a new month, February, let's sit at His feet with Wanda as she challenges us to "grow stronger."

Thank You, Father, for taking the grains of sand in our lives and making pearls. Help us to continue to walk with You and grow stronger.

NOTES

February

Staying Strong
Wanda Gore Griffith

Wanda Gore Griffith is the author of *Sand in My Shoes*, published by Pathway Press in 1994. She has written many articles for the *Church of God Evangel* and the adult Sunday school curriculum's Life Related Learnings. She and her sister, Evaline, have spoken at state ladies retreats, Prayer and Praise Conferences, and writers workshops. She has a master of science degree in educational administration and supervision from the University of Tennessee in Knoxville.

Most of Wanda's career was spent at Lee College, where she served as registrar and part-time teacher until 1991. After serving for a short time as editorial assistant in the International Ladies Ministries Department, she then moved to the Church of God Publishing House, where she presently serves as administrative assistant to the general director.

Wanda and her husband, Bob, live in Cleveland, Tennessee. They have two sons, Rob and Mike, and three grandchildren—Vance, Jennifer, and Emily.

February 1

Scripture: "The eyes of the Lord range throughout the earth to strengthen those whose hearts are fully committed to him" (2 Chronicles 16:9).*

The telephone rang. It was Debbie, my daughter-in-law. She was sick and would not be driving home for the holidays. "Did you receive my gift?"

"Yes," I said. "But I haven't opened it yet. Do you want me to open it now?"

"Please, would you? I want to hear your response."

I knew the package was a book. The size and weight was a dead giveaway. My friends and family often give me books because they know how much I enjoy reading. I thought, *I probably already have this book.* However, I told myself, *Wanda, act excited! It's the thought that counts!*

The gift was indeed a book—one I was using in a Bible study group each week. But this book was special. Debbie had stood in line over an hour to meet the author and get his autograph for me.

Debbie's voice came back on the line, "I know you already have the book because I saw it in the backseat of your car. But I still think you will like this particular book. Open it."

As I opened *He Still Moves Stones,* I found this personal note from the author written on the inside: "Wanda, stay strong. Max Lucado."

I couldn't believe it. My hero! My favorite writer.

And the message . . . meaningful, challenging! I couldn't get away from it. He may have written the same words to hundreds of others, but I received them as my own private instructions. Almost a command—"Stay strong."

To focus on this staying power, I hastened to develop this acrostic:

Staying . . . in His presence.
Trusting . . . His unfailing love.
Resisting . . . those things that divert my focus and purpose.
Obeying . . . His Word.
Nourishing . . . fruitful relationships.
Growing . . . stronger each day.

Father of all strength, I commit my life to You. Strengthen me and help me stay focused on Your Word so that each day brings me into closer relationship with You.

*The Scripture references used for this month's devotions are from the *New International Version* unless otherwise indicated.

February 2

Scripture: "Be strong in the Lord and in the power of His might. Put on the whole armor of God, that you may be able to stand against the wiles of the devil" (Ephesians 6:10, *NKJV*).

As we embark on the 21st century, we find that women comprise over half the workforce in this country. The U.S. Census Bureau shows that the number of working women has more than doubled in the last four decades.

Staying strong in this environment demands a strong commitment to juggle many responsibilities. We wear so many hats; handle so many different agendas; and most of the time burn the candle at both ends. You are probably thinking, *How can I stay strong when my strength is used up on my job, in choir rehearsals and performances, Bible study groups, and taking care of my family?*

There are times we feel like throwing in the towel. Yes, just quitting. Our world is topsy-turvy with upheaval and change. Little by little our full DayTimers and tight deadlines squeeze every bit of energy out, including our priority to stay strong.

Here is a poem by an anonymous writer that expresses these sentiments:

> When things go wrong, as they sometimes will,
> When the road you're trudgin' seems all up hill,
> When the funds are low, and the debts are high,
> And you want to smile, but you have to sigh,
> When care is pressing you down a bit,
> Rest if you must, but don't you quit.

Charles Stanley, in *The Source of My Strength*, reminds us that the Bible has much to say about those who endure. Staying strong means running the race all the way to the end. Stanley summarizes Ephesians 6:10-18 by saying: "Finally, being fully armed and in prayer, persevere. Don't give up. Don't give in. In fact, don't give an inch. Hang tough for the Lord."

Moses was one who hung tough, who refused to give in or give up, who decided that no matter what the odds were against him, he would not surrender. He had staying power.

I heard a Lee College student speak about the four words her father whispered in her ear when he brought her to college as an insecure freshman. Those four words sustained her through many difficulties. What were they?

"Just hang in there!"

Thank You, Father God, for providing the armor and equipment for us to endure the hard times. Help us to hang tough when tough times threaten to hang us. May we be reminded that You strengthen our faith and refine us for Your purposes.

February 3

Scripture: "With Him are wisdom and strength, He has counsel and understanding" (Job 12:13, *NKJV*).

One day I caught my 4-year-old son with a towel tied around his neck, raising his window on the second floor. He was preparing to fly just like Superman.

We must appear just as foolish to God at times—making our "to do" lists, filling in our DayTimers, spinning and whirling like Wonder Woman in her all-American red, white, and blue outfit. Why do we try so hard to measure up to the standards of the virtuous woman described in Proverbs 31? She "works with her hands . . . brings her food from afar . . . rises also while it is still night . . . considers a field and buys it . . . extends her hand to the poor. . . . Her clothing is fine linen. . . . She smiles at the future. She opens her mouth in wisdom. . . . Her children rise up and bless her; her husband also, and he praises her" (*NASB*).

Wow! Talk about Wonder Woman. My children have called me names, but "blessed" was not among them. I wondered about this Wonder Woman in Proverbs. I'm sure she didn't wear a red, white, and blue suit with crowning tiara, but how could she be all things to all people? Then I realized that maybe this passage of Scripture is not describing one day's activities. Maybe it describes what she accomplished in her lifetime. I hope so.

When the dust settles from our tailspin of "doing," we slump in a cloud of guilt and defeat because every item on the list did not get checked off. We becomes slaves, shackled with self-imposed chains—too many things to do!

Staying strong does not mean proving we are Wonder Woman. God doesn't expect it, so who are we trying to please? Then I remember His promise:

"Trust in the Lord with all your heart, and do not lean on your own understanding" (Proverbs 3:5, *NASB*).

Why can't we just relax and trust His Word, which tells us, "Be still, and know that I am God" (Psalm 46:10). After all, He alone provides strength for our weaknesses. I think He is saying to me today, "Be still and know who I am. I will show you what is important to do today. I will provide strength for every task."

And I respond, "OK, Lord, I understand."

Then I add this entry to my "to do" list:

Take off Wonder Woman outfit. The Lord is my strength!

Thank you, Father, for not expecting me to be Wonder Woman. I know I try at times, but I fail miserably when I get my priorities out of order. I want to trust You for the strength to do the things I can do today and not be defeated by those things left undone. Your wisdom will guide my decisions.

February 4

Scripture: "Do not forsake me when my strength is gone" (Psalm 71:9).

A few years ago my husband and I drove a BMW. We inherited this flaming red vehicle equipped with five in the floor, sunroof, bucket seats, blasting stereo speakers (and monthly payments) from our son, a sophomore in college. While making his first "big money" on a co-op job at TVA, Rob purchased this preppie car, assuring us he could sell it for more than he paid for it. Yes, we've all experienced this I-know-more-than-you-do attitude from our children.

Although this car did not match our forty-something lifestyle, we drove it for several years. Toward the end of its tenure with the Griffith family, the Beamer (we named it this before it stopped beaming) developed a serious problem. Right in the middle of five lanes of traffic, it would just stop. No warning. No lights, whistles, or bells. It just stopped and would not start.

My husband, who is a number one shade tree mechanic, could not figure out what was wrong. He replaced the battery, alternator, electric starter, and many other parts not familiar to me. Some of my most embarrassing moments in life are flashbacks of Bob and me pushing this BMW down the streets of Ft. Worth, Texas, in 102-degree temperatures where 10,000 friends (and former friends) congregated around the General Assembly auditorium. I prayed for the earth to open and let me disappear. But no such luck. I had to face my friends and listen to their jokes.

This unreliable, unpredictable, unfixable car almost cost me my sanctification. Almost? Well, you figure. I wanted to personally box it up and ship it back to wherever BMW's come from. "Please," I begged my husband, "buy me an American car that will keep running once it's started. I don't care what color, how sporty, or flashy—just as long as it keeps running!"

As I climbed down off my soap box, I remembered how some of Christ's disciples were just as unpredictable as my old BMW. They started fine, but when the pinch came—when stress mounted—they ran out of go. Take Peter, for example. He always started strong. His attempt at wave walking went well at first. However, not too many steps out, he lost his focus and found himself treading water.

Earlier this year I was sitting at a ladies seminar on "The Spirit-Controlled Temperament," taking a test to determine my personality type. The leader cleverly labeled each category biblical characters: Paul for choleric (doer); Peter for sanguine (influencer); Barnabas for phlegmatic (relater); and John the Baptist for melancholic (thinker). As I tallied up my score, my sister Evaline looked over at me and asked which personality type the test labeled me.

"Peter," I said. "Watch your ear!"

Of course she turned out to be Barnabas—steady, deliberate, predictable, patient. Pretty disgusting if you ask me. Then I remembered that even though Peter was impulsive, emotional, persuading, and enthusiastic, he turned out to be strong—a rock, a "chip" from the greater foundation rock upon which Christ built His church. Not a bad finish for a sanguine. But Jesus never gave up on him. He prayed that Peter would not fail. And guess what? He does the same for you and me.

Thank You, Father, for not giving up on me. Help me remember the lessons You teach me.

February 5

Scripture: "The people that do know their God shall be strong, and do exploits" (Daniel 11:32, KJV).

What causes us to become satisfied with the status quo? Why do we lose the initiative and hunger to stretch ourselves, to grow stronger? One characteristic of people who stay strong is that they have a genuine passion for what they're doing—they believe in their mission.

Billy Graham, one of the most highly respected religious leaders of the 20th century stands out as an excellent example of someone who stayed strong when others all around him fell from their pedestals. How has he stood with the strength of a giant, escaped the criticism from the inquisitive press, and been chosen one of the "Ten Most Admired Men in the World" 32 times?

After attending Bible school at Bob Jones College, Florida Bible Institute, and Wheaton College, from which he later graduated in 1943,

Graham started speaking for Youth for Christ. He never attempted to be a spectacular, motivational, I've-got-a-new-revelation type of speaker. He just stayed strong in the Word and preached the gospel.

Through the years, Billy Graham remained true to his belief that if he will present the Word, God will bring the increase. Since his first crusade in 1949, literally millions around the world have responded to the simple, but profound message of God's love. His Global Mission crusade (held March 14-18, 1995, at a baseball stadium in San Juan, Puerto Rico) was sent around the world by satellite, television, and videotape to reach an estimated one billion people. Interpreters translated Graham's messages into 116 languages, and technicians used 30 satellites to beam them across every time zone. Reports from various nations describe decisions for Christ and a renewed enthusiasm and unity among believers. If response rates matched those recorded during previous Graham crusades, more than 100 million people made decisions for Christ (*National & International Religion Report*, April 3, 1995).

When asked if he has ever considered changing or updating his methods, Graham responds, "No, I've not considered changing because my message is the same and the method works. I have often been asked the secret of my crusades," he said. "There are three secrets: prayer, prayer, prayer."

What staying power!

Dear Father, I thank You for faithful servants like Billy Graham who refuse to compromise their message, and stay strong for You. Raise up more prayer warriors with staying power to reap the harvest in these last days.

February 6

Scripture: "Stand fast therefore in the liberty by which Christ has made us free, and do not be entangled again with a yoke of bondage" (Galatians 5:1, *NKJV*).

A new yoke of slavery is offered every day by life's temptations and challenges. So how can we stay strong and free of this yoke?

I read a lovely story of a young man visiting a small village. It was what we might refer to in Alabama as just a wide place in the road, with maybe only one traffic light. The young man asked an older village dweller what it was about this place that made it significant. "Young man," the villager responded, "this is the starting place for any place in the world. You can start from here and go anywhere— anywhere at all."

Isn't that what Christ says to us? Is it not what He said to the woman caught in adultery in John's Gospel (7:53—8:11)? What about the woman at the well? Did He not offer her "a well of water springing up into everlasting life"? (John 4:14, KJV).

Amazing! In both of these instances, the sin is not condoned, but there is no condemnation. The women who found themselves at Jesus' feet are forgiven and offered hope—everlasting life.

There are times when we find ourselves in both the skin of the accusers and the accused. We hold unresolved guilt, ready to hurl rocks, just like those scribes and Pharisees. Our failures may not be as obvious or easily categorized as the woman's, but what we are and have done is no less serious to our Lord. We try to fool ourselves by attaching fancy labels to our problems and failures, refusing to look at the real culprit—sin.

Staying strong means having the strength to drop the stone. Accept His forgiveness. Stand fast in His liberty. And refuse to become entangled with a yoke of sin's bondage.

I'm starting today! Want to join me?

Thank You, most gracious Father, for providing this highway of redemption and liberty. I refuse to become entangled with sin's yoke of bondage. I choose to accept Your forgiveness, strength, and freedom.

February 7

Scripture: "But one thing I do, forgetting what lies behind and straining forward to what lies ahead, I press on toward the goal for the prize of the upward call of God in Christ Jesus" (Philippians 3:13, 14, *RSV*).

One of my dad's spiritual "checkup" questions was "Wanda, have you got the victory?"

Victory? No way. He knew I didn't, or he wouldn't have asked. I could never fool my father for one minute. His discerning eyes X-rayed my spiritual condition with an insight that only God could top. More often than not, the diagnosis was not one of victory but of a struggling child, pursuing ways to stay strong and victorious.

It was difficult for me because I erroneously thought living victoriously meant you were on the mountaintop all the time, shouting "Victory!" That is probably the reason I backslid (or so I thought) all the time. Much later in life I discovered the presence and work of God in my life were based on something much deeper than feelings.

How do we fuel this passionate search for victory and strength? What curious stuff within us keeps pressing for the extraordinary? A favorite book of mine is *Restoring Your Spiritual Passion*, by Gordon MacDonald. It was a birthday gift from my sister Evaline in 1986. I have read this book many times, rereading parts with frequent regularity.

In one chapter, MacDonald refers to this passion for victory as a killer instinct, the way of the hungry boxer. To the business person, it's an eye for the top; to the academic, it's the untarnished quest for truth; to the soldier, it's the gung ho; to the artist, it's a kind of mystical perfection; and to a mother, it's that faint whimper in the middle of the night coming from the room of a sick child. There is something about passion that tranquilizes the senses of fatigue, pain, and even a sense of well-being, causing some to pay incredible prices for certain goals.

When our two sons played football in high school, their team went to the state finals two years in a row. Bob and I sat on the sidelines in rain, sleet, and snow during these long football seasons, cheering them on. Without exception, one or the other got hurt every game with minor, and not-so-minor, injuries. At the time, however, the injuries were not important to them, the pain totally insignificant. They played with a passion; their goal was to win!

This passion to win is necessary if we stay strong in our Christian walk. Even when we lose this passion that should be strongest and allow weaker passions to rule us, God reveals Himself to those who want to know Him more than they want anything else. It was from a wellspring of this kind of passion that the apostle Paul penned these words in Philippians: "But one thing I do, forgetting what lies behind and straining forward to what lies ahead, I press on toward the goal for the prize of the upward call of God in Christ Jesus."

Martin Luther demonstrated this passion when he stood before the intimidating power of the papal legates from Rome and announced, "Here I stand; I can do nothing else." Being branded as a heretic did not keep him from pressing forward; it added fuel to the fire. The spark he ignited by hammering the Ninety-five Theses to the door of the Wittenberg church caused the Reformation to burst into full flame.

What can we say about this kind of passion for strength? I say, "Help us press forward—always forward—with a passion that dares not remain the same, but grows stronger because we have the presence of a living and victorious Lord in our lives!"

Heavenly Father, ignite my passion for more of Your strength. Help me remember that victory is not always a mountaintop experience but an overcoming life that keeps pushing toward the prize of Your high calling.

February 8

Scripture: "To draw near to listen is better than to offer the sacrifice of fools" (Ecclesiastes 5:1, *RSV*).

Saturdays around the parsonage were "preparation day" for Sunday. Six long-haired women presented a challenge for the hair products—shampoo, styling gel, wave clamps, metal curlers, and hair spray. We could stack those hairdos so well they would stay for days, and with the help of a hair net maybe a week.

Daddy spent Saturdays studying and meditating. Often his "meditations" turned into naps. We would find him stretched out on the sofa in the den with his Bible open on his chest and his sermon notes on the floor.

Throughout the centuries, Christians have related a variety of ways of staying strong by drawing near and listening to God. The accumulated wisdom of their experiences gives us insight as we seek stronger intimacy with God.

The meditation of Scripture centers on internalizing and personalizing the passage. The written Word becomes a living word addressed to us personally. Take a single event, or a parable, or a few verses, or even a single word and allow it to take root. As we open His Word, we become one of Christ's disciples, and sit at His feet.

In the fullness of time, Jesus came and taught the reality of the kingdom of God, demonstrating what life could be like in that Kingdom. In His intimate relationship with the Father, Jesus modeled for us the reality of hearing and obeying. "The Son can do nothing of his own accord, but only what he sees the Father doing; for whatever he does, that the Son does likewise" (John 5:19, *RSV*).

When Jesus told His disciples to abide in Him, they understood what He meant because He was abiding in the Father. He said He was the good Shepherd and His sheep knew His voice (John 10:4). He told them the Comforter would come, the Spirit of truth, who would guide His children into all truth (John 16:13). He says the same thing to us today.

In the Book of Acts we see the resurrected and reigning Christ, through the Holy Spirit, teaching and guiding His children: leading Philip to new unreached cultures (Acts 8), revealing His messiahship to Paul (Acts 9), teaching Peter about the Jewish nationalism (Acts 10), guiding the church out of its cultural captivity (Acts 15).

What we see again are God's people learning to live from hearing God's voice and obeying His Word. This forms the biblical foundation for meditation. The wonderful news is that Jesus has not stopped acting and speaking. He is working in our world. He is alive to keep us strong!

Thank You, Father, for serving as our High Priest to forgive us, our Prophet to teach us, our King to rule us, our Shepherd to guide us.

February 9

Scripture: "Oh, how I love your law! I meditate on it all day long" (Psalm 119:97).

The New Age emphasis on meditation has almost made us afraid to talk about Christian meditation. However, Christian meditation and that centered in Eastern religions stand worlds apart.

Eastern meditation is an attempt to empty the mind; Christian meditation is an attempt to fill the mind. Eastern forms of meditation emphasize becoming detached from the world—losing personhood and individuality, merging with the "cosmic mind." There is a longing to be freed from the burdens and pains of this life and to attain the blessedness of oblivion in Nirvana. Personal identity is lost. In fact, personality is seen as the ultimate illusion. Followers seek escape from the miserable wheel of existence, as well as from a god to be attached to or hear from. Detachment is the final goal of Eastern religion.

Christian meditation goes far beyond the notion of detachment. Jesus indicated that in His story of the man who was emptied of evil but not filled with good. "When the unclean spirit has gone out of a man . . . he goes and brings seven other spirits more evil than himself, and they enter and dwell there; and the last state of that man becomes worse than the first" (Luke 11:24-26, *RSV*).

No, detachment is not enough; we must go on to attachment to God. Christian meditation leads us to the inner wholeness necessary to give ourselves to God freely. After each encounter with God, meditation sends us into our ordinary world with stronger and greater perspective and balance.

Warren Wiersbe, a great writer and Bible teacher said, "What digestion is to the body, meditation is to the soul. If you ate nourishing food but never digested it, you would slowly die." The blessed man— or woman—described in Psalm 1 meditated on the Bible and its truths day and night. How? The bridge between learning and living is meditation—praying over the Word, pondering it, applying it to our lives. Only then can we grow stronger as we plumb the inner depths of His love and strength.

Holy Father, help us locate those safe places where we can listen for Your voice, where You can speak to us through Your Word, by Your Spirit.

February 10

Scripture: "The joy of the Lord is [my] strength" (Nehemiah 8:10).

One day I was home during the lunch hour praying for my family. The big chair in my living room quickly converted to my altar for the hour. The phone rang. I started not to answer it, but I decided to go ahead and interrupt my prayer.

The voice on the other end was a close friend calling from Arizona, two time zones away. I told him, "Bob isn't here. I came home by myself." He answered, "Wanda, I don't want to speak to Bob. I was praying and felt that I needed to call you and tell you I'm praying for you and your family."

He did not know the problem I was facing, but he continued: "Wanda, don't let the devil steal your joy. 'The joy of the Lord is your strength.'" Then he prayed over the phone that God would give me guidance and new strength. Twelve years have passed since that call interrupted my time of prayer and despair, but I remember it when I become discouraged and feel my joy slipping away.

The prophet Nehemiah built the walls of Jerusalem "even in troublesome times" (Daniel 9:25, *NKJV*). Yet he found the true source of joy. He celebrated God's goodness.

One writer described joy as the motor that keeps everything else going. When it is missing, we have to go back to the Master Mechanic. We cannot continue long in anything without joy. Women endure the problems of pregnancy and pains of childbirth because the joy of motherhood is not far away. Young married couples struggle through the first difficult years of adjustment because they value the promise of a long life together. Parents hold steady through the terrible teen years, knowing their children will one day grow up and get it all together.

God commanded Israel to gather together three times a year to celebrate His goodness. These festivals of praise gave strength and cohesion to the children of Israel. Without such cohesion, life falls apart. When we celebrate God's goodness, His joy becomes our strength, fortifying us with energy and power.

Joy keeps us strong even when our problems continue.

No other name, Father, but Yours alone, has the power to strengthen us by empowering us with Your joy. Even in times of discouragement, doubt, and disillusionment, we refuse to let the devil steal our joy! We will praise Your name.

February 11

Scripture: "In the fear of the Lord there is strong confidence, and His children will have a place of refuge " (Proverbs 14:26, *NKJV*).

Recently I was preparing to leave town for a weekend conference. In my haste to pick up last-minute items, I failed to see the big, white Chrysler coming toward me as I was turning left out of the shopping center. Wham! she hit my side of the car! My tape player was blasting, "Cast your cares on Him, for He cares for you."

Stopping the tape, I crawled out on the other side of the car to survey the damage. It was bad! I knew Bob was going to be upset with me for not going the extra distance to the light to cross the intersection. How many times had he told me? Many.

The first person who stopped to check on the accident was a home-care nurse. My face was red, my heart pounding. The only question she asked me was the important one, "Do you have high blood pressure?" Following an affirmative nod, she put me in her air-conditioned car to cool down and escape the 96-degree temperature. After calming me down and checking my blood pressure, she stayed with me until Bob arrived. She provided a place of refuge, a quiet peace in the midst of screaming sirens and police cars. I was fortunate to escape with very minor injuries. The nurse (my guardian angel) kept assuring me that cars are easily repaired; people are not.

Through this traumatic experience, I felt the strong arm of God. He was my confidence during a time of uncertainty. Watching the wrecker tow my car away, I remembered the song playing in my tape machine. The words still ringing in my head reminded me that when I am weak to "let the mighty hand of Jesus carry you."

When our strength is gone, we are forced to trust God completely, letting go of the props and supports. It is then we can rely on Him to care for us and provide a place of refuge.

Thank You, Heavenly Father, for protecting me and providing a place of refuge—even when I'm weak and careless, not watching the traffic closely enough. You are a present help in time of trouble.

February 12

Scripture: "The name of the Lord is a strong tower; the righteous run to it and are safe" (Proverbs 18:10).

As I pop the Homecoming and Reunion videos into my VCR, I reach for the box of tissues. Here come beautiful moments of nostalgia and buckets of tears. Bill and Gloria Gaither touch millions of hearts with these video productions of the "old timers." I am no exception.

Each time I watch one I think, *This time I won't cry.* But I always do. To see and hear my heroes of the all-night sings testify of God's faithfulness to them renews and strengthens my faith. It also brings a note of sadness when I realize my children and grandchildren do not know these great gospel songs of the 1950s and '60s.

When I talk about the different singers in the groups, my husband says, "Jake who? And Hovie who?" He didn't grow up as a preacher's kid whose number one form of entertainment was the monthly all-night sings.

"First names, huh? You'd think you are close friends, or kissing cousins," he teases. Well, I feel like we are close friends. I worshiped with all their songs and sang them in church and camp meetings as a teenager. Today scrapbooks filled with autographed pictures of the Statesmen and Blackwood Brothers are somewhere in my basement. I even have a piece of the wrecked airplane that killed R.W. Blackwood and Bill Lyles (members of the Blackwood Brothers Quartet) in Alabama in the early 1950s.

Recently while rocking my granddaughter, I sang along with the *Revival* video. Jennifer looked up at me with those beautiful blue eyes and said, "Granna, you know *all* the songs, don't you?" For over an hour we rocked and sang.

These sing-along videos preserved a portion of my gospel heritage, capturing on tape remnants of childhood memories and moments of strength flowing from the Southern Gospel lyrics. Most of the songs are personal testimonies of God's love and grace to His children.

He is our strong tower. We have the privilege to call on His name—our refuge—in times of trouble. Let's keep singing!

Thank You, Father, because You are our strong tower. You are our refuge in times of difficulty and trouble, and You are our song.

February 13

Scripture: "What strength do I have, that I should still hope? What prospects, that I should be patient? (Job 6:11).

My younger sister Carolyn has a wonderful testimony of how the Lord healed her broken heart. After Mother died, she went through a period of depression and heartbreak. In her own words she relates how the Lord strengthened her and gave her a new song:

I still remember the Sunday I stood in church and sang "Whatever It Takes." I had never really surrendered my life to sing part of the words of this song that gave my willing assent for God to take the thing dearest to me. At that time I thought my youngest child, who was only 2, was the dearest person to me. But Jesus knew better. He knew I had depended on my mother more than I had Him. So when she was taken, I was lost. I became depressed, bitter, and angry. Even though I had served the Lord most of my life and given him years of service, I felt He had rejected me; I was alone.

Then one day, after months of suffering, God gave me a song—"A Different Song." As I recorded the words, I began to sing the melody. It was at this moment He started a process of healing my broken heart and gave me a new song to sing.

Many times I had sung the song "The Healer," taken from Isaiah 53:4, 5, which says, "By His stripes we are healed." Now I truly believed His Word and I began clinging to Him until the healing was complete. The hopelessness and despair were replaced by joy.

The Lord gave me "A Different Song" in 1979. In 1990, just before Christmas, I received a gift I will never forget. A letter arrived from Pathway Music saying my song would be published in their new book, *Adoration*. Oh, what joy fills my heart every time someone tells me, "I sang 'A Different Song,' and it blessed my heart." I am reminded how God healed my broken heart and truly gave me a different song.

A Different Song

I had walked with Jesus for so much of my life,
I thought I had known Him and had walked in the light;
But He helped me see where I was walking wrong,
And He gave me a different song.

Chorus

A different song, I have a different song,
Since Jesus changed my life He gave to me a different song;
Now I can walk with Him, now I can talk to Him,
For Jesus healed my broken heart, He gave to me a brand new start.

I was low in despair, felt that no one really cared,
But He spoke to me, said that I could be free;
He changed me that day, and now I praise Him all the way,
For He gave me a different song.

—Carolyn Gore McElroy

Heavenly Father, You are the healer of broken hearts and the giver of life. Thank You for giving us a different song and restoring our strength.

February 14

Scripture: "By this we know love, because He laid down His life for us" (1 John 3:16, *NKJV*).

This is Valentine's Day, a holiday honoring lovers, named for the patron saint of lovers, St. Valentine. It's a special day to express our love by giving cards and gifts. It's also a time for remembering.

Remember your first love? Every woman does (men do too; they just don't talk about it). First loves are different from first crushes, first dates, first kisses, first anything else romantic. Why? Because your first love is reciprocal. It is not one-sided. It's the first time you love someone and that someone loves you back. It's special. Many people do not marry their first love, but they never forget them.

At a writer's conference a few years ago, the leader gave us an assignment to write two pages about our first love. Because I knew the speaker (he was a former student at Lee College), he asked me to read my paper to the class. As I described the handsome, intelligent, athletic, dreamboat that broke all the girls' hearts in high school, the speaker said, "Yes, that's Bob."

"No, it wasn't," I said. Even though Bob has all these attributes, I had to tell my instructor, in front of God and everybody, that the first love in my story was not my husband.

As Christians, our first love relationship is to love the Lord our God with all of our heart, soul, mind, and strength. No competitors. However, God always takes the initiative in this love relationship. He came to Adam and Eve in the Garden of Eden. He came to Noah, Abraham, Moses, and the prophets. Jesus came to the disciples and chose them to be with Him. He told them, "You did not choose Me, but I chose you. . . . You are not of the world, but I chose you out of the world" (John 15:16, 19, *NASB*).

God determined to love you and me. Otherwise, we could never have come into this love relationship. We are His first love. This unconditional love beckons us: "Behold, I stand at the door and knock; if anyone hears My voice and opens the door, I will come in to him, and will dine with him, and he with Me" (Revelation 3:20, *NASB*). Our part is to sit at His feet and commune with Him. That's where we feel His love and receive strength.

Today, dear Father, I give You my love, my life, my past with its failures, fears, and pride. Thank You for loving me first.

February 15

Scripture: "Go in the strength you have. . . . Am I not sending you?" (Judges 6:14).

We've all heard the statement "A chain is only as strong as its weakest link."

In a society that places so much emphasis on numbers, we forget the importance of the individual. But the Bible is filled with examples of God's appointing one man or woman with special strength to do His work.

Remember how Mary of Bethany brought her offering to her Lord in the privacy of a home? Jesus responded by saying that her act of worship would have spiritual influence around the world (see Mark 14:9).

God set His great plan in motion to redeem a lost world when He called Abraham. He called one man, Moses, to free His people from the bonds of slavery; and He called Joshua, the son of Nun, to lead the Israelites across the Jordan to claim their inheritance.

Church historians remind us that the Roman Empire was conquered for Christ not only by the endeavors of the great missionaries but also by the daily witness of individual believers.

During my first year at Lee, I was invited by the Pioneers for Christ Club to go to the Bradley County Work House to play the accordion for a service. It was my first jail service and, as it turned out, my last. Richard Ussery, the student leading the service, asked me to testify. I had not been given advance notice, so I just winged it. Everything was going fine until the end. I didn't know how to end my testimony. So I just said what I would have said in a Wednesday night testimony service back in Alabama: "You all pray for me." Not the most appropriate place to request prayer, perhaps.

Nevertheless, God has an important place for each of us to fill. Maybe it's not a jail ministry. However, if we stay strong in the faith, and keep our part of the chain strong, He will accomplish His work and His will through us. Yes, you and me!

It's comforting, O Lord, to see Your witness through us, Your children. Help us to personalize Your Word, remembering that You use individuals to carry out Your work here on earth. I thank You that I am important to You.

February 16

Scripture: "And who knows but that you have come to royal position for such a time as this?" (Esther 4:14).

When the TV camera focuses in for a close-up mug shot, why does the person always say, "Hi, Mom?" Not "Hi, Dad" or "Hi, Pop." It's always Mom.

In a poll conducted by the Search Institute of Minneapolis, and reported by the Associated Press, 10,000 people were asked, "Who has had the most positive influence on your religious faith?" From every age group, "My mother" was the most frequent answer. "My wife," was the second-place response from men. The survey also revealed that women have a higher faith level than men.

This poll confirms what we already knew: Women have a great deal of influence for God. Queen Esther is a biblical example of the influence and strength of one woman. She put her life on the line for her people. During crisis that threatened the annihilation of the Jews, she called for a period of fasting and prayer before she took action. Then she went to the king and intervened for the lives of her people. God granted Esther favor with the king and reversed the curse against the Jews.

Today we can be strong women for God and His kingdom. We can make a difference. The Holy Spirit empowers us with strength "for such a time as this." Go ahead, ask me, "How? Give me a royal position—something to stand on when I'm weak." OK, here it is.

His indwelling Spirit . . .

- Teaches us (Luke 12:12; 1 Corinthians 2:13).
- Guides us (Matthew 10:19, 20; John 16:13).
- Comforts us (John 14:16, 17; Acts 9:31).
- Reveals the Father's will to us (John 14:20; 1 Corinthians 2:9, 10).
- Gives us joy (John 15:11; Romans 14:17).
- Gives us spiritual gifts (1 Corinthians 12:4-31).
- Gives us power for service (Luke 4:14; Acts 1:8).
- Intercedes for us (Romans 8:26; 1 Corinthians 14:14, 15).

What more do we need to stay strong in the fast-approaching 21st century?

Absolutely nothing!

Holy Spirit, thank You for strength, for power, wisdom, and guidance. Help me accept whatever difficulties I meet, knowing that with Your enablement I can be a woman for such a time as this.

February 17

Scripture: "Guard the fortress, watch the road, brace yourselves, marshal all your strength!" (Nahum 2:1).

Sometimes I think the Lord forgot to include the compass when he made me because I have no sense of north, south, east, and west. My husband says I'm the only person he knows who gets lost in a hotel lobby. Invariably, when the elevator door opens, I turn the opposite direction from where my room is located.

My sister Evaline is equally directionless. Put the two of us on the road and there's not a map in the country that can keep us on the right track. Evaline will say, "They must have changed the road numbers since this map was printed." Sure. Every trip?

We inherited this from our father, but with one difference. He would never stop and ask directions. He just kept driving until he finally somehow reached his destination. I once wrote an article called "No Shortcuts" that was printed in the *Evangel*. The byline, which I didn't see until it was in print, was written by an editor with a great sense of humor. It said something like "Wanda lives in Cleveland and seldom gets lost on out-of-town trips." As soon as the *Evangel* was distributed, my phone started ringing. Anyone who had ever traveled with me thought this was the biggest joke of the year.

Recently Evaline and I were on the North Georgia campground for a ladies retreat. We asked the state overseer for directions back to our motel. He rattled off some of those Atlanta-type instructions: "Go back to the second red light, cross the railroad, go under the freeway . . ." and so forth. I thanked him with a puzzled look on my face. After he walked away, his wife asked, "Do you understand?" (a question men never ask). I whispered to her, "Which way do we turn out of the parking lot?" So she asked someone to *lead* us to the motel. Good idea. We follow cars better than verbal instructions. We have given Trivial Pursuit a whole new meaning.

You're probably wondering, *Is there a spiritual lesson buried somewhere in all this?* I certainly hope so. I don't want to lose my way like the Israelites did in the wilderness and wander around for 40 years because of disobedience. God did not forsake them during their wandering and complaining, but look at the terrible consequences they paid.

The prophet Jonah took a three-day detour to the Hotel Whale's Belly because of his unwillingness to follow God's direction to preach to the city of Nineveh.

I don't want to waste my time on earth with a bunch of dead ends, wrong turns, and aimless detours. I want a life that makes sense, a life that points toward a destiny beyond time. Like a road map guiding us away from fear and uncertainty and toward confidence and strength, God's Word reassures us we're going the right way. Thanks to my *BibleSoft* (computer software), I found an itinerary that promises a successful destination. Joshua 1:7 says: "Be strong and very courageous. Be careful to obey all the law my servant Moses gave you; do not turn from it to the right or to the left, that you may be successful wherever you go."

That sounds like a pretty good road map for me—be strong, obey God's law, do not turn from it to the right or to the left. This road map is for our temporal life to lead us to our eternal life with God. He gives us the road map of His Word, along with fellowship with other believers, and communication with Him through prayer. There is no reason for taking shortcuts or detours. Bon voyage!

Eternal Lord, keep us through all the turns and twists of this life. But if we make a wrong turn, we know You are there to give us new direction.

February 18

Scripture: "Thy word have I hid in mine heart, that I might not sin against thee" (Psalm 119:11, KJV).

Recently I read about a new 900 phone number that connects the information-superhighway generation with the Father. As my nephew Josh says, "No, I'm not joshing you." With the latest technology in place, you can now call 1-900-226-POWR on a Touch-Tone phone any time of day, seven days a week from anywhere in the world. What is the message? For two minutes you will hear a Bible verse and blessing. The total cost of the call is $1.95.

My first reaction was "What's new? I've known about the royal telephone all my life." We used to sing a song that said: "Central's never busy, always on the line. You may hear from heaven almost any time." I guess the *almost* has been dropped with this 24-hour *anytime* number. And I wonder if you ever get a busy signal. Even with the best technology (judging from my experience with computers), there will probably be hours when you can't get through on this powerline.

But why pay to hear God's Word read electronically when you can carry it in your purse or, better still, hidden in your heart? Leslie Rishel, president of the Powerline, says "The primary user will be the solid Christian who understands the power of hearing Scripture in the midst of a hectic day. But we also see this as an evangelical tool to draw borderline Christians or even nonbelievers to the Scriptures and eventually to church fellowship" (Quoted in *Virtue*, July, August 1995).

To stay strong in our commitment to promote the gospel and win the lost, we cannot ignore the information superhighway. We must use every new innovation and technology available. Otherwise we will be bypassed—left behind with the out-of-date models.

Whatever we need to do to keep pace with the strong is what we must do. Most colleges offer night classes in computers, and there are hundreds of seminars and workshops. It might even be feasible to hire a tutor, or if you have children, ask them to teach you. The options are out there. Go for it!

Father, help us utilize every method and opportunity to stay in the race, strong and viable for Your cause.

February 19

Scripture: "Therefore I am well content with weaknesses, with insults, with distresses, with persecutions, with difficulties, for Christ's sake; for when I am weak, then am I strong" (2 Corinthians 12:10, *NASB*).

We learned in Childhood 101 the art of throwing pity parties. "Mama, Carolyn didn't work as hard as I did. Why does Evaline get to go and I don't?"

As adults we continue this pattern, recounting all we have done for the Lord, and wonder, *Why do I bother? Does anybody even give a hoot?*

If anyone in Scripture earned an honest-to-goodness pity party, it was the apostle Paul. Frustrated with the complaints and insults of the supersaints of his day, he told them:

> I have worked harder [than any of you].
> I have been in prison more frequently.
> I have been flogged more severely.
> I have been exposed to death again and again.
> I have been beaten by the Jews with forty lashes minus one.
> I have been beaten with rods three times.
> I was stoned once.
> I have been shipwrecked three times.
> I have spent a night and a day in the open sea.
> I have been constantly on the move and in danger from rivers, from bandits, from my own countrymen, and from Gentiles.
> I have been in danger in the city, in danger in the country, in danger at sea, in danger from false brothers.
> I have labored and toiled and often gone without sleep. I have known hunger and thirst, and have often gone without food.
> I have been cold and naked.
> Besides everything else I face daily the pressure of my concern for all the churches (adapted from 2 Corinthians 11:23-29, *NIV*).

Can anyone top this list? No way. Our lists look insignificant, to say the least. And what about Paul's conclusion? "Therefore I am well content with weaknesses. . . ." Well content? How is this possible? Read on. "For when I am weak, then am I strong."

This is a strange formula for a culture that buys into the philosophy that what we possess is a sure measure of our strength. Our list of possessions includes wealth, health, education, employment, prestige, fame, security, and acquired skills. But contentment? The apostle Paul discovered contentment in the midst of distresses, persecutions, and difficulties. In weakness he found inner strength.

Think about it. Cancel the pity party!

Heavenly Father, help us be content. It's difficult. You understand us when we grow weary, but You promise strength in exchange for our weaknesses. We give it all to You today!

February 20

Scripture: "I am the vine; you are the branches. If a man remains in me and I in him, he will bear much fruit; apart from me you can do nothing" (John 15:5).

Only a few hours remain. The sense of urgency grows inside the crowded room. Jesus is about to leave His disciples, but He wants to prepare them for the days ahead. Foreseeing the fierce trials, opposition, hatred, beatings, and executions His disciples will face, Jesus uses an allegory, a parable from nature to make His point: "I am the vine; you are the branches."

"In order to bear fruit like the luscious grapes," Jesus said (and I paraphrase), "one thing is essential: You must stay connected to the vine. The branches that become disconnected from the vine lose their source of nourishment. They are swept away in a heap for burning. So remain in Me and stay strong!"

The disciples probably did not completely understand all Jesus was saying to them. After all, He was still with them. But after His ascension they would remember this symbolic lesson with its abrupt contrast between juicy grapes and withered branches. This would stay with them, reminding them of their source of strength.

As we close in on the 21st century, this allegory is just as applicable today as it was in the first century. Jesus is the vine; we are the branches. Without this vital link we cannot stay strong; we will be like the withered branches—lifeless!

In a seminar on the fruit of the Spirit, I used this scripture in John 15:5 to illustrate how a Spirit-filled Christian can become a fruit bearer. Just as natural as the air in summer is transfused with sunshine, so must our lives be transfused with the Holy Spirit, bearing the fruit of love, joy, peace, patience, kindness, goodness, faithfulness, gentleness, and self-control. And there is never a power shortage. We may unplug ourselves from the source, but His source is never exhausted; it never runs down.

Many people operate on what I call the "battery system." They attend a convention and when they return they are altogether different—for about three weeks. Or they read an inspirational book and say, "I'll never be the same again," and they're not, for about three weeks. Or they have an all-night prayer meeting in the midst of a crisis. They are transformed—for about three weeks. But each time, they lapse to the dull average again. Why? Because they are relying on crisis experiences to charge their batteries instead of the strength of the Holy Spirit.

The Spirit-filled life was never meant to run on batteries. To stay strong we must operate on the electric circuit principle. Put simply, this means continuous current through continuous contact. How do we maintain continuous contact with the heavenly current, the Holy Spirit? By communicating in prayer, daily meditation on the written Word, and obedience to the Spirit.

We cannot create fruit within ourselves. He has not called us to be creators. We are continually replenished by the Holy Spirit, provided we stay connected to the Vine.

Strengthen us, Lord, with Your never-ending source of strength and power.

February 21

Scripture: "Then Nebuchadnezzar said, 'Praise be to the God of Shadrach, Meshach and Abednego, who has sent his angel and rescued his servants! They trusted in him and defied the king's command and were willing to give up their lives rather than serve or worship any god except their own God'" (Daniel 3: 28).

One Sunday after arriving home from Sunday school, my daughter-in-law, Martha, asked my 3-year-old granddaughter, "Jennifer, what did you learn today?"

"I learned that God made Adam and Even," she said. That's close.

Many of us cut our teeth on familiar Bible stories. One of my favorites is the story of the three Hebrew children. Imagine the scene: We are standing on the plains of Dura, outside the palace of mighty King Nebuchadnezzar. Shadrach, Meshach, and Abednego are summoned to stand on a platform overlooking the crowds. A golden figure (perhaps Nebuchadnezzar) is set on a raised altar. The moment of truth arrives.

The chief musician lifts his baton to the sound of music—"all kinds of music" (v. 15), the Bible says. The multitudes bow—faces to the ground. Then one from the king's court looks up. He is shocked to see that Shadrach, Meshach, and Abednego are still standing.

The three are dragged before the outraged king who threatens to burn them alive in a furnace. How dare anyone defy the king? Without arrogance, one speaks up, "We have no need, O king, to defend ourselves to you. We will not bow to an idol. Whether or not you cast us into a fiery furnace is your affair. Our God is able to deliver us. But even if He doesn't, we will still trust Him."

Nebuchadnezzar's anger grows. "Who is this god who can save you?" he yells. The music sounds again. The Hebrews stay strong and refuse to bow. The furnace is heated seven times hotter than normal, and the three men are bound and carried to it. So hot is the blaze that the guards who throw them in are consumed.

Then the miracle! An angel of the Lord appears. The ropes are consumed by the flames, but not a hair on their heads is singed. The king is humiliated. Their clothes do not even smell smoky.

These young heroes in Hebrew history demonstrated a strength that was stronger than peer pressure, stronger than the fear of disobeying the highest authority in the land, even stronger than the fear of losing their lives.

Every time I read this account in Scripture I want to don my old cheerleader outfit, pick up the megaphone, and join King Nebuchadnezzar in leading a cheer, "Praise be to the God of Shadrach, Meshach, and Abednego, who has sent his angel and rescued his servants!"

What valiant strength!

Holy Father, may these examples in Your Word never become just another story to read to my grandchildren. I do praise You for rescuing Your servants.

February 22

Scripture: "The Lord turned to him and said, 'Go in the strength you have and save Israel out of Midian's hand. Am I not sending you?'" (Judges 6:14).

Throughout history God has picked the weak, the least likely to succeed, to accomplish His plan. None of us would have chosen Gideon to end the Midianites' seven-year siege on Israel. Gideon was probably

72

in shock when the Lord himself appeared with the message that he was to be the commander in chief of Israel. *Who, me? The weakest member of the weakest clan of the weakest tribe in the weak nation of Israel?*

To be sure God was with him, Gideon tested Him with the wet and dry fleece (you know the one every minister tries at some time in the ministry). Confident that God was with him, Gideon did what any smart general would do. He gathered a large army, 32,000 in number, to go against the enemy so great in number their "camels could no more be counted than the sand on the seashore" (see Judges 7:12).

Hundreds of sermons have related how God reduced Gideon's large army to a mere 300 men who lapped water from their hands like a dog. What was God's purpose in doing this? The answer is clearly given in verse 2—"in order that Israel may not boast against me that her own strength has saved her."

Many of us identify with Gideon, admitting we are not the strongest in our circle of friends. We'll never be the featured speaker at the Church of God General Assembly. Our name will not be inscribed in the Pentecostal Hall of Fame or as Distinguished Alumnae of Lee College. We will probably never be front-page news for our local newspaper. But let's look at a New Testament passage of Scripture:

"Brothers [sisters], think of what you were when you were called. Not many of you were wise by human standards; not many were influential; not many were of noble birth. But God chose the foolish things of the world to shame the strong. He chose the lowly things of this world and the despised things . . . so that no one may boast before him" (1 Corinthians 1:26-29).

From Genesis to Revelation we find the weak becoming strong. None of us would have chosen the teenage shepherd to slay the mighty giant who was oppressing Israel. Neither would we have selected Sarah from the membership of AARP to be the mother of a new nation. He picks you and me with all our weaknesses, inadequacies, and fumbling of opportunities to do His work today.

I accept. How about you?

Father, we don't understand Your ways, but we give to You all that we are as we sit at Your feet. Use us in Your work, for Your glory and Your honor.

February 23

Scripture: "So do not fear, for I am with you; do not be dismayed, for I am your God. I will strengthen you and help you; I will uphold you with my righteous right hand" (Isaiah 41:10).

"Worry is like a rocking chair," someone has said. "It will give you something to do, but it won't get you anywhere." We worry about our families, our finances, our work, our relationships, knowing the Bible tells us "not [to] worry about tomorrow, for tomorrow will worry about itself. Each day has enough trouble of its own" (Matthew 6:34), but we continue asking the big "What if . . ." questions.

In their book *Helping Worriers*, James R. Beck and David T. Moore list the negative consequences of worry:

- Worry interferes with performance.
- Worry produces physiological changes.
- Worry impairs judgment.
- Worry fuels anxiety.

There are many theories on the nature of worry and its effects on individuals. Beck and Moore list a variety of effective remedies for the chronic worrier which range from working with therapists in skills training and problem solving to something as simple as relaxation.

The Bible has a great deal to say about worry. But isn't the bottom line the issue of faith? Why? Because faith is the exact opposite of worry. After reading the faith chapter again (Hebrews 11), I was drawn to the last two verses, "These were all commended for their faith, yet none of them received what had been promised. God had planned something better for us so that only together with us would they be made perfect" (vv. 39, 40).

What is this "something better" God planned for us? I believe it is found in Philippians 4:7: "And the peace of God, which transcends all understanding, will guard your hearts and your minds in Christ Jesus." Could the enemy of our hearts and minds be worry? If so, His Word promises to protect our minds with a peace that transcends all understanding. We can answer worry with faith.

When Worry says, "What about my child's spiritual condition?"

Faith says, "Cast all your anxiety on him because he cares for you" (1 Peter 5:7);

When Worry says, "What about those lab reports from the doctor?"

Faith says, "Do not be anxious about anything, but in everything, by prayer and petition, with thanksgiving, present your requests to God" (Philippians 4:6, 7);

When Worry says, "What if something happens to my companion?"

Faith says, "Surely I am with you always, to the very end of the age" (Matthew 28:20).

This is how Jesus taught us to handle worry. When Worry knocks on the door, send Faith, supported by His Word, to answer the knock. The amazing result is *peace*. If we are peaceful, we are not worrying; if we are worrying, we do not have peace.

May His peace strengthen you today! Pray with me:

Father, I refuse to allow worry to erode my faith and rule my life. I accept Your peace as a gift to me, the worrier. On the basis of what You have done for me in the past, I step out into new arenas of faith and worry-free living.

February 24

Scripture: "Restore us, O God; make your face shine upon us, that we may be saved" (Psalm 80:3).

My 4-year-old grandson, Vance, has trouble pronouncing his *l*'s (he pronounces them as *y*'s). Of course Granna thinks anything he says and does is adorable. Recently we were singing the nursery rhyme, "Mary Had a Little Lamb." Vance's version goes like this: "Mary had a yittle yam, yittle yam, yittle yam." Then I thought of another song to teach him. As we sang, "This yittle yight of mine, I'm gonna yet it shine," his dad caught us. "Mother," he scolded. "Vance is never going to learn to pronounce his *l*'s as long as you keep reenforcing the incorrect pronunciation."

All of us have weaknesses. They may not be as obvious as Vance's *l*'s, but they are there. To reenforce them or to accept them as "That's just the way I am" is not God's plan for our lives. We must go beyond those self-defeating voices to overcome our weaknesses.

There are also strengths and potentials inside each of us we need to discover and use. We have God's permission to move from strength to strength in this life, from glory to glory (see Psalm 84:7).

A few years ago I became fascinated with a unique gemstone, the opal. It is not found in nature in the form of crystals like diamonds, but in irregular patches, often filling cavities in rocks. Gemologists speak of an opal as a hydrated silica gel, because it contains water along with the silica. The water content makes some opals a risky buy. Many of them "check" (crack) after a long time in dry air. The checking occurs as the water in the gel dries out.

There are many different kinds of opals. They are classified according to the color of their background and the brilliance of the light rays they reflect. Opals that give off brilliant flashes of color are precious opals.

Since the beauty of the opal lies in its internal color flashes, it is never cut with facets like a diamond. Instead, it is cut with a gentle, rounded convex surface.

Barbara Johnson in *Splashes of Joy in the Cesspool of Life* describes the opal as "the lamp of fire" because, she says, the breath of the Lord is in it. She points out that an opal will lose its luster if it is kept in a cold, dark place, but the luster is restored when it is held in a warm hand or when light shines on it.

There will be times when we are weak—the luster in our lives gone, our strength depleted. How do we become restored? The same way we restore the luster to our silver trays or brass ornaments when they become tarnished. We get out the tarnish remover and start rubbing. First we remove the tarnish, and then apply a coat of polish to bring back the shine.

To restore the luster and strength in our lives requires cleansing, asking for forgiveness. Getting rid of the tarnish. God's love is complete, without blemish or defect. It rids our lives of the film of frustration, the rust of resentment, and the varnish of vanity. When we are warmed by His love, we take on color through our weaknesses and defects. Then His Holy Spirit flows through us and polishes our lives so we can give back the lovely hues of His light to others. We can become precious gems—shining strong vessels for His service.

Dear Lord, help us discover those hidden strengths within each of us. We give them to You for cleansing, for polishing, and for use in Your kingdom.

February 25

Scripture: "The fruit of righteousness will be peace; the effect of righteousness will be quietness and confidence forever" (Isaiah 32:17).

Someone told me recently, "I just had to get away and spend time alone."

I think we all get to this place occasionally. We need solitude. Solitude gives us time for careful and constructive self-examination. When we are among people, we usually wear a mask that more or less conceals our real self. But alone, the shackles of hypocrisy fall away, the sham dissipates, and we see ourselves as we really are—the way God sees us all the time.

We have vivid biblical examples of those who were chosen for special purposes. They were given new strength.

- A hot-tempered Moses, a prince in Egypt with all the privileges and power of the court, became a meek man after 40 years in the lonely desert of Midian. There he gained the strength of character needed to accomplish his mission in life.
- Elijah did not hear God in the mighty and threatening powers of nature but in the "still, small voice," or, as someone has said, "in the sound of gentle stillness."

- It was not until Paul retired to Arabia that he was fully equipped to become an effective missionary.
- Jesus found the nights on the lonely mountain or in a secluded desert place to be ideal for fellowship with His Father.

Why are we afraid of the silence, of being alone with our thoughts? We need to develop anew the art of contemplation and reflection. Silence can be a great force for good, because out of the silence God still speaks with the "still, small voice"—if we are willing to listen.

This power of tranquility and aloneness with God is packaged with strength. In a world filled with loud, spectacular events, we must learn that God works in the same quiet way He has from the beginning.

Sitting quietly at His feet is a discipline we need to cultivate. Intimacy with God, like the oak tree, grows slowly. It is during these times of quiet devotion that He consoles, constrains, and at times, convicts us. It is also in this place that strong Christian character is built. Accept His invitation: "Be still, and know that I am God" (Psalm 46:10).

Help me wait on You, dear Father, and not be frightened of the silence. I thank You for the confidence I have in knowing that Your hand is on my life.

February 26

Scripture: "Look to the Lord and his strength; seek his face always" (1 Chronicles 16:11).

Staying strong calls for constant renewal. All the management books point out that among the resources—machinery, materials, money, methods—men and women are the primary resource in any company. It's up to these key people (or managers) to plan, organize, control, and lead the business. Words like *inspire, motivate, demonstrate, delegate,* and, most of all, *communicate* surface in every manual or training session. The leader in one seminar I attended kept emphasizing, "Don't kill the spark of individuality. The vitality of the organization rests on the ideas of creative, innovative employees."

If the professional business world recognizes this principle of renewal and vitality of the individual, shouldn't we in the Christian world?

I lead a prayer/share group made up of ladies from Lee College and the Publishing House. Once a year in the spring we have an out-of-town retreat. This is a time when we get away from normal, everyday responsibilities for a time of refreshment and renewal. Since the first retreat 10 years ago, we have grown numerically but, more significantly, spiritually. Just in the last two years, different members of the group have gone on short-term mission trips to the Ukraine, the Netherlands, China, France, South Africa, and Israel.

I recently spent 10 days in the Holy Land. One of the purposes of the trip was to attend the 17th World Pentecostal Conference and interview several missionaries for articles to be published in the *Evangel*. One of the individuals I interviewed was Dr. Olly Mesach from Indonesia. When I asked her to tell me about her work, she replied, "Which area? I wear so many hats." And does she ever! In addition to serving as pastor's wife to the 2,500-member Bethel Church of God, she is a medical doctor and operates a community health clinic where she teaches hygiene, nutrition, and meal planning.

After we talked for 30 minutes, I couldn't believe the different ministries Dr. Mesach supervises. But the topic she wanted to talk about most was a recent revival where she and all the members of her church received renewal and a new anointing. "In a country filled with evil and the occult," Mesach continues, "we saw the real power of God manifested in conversions, healings, visions, and the gifts of the Spirit. We are now seeing many of the Muslim leaders come to the Lord. It's an exciting time to work for the Lord."

The Holy Spirit renews our strength and empowers us all for service, not just Dr. Olly Mesach. Are you hungry for renewal? I am.

Holy Spirit of God, renew us with Your Spirit through personal revival and greater service for Your kingdom work.

February 27

Scripture: "'My grace is sufficient for you, for my power is made perfect in weakness.' Therefore I will boast all the more gladly about my weaknesses, so that Christ's power may rest on me" (2 Corinthians 12:9).

One little boy went to a new Sunday school class. When he came home, his mother asked him about his teacher—who she was, if he liked her, and so forth. The little boy didn't have many answers. He said, "I don't know her name, but she must have been Jesus' grandmother because that's all she talked about."

It is difficult not to talk about your grandchildren, especially when they talk about Jesus. When my grandson was 3, he came home from Sunday school and said, "Jesus is the Son of God." Rob grabbed the phone. "Quick, we've got to call Granna and tell her what Vance learned in Sunday school today." When I answered the phone, Rob said, "Mother, Vance wants to tell you something that will make you turn a few back flips."

A best-selling book in 1995 supports this idea of recounting the good times and looking at how well our successes are celebrated by those close to us. In *LifeMapping*, John Trent says that the first element is recognizing our strengths, successes, and acceptance level. Why start with strengths and successes? "Even Christians often have an easier time coming up with a list of weaknesses than they do clearly recounting strengths," says Trent.

He explains further that for life-mapping purposes, our strengths are those God-given abilities, talents, desires, and sensitivities that He has chosen to make a part of our lives. Trent continues by saying that it is the degree to which our strengths are celebrated that primarily determines the acceptance level we live with every day.

Even if our strengths are not celebrated, God invites us to look into His mirror and see all the good things we can become in His Son, regardless of where we have been.

Just think! The God of unsurpassed strengths finds and invests tremendous value in you and me.

Keep boasting!

Heavenly Father, thank You for every good gift that comes from above. We celebrate every strength and God-given ability, dedicating them to Your glory and honor.

February 28

Scripture: "His divine power has given us everything we need for life and godliness" (2 Peter 1:3).

Staying strong is a by-product of a Christlike lifestyle, one that calls you and me into deeper intimacy with our Savior. We must choose to sit at His feet just like the crowd that gathered around Him in Mark 4:1. Let's imagine having a ringside seat when He gets into a boat and teaches from it a short distance out in the lake. Multitudes line the shore, straining to see and hear this Teacher who speaks in mysterious parables.

We listen, not quite understanding about a farmer scattering seeds among rocky places, thorns, shallow and good soil. The story ends, the crowd disperses, and the Teacher says, "He who has ears to hear, let him hear" (v. 9).

We feel puzzled, but something summons us to stay, to find a closer spot, to ask Him the meaning of the parables.

"The secret of the kingdom of God has been given to you," Jesus says (vv. 10, 11). And there, away from the busyness of life, with fellow seekers, the Lord unravels His innermost desires and plans for our lives. Through the parable of the sower, He tells us that we, like the good soil, must "hear the Word, accept it, and produce a crop—thirty, sixty or even a hundred times what was sown" (v. 20).

What was the answer Jesus gave to the teacher of the law who asked Him, "Of all the commandments, which is the most important?" (12:28). Listen to Jesus' answer: "Love the Lord your God with all your heart and with all your soul and with all your mind and with all your strength. The second is this: 'Love your neighbor as yourself.' There is no commandment greater than these" (vv. 30, 31).

We are filled with such wonder and awe to be "seated . . . with [Christ] in heavenly realms" (Ephesians 2:6), experiencing His words, His wisdom, His strength. With a deeper level of determination, we resolve to stay strong when everything is falling apart . . . to stay strong when our enemies seem to prosper . . . to stay strong in times of crisis . . . to stay strong when big people act contemptibly small . . . to stay strong when people demand authority they don't deserve . . . to stay strong when the wicked appear to be winning.

What a bumper crop of strength!

Thank You, eternal Father, because we still have the privilege to sit at Your feet, digest Your Word, and know Your strength.

February 29

Scripture: "Let the words of my mouth, and the meditation of my heart, be acceptable in thy sight, O Lord, my strength, and my redeemer" (Psalm 19:14).

What a powerful prayer to end the month of February. This scripture serves as the Lee College benediction and has for many years. It acknowledges the source of our strength—our faithful Lord. A line from my favorite hymn, "Great Is Thy Faithfulness," by Thomas Chisholm, promises "strength for today and bright hope for tomorrow."*

We have to take life one day at a time. If we allow Him, God will give us wisdom and strength for each day—wisdom to know what to do and strength to do it. The writer of Hebrews urges us to "hold unswervingly to the hope we profess, for he who promised is faithful" (Hebrews 10:23). To stay strong and be acceptable in His sight requires going back to the basics. The Word of God, not circumstances, becomes our frame of reference for who God really is. His faithfulness is not based on a sliding Dow Jones average or a rising Richter Scale. "God is our refuge and strength, an ever-present help in trouble. Therefore we will not fear, though the earth give way and the mountains fall into the heart of the sea, though its waters roar and foam and the mountains quake with their surging. . . . The Lord Almighty is with us; the God of

Jacob is our fortress" (Psalm 46:1-3, 7).

The words of our mouths and the meditations of our hearts reveal our level of trust in His faithfulness. It is critical to understand the powerful effect our words have. From our toolbox of talents and tactics nothing has the same dynamic as the words we speak.

I want to conclude my devotions with the words of another favorite hymn that says:

> Then in fellowship sweet
> We will sit at His feet,
> Or we'll walk by His side in the way;
> What He says we will do,
> Where He sends we will go,
> Never fear, only trust and obey.

—Daniel B. Towner (Words), and John H. Sammis (Music), 1887.

God wants us to realize that time is His gift to us, and it is a sin to waste it or merely spend it; we must invest it by sitting at His feet and doing His will.

This prayer will help you and me evaluate our level of development as strong disciples:

- I cannot say, "our" if I live only for myself.
- I cannot say, "Father" if I do not endeavor each day to act like His child.
- I cannot say, "which art in heaven" if I am laying up no treasure there.
- I cannot say, "hallowed be thy name" if I am not striving for holiness.
- I cannot say, "Thy kingdom come" if I am not doing all in my power to hasten that event.
- I cannot say, "Thy will be done" if I am disobedient to His Word.
- I cannot say, "in earth, as it is in heaven" if I don't serve Him here and now.
- I cannot say, "Give us this day our daily bread" if I am dishonest or seeking things by subterfuge.
- I cannot say, "Forgive us our debts" if I harbor a grudge against anyone.
- I cannot say, "Lead us not into temptation" if I deliberately place myself in its path.
- I cannot say, "Deliver us from evil" if I do not put on the whole armor of God.
- I cannot say, "Thine is the kingdom" if I do not give the King the loyalty due Him from a faithful subject.
- I cannot attribute to Him "the power" if I fear what men may do.
- I cannot ascribe to Him "the glory" if I seek honor only for myself.
- I cannot say, "for ever" if the horizon of my life is bounded completely by time.

—Author unknown

March

Heritage of Faith

Mary Ruth Stone

Mary Ruth Stone is a former executive director of the Department of Ladies Ministries at the Church of God International Offices. She received an associate of arts degree from Lee College in 1962, a bachelor of arts degree from the University of Arkansas at Little Rock in 1973, a master of science degree at Radford University in 1977, and a doctorate in education at the University of Alabama in 1985.

Mary Ruth's ministry includes speaking at various functions and organizing and implementing programs in her role as state Ladies Ministries president for the Pacific Northwest. Presently she and her husband, the Reverend Lynn Stone, state overseer of the Pacific Northwest, are placing emphasis on training of ministers and their spouses.

The Department of Ladies Ministries recently published a Bible study book titled *One Woman Before a King*, written by Dr. Stone. She and her husband have four sons: Ken, Tim, David, and Jon; and one granddaughter, Jordan.

March 1

Scripture: "So it shall be, when the Lord your God brings you into the land of which He swore to your fathers, to Abraham, Isaac, and Jacob, to give you large and beautiful cities which you did not build, houses full of all good things, which you did not fill, hewn-out wells which you did not dig, vineyards and olive trees which you did not plant—when you have eaten and are full—then beware, lest you forget the Lord who brought you out of the land of Egypt, from the house of bondage" (Deuteronomy 6:10-12).*

Beware! That is a warning that is often used to get the attention of the public in order to avoid danger, injury, and even death.

Moses used the word *beware* in this scripture. And, sure enough, he was sounding a warning to the children of Israel. He wanted them to avoid a tragedy, the tragedy of unthankfulness and forgetfulness toward God, who recently had delivered them.

Moses reminded the people that they must love the Lord and obey Him. In order to do that, they must constantly be aware of His words. His words must be in their hearts. He reminded them that God had promised them a land flowing with milk and honey. And then he raised this caution—they must remember the Lord, who brought them out of Egypt and gave them the wonderful land toward which they were heading.

That same warning is appropriate for Christians today. We *must* remember the Lord, who brought us out of the bondage of sin, which is analogous to Egypt. We must remember His words. We must obey His commandments. We must love Him with all our hearts. We must worship no other gods. We must give Him first place in our hearts and in our lives. If we forget that God is the One who delivered us, if we forget that every good thing that we have in our lives ultimately came from His giving hand, then we are in danger of transgressing in every other way.

For that reason, you, the reader, are being led this month to reflect on your heritage. The devotions which involve the writer's heritage should serve to lead you in reflecting on your own heritage, the heritage of your local church, and the heritage of Christians everywhere.

Beware, lest you forget the Lord and what He has done for you.

Dear Lord, I praise You today for Your many blessings to me. Thank You for the gift of salvation. Thank You for Your Word. Thank You for my Christian heritage.

*The Scripture references used for this month's devotions are from the *New King James Version* unless otherwise indicated.

March 2

Scripture: "However, when He, the Spirit of truth, has come, He will guide you into all truth; for He will not speak on His own authority, but whatever He hears He will speak; and He will tell you things to come" (John 16:13).

It was the late 1920s when the message of Pentecost was first brought to my hometown in Maryland. The small Eastern Shore fishing village was a religious community with a strong Methodist heritage rooted in the Wesleyan traditions. My ancestors were no exception and were deeply troubled by the new doctrine that had come to town and was being proclaimed from a gospel tent.

During lunch one Wednesday, my great-great-grandparents, my great-grandparents, my grandparents, Granddad's siblings, and my father (who was a very small boy) were sitting around the table questioning aloud the validity of the doctrine coming from the tent. They wondered if it had anything to do with them.

Shortly, they saw a woman walking up the dirt road leading toward their house. "That looks like May Wilson. Wonder what she could have walked all the way out here for? Maybe she needs to borrow a little money," Great-granddad speculated, knowing that Mrs. Wilson was a widow with several children to support. She worked in a garment factory for meager wages. The factory closed on Wednesday afternoons to give the women who worked there time to attend to their households. It was a three-mile walk from the factory to the Morris farm.

Finally Mrs. Wilson knocked on the door and was invited in. She was offered some lunch but nervously declined. "No. I don't want anything to eat. While I was sewing this morning, the Lord told me to come out here this afternoon and bring you a message."

"Then by all means, tell us what it is," came the quick reply.

"He told me to tell you, 'The Holy Ghost is real,'" she said with a quiet confidence. "That's all. The Holy Ghost is real." With that, she excused herself, again declining the offer of lunch.

That was all it took. The question was answered. Within a few short weeks, four generations of Morrises experienced the baptism of the Holy Spirit.

God is looking for open and honest hearts. He will use any and all means necessary to bring the truth to a seeking heart.

What are your questions? The Holy Spirit has been sent to guide us into all truth. Listen to Him today.

Holy Spirit of God, speak to me. Help me to hear the message of truth You know I need to hear today.

March 3

Scripture: "John answered, saying to all, 'I indeed baptize you with water; but One mightier than I is coming, whose sandal strap I am not worthy to loose. He will baptize you with the Holy Spirit and fire'" (Luke 3:16).

The weeks following May Wilson's visit to the Morris farm with her message of truth were exciting ones. Grandmother was the first to venture inside the tent, walk the sawdust aisle to salvation, and subsequently receive the baptism of the Holy Spirit with the evidence of speaking in another tongue.

It wasn't long until her husband, her father-in-law, and her son followed in her footsteps. Shortly thereafter, her mother-in-law and other family members followed along as well.

Then the family faced another decision: Would they rest on their old experience of water baptism by sprinkling, or would they follow the custom of water baptism by immersion being taught in the tent revival? Every night after hearing the latest sermon, they would search the Scriptures in order to test the validity of the new doctrines. They decided they would follow the Lord in baptism by immersion. It was in the Bible; Jesus himself partook.

Margaret Morris, the matriarch of the family, was in her 70s at the time and had developed a habit of conversational prayer as she went about her household chores. She was overheard having this conversation with the heavenly Father on the day before her water baptism:

> Now Lord, You know that my son and his wife, my grandson and his wife, and some others here in my family have received this experience of being baptized in the Holy Ghost and speaking in tongues. Now You also know that I am planning on being baptized in water tomorrow. I haven't been baptized in the Holy Ghost yet. And it seems to me that tomorrow when I am baptized in water would be the perfect time for You to baptize me in the Holy Ghost. So I'll be believing tomorrow that when the preacher baptizes me in water that You'll baptize me in the Holy Ghost and fire.

The deal made, she went on about her duties and prepared for Sunday's baptism. Sure enough, when Great-great-grandmother came up out of the water the following day, she was speaking in a heavenly language.

Believing God to fulfill His Word is a simple exercise in faith. Sometimes we make it something hard to do. Hear the Word of God today. Believe He will do what He said He will do.

Father, I thank You for the promises in Your Word. I am trusting You to bring them to pass in my life today.

March 4

Scripture: "And my God shall supply all your need according to His riches in glory by Christ Jesus" (Philippians 4:19).

From the time my great-grandfather was filled with the Spirit, he began a rich prayer life and began to trust God for all his needs. He prayed three times a day—morning, noon, and evening. Nothing interrupted his prayer time. He depended on God for guidance in all matters both small and great.

God never let him down, and our family's oral history is rich with accounts of answered prayer. One of the most colorful testimonies involved, of all things, a set of missing dentures.

It was during the 1930s, and my great-grandfather owned a seafood packing business. It was common for him to be out on a portion of the Chesapeake Bay tonging for oysters along with his crew. For some reason known only to him and understood only by those who have experienced ill-fitting dentures, he was working with his false teeth in his shirt pocket rather than in his mouth. Predictably, sometime during the day his dentures fell into the murky waters of the Chesapeake Bay.

That evening he was distressed at the loss of his teeth and wondered how he could replace them. He prayed for guidance and for the return of his teeth.

The next day he set out on his boat asking God for direction. He steered his boat to the general area where he had been working the day before. He said another prayer about his teeth, and lowered the tongs into the water.

Oyster tongs are similar to two rakes fastened together in scissor-like fashion. They are about 10 to 15 feet long. On the very first dip into the waters, my great-grandfather pulled the tongs into the boat and released his catch onto the culling board. There among the oysters, shells, and mud were his dentures—both top and bottom teeth, smiling, as it were.

Needless to say, there was a great hoopla of praises and shouting on the boat. Every oyster boat in his small fleet bore testimony to the miracle of the finding of the false teeth.

Though this incident took place before my birth, eyewitnesses to the miracle told the story in my presence many, many times. How marvelous it is to serve a God who cares, not just about meeting our spiritual needs but also about meeting our tiniest material needs as well.

Do we live beneath our privileges as children of God? Could it be that God would meet us at our point of need more often if we would only invite Him there?

Father, Abba Father, I come to You today as a little child approaching a parent. Look into my heart and life and supply all of my needs according to Your knowledge and Your riches.

March 5

Scripture: "But without faith it is impossible to please Him, for he who comes to God must believe that He is, and that He is a rewarder of those who diligently seek Him" (Hebrews 11:6).

I love the "Abba Father" concept of God. I had a wonderful father who provided a great model of what God as Father can mean in the life of a believer. Perhaps I learned to appreciate the presence of my father because of the unique history of our relationship.

I was born a few months after my father was drafted into the U.S. Army and had left for World War II. Soldiers were not drafted for a specific period of time in that war. They were told at induction that their period of service would be "for the duration" of the war. For my father, "the duration" was three and a half years.

My father's family lived in Maryland, and I was their only grandchild. My mother's family lived in Florida, and Mother and I spent most of the war years living with them. My maternal grandfather worked for the railroad and provided free passage for Mother and me between the two families so that I could grow up knowing both sets of grandparents. They didn't know how long "the duration" might be.

My entire life seemed to be controlled by the war. Many of our male relatives were in various parts of the world serving in the U.S. Army. My mother, Ruth Morris, and my aunts worked in the war effort at the draft board, at the shipyards, and in various war-supporting capacities. Our windows were covered at night with the thick, dark-green shades of the blackouts. The radio with its ominous stories of death and destruction alternately frightened us or gave us hope. Reports of German submarines patrolling our coastal waters terrified us.

I grew up with adults who speculated when or whether I would ever know my father. Mother sent Dad monthly pictures of me so he could watch me grow. She faithfully taught me who my daddy was from photographs of him—mostly in uniform.

One day as Mother and I traveled from Florida to Maryland by train, we were delayed at a station where thousands of men in the familiar army green were loaded and unloaded onto troop trains headed for various military bases. Mother says that I stood with my face pressed against the window for a very long time. I was motionless as my eyes scanned the throngs of soldiers looking for that one familiar face I knew only in a photograph but longed for with all of my heart.

Finally, turning to her with a painful expression on my little face, I said plaintively, "Looks like one of them could be my daddy."

I was a little girl longing for my natural father. But the human heart that remains devoid of the heavenly Father makes that same search, groping here and there, empty and unsatisfied until right relationship is established. No human heart is fulfilled outside of relationship with the heavenly Father. Seek Him today while He may be found.

Dear heavenly Father, my heart longs for You. I am incomplete and unfulfilled without You. Reveal Yourself to me today.

March 6

Scripture: "Let your waist be girded and your lamps burning; and you yourselves be like men who wait for their master, when he will return from the wedding, that when he comes and knocks they may open to him immediately. Blessed are those servants whom the master, when he comes, will find watching" (Luke 12:35-37).

Are we watching for the Lord to come with great expectation for His appearing?

I can remember as a little girl waiting for my mother to come home from work. I stayed at home with my grandmother all day. She loved me dearly and was attentive to my every need. I loved her in return. However, there was something special every afternoon when it was time for my mother to come home.

Granny wanted me to be wearing a clean outfit, have clean hands and face, and have my hair combed for Mother's homecoming. The last half hour would be filled with preparations. Then, I could wait on the front porch, or once in a while I was allowed to walk about a half block and wait for her at the corner.

The waiting rules were very strict. I could only go to the end of our block. Under no circumstances could I cross the street. Granny would stand on the porch watching to see that I obeyed the rules.

Mother rode the city bus home. I could see the bus stop from the corner where I waited. I can still remember the excitement when the bus stopped. She would be on the other side when it pulled away, but it took only a minute or two for her to walk to where I was and scoop me up in her arms.

Once in a while, I would get to the corner too soon and a bus or two would come and go without the familiar figure appearing. There would be a momentary disappointment, and then another bus would pull up to the curb, disgorge some riders, and pull away.

Finally, there she was. She would have to wait for the traffic light to allow her to step into the crosswalk, and then she would head my way. Sometimes I felt shy and subdued and leaned quietly against the concrete marker that named our street. But most days I jumped up and down with excitement.

Wonder if she'll bring me a surprise? Sometimes she did. Most times she didn't. It really didn't matter. It wasn't a surprise I was anticipating. It was Mother's smile, Mother's wave, Mother's hug. It was Mother's love I wanted. And I wanted it in the fullness of her personal presence.

I was never disappointed. I was never left standing at the corner alone.

Are you looking for the appearance of our Lord and Savior Jesus Christ? Look in quiet anticipation, or jump for joy as you wait. But don't despair. He is coming!

Lord, we pray with John the Revelator, "Even so, come, Lord Jesus." Help us to be watching, waiting, and ready for Your appearance.

March 7

Scripture: "For now we see in a mirror, dimly, but then face to face. Now I know in part, but then I shall know just as I also am known" (1 Corinthians 13:12).

For three years, I learned what my father looked like through pictures. I could not hear his voice. I could not feel his touch. Even the letters he wrote were censored because of wartime security constraints. I knew him only by pictures.

His knowledge of me was based on pictures as well. Mother faithfully took me to a studio every two months for new ones. She sent him snapshots. She wrote him letters every day, describing my growth and development. My dad knew a whole lot more about me than I knew about him.

My immaturity caused misunderstanding as well. When I asked for certain things such as our own house, a puppy, a little brother, and so forth, I was told that we had to wait until "Daddy comes home." So I came to believe that if and when he ever came home, I would have everything a little girl could dream of.

Finally, in November of 1945, the long-awaited day came. Germany surrendered. Japan surrendered. Then it was a matter of time, seniority, and logistics in combination that determined when Dad would be home.

We got a call that he was in New York. It wouldn't be long, but he would have to go through Fort Meade, Maryland, where he had been inducted to be mustered out. We should wait for a call at his parents' home in Maryland. Then one night, the big call came. He was in Salisbury, Maryland, 35 miles away at my great-uncle's restaurant. We should pick him up as soon as possible.

The excitement in that household was indescribable. His parents were beside themselves with joy and relief. Mother was ecstatic, and joy expressed itself in tears. My uncle, only 4½ himself, and I mimicked the adults.

I clearly remember riding to Salisbury in the backseat of a 1939 maroon Plymouth and pulling onto the parking lot of the restaurant. I recall seeing a man in a green U.S. Army uniform through that window.

It was my father. I knew it. I was seeing my father for the first time in my life, and I was seeing him through a window.

Doors flew open on the car. A door sprang open to the restaurant. Mother and I were scooped up in those strong arms that we had longed for and wondered if we would ever feel. Parents, spouse, child, brother, aunts, uncles, grandmother, a returned warrior—we all laughed and cried and hugged and kissed and tumbled around with each other in a mass of joy, excitement, and relief.

I finally had met my father—face-to-face!

Every human soul longs to know the Father in heaven. And it longs to know its Creator face-to-face. Today we can know Him intimately by His Spirit. That is wonderful. But we long to know Him in His fullness, face-to-face.

Lord Jesus, thank You for revealing Yourself through Your Word. Keep us safely in Your love until the day that we meet around Your throne.

March 8

Scripture: "By this we know that we love the children of God, when we love God and keep His commandments. For this is the love of God, that we keep His commandments. And His commandments are not burdensome" (1 John 5:2, 3).

I shall never forget riding home that night in the backseat of the old Plymouth. Now there were three of us, not just two. But I recall the excitement slowly dissipating as we rode along. In its place came a sense of self-consciousness and, perhaps, a foreboding of uncertainty. Quietly I slipped from between my parents and wiggled in between Mother and the door. I was hiding from the father I had been longing to see.

The next morning things were really changed. There was not the familiar uniform like the one in the pictures. Maybe this man that we had picked up the night before was not my daddy after all. Besides, Mother was no longer mine and mine alone. She had to be shared. Besides all of that, there was no puppy, no new house, and no baby brother. Had I been misled?

As time went on, new expectations became all too apparent to me. No longer were grandparents suggesting indulgence rather than discipline. No longer was a 98-pound young mother my sole boss. Now there were two. And this new one was a lot more demanding, a lot less vulnerable to grandparents, and a whole lot bigger and stronger. Hmm. This relationship was not turning out as fantasized.

Do we sometimes want the heavenly Father on our own terms? Do we fantasize about having Him supply our needs and even our wants without thinking about our reciprocal responsibility? Are we resentful about the ways that living a life pleasing to the Father impacts our time, our behavior, our attitudes, and even our relationships with other people?

I can remember as a 3-year-old wanting my earthly father on my own terms. I wanted him to give me things. I wanted Mother to be happy spending time with him as long as it didn't infringe on the time she spent with me. I wanted to behave in my own selfish, self-centered way without his interference, and certainly without his discipline.

Dad and I struggled for several months as we each sought to know the other. We stumbled as we learned to love the reality of who each other was rather than the fantasy that each of us had created about who the other was.

Babes in Christ must learn to know the Father in much the same fashion. We revel in the blessings that flow from His hand—yes. But we also must learn to appreciate the loving demands He makes. We must learn to feel safe in the predictability of His discipline. All of His demands are because of love, and they serve to protect us from evil.

My love for Dad grew strong, as did his for me. We learned to love and appreciate each other for all the right reasons. We forgot about our fantasies and learned to love the reality.

Father, I want to know You fully. I want to love You and obey You. Help me to cherish the security of Your commandments.

March 9

Scripture: "Every good gift and every perfect gift is from above, and comes down from the Father of lights, with whom there is no variation or shadow of turning" (James 1:17).

I remember rejecting a gift when I was about 3 years old. My uncle, the gift giver, never let me live down this incident, which was born of immaturity and plain old stubbornness.

It was 1945, and Uncle Harold had just returned from World War II. He was attempting to make friends with his niece when we met for the first time. He drove me to the ice-cream parlor and asked, "What kind of ice-cream cone do you want, Sugar Foot?"

"I want one dip of vanilla," I answered. That seemed straightforward enough to me.

He must have thought that if one dip would make me happy, two dips would make me doubly happy. Wrong! I refused to accept his double dip. It wasn't what I asked for, and I was not about to eat it. Needless to say, he was very disgusted with his spoiled little niece— and well he should have been. (His revenge was to remind me of the incident throughout my life and then to relate it to my children as soon as they were old enough to understand what a brat their mother had been when she was 3.)

That is an incident I might be able to forget, if only I didn't respond to the gifts of God in the same immature and stubborn way from time to time. Am I alone? Have you ever rejected the gift of God when He answered your prayer in a fashion other than what you had in mind?

Have you ever prayed for a financial windfall, only to receive a job? The labor was difficult, but your needs were met. The sweepstakes would have been the perfect gift. (One dip or two?)

Have you ever prayed for healing only to receive the grace of God sufficient to bear the infirmity? Paul did. See 2 Corinthians 12:8-10. (One dip or two?)

Have you ever prayed for a new car only to receive a well-used one? Or perhaps you prayed for a good used car when God really wanted to provide a brand new one. (One dip or two?)

Did you ever pray for an opportunity to serve the Lord in your local church only to be called by God to minister in a position far, far away from your family and friends? Perhaps you found it hard to make the transition. But as time went on, you found your ministry much more fruitful than it would have been at home. (One dip or two?)

When the gift comes from God, it is always the best gift. Don't reject what comes down from Him just because it isn't exactly what you

93

prayed for or what you imagined. It will be much better in the long run. Paul described God as the One "who is able to do exceedingly abundantly above all that we ask or think, according to the power that works in us" (Ephesians 3:20).

Father, I do not deserve any of Your gifts, but I receive them with gratitude and with the understanding that You always know what is best for me.

March 10

Scripture: "Search me, O God, and know my heart; try me, and know my anxieties; and see if there is any wicked way in me, and lead me in the way everlasting" (Psalm 139:23, 24).

Dad bought me a bicycle for Christmas when I was 6 years old. It wasn't a small bike. My feet wouldn't actually touch the pedals for the full revolution of the wheel. But he was sure I needed one that large. Wobbly training wheels and Dad's willingness to run up and down the street supporting me finally made it possible for me to ride that blue bicycle. Soon the training wheels were gone, and Dad could watch and not run.

The practicality of that large bike was that it lasted. I never outgrew it.

One Sunday afternoon when I was about 10, my parents decided to go out for a ride. I stayed home. As Dad was backing out of the driveway, he stopped and said, "If you ride your bike, don't ride in the water because it's salty and will cause it to rust.

"OK. I won't," I promised. It seemed reasonable enough. The ditches were overflowing onto the roads as a result of high tides from a recent hurricane. No problem.

A half hour or so later when boredom was setting in, along came four of my friends and invited me to go bike riding. Great! The only problem was that they headed straight for a section of country road where the water not only edged the roadway, it completely covered it. I stopped short of the water and declined to follow them in. They called for me. I noticed how neat it looked as their tracks left water trails like wakes behind them as they rode back and forth through the salty water. How enticing!

And then the irresistible, unsurmountable happened. "You're not scared, are you?"

"No. My dad told me not to ride in the salt water, that it would cause my bike to rust."

"Don't worry about that. We'll help you clean it up. He'll never know."

That was all it took. I was in fast pursuit of the others making my own neat little water wakes.

They helped me clean the bike, all right. It was so clean and sparkling from tires to handlebars when Dad came home that it attracted his attention immediately.

"Why did you ride in the salt water when I told you not to?"

I was totally shocked. How did he know? The bike was clean. And that was the answer—it was too clean. He knew that I had covered my disobedience by removing the evidence. Guilty. There was no need to try to lie out of it. Confession. Forgiveness.

Trying to fool my earthly father never worked. But now and again I would give it another futile try. How much more foolish are we when we seek to fool and to deceive our heavenly Father, who sees not only our overt deeds but the very thoughts and intents of our hearts (Hebrews 4:12, 13)?

Let us pray today and every day the prayer of David: *"Search me, O God, and know my heart." Forgive me, Father. Cleanse me.*

March 11

Scripture: "For I know whom I have believed and am persuaded that He is able to keep what I have committed to Him until that Day" (2 Timothy 1:12).

My great-grandfather trusted God for everything. He trusted the Lord for his business decisions, for the healing of his body, for his personal property—for everything. He had various small businesses, and God prospered him and blessed the work of his hands.

In today's world, and perhaps even then, many people would have judged some of the decisions that he based on trust to be unwise. Perhaps . . . but he and God had an intimate relationship, and God never let him down.

Take the chicken-house incident for an example.

Great-granddad Morris had three large poultry houses in which he raised several thousand chickens at a time. When one lot matured and was sold, he started another. The interesting thing is that he did not carry insurance on either the chickens or the buildings. This was not a source of worry or concern to him. He lived in absolute and total trust. It did worry his son, my granddad, who was in the same business on an adjoining farm. "Dad, you ought to have insurance," was the frequent warning.

It was the '40s, and the chicken houses were heated with coal-burning stoves spaced every 10 or 15 feet throughout the long buildings. There was a new litter of several thousand baby chicks occupying each house. Fresh, new wood shavings, dry and tender covered the flooring.

Great-granddad went out to one of the chicken houses early one morning to feed the chicks. And there he saw a sight that astonished him. One of the coal-burning stoves had somehow burned out of control. The fire had escaped and had burned about a four-foot diameter circle all around the stove. Then, amazingly, it burned itself out. Incredible, since the floor was covered with dry wood shavings. Not a chick was singed!

Of course, he gave God glory for saving his building and his thousands of baby chicks. And he called for his son to look at the phenomenon. The conversation went something like this:

"Well, you've got a lot to be thankful for since you don't have insurance."

"I would say I've got a lot to be thankful for, since I have the best insurance."

No argument ensued. Both father and son were convinced of the protecting hand of God. Now in the day and age in which we live, to hold uninsured property is definitely not recommended. However, above and beyond all human precautions that we might take, ultimately we still must trust in God. He is our protection. He is our strong tower. He is the One on whom we must depend.

David said it best: "I will love You, O Lord, my strength. The Lord is my rock and my fortress and my deliverer; my God, my strength, in whom I will trust; my shield and the horn of my salvation, my stronghold. I will call upon the Lord, who is worthy to be praised; so shall I be saved from my enemies" (Psalm 18:1-3).

March 12

Scripture: "For I am the Lord who heals you" (Exodus 15:26). "Who Himself bore our sins in His own body on the tree . . . by whose stripes you were healed" (1 Peter 2:24).

Divine healing has been a part of the doctrinal foundation of the Pentecostal church ever since the modern-day outpouring of the Spirit. The New Testament church believed in and practiced divine healing. Scripture is full of such incidences. The ministry of Jesus on earth involved many, many healings. God provided healing for the children of Israel in the wilderness. God heals.

During my growing-up years, my home church quite often followed the advice of James 5:14, 15: "Is anyone among you sick? Let him call for the elders of the church, and let them pray over him, anointing him with oil in the name of the Lord. And the prayer of faith will save the sick, and the Lord will raise him up."

My great-grandfather, known as a man of prayer, got many such calls. Our family also relied on his prayers to a great degree.

I clearly remember one such day. Mother, Dad, and I had just finished dinner and were cleaning off the table. Mother suddenly was struck with an abdominal pain so intense that she fell to the floor. She was in agony. "Call Granddad," she groaned.

If we had lived in a city, I would say that we lived about two blocks from him. Since we lived in the country, it might be accurate to say that we lived in sight and in hollering distance of him. Dad stepped outside the house and saw his grandfather walking around in the yard, hollered to get his attention, and beckoned for him to come. He came at once.

Dad had lifted Mother from the floor and laid her on the couch. She still was in excruciating pain. When Great-granddad walked in the door and into the room, he looked at her and said, "Ruth, I prayed for you while I was walking over here. You're healed." A broad smile of confidence covered his face.

Mother responded immediately. "Yes, I am!" she said, and stood to her feet. That was it. We have never known the source of that pain. We only know two things about it: First, it was debilitating for about 15 minutes. Second, God delivered her from the pain and healed the source in an instant.

God still heals today. Human beings have been unable to explain why some people are healed and others are not. No one understands why the same individual may be instantly healed on one occasion and have to suffer for a long time on another. We do not know why God sometimes heals through the prayer and anointing process and at other times chooses to heal through the hands of a physician who may or may not know he or she is being used by God. But this we know—God is a healer.

Lord, I praise You today that healing has been provided for us through Your death and suffering. I ask you now to heal my infirmities, heal my diseases, and, Lord, if I have committed sins, forgive me. Thank You for healing from sin-sickness, for that is the greatest healing of all.

March 13

Scripture: "Precious in the sight of the Lord is the death of His saints" (Psalm 116:15).

It has been said that the purpose of this life is merely to prepare for the life to come. So the Christian faith is as much about death as it is about life.

Death seems so frightening and mysterious that we often try to protect the young from its reality. We seek to shield them from a knowledge of death as long as possible.

I remember learning about death. Once again, the lesson was taught by my great-grandfather, and it was delivered eloquently.

I was 8 years old. Great-granddad became ill and said that God had shown him that his sickness was a "sickness unto death." It was not his practice to seek help from physicians. He had not done so for more than 20 years. However, since he knew that his time to die had come, he thought it prudent to have a physician come to call. He reasoned that after his death, his family would be criticized for not doing everything possible to save his life. So Dr. George Coulborne was summoned to the home.

House calls were quite common in that time and place. Besides, "Dr. George," as we called him, had been our family physician for years and had delivered two generations of Morrises. He came willingly and quickly. I remember the visit well. He came out of the sickroom with tears in his eyes. He said there were some things he might do. "However," he opined, "when a man is as close to his Maker as this man is and the two of them have agreed that it's time to die, there is really nothing a man like me can do to prevent it. I won't try. Let's keep him as comfortable as we can."

For the next couple of weeks, Great-granddad prepared for his homegoing with great anticipation and quite a bit of ceremony. He called his children and grandchildren in and said, "I've done my best to show you how to live. Now I'm going to do my best to show you how to die."

And that he did. He praised God. He exhorted his visitors. He forgave his debtors of their debts. He prayed for all of us and for our children and for our children's children. He comforted the family members who were having difficulty letting him go. He enjoyed his favorite foods and told my mother, who had prepared his last meal, a special favorite of his, "Ruth, you've cooked me many delicious things since you came into our family. And I thank you. Now this meal is my last nourishment."

During the last few hours he lived, he prayed for us all. He reassured us that he was delighted to be going home. He communed with God in a heavenly language. And then, gently, he was gone. His parting words rang in our ears: "This old-time religion is good to live by, but it's better to die by."

I believe him. His own life and the Word of God bear witness that he spoke the truth.

Lord, help me to live the rest of my life in such a manner that I will approach death with joy and not regret. May I look forward to the day when I will meet You and join my loved ones.

March 14

Scripture: "If you then, being evil, know how to give good gifts to your children, how much more will your heavenly Father give the Holy Spirit to those who ask Him!" (Luke 11:13).

My dad was a great gift giver. He returned from Europe and World War II in November of 1945. I met him for the first time. For most of my young life, I had wanted a puppy. At each request, I was put off by "You'll have to wait until your Daddy comes home." I halfway thought he might bring the puppy with him.

My late November birthday and Christmas that year run together in my memory. I can't be sure what gifts went with which occasion, but there is one thing I know. The first gift I can remember receiving from my father's hand was a puppy. She was a little black-and-tan terrier and was immediately named Skippy.

From that time until my father's death, he delighted in buying and giving gifts to me and to others. Giving was such joy to him, almost a game. He seemed to get more pleasure than the recipient did in his giving.

Christmas, of course, afforded him great opportunity for gift giving. He would tell Mother, "Buy lots of little gifts for everybody so that we can open some early." Then several days before Christmas when all the gifts were wrapped and safely under the tree, Dad would come in and say, "Let's everybody open one gift." It was a ritual we planned ahead for.

Giving was his lifestyle. In fact, when he died December 2, 1979, he had much of his Christmas shopping done. He had accomplished this from his wheelchair in the more-elaborate-than-usual gift shop of the hospital.

All of these years after his death, I have had people to whom Dad ministered tell me about special gifts he gave them. A pastor in Trinidad, West Indies, told me Dad gave him the first turkey he and his family had ever had so that they could have an American-style Thanksgiving. He brought it in his hands from the United States through customs—frozen. He made giving and receiving fun.

As generous as Dad was, his giving spirit cannot be compared with the giving nature of our heavenly Father. The ultimate expression of

God's generosity is articulated in John 3:16: "For God so loved the world that He gave His only begotten Son, that whoever believes in Him should not perish but have everlasting life."

Have you asked your heavenly Father for a gift He has not given? Then He must have known that it would not be good for you.

Have you asked for a gift you know by His Word is His will for you? Then follow the advice of Jesus and keep on asking: "Ask, and it will be given to you; seek, and you will find; knock, and it will be opened to you. For everyone who asks receives, and he who seeks finds, and to him who knocks it will be opened" (Matthew 7:7, 8).

Father, giver of life and redemption, give to me the gifts You would have me receive. I will accept them from Your bountiful hand with thanksgiving.

March 15

Scripture: "Likewise the Spirit also helps in our weaknesses. For we do not know what we should pray for as we ought, but the Spirit Himself makes intercession for us with groanings which cannot be uttered" (Romans 8:26).

The Holy Spirit is a gift from God. The baptism of the Holy Spirit with the evidence of speaking in other tongues is available to believers today. As May Wilson told my ancestors four generations ago, "The Holy Ghost is real" (see March 2).

There have been many, many times in my life when the Spirit of God has spoken during family, as well as private, prayer times. He has been our comfort, our guide, our friend.

The manifestation of the Holy Spirit through speech in an unknown tongue is a legitimate biblical experience. It is not the result of overactive emotions in which people become overwrought and engage in some type of meaningless babble. It is communication with God.

In 1966 my family and I had a beautiful opportunity to hear the Spirit intervene in the best purposes of Romans 8:26. My grandfather lay dying in Johns-Hopkins Hospital in Baltimore, Maryland. He knew and we knew that his time was short. He had expressed joy in his expected homegoing. He had reaffirmed his father's parting words, "This old-time religion is good to live by, but it's better to die by." He was waiting.

Heart monitors were a relatively new phenomenon in those days. For the first time in our family experience, we were able to watch the jagged lines moving across the screen letting us know that someone we loved very much was slipping away from us.

One day an attending nurse spoke to my uncle about something that was puzzling her. "Your father is quite lucid," she said. "He makes perfect sense when he talks to us. Every now and then, however, he becomes incoherent, and we can't understand his speech. That is not unusual in his condition," she continued. "What we can't understand is that when his speech is incoherent, his heartbeat is at its very best."

By then my uncle was smiling. "I can explain that," he said. "You see, we're Pentecostal. We believe in an experience whereby we can speak directly to God in a language known only to the Spirit. So, you see, when he appears to be incoherent to you, he is communing with God in a very special way."

She shook her head with understanding as tears formed in her eyes. "Then that explains the regular heartbeat and improved vital signs as well," she said softly. She turned to leave and then turned back. "You say your brother pastors a church here in Baltimore?"

"Yes. In Essex."

"Give me the name and address, please. I think I'll start going there."

And she did.

Holy Spirit of God, pray for me. I am weak and do not know how to pray for myself. Bring my petitions to the throne according to the will of God.

March 16

Scripture: "He said unto them, Have ye received the Holy Ghost since ye believed? And they said unto him, We have not so much as heard whether there be any Holy Ghost" (Acts 19:2, KJV).

The Pentecostal heritage in my husband's family is rich. Grandma Stone went to a tent revival in Whitwell, Tennessee, in 1913. They were teaching a "new" doctrine about the Holy Ghost. They said that after people were saved, they needed to be sanctified and filled with the Holy Ghost. Furthermore, they said, when one is filled, he or she will speak in tongues in a language never learned.

Grandma was interested. She even heard people speaking in this new tongue. They seemed so happy and free! She wanted the experience too.

Grandpa Stone was much taller than his wife and was 15 years older. He was a coal miner who prided himself on loading more coal than was expected of an average man. His reputation in the little mining town was important to him. Religiously, he was a staunch believer in "once in grace, always in grace." He had been baptized as a boy. He accepted God's grace at that point. Therefore, he was still "saved" no matter what he did or didn't do. There was no need of tent meetings and new experiences for him.

When Grandma returned home excited about what she had seen and heard, her husband was furious. He warned her *never* to go to that tent again. After all, if his wife was seen at that "Holy Roller" meeting, what would people think? He would be disgraced.

"If you ever go to that tent again, I'll kill you." That was his final word on the matter!

The following day was one of mixed emotions and agonizing indecision for Grandma. What should she do? She'd better obey her husband, yet something kept tugging at her soul to go back to the tent. When church time rolled around, Grandpa was not at home, and the soul tug won. She went back to the tent.

That night Grandma received the baptism of the Holy Spirit. She was ecstatic. The rejoicing went on for quite some time, and it was late when she walked up on her front porch. There sat her husband, his empty bottle on the floor. He was livid.

He grabbed her by the throat, towering over her. He put a hawk-billed knife to her throat. The smell of alcohol permeated his breath as he growled, "I told you not to go back to that tent. You did it anyway, and now I'm going to kill you."

Grandma was pretty sure she was about to meet the Lord. And she was absolutely sure that she was ready! Her little feet began to pat up and down on the floor as she danced in the Spirit. Then she began to speak in a heavenly language. The next thing she knew, the knife went one way and her husband the other. She remained a member of the Church of God until her death at age 93.

"And do not fear those who kill the body but cannot kill the soul. But rather fear Him who is able to destroy both soul and body in hell" (Matthew 10:28).

Thank You for the power of Your Spirit. Fill me anew today. Give me a biblical fear of You and fear of nothing else.

March 17

Scripture: "Casting all your care upon Him, for He cares for you. Be sober, be vigilant; because your adversary the devil walks about like a roaring lion, seeking whom he may devour. Resist him" (1 Peter 5:7-9).

The decade was the '40s. The woman who would become my mother-in-law was extremely ill. She had been treated to no avail. She had spent considerable time in the University of Virginia Hospital, where the state's most competent physicians had little optimism for her future. Prayers seemed ineffective.

The suffering itself was a heavy burden. In addition, she was a pastor's wife and the mother of four little boys whose ages ranged across a six-year span. They needed more from her than she had strength to give. The pain and inadequacy were overwhelming.

As weak as she was, she went to a revival where the evangelist was emphasizing divine healing. She joined the prayer line. She felt victory. She really believed she was healed and began to testify of that.

To her disappointment, there were no immediate physical signs of healing. The weakness and pain continued. She gained no weight. Some days she wondered if she was regressing.

One particular Sunday morning, she helped the boys dress for Sunday school and, in exhaustion, had to go back to bed. There in the parsonage, she sunk to her lowest ebb. Then she sensed that she was not alone. She was aware of the invisible, evil presence of Satan. "You testified that you were healed. You're not healed. Just look at you."

She conceded, "Well, I guess I'm not. I'm no better."

Satan went on, "Besides that, you don't have the Holy Ghost."

More discouraged, she responded, "Perhaps I don't have the Holy Ghost. It's been a while since I have heard Him speak."

"Furthermore," Satan reasoned, "You're not sanctified."

"Probably not," she agreed. "I've been impatient."

Satan pressed on, sure that he had the upper hand. "In fact, you're not even saved. If you die, you won't go to heaven."

Suddenly faith stirred in her heart and Satan was revealed as the liar that he is. She sat up and responded with conviction: "Devil, I know I'm saved. You lied about that. If you lied about that, you lied about sanctification. I know I'm sanctified, and I know I have the Holy Ghost. Furthermore, you lied about my healing too. I am healed."

Immediately the evil presence fled the room, and it was filled with a heavenly brightness. The Lord came and said, "Do not be afraid: I am Alpha and Omega, the first and the last. I am He who lives and was dead; and, behold, I am alive forevermore. And I have the keys of hell and of death" (see Revelation 1:11, 18).

From that time forward, she was strengthened and restored to complete health. At her lowest point, the Spirit renewed her faith, and Satan was resisted. Later, God blessed her with a daughter, and at this writing, my mother-in-law is in her 80s, is firm in her faith, and gives testimony of healing. (Interestingly, March 17 is her birthday.)

Thank You, Father, for each stripe of pain You paid for our healing.

March 18

Scripture: "Lord, help me!" (Matthew 15:25).

Lynn, my husband, spent his early years in the mountains of Virginia. He and his three older brothers loved nothing more than climbing the mountains and playing in the crystal streams near their home. The four boys were close in age and attachment.

Somewhere about 1944, when Lynn was about 3, the boys were asked to carry some items to one of the neighbors. En route they had to cross a stream on a narrow, wooden footbridge. They had made the crossing many times in uneventful fashion. On this day, however, the little stream was flooded. It was a muddy, rushing torrent. The wooden planks barely cleared the deluge.

Frightened, Lynn hung back. "I'm afraid," he whimpered. "Hoyt, I'm not going unless you carry me."

"We have lots of bundles to carry. You're big. You can walk," Hoyt encouraged. Lynn's reply was a whine and a refusal.

"I'd rather carry him than all this stuff," his next brother, Neil, said, swinging Lynn onto his shoulders. That was fine with the 3-year-old. Neil was bigger than his older brother anyway. So the procession started across. Hoyt was first with the parcels; Neil with Lynn on his shoulders was next; Jimmy was last.

Things went well until Hoyt reached the other side and gave a jump as he left the bridge. Vibrations traveled the length of the boards. Neil wavered to the left and to the right. Struggling in vain to regain his balance, he dropped his little brother into the raging stream.

"Ahhh-gug!!!" Lynn screamed as he tumbled, choking on water as he began to bob under and over the surface of the murky, muddy, raging stream. No intelligible words were spoken, just a desperate cry for rescue.

The three brothers looked on in horror as their baby sibling was swept away. They were helpless.

Fortunately, there was a soldier on furlough walking along the river. He heard the scream, visually assessed the situation, ran to the next bend in the river, and waited. When the time was right, he stretched out his hand. The terrified child responded in kind.

In Matthew 15:25, a desperate woman made a well-structured speech to the Lord and was ignored. Then she cried in desperation, "Lord, help me!" The etymology of the word *help* in the original Greek writing contained the picture of someone running in response to the screams of another. She had to have help for her daughter who was demon-possessed. This cry of desperation elicited the desired response. Her daughter was delivered by Jesus.

Similarly, the soldier heard Lynn's screams and rescued him. Do you have a desperate need today? Jesus does not require a well-structured petition. But He does respond to cries of the heart.

Lord, help me today. You see the desire of my heart. Grant it according to Your will.

March 19

Scripture: "For the Lord Himself will descend from heaven with a shout, with the voice of an archangel, and with the trumpet of God. And the dead in Christ will rise first. Then we who are alive and remain shall be caught up together with them in the clouds to meet the Lord in the air. And thus we shall always be with the Lord. Therefore comfort one another with these words" (1 Thessalonians 4:16-18).

It seemed like a reasonable request. After our wedding and the reception, I wanted to drive away for our honeymoon with no graffiti on the car, no tin cans or old shoes, no shaving cream, nothing. There would be no practical jokes involving our luggage, our possessions, our persons.

"But you don't understand. I am guilty of doing those very things to my older brothers," Lynn explained.

"But marriage is sacred, not to be spoiled by practical jokes. Besides that, I have a plan; just do your part," I begged.

Eager to please, he listened. This was the plan: Before our evening wedding, he would put his car with our luggage in the garage of my friend who lived near the reception hall. My mother would pick him up. She would tell no one. After the reception, we would go to a room to change. Instead of coming back to say good-bye, we would slip out a back door and walk in the dark to the garage where his untouched car was hidden. He agreed.

The wedding and reception went as planned. At the appropriate time, we left to change. Mother went along to help. She returned to the festivities in what seemed an appropriate time and made small talk.

In the meantime, we finished dressing and went to the back door. The door no longer in use, the steps had been removed. But the four-foot drop wasn't bad even in high heels. My new husband helped me. Then we crossed a ditch, but it didn't have much water.

We walked the distance of a city block. But it wasn't an ordinary block; it was a cemetery, and the night was very dark.

"Someone's coming," Lynn whispered looking back toward the reception hall. Sure enough his oldest brother was walking alongside the building. He looked at the door and across the cemetery. But he didn't see us, because we were hiding behind a convenient tombstone. Still dissatisfied, he went to get another brother.

But we were gone. We ran through the cemetery into the garage, hopped in our car, and were on our way. My unusual request had been honored, and we were riding along toward our honeymoon in a clean car with no practical jokes—just a happy bride and groom alone together.

The incident has been an inspiration to us through the years. Nowadays we compare it to the time when we shall escape the sleaze and pettiness of this world to be with the Lord for the marriage of all marriages. Sure, we may have to "hide" behind a tombstone for a time before the marriage of the bride, the church, and the Bridegroom, Jesus Christ, is consummated. But death is only for a season. Then life will be eternal!

Lord, wash me from all sins of this world so that I may be part of Your spotless, unblemished bride.

March 20

Scripture: "Behold, children are a heritage from the Lord, the fruit of the womb is a reward. Like arrows in the hand of a warrior, so are the children of one's youth. Happy is the man who has his quiver full of them; they shall not be ashamed, but shall speak with their enemies in the gate" (Psalm 127:3-5).

How can a parent describe the birth of a child? It is not possible to describe. It must be experienced.

I am an only child. My one sister lived just five hours. In my extended family, there were several who were never blessed with children and several more who knew the sorrow of losing a child at birth. Not surprisingly, I grew up believing that having a child was a rare privilege, a cherished gift.

Our first son was born about a year and a half after we were married. He weighed only five pounds. I shall never forget the overwhelmingly powerful love that swept over me when that tiny little bundle was placed in my arms. As the hours went on, I was literally amazed at how much totally unselfish love I felt for him. In that regard, I was no different from other parents. New parents, almost universally, express similar emotions.

It was a little scary to know that such a vulnerable creature was totally dependent on his daddy and me for his survival. He weighed 4 pounds and 13 ounces when we took him home from the hospital. Even preemie clothes left him growing room.

When our second son came along just 18 months later, we weren't surprised by the immediate love that we felt, but we were just as enchanted by him. Another five-pounder, he had amazingly bright eyes for a newborn. "Stoney" was what the preemie nursery attendants called him. They seemed reluctant to let him go when the doctor finally dismissed him at 5 pounds, 8 ounces.

Four and a half years went by, and another little boy was born. He seemed beautiful and big to us at 7 pounds. Right away we were enamored. The other boys were old enough to share our joy.

Five years later our fourth and last son came along and weighed in at 7 pounds and 10 ounces. No longer surprised by the immediate and powerful love, we just let it wash over us. What a joy that baby was!

A house full of boys can be a boisterous place, an exciting place, a disorderly place! We have experienced a vast array of events and emotions just as other parents have. Love and joy are basic to them all.

In reflecting on my love as a mother, I am awestruck to know that my heavenly Father loves me far more than I am capable of loving my own children. I am comforted to know that He loves my own children more than I am capable of doing. He will care for them long after I am gone.

Yes, children are a blessed gift from the Lord. We—as parents, as Christians, as good neighbors, and as good citizens—should appreciate and love the children of our homes, our churches, and our communities. We should feel a responsibility for them.

Dear Lord, help me to love all children everywhere. Inspire me to nurture them physically and spiritually.

March 21

Scripture: "Has the Lord as great delight in burnt offerings and sacrifices, as in obeying the voice of the Lord? Behold, to obey is better than sacrifice, and to heed than the fat of rams" (1 Samuel 15:22).

Early in January of 1970, something totally unpredictable happened to my father. He was called by God to leave his large, comfortable pastorate and go to the West Indies.

It happened like this. He took a trip with his uncle who was going to preach a convention in Trinidad. He was merely to be an observer, a visitor. He fell in love with the people of the islands, and God began dealing with his heart. Never for a moment from that time on were the people of Trinidad far from his mind.

Finally, the Lord made Himself very clear. The calling was undeniable. World Missions was contacted. All the details were worked out, and the appointment was made. Soon the church was informed and the whole community began to hear the news—one of the local pastors was leaving his parish to become a missionary. Expressions from the community were overwhelmingly positive. The consensus was that they all hated to lose Mother and Dad, but they were pleased that he was following the leading of the Lord.

Interestingly, the only negative responses came from the ministers of his own denomination. Did he know what he was doing? "This is not a good career move. . . . You won't be able to get a church to pastor when you're ready to return to the U.S. . . . This is a real step-down for you. . . . How will you manage the huge pay cut?" The negative feedback was beginning to be painful.

Finally, one of Dad's good friends said to him, "What happened to you, Ralph Morris? Did you fall on your head?" (He was suggesting mental incompetence, of course, questioning the decision.)

The reply was quick: "No. I fell on my face before God. You should try that. Who knows? You might get a call."

One thing is for sure—a true calling from God is unlikely to come to those who do not seek His will.

The apostle Paul is an example of a biblical character who constantly sought the will of God. It was God who directed him from city to city. It was God who called him into Macedonia. It was God who enabled him to press on to Jerusalem, where he would be arrested. It was God who led him to Rome, where he would be imprisoned and ultimately would die.

Seeking, hearing, and obeying the voice of God is paramount for the committed Christian. He has a plan for each one. To follow that plan obediently is the highest service one can render. It is the highest office one can fill.

Father, obeying You is more important to You than anything I could possibly give You. Obeying You is important to me as well. Let me fulfill that acceptable, good, and perfect will of God.

March 22

Scripture: "If I take the wings of the morning, and dwell in the uttermost parts of the sea, even there Your hand shall lead me, and Your right hand shall hold me" (Psalm 139:9, 10).

My parents, Ralph and Ruth Morris, spent the summer of 1970

sorting through their belongings, selling the unnecessary, storing the sentimental, and packing the rest in huge barrels for Trinidad. Eventually everything was properly sold, stored, or shipped. All that remained could be checked on the plane when they actually traveled. Immunizations complete, immigration requirements met, blessings of the church bestowed, they boarded a plane headed south over the Caribbean Sea. Expectation and trepidation battled within them, but they were absolutely sure God had called them.

They landed at Piarco Airport, Port-of-Spain, Trinidad, on a hot September evening. A large group of Church of God members lined the visitors' gallery to welcome them. Beautiful, smiling faces bolstered their confidence as they crossed the tarmac.

Inside, they approached the immigration desk. Mother laid her papers on the desk first. The officer looked at the documents, asked a few questions, and marked her papers with a large "X."

"What does that mean?" Mother's voice quavered.

"It means you've been denied entry into the country of Trinidad. Wait right over here. We will bring your luggage; you must return to the United States on the next flight. In the meantime, you are restricted to this area," came the terse reply. The exact same process was repeated with Dad.

He protested, insisting that their visas and other documents were in order. They *must* be admitted. He persuaded the officer to let them stay 24 hours. For now, they were free to travel to the mission house, but they must depart the country within 24 hours.

Predictably, there was no sleeping that night. They walked the floors and prayed. They questioned their understanding of God's calling. Perhaps those who had discouraged them had been right after all. They were at the tip of the West Indies, unwelcomed by the government. Their belongings were on a ship. Their lovely church was being pastored by someone else. What were they to do?

The Lord led Dad to the 139th Psalm. With his arms around Mother, he read it entirely. Verses 9 and 10 stood out. Then he prayed, "That is what we have done, Lord. We took the wings of a jet plane and came to this island in the sea. Now You must lead us and hold us." With that, they determined to be at the immigration office in the national capital when it opened.

They were shuttled from office to office all day long. At the end of the day, they were sent to an office said to be their last hope. When the door opened, there sat the man who had put the "X" on their papers the night before. Something had changed. He now was willing to give them 30 days to stay in Trinidad.

Dad determined to do everything he could in those 30 days. God blessed. Extension followed extension, and those original 24 hours stretched into six years of very fruitful ministry.

God never makes mistakes. God never calls without enabling. He is faithful!

Thank You, Lord, for the assurance that no matter how far from "home" we are or how complicated the circumstances, there is never a moment or a place that You are not with us—directing us and leading us.

March 23

Scripture: "The steps of a good man are ordered by the Lord, and He delights in his way. Though he fall, he shall not be utterly cast down; for the Lord upholds him with His hand" (Psalm 37:23, 24).

Mother and Dad were due for a few months' furlough during the summer and early fall of 1974. Their weeks were filled with a whirlwind of appointments in churches all over the eastern U.S. They shared the needs of the work in Trinidad. Along with cash offerings and mission pledges, a number of people donated "gifts in kind," items Dad had mentioned that were urgent needs.

The weeks flew by, and it was time to return. The number of suitcases, boxes of supplies, equipment, and so forth, was staggering. Dad and Lynn finally got it all into the car, Mother and Dad squeezed in, and they were off to the airport. I couldn't even find room to go along to say one last good-bye.

On the way to the airport, Dad said, "You know, the overweight charges on all of this are going to be horrendous. We've got this gasoline generator, an electric keyboard and amplifier, a copier, all kinds of stuff besides our suitcases."

"Well, how much do you think it will be?" Lynn inquired.

"Oh, several hundred dollars, I'm sure," Dad answered.

"Do you have the money?" Lynn asked the obvious question.

"No," Dad answered, a broad smile covering his face.

"Well, I don't either. What will you do?"

"I don't know. The Lord knows."

Lynn was nervous. It wasn't exactly his problem, but somehow it seemed like it was. He felt guilty about being unable to come up with the money to pay the excess. He breathed a prayer. Most likely everyone was praying, because the car grew quiet.

At the airport, all the parcels were lugged up to the ticket counter. It was a massive, irregular pile. The agent peered over the counter. "All that yours?" Dad nodded in the affirmative. The agent responded with a nod in the negative. "OK, start putting it up here on this scale. We'll add it up."

The first piece went onto the scale, and the needle did not move. The second piece went on; no movement.

"Hey, Bob!" the agent called into the back room as he kicked and rattled the scale. "What's wrong with these scales? The needle's not moving."

Bob came out of the back. "They're broken. A man came in last night and stepped on them. He was huge, exceeded the capacity, and they broke. We've called for a repairman. He can't come until tomorrow." Bob returned to the back.

"Well, sir," the agent said in disbelief. "This is your lucky day. I can't charge you for excess if I can't document the weight. I'll just have to check you on through."

"What is the capacity of that scale?" Dad asked.

"Three hundred pounds."

Dad turned to Lynn with a grin, "You ever seen a three-hundred-pound angel of the Lord?"

Father, I don't know what obstacles may fall in my path today, but I trust You to remove them all according to Your will.

March 24

Scripture: "Let Your work appear to Your servants, and Your glory to their children. And let the beauty of the Lord our God be upon us, and establish the work of our hands for us; yes, establish the work of our hands" (Psalm 90:16, 17).

Dad's first 24 hours granted by the immigration official in 1970 (see March 22) stretched into six years. The work in Trinidad, Tobago, and Grenada had flourished. The number of churches and members greatly increased. The ranks of the ministry grew. Properties were improved. Mother and Dad were thankful.

Even though Dad was only 55, his health was clearly failing. Reluctantly, he notified the World Missions Department that he would have to return to the U.S. They commended his work, told him they would locate a pastorate for him in the States, and asked his assistance in arranging the appropriate visas for the man who would replace him. He agreed.

There was a strong anti-American atmosphere in the islands at that time. Immigration officials decided not to approve any more U.S. missionaries. Dad pressed for approval for his successor.

"And just why do you think an American can love Trinidadians as much as our national ministers can love them?" asked the impatient bureaucrat.

"Because I do," Dad responded with passion.

"It's easy to talk about loving," was his retort. "It's more difficult to prove. What evidence do you have of your love?"

Dad stretched his hands across the man's desk. "These," Dad answered softly, sincerely, his eyes filling with tears. His hands were hard and calloused. They were cracked, bruised, and scraped from many hours of mixing mortar, laying blocks, finishing cement, and other labors of the builder's trade. The tops of his hands and arms were deeply tanned from day after day in the tropical sun.

He offered this commentary on his hands: "My denomination sent me here to oversee the New Testament Churches of God in Trinidad, Tobago, and Grenada. I could have done that to their satisfaction from my air-conditioned office and my air-conditioned car. My pay would have been exactly the same as it has been. But because of love, I built and remodeled numerous churches, built and remodeled houses, planned and built a Bible school and a convention center. I did not merely oversee those jobs. I worked on them with these hands. These hands are proof of my love."

The official lowered his eyes and examined the outstretched hands. Silently, he picked up his pen and signed the documents admitting another American missionary to his country.

Three and a half years later those hands were folded in death. They had built one more beautiful church after returning to the U.S. Shortly before his death, he exhorted my mother, "Don't ever let the devil tell you I shouldn't have worked so hard in the islands. Those were the more satisfying years of my ministry."

It seems to me I remember another pair of hands scarred and wounded by acts of love. We'll touch them in eternity.

Thank You, Jesus, for Your unequaled love. Help me to love others in return. Help me to serve You by serving them.

March 25

Scripture: "Blessed are the dead who die in the Lord . . . that they may rest from their labors, and their works follow them" (Revelation 14:13).

No one in our family had visited Trinidad since my parents left in 1976. General Assemblies were always happy reunion times with those who were able to attend. Then in 1995, an opportunity developed to return to the islands. The overseer arranged for Lynn and me to conduct regional workers seminars around Trinidad and Tobago. To say we were excited would be an understatement.

The apostle Paul taught us that some Christian workers plant seed for the Kingdom while others water those plants and still others do the reaping. God is the One who gives the increase. Dad and Mother did some joyful reaping in the West Indies, but they did a lot of planting and watering for a future increase (1 Corinthians 3). The fruit of their labor was bountiful, and we were privileged to see it during our return visit.

The overseer himself continued to speak of Dad's positive influence on his life. The church that he pastors is one that Dad enlarged and remodeled. Since those days, the Lord has filled the building to capacity.

A member of the territorial council shared that Dad had given him a scholarship to Bible school after he converted from Hinduism. The young man had been an artist who sculpted Hindu gods before his conversion. He remembered how Dad watched with tears as he painted a picture over the baptistery of the newly constructed convention center in 1975. Much of the scholarship money came from Dad's own pocket. A good investment since that same artisan is now the pastor in a church of over 700.

Another territorial councilman shared how Mother fed him and Dad bought him a motorcycle when he was thrown out of his home for converting from Hinduism to Christianity. He gained ministerial credentials, began a Bible school, and accepted his first pastorate under Dad's leadership. A good investment since he now pastors a church of over 400 in a spot where only about 10 members worshiped in 1970.

Mothers brought sons and daughters to meet us and told of weddings, births, dedications, ministerial credentialing, and so forth, at which my parents had been influential or inspirational. Lynn delivered the commencement address at the Bible school. As I sat there in the building that Dad had built and looked at the work of his hands, I also looked at the people he had influenced and saw the work of His heart.

What could he have done with six of the last nine years of his life that would have been more profitable? How glad I was he answered the call of God. How sure I was that his works now follow him. The planting and the watering have come to full fruition.

"Therefore, my beloved brethren, be steadfast, immovable, always abounding in the work of the Lord, knowing that your labor is not in vain in the Lord" (1 Corinthians 15:58).

Lord, may all of my works be unto You and not just unto humankind.

March 26

Scripture: "Now to Him who is able to do exceedingly abundantly above all that we ask or think, according to the power that works in us, to Him be glory in the church by Christ Jesus to all generations, forever and ever. Amen" (Ephesians 3:20, 21).

It was 1971, and Lynn was the state youth and Christian education director of Arkansas. The ministers and laymen had spent long, hard hours building a youth camp. Hired workers had been few. Labors of love had gone on for most of a year. Camp was scheduled to begin in two weeks, and dorms were getting their finishing touches.

Weeks ahead, arrangements had been made to purchase 200 surplus beds from the U.S. Army. The letter of agreement was filed. All that remained was to pick them up at Fort Leonard Wood, Missouri. Lynn called to arrange the pick-up time.

"I'm sorry, sir," said the feminine voice on the other end of the line. "We have no records of that agreement."

"But I'm holding the letter in my hand," he protested.

"No doubt that you have a letter, but we don't have 200 beds. We have 129 beds, but they will be sold at auction day after tomorrow. You might have a shot if you are here at 8 a.m."

The next day Lynn boarded a commuter plane in Little Rock and headed out on a circuitous route to the base. Several hours and a few planes later, they were making their descent. Suddenly the plane lurched in a terrific shudder. Lightning flashed, and the plane climbed. They circled. The sequence was repeated. A third time. An announcement came: "Due to the storm, we must land in St. Louis. There will be a bus to drive you to Fort Leonard Wood."

Lynn asked the flight attendant, "When will the bus arrive?"

"About 5 a.m." All right. He would have time to spare.

In St. Louis, they headed for the bus, and Lynn was stopped, "Where are your orders?" he was asked. "Are you Army?"

"No. But the flight attendant said I could ride this bus."

"Sorry, sir. Military only."

"But you don't understand . . ."

"No, *you* don't understand. This bus belongs to the U.S. Army. Go to the terminal and ask when's the next flight."

The next flight was at 9 a.m., one hour *after* the beds would be sold. Far from home and farther from the base, he grumbled to God. Finally, there was prayer in the Spirit, and sleep came.

Lynn arrived at the base two hours after the 129 beds had been sold. They were stacked with the buyer's name attached.

Discouraged, Lynn looked for a telephone and called a cab. As he hung up, an officer behind the counter asked, "What brings you to Fort Leonard Wood?" Lynn told his whole pitiful story.

The officer picked up the phone and said, "Bob, there's a man coming over. Sell him 200 beds for $5.00 each." He hung up, wrote a requisition, and handed it to Lynn. "There, sir. Your taxi's here. Go to building C and give them this order."

That was it. We don't know who the officer was or where he got the beds. We do know God provided 200 beds rather than 129.

What is your need? Ask God. He is able to provide more than we ask according to the power of the Spirit.

Thank You for Your intervening power. When we have exausted our resources, You are right on time, never late.

March 27

Scripture: "Be strong and of good courage, do not fear nor be afraid . . . for the Lord your God, He is the One who goes with you. He will not leave you nor forsake you" (Deuteronomy 31:6).

In the summer of 1991, my husband experienced chest pains, and I insisted he see a doctor. X-rays showed a spot on his left lung. Time passed as various attempts to sample the lesion failed.

"I hope it isn't malignant; I don't think it is. But I am reluctant to bet your life that I'm right," the surgeon said. And remembering his brother who had died of cancer, Lynn agreed.

Lung surgery was scheduled. By then it was mid-October. Blood was collected from family. Everyone was briefed. Lynn was admitted, and by noon it was over. A wedge of lung was excised, and the cone-shaped lesion identified as benign before the rib spreader was removed. An epidural was inserted for pain control and would remain there for a few days to make his recovery "almost pain free."

Lynn was settled into a private room. As he regained consciousness, he complained of terrible pain. The dosage to the epidural was increased. Pain remained. Another increase. Puzzled the surgeon, the anesthesiologist, and the pulmonary specialist conferred. They increased the medication significantly for 20 minutes then brought it back down to the normal range. Still no relief. The dosage remained very high.

The evening R.N. spent a lot of time with Lynn and seemed concerned. About 10 p.m., she spoke to me. "I will be leaving in an hour. I'm worried about your husband's breathing. It isn't right. Watch him carefully. Wake him every few minutes. If he does not rouse when you speak his name, get help. Count his breaths; if he takes fewer than eight a minute, call for help."

I took her warning seriously and followed every instruction. About 2 a.m., I called Lynn's name and got no response. Again, no response. I pushed the nurse's call button and told her he was barely breathing. I slapped his hand. No response.

By the time the nurse arrived, he was in respiratory arrest. A "Code Blue" call was issued. As if from nowhere, the team filled his room, and I stood outside the door. A nurse from the next ward came and allowed me to use her phone to call my brother-in-law. A student from the college where I taught came from her night job in the lab to sit with me.

Meanwhile, Lynn was having a classic near-death experience. He saw himself leave his body and float painlessly upward. He watched the ball of light that was Earth grow small. Then suddenly he returned. The bright lights were on him, the pain unbearable. The medical team had cancelled all painkiller from his body in order to restore his breathing. For one and a half hours, he was postoperative with a huge incision, large drainage tubes, and many staples inside and out of his body. Each breath was torture.

That was when the Lord came. Seen only by Lynn, Jesus came and placed His hand ever so gently on his side. Lynn remembered the piercing of His side and knew that since Jesus was there, he could endure the pain. And he did. After all, He knew the pain.

Lord, I thank You for Your omnipresence!

March 28

Scripture: "Sing praise to the Lord, you saints of His, and give thanks at the remembrance of His holy name. For His anger is but for a moment, His favor is for life; weeping may endure for a night, but joy comes in the morning" (Psalm 30:4, 5).

This scripture is from a psalm of David and was written for the dedication of his house. David had a relationship with the Lord that was deep and constant. This relationship endured sin and punishment. It endured persecution and exaltation. It endured war and peace. It endured caves and palaces. It endured disgrace and honor. Yet David remained a man after God's own heart. God never forsakes those who are in relationship with Him—even though He is sometimes forsaken by them.

My relationship with God has spanned most of my life. I was born into a Christian family and brought up in church. My friendship with Him deepened when I received the baptism of the Holy Spirit at age 12. While I have not been 100 percent faithful to Him all these years, He certainly has been totally faithful to me!

It is healthy to share one's Christian experiences and testimonies as this month's devotions have done. However, I find the deepest, richest, most meaningful times with God are too personal and too precious to share in their entirety.

Sometimes sharing gives the wrong impression of others because of being told from one perspective without the balancing influence of the other viewpoint. Often the supernatural can't be described in earthly terms. And there are those times that are meant to remain between an individual believer and God alone.

Today, will you join me in thanking God for those deepest of all experiences you have had with Him? Yours are as meaningful to you as mine are to me.

Thank Him for the times that you have felt the anointing of His Spirit pour over you just as Samuel's oil poured down the face of David. Thank Him for the times He has multiplied your faith and your strength and allowed you to slay your Goliaths and to kill your ten thousands. Thank Him for His comfort in times of persecution. Thank Him for the caves as well as the palaces. Thank Him for strength to resist sinning. Thank Him for forgiveness when sins have been committed. Thank Him for being your Good Shepherd.

After reviewing your past experiences with God, thank Him for your hopes and dreams for the future. Rejoice that He has promised to be with you to the very end. He plans to walk with you through the valleys of life as well as the valley of the shadow of death. He will answer your prayers that are prayed according to His will. Is this a day of sorrow for you? If so, rejoice that sadness only lasts for a season. Joy is in your future. Is this a day of loss for you? If so, rejoice. Restoration is in your future. Share your secrets with the Lord. He has some secrets for you. Keep them in your heart—between you and Him alone.

Lord, thank You for Your willingness to relate to me on a personal level. I treasure Your friendship.

March 29

Scripture: "'Then it shall be, when many evils and troubles have come upon them, that this song will testify against them as a witness; for it will not be forgotten in the mouths of their descendants, for I know the inclination of their behavior today, even before I have brought them to the land of which I swore to give them.' Therefore Moses wrote this song the same day, and taught it to the children of Israel" (Deuteronomy 31:21, 22).

Moses had come to the end of his life. He had a heritage to pass on to Israel. He hoped they would remember the blessings of God and worship Him. He feared they would forget and turn from Him. So he wrote a powerful song (Deuteronomy 32). Then he spoke its words to an assembly of Israel. He hoped his song would remind them to be thankful and would restore them should they sin.

Every Christian family has a song just as Israel had a song. Every family has a story, a history. Every Christian person has a song to sing and a story to tell. It is important to sing it and tell it. It will give descendants the courage to remain faithful. It will give prodigals the inspiration to return to the Father's house.

Give your testimony. Give it to your children. Give it to your friends. Give it to saints and sinners. It will strengthen those who hear it and strengthen you as well. Various scriptures support sharing one's heritage, giving one's testimony.

Deuteronomy 6 urges parents to teach their children God's law. The same chapter admonishes parents to tell their children the story of God's deliverance: "When your son asks you in time to come, saying, 'What is the meaning of the testimonies, the statutes, and the judgments which the Lord our God has commanded you?' then you shall say to your son: 'We were slaves . . .'" (vv. 20, 21).

Paul taught the Romans that testifying is a part of salvation: "If you confess with your mouth the Lord Jesus and believe in your heart that God has raised Him from the dead, you will be saved. For with the heart one believes unto righteousness, and with the mouth confession is made unto salvation" (Romans 10:9, 10).

John the Revelator heard a voice from heaven talking about the value of one's testimony as a weapon against the devil: "Now salvation, and strength, and the kingdom of our God, and the power of His Christ have come, for the accuser of our brethren, who accused them before our God day and night, has been cast down. And they overcame him by the blood of the Lamb and by the word of their testimony'" (Revelation 12:10, 11).

Jesus himself said that He would testify for us if we would testify for Him: "Therefore whoever confesses Me before men, him I will also confess before My Father who is in heaven. But whoever denies Me before men, him I will also deny before My Father who is in heaven" (Matthew 10:32, 33).

So tell your story. Sing your song. Give your testimony. You, your children, and others will gain inspiration to obey, courage to stand, and strength to overcome.

Lord, anoint me to speak of Your many blessings to me.

March 30

Scripture: "Now Martha said to Jesus, 'Lord, if You had been here, my brother would not have died. But even now I know that whatever You ask of God, God will give You'" (John 11:21, 22).

There is a healthy way to reflect on the past. Healthy reflection inspires thankfulness, induces repentance, fosters wisdom, and shines a light on the path to the future.

In today's Scripture lesson, Martha was speaking to Jesus about the death of her brother, Lazarus. Jesus had been called when Lazarus first fell ill but had delayed going to Bethany, where the sisters hoped He would heal their brother. Now he was dead.

At first, Martha had a typical human response—if only. If only Jesus had been there at the right time, her brother would not be dead.

Have you ever found yourself living in an "if only" state of mind? I have, many times. "If only I hadn't done that. . . . If only you had done that. . . . If only I had more. . . . If only I could. . . . If only. . . ."

No state of mind is less productive than the "if only" state of mind. It is unhealthy to focus on the past to the point of getting stuck there. It can be dangerous emotionally. It can blockade the future.

The "if only" state of mind is analogous to the driver who looks in his rearview mirror too long and has a head-on collision with an approaching vehicle. Fortunately, Martha did not remain in that frame of mind. In the presence of Jesus, she moved quickly to the "but even now" way of thinking.

There is a conscious decision involved in moving from "if only" to "even now." One chooses to shake off the memories and conditions of the past. One chooses to focus, instead, on the future and how the present circumstances might be overcome in order to move toward a more positive tomorrow.

Forcing oneself to let go of the past and reach toward the future isn't always easy. However, it can be accomplished. And it can be accomplished most easily in the way that Martha did it. Martha left the house of mourning and went to meet Jesus. In His presence, she was able to make the transition. Hope revived.

There are people all around us who have made such terrible messes of their lives that no other human being alone could get those lives back in order. But nothing is too difficult for Jesus. He had the answer for the woman at the well in spite of her tangled past—marital problems. He had the answer for the woman caught in the act of adultery—sexual sin problems. He had the answer for Zacchaeus—crooked business practices. He had the answer for Martha—grief. And He has the answer for *you*.

Strange how some people run *away* from the Lord when they get in trouble. Martha did not make that mistake. She ran *to* Him.

Are you displeased with your past? Are you frustrated by your present? Run to Jesus, praying, "But even now I know that whatever You ask of God, God will give You."

Lord, thank You for my heritage. Thank You even more for my future. Help me to see both in the light of You.

March 31

Scripture: "My frame was not hidden from You, when I was made in secret, and skillfully wrought in the lowest parts of the earth. Your eyes saw my substance, being yet unformed. And in Your book they all were written, the days fashioned for me, when as yet there were none of them" (Psalm 139:15, 16).

Knowing who our family is and what it has accomplished is important to a sense of personal identity. Knowing the history and doctrines of our church is valuable to our Christian identity. But no personal heritage, corporate history, or self-understanding can compare to the sense of well-being, faith, and security that comes from knowing who we are in Christ Jesus.

Psalm 139 is a marvelous place to begin looking for knowledge of who we really are. David said, "You formed my inward parts; You covered me in my mother's womb. I will praise You, for I am fearfully and wonderfully made" (vv. 13, 14).

Do you know what that means? That means that the great God of creation was present, presiding over your conception. Your mother probably had about 480 ova to mature during her childbearing years. God chose which one would be mature at your conception. Your father likely provided somewhere around 400 million sperm cells from which the other half of you could be selected. Chromosome pairings and genetic trade-offs followed. Finally, you were selected out of the approximately 700 billion chances of who you might have been. You won out over all the others! God chose you! You are a winner, indeed.

Some people were conceived under sinful circumstances. Does that mean that God did not choose them? Absolutely not. The sin problem was between the parents and God. The little baby being formed was chosen by God separate and apart from its parents' behavior.

"Such knowledge is too wonderful for me; it is high, I cannot attain it," David wrote (v. 6).

And God didn't stop there. He fashioned my days for me (v. 16). Think of that, and you will want to say with David, "When I consider Your heavens, the work of Your fingers, the moon and the stars, which You have ordained, what is man that You are mindful of him, and the son of man that You visit him?" (Psalm 8:3, 4).

But what about sin? Sometimes we mess it all up. We spoil what God intended to do. True. Let's go to Romans 8 to deal with that: "There is therefore now no condemnation to those who are in Christ Jesus, who do not walk according to the flesh, but according to the Spirit. For the law of the Spirit of life in Christ Jesus has made me free from the law of sin and death. . . . For as many as are led by the Spirit of God, these are sons of God. For you did not receive the spirit of bondage again to fear, but you received the Spirit of adoption by whom we cry out, 'Abba, Father.' The Spirit Himself bears witness with our spirit that we are children of God, and if children, then heirs—heirs of God and joint heirs with Christ" (Romans 8:1, 2, 14-17).

Formed by God. Redeemed by Jesus. Heirs of God. Joint heirs with Christ. There is no greater heritage!

God my Creator, how can I thank You enough for Your thoughts toward me? My vocabulary is inadequate. Please read my heart and know that I am grateful for Your work in me!

NOTES

April

Seasons of Change

Oleda Glenn Atkinson

Oleda Glenn Atkinson has served as state president of Ladies Ministries in Mississippi, Kentucky, and Alabama. She is also a popular speaker for Ladies Ministries retreats, seminars, and camp meetings. She has also written for various church publications. Oleda has an associate of arts degree from Lee College and a bachelor of arts degree in elementary education from Clemson University. She also has additional work on the master of arts degree at the University of Tennessee at Chattanooga.

She taught in the public-school system in Anderson, South Carolina, and in a private school in Jackson, Mississippi. In Cleveland she served as information specialist in the Public Relations Department at the Church of God International Offices.

She presently serves as a member of the Advisory Council to the Ladies Ministries Department. She has served alongside her husband, Dr. Walter P. Atkinson, as evangelist, pastor, state youth and Christian education director, state overseer, and presently as general secretary-treasurer. The Atkinsons have three children: Reita Ball, Renea Medlin, and Rhonda Parris; and four grandchildren—Brittni Ball, Taylor and Tori Medlin, and Clay Parris.

April 1

Scripture: "To everything there is a season, a time for every purpose under heaven" (Ecclesiastes 3:1, *NKJV*).

There are life-changing lessons to be learned from the seasons of life. The word *season* itself means change, transition, an indefinite period. Someone has said, "It is only through change that we grow." At each stage of life, we experience feelings of inadequacy, frustration, and worthlessness. We often become dissatisfied with who we are and what we do. We may even wish for a fleeting moment that we could be someone else.

We are not accidents. God is the Creator of all, and He is aware of each life from conception to death—throughout all the seasons of our lives. He provides the necessary essentials for an effective, fulfilled, meaningful life. Colossians 2:10 tells us, "[We] are complete in Him, who is the head of all principality and power" (*NKJV*).

Springtime is my favorite season. Spring brings freshness and anticipation, newness, hope, and the joy of new beginnings. Wouldn't it be wonderful if we could linger longer in the spring season of our lives! As I observe my grandchildren, I reflect on the carefree days of childhood. Schedules, financial stress, and weighty decisions are strangers to them. Endless hours of laughter and play comprise their days. They simply trust the adults in their lives to keep their world orderly and safe. I am reminded that I too can trust my heavenly Father to do that for me. How much less stressful my days would be if I could employ that childlike trust instead of fretting, worrying, and straining to fix my world myself!

Make yourself a promise to walk again in the rain and allow the fresh aroma of God's goodness to permeate the staleness of your mind. Then return to experience a new awakening of the goodness of God and the assurance of His marvelous love as you sit at His feet.

Thank You, God, for the springtime of my life and for the promise in Psalm 103 to renew my youth like the eagle's.

April 2

Scripture: "Therefore, if anyone is in Christ, he is a new creation; old things have passed away; behold, all things have become new" (2 Corinthians 5:17, *NKJV*).

In the springtime of life, each experience is exhilarating, challenging, exciting. Every day holds a new opportunity to explore, grow, and learn.

The birth of a baby brings indescribable joy. However, birth also involves pain. The birth of two grandchildren just seven months apart brought me face-to-face with the reality of both the pain and pleasure that a new life brings. But new mothers have the ability to quickly forget the pain. The accompanying love and happiness far outweigh the pain! The smile of their infant—grasping, trusting—quickly erases the traumatic hours prior to the baby's birth.

Spiritual birth is an awakening, a renewal, a refreshing change. The pain of sin is erased, and the new convert moves into a life that finds its richest meaning in Christ, who gave the new life.

What a joyous privilege to know we have moved from pain to pleasure, from heaviness to happiness, from dread to delight, and from death to life as a new creation in Christ.

As a child is born and comes forth to commence a brand-new life, we likewise experience the dawning of a new day when we accept Christ. The past is forgotten, the future is eternal hope.

Lord Jesus, thank You for Your gift of life and the glorious opportunity to step out of darkness into Your marvelous light.

April 3

Scripture: "Blessed is the man who trusts in the Lord, and whose hope is the Lord. For he shall be like a tree planted by the waters, which spreads out its roots by the river, and will not fear when heat comes; but its leaf will be green, and will not be anxious in the year of drought, nor will cease from yielding fruit" (Jeremiah 17:7, 8, *NKJV*).

Growth isn't easy. Jesus said, "Most assuredly, I say to you, unless a grain of wheat falls into the ground and dies, it remains alone; but if it dies, it produces much grain. He who loves his life will lose it, and he who hates his life in this world will keep it for eternal life" (John 12:24, 25, *NKJV*). We must decrease and He must increase.

As an elementary schoolteacher, I observed my fifth-grade students who carefully placed large lima beans in containers to complete their study of germination. To their amazement, they learned that before a seed can sprout, it must first "die."

In "dying" we live. In "dying" we grow. In "dying" we produce fruits of pleasure for the Creator. It may be necessary to arrange "funeral services" daily for the anger, strife, resentment, or critical attitudes.

A young child quickly learns the meaning of "No" as he tests his parents and his environment. He soon learns what brings pleasure or pain and adjusts his behavior accordingly. Likewise, adults must die to selfish ambitions to walk according to God's plan.

Someone has said that life is like a piece of expensive tapestry that is woven with many exquisite strands. Some of the threads may be gold with success and other threads may be red with suffering, while others may be dark threads of pain. It is strengthening to know that through all the seasons of our life the Holy Spirit is ready to weave the threads of time and experiences into a beautiful, exquisite, brightly colored pattern of loveliness.

Heavenly Father, help me to put off any hindrances to my service for You. Please help me sink my roots deep into Your love and grace.

April 4

Scripture: "And He said to them, 'Come aside by yourselves to a deserted place and rest a while.' For there were many coming and going, and they did not even have time to eat" (Mark 6:31, *NKJV*).

God has prepared green valleys for His sheep. He knew there would be days when life flashes a "no exit" sign and we would need a place to be nurtured and renewed. He knows all about stress, pain, trauma, and frazzled nerves.

Rest sometimes means that we must shut our mouths in His presence. Rest is not governed by a geography; it is, rather, a condition of the soul, a relationship with God.

It is on those days when we are completely overwhelmed by the demands, duties, deadlines, and disappointments that we can pull aside in our green valley and just allow the warmth of His Spirit to bathe our spirits.

In those days when I was a young mother, every day was a rush to make breakfast, get the girls ready for school, straighten the house, and take care of dozens of other responsibilities. It seemed impossible to set aside a consistent time for spiritual nurturing. However, I soon realized that I had a choice to make. It became imperative to boost my spiritual diet with God's Word. My spiritual muscles needed to be firmed by the exercise of prayer.

Housecleaning took on new meaning as I began to pray for family members and friends whose names came to mind as certain objects were dusted or clothes were laundered and folded. Inspirational music provided strength and refreshing as I performed household tasks. As my spirit was nourished and nurtured, it became easier for me to exercise my maturing skills to my family. One cannot give from an empty container. We must be filled before we can overflow onto others.

Only through prayer and meditation in His Word is God given the opportunity to fulfill His plan and purpose for your life. Allow His pruning to work. Pay attention to His gentle nudgings.

Paul described what we could be like with the Holy Spirit's power working in our lives: "But when the Holy Spirit controls our lives he will produce this kind of fruit in us: love, joy, peace, patience, kindness, goodness, faithfulness, gentleness and self-control" (Galatians 5:22, 23, *TLB*).

Dear God, You are the Master Gardener. Please overshadow me with Your grace and love. Renew and refresh me as I spend time with You in sweet communion.

April 5

Scripture: "I am like a broken vessel" (Psalm 31:12, *NKJV*).

The phone rang and the friend sobbed, "Today, the divorce is final."

The pain is obvious in the face of the young couple as they relate, "We just lost our unborn child."

"I've been diagnosed with a terminal illness."

"We just lost all our financial security."

Shattered dreams, interrupted plans, and crushed spirits are common in this world. Isaiah 40:31 gives hope: "But those who hope in the Lord will renew their strength. They will soar on wings like eagles; they will run and not grow weary, they will walk and not be faint" (*NIV*).

My grandson Clay is a toddler learning to explore his surroundings with great delight. His plump little legs support him briefly, but he often "wipes out" and lands on his backside with accompanying yells and tears. It is all a part of growing.

All of us will experience wipeouts as we strive to attain and reach new goals, new heights, new dimensions. No one likes to fall. No one likes to break things. It is almost impossible to repair broken objects to their original condition. The good news is, God can take the glue of the Holy Spirit and put us back together and make us useful for His service again. Once we have been restored from our brokenness, we can offer compassion and empathy for other broken vessels.

Prayer is the ladder out of brokenness. Praise is the means by which we can be restored. God knows all about weakness, failure, and discouragement. He desires that we energize and encourage ourselves in the Lord. "Trust in the Lord with all your heart and lean not on your own understanding" (Proverbs 3:5, *NIV*).

These are uncertain times. Every life has clouds. Change is constant. They are facts of life. Just as an airplane soars above the dark clouds that block our view of the sunshine from earth, God enables us to soar above the darkness in our life as we lean on Him.

Bumps, bruises, and brokenness are all part of this life. They simply offer opportunities for us to grow and mature both physically and spiritually. We just have to get up and try again.

Heavenly Father, help me to understand that You work in my adversities to bring good to my life.

April 6

Scripture: "Rejoice in the Lord always. Again I will say, rejoice!" (Philippians 4:4, *NKJV*).

One of my favorite pastimes as an elementary student was to join my friends in the delightful game of jump rope. We were good! The memories of the young girls gleefully jumping rope to the singsong chant is still vivid in my mind. Chores, assignments, and responsibilities were momentarily forgotten as we happily jumped for joy.

As the years have come and gone, jumping rope no longer holds the same fascination for me that it did in those early years. However, I still have days when I "jump for joy." Joy is often elusive, and laughter is lost in the daily grind. Responsibilities crowd out relaxation time. Nevertheless, I can choose to be joyful in spite of pains, perplexities, or problems. The memory of the pain of childbirth quickly passed when I looked in the faces of each of my newborn daughters. Now I watch those daughters faithfully and joyfully mothering their own precious treasures. In much the same way, God ministers joy to our spirits even as we are enduring unpleasant circumstances.

Fanny Crosby chose to jump for joy in spite of her loss of vision and personal pain. She moved into a remarkable spiritual discernment as she wrote, "I shall see Him face to face." We can turn our burdens into blessings. It is all in the attitude. It is all in the choice.

Professional woodworkers, I have been told, look for trees that bear the marks of storms and strife. Trees that grow along the steepest cliffs produce the strongest woods—trees whose lofty branches reach high into the blue sky and whose roots sink deeper into the dark earth.

When the storms of life assail, sing! When your life produces pain, persevere! When your life brings adversity, advance! When your life is just a jumble, jump for joy!

Dear God, You bring such joy into my life. I praise You for the renewing and refreshing that comes from simply praising Your wonderful and majestic name.

April 7

Scripture: "From the end of the earth I will cry to You, when my heart is overwhelmed; lead me to the rock that is higher than I. For You have been a shelter for me, a strong tower from the enemy" (Psalm 61:2, 3, *NKJV*).

The years of innocent childhood and youth are so brief. From this stage of bright faces, active imagination, and energy in motion, one is suddenly projected into the world of broken hearts, restlessness, pressure, and competition. It is important to "look and act cool."

The unspoken message is clear. Physical desirability determines one's worth. Being overweight, or underweight, means rejection. This image of physical beauty and material wealth is portrayed as the measurement of success. Disillusionment replaces innocence in the pursuit of a redefined perfection. Student suicides are at an all-time high; self-esteem, at an all-time low. Society, perhaps unwittingly, has devalued the uniqueness of each individual life.

The scripture in Matthew 19:19 clearly tells us that God wants us to love ourselves. "Thou shalt love thy neighbour as thyself" (KJV). Although we are not to overvalue ourselves, we need a healthy, not haughty, self-esteem.

It is important to know that we are special. There has never been, nor ever will be, anyone exactly like you. No one has your lip prints, your fingerprints, or your voice prints.

There will always be those who will outachieve us in some way, but there is no one who has the exact unique qualities, abilities, and talents you have.

Rejection is disappointing, indeed, but God will never reject you. Remember the One who created you loves you and values you for yourself. Stop negative self-talk. Paul said, "Do not conform any longer to the pattern of this world, but be transformed by the renewing of your mind. Then you will be able to test and approve what God's will is—his good, pleasing and perfect will" (Romans 12:2, *NIV*).

Dear Jesus, You created me a masterpiece. Help me to understand that the molding process is sometimes painful but the finished product will be glorious.

April 8

Scripture: "He commanded our forefathers to teach their children, so the next generation would know . . . and they in turn would tell their children" (Psalm 78:5, 6, *NIV*).

Mom was an avid gardener. Often she arose before dawn and sat in her chair, waiting patiently for daybreak so that she could once again do what she loved so much to do—pruning, nurturing, and cultivating her beloved flowers. She followed the same concept in spiritual matters. Being her only child, I had the wonderful opportunity to benefit from her scriptural knowledge and training as we went about our daily activities.

Teaching a difficult group of children in Sunday school was simply a challenge to her. Filling their heads with biblical knowledge was just one of her many talents. They responded to her gentle cultivating like tender young plants in her garden. She fully believed in the principle "Train up a child. . . ." Today many of her students have become mature, sturdy blossoms for the Lord.

As spring evolved into summer, tiny seeds grew into sturdy plants that produced buds, which in turn opened into full bloom. Warm sun rays, the moisture of the rain, and the undaunted efforts of Mom—the devoted gardener—helped tiny buds unfold into bright and beautiful blooms. Their fragrance was released and the visual delight breathtaking.

Titus 2:4, 5 stresses the importance of mentoring. God had a purpose in His instructions to teach and train. Young "buds" must be encouraged to "hang on the vine" and do what a flower is supposed to do: grow, unfold, lift petals, sink roots deeper to become blossoms of blessings. Mentoring is a two-way street. The older and younger can each share observations of life and courage gained from each experience.

It is regrettable that some young plants are "nipped in the bud" and never reach their full potential. Likewise, some people never have the opportunity to reach spiritual maturity or "blooming" because of difficult circumstances, lack of quality care, and failure to mature spiritually. In order to be productive, one must draw deeply from the wells of God's love and His great mercy. God is the master designer, and it is His will that each life be faithful and fragrant.

Young plants, new buds, and tender blossoms must be nurtured to become mature, glorious, and strong. Then they will be able to withstand the winds of adversity while their breathtaking fragrance continues.

The process works! All who follow Christ have the potential to bloom and to produce. It just takes the determination of a common deep-rooted dandelion. They are survivors! They continue to grow in spite of difficulty. They continue season after season. So must we!

Dear Lord, help each of us to follow the spiritual pattern of mentoring. May we be steadfastly nurturing those entrusted to our care.

April 9

Scripture: "If I take the wings of the morning, and dwell in the uttermost parts of the sea, even there Your hand shall lead me, and Your right hand shall hold me" (Psalm 139:9, 10, *NKJV*).

Have you ever wished you could just be transformed into a bird and fly away? Some people "fly the coop" with drugs, alcohol, and extramarital affairs in an attempt to escape the realities of a painful existence. But this type of flight from reality just is not the path to take.

There is often a deceptive attraction in the temptation to escape problems, hectic schedules, and crises in our lives. However, escape is just not usually what God has in mind for us; instead, He provides us with His strength to weather the storm and live through our painful circumstances.

Sitting at His feet teaches us to adapt, endure, and face whatever life serves us. There is no dodging or ducking. Concentration on the Captain, and not the crew, gives us the ability to let go and forgive, to cope, surrender, and survive!

There have been times when demands upon my time were almost unbearable. I was one of those mothers who thought she could handle it all. Why, it would be a cinch to finish that college degree, perform functions as the wife of a pastor, and always "be there" for my husband and children. After a hectic and demanding week at the university where I was a student, plus all the other dozens of duties that demanded my attention, I loudly announced, "I need a break. Let's go to the mountains." My well-intentioned plans for a peaceful and quiet getaway turned instead into a terrible hailstorm en route and a downpour upon arrival.

Somehow, I suspect that most of us need to learn that rest is not a place but a relationship of the soul with our Creator. When our carefully laid plans for a restful retreat turn soggy, as they sometimes will, we can still sit at the feet of our Master and He will be for us that greatly needed "haven of rest." All of us need refreshing and renewal. Stop, surrender, and soak up His precious Spirit.

Dear Father, thank You for providing rest for my exhausted emotions. You are the peace speaker who calms all my fears and brings sweet peace to my being.

April 10

Scripture: "For this reason a man will leave his father and mother and be united to his wife, and they will become one flesh" (Genesis 2:24, *NIV*).

It is natural and normal for young people to make a lifetime commitment of love. Suddenly, almost without warning, a young person's heart is smitten and the selfish singleness moves into yet another change in life. Now, it is no longer "I" but "we."

Adjustments are necessary. Priorities change. There are frequent frustrations. Often expectations are dashed on the shores of reality. The knight in shining armor turns out to be a husband with a used and not-paid-for automobile. The "white cottage with flowers" turns into a crowded apartment, and visions of breakfast in bed turn into a ham biscuit on the run.

It is the plan of God that a man and a woman "leave and cleave." No longer are they under the protective shelter of parents, but together they establish a new family unit.

Marriage is God's plan. It is His desire that one man and one woman join in a faithful and permanent union. Marriage is a covenant entered into by two people who make a commitment to love and honor.

A successful marriage takes much work, patience, and "bearing with one another." Agape is strong love, and strong love is required if a marriage is to succeed. A marriage needs the Holy Spirit to energize the relationship.

Marriage cannot be set on automatic pilot—it demands the full attention of both partners to prevent the flight from crashing. The word submission has fallen into disfavor among the "my rights" crowd. Nevertheless, it is still God's command for His children. Submission does not mean allowing yourself to become abused, or belittled. But submission does mean that we will be accountable to another and that we will do everything in our power to make another succeed.

Satan has made it his business to destroy marriages. Marriages fall prey to troubles, and the Enemy tells the couple their problems will be solved by dissolving the relationship and starting over. But God clearly says to keep on trying, keep on loving, keep on praying. We may not be able to change the circumstances, but our great God will move in beside us as we move closer to Him. Marriage offers the opportunity to grow out of self-centeredness and function as an adult, to give and share love, to suffer together, to sacrifice, and to work out a relationship that glorifies God.

Heavenly Father, please help me glorify You in my marriage commitment and covenant.

April 11

Scripture: "And do not be conformed to this world, but be transformed by the renewing of your mind, that you may prove what is that good and acceptable and perfect will of God" (Romans 12:2, *NKJV*).

The story is told of two caterpillars in deep conversation as they inched their way across the lawn. One caterpillar, referring to the butterflies flitting gracefully from flower to flower, said, "There is just no way to get me up in one of those things." Little did he realize that his destiny would one day take him soaring above the dust and grass and that he would be delighted in doing the very thing he had previously disparaged.

The caterpillar story reminds me of the limited vision of the children of God. We are so preoccupied with being crawlers instead of flyers that we fail to see the big picture of our marvelous destiny. Life is full of dilemmas, decisions, and discouragements; but when we learn to trust God with the outcome of our lives, we will fret less and be more productive in our service to Him.

Mothers see the big picture. The nine months of pain, nausea, backaches, swollen feet, ill-fitting clothing all take a backseat because they know that soon a wonderful creation of God will arrive. Soon anticipation is rewarded by soft skin, shy smiles, and tiny fingers of hope.

Youthful, carefree days and endless hours of pleasure are quickly spent. Days become challenging, life becomes a constant schedule, and decisions occupy much of one's time.

Just as a life-changing transformation occurs in a caterpillar, we too undergo a "metamorphosis" as we allow the love of God to change our lives. The trouble occurs when we try to expedite the process. Attempting to assist a caterpillar in its transformation is to invite disaster. Why can we not trust God to work out the problems in our lives in His own perfect time? It reminds me of our second daughter, Renea, during a family holiday in a mountain condo. A terrible storm occurred and the loft bedroom where she and her husband, Don, slept began to sway in the wind. She announced to the huddled family group on the lower level as she quickly descended from the loft, "I've turned it over to God three times." Once is all that is necessary, but how hard it is for us to learn the valuable lesson that God can be trusted!

Jesus, thank You for Your transforming and renewing power. Help me to learn to simply trust You for all my decisions and destiny. Thank You for Your love and concern for us during the summer season of our lives.

April 12

Scripture: "My grace is sufficient for you, for my power is made perfect in weakness" (2 Corinthians 12:9, *NIV*).

My oldest daughter, Reita, announced to her dad after the birth of her daughter, Brittni, "It has just dawned on me that I'm responsible for this child for the rest of my life." The impact of this realization suddenly made her a student in the course "Managing Motherhood 101."

Suddenly, impossible demands, endless schedules, anxieties, and conflicts loomed on the horizon. How would she balance all those demands?

P atience
R esist perfectionism
A llow for failure
Y ield personal ambitions
E liminate negatives
R elax

Set goals that are reachable and strive to be excellent within your own capabilities. Isn't it beautiful to know that young mothers can sit at His feet even while mounds of clothing are being folded or bottles of formula are being prepared. For students in "Managing Motherhood 101" there is no free time. But in the 24 hours, 1,440 minutes, or 86,400 seconds, she can put her own unique stamp upon the ones entrusted to her care. What a wonderful opportunity to weave her story upon the fabric of her child. The gift of time must be used to its best advantage. Priorities must be set and circumstances or conditions of the day must not rule our relationship with Christ.

What ecstasy can be felt in the smile of a child who has succeeded or received comfort! What reward when a child simply and without provocation says, "Mommy, you are my bestest friend!" There is no greater achievement than to show by your lifestyle that God really is someone to be loved, trusted, and served. Careers, personal ambitions, and a rested body may have to be sacrificed for a brief time, but be encouraged by the fact that Managing Motherhood 101 is part of God's curriculum. Refuse to quit. Weave, mold, "cocoon," and love your child. God will provide the grace to create a masterpiece.

In the spring of your child's life, enjoy the time of cuddling. Walk slowly and see the world through your child's eyes. In the summer of your child's life, plant, water, nourish, and explore. During the rainstorms and deluges of this season, persevere! In the fall of your child's life, give your child the space to fly on his or her own. In the winter of childhood, when the nest is empty, reflect and respect. Watch for spring and the arrival of a new beginning!

Heavenly Father, may I never take for granted the awesome responsibility placed upon me. Help me do my very best to submit to Your will and to perform my responsibilities accordingly.

April 13

Scripture: "And all thy children shall be taught of the Lord; and great shall be the peace of thy children" (Isaiah 54:13, KJV).

Someone noted that an entire week is designated to honor secretaries and even pickles, but moms and groundhogs receive only one day of honor! Nevertheless, the privilege of motherhood is exclusive and unique. What weaving and molding! What tender nurturing!

It has been my privilege to be present when all three of my daughters became mothers. In each situation, my heart was filled to overflowing for the goodness of God and for the awesome miracle of the arrival of their treasures. In such a brief span of time, daughters become mothers and another generation begins. The tiny seed of a tiny new life grows inside until the momentous moment when, with a final push, a small, slippery, wrinkled body enters the world and is placed in the arms of a waiting mother. What responsibility lies ahead! Nothing will ever be the same again. A tough assignment! Only God can provide sufficient grace to mold each masterpiece.

My 4-year-old grandson, Taylor, was very much a part of the anticipated arrival of his little sister, Tori. And just in case she didn't know it, he constantly made her aware of the awesome God who formed her. He would snuggle up to his mom, Renea, in the months prior to Tori's birth, placing his face against her protruding stomach and loudly proclaim with his best-singing voice, "What a mighty God we serve!"

Although Taylor may not know the full impact of his proclamation, this mighty God is the provider of the stamina, strength, and solace needed to make the transition from daughter to mom. Only by leaning on His strong arm will any mother succeed in the fantastic marvel of motherhood.

A young mother must decide that her family will truly be a family! God has promised His protection and grace, but He expects us to literally snatch our families from the mind-set of this society. It will take strength. It will take rolled-up sleeves. It will take *agape* love. It will take high standards. It will take established values. It will take fortitude. Decide to swim upstream! Go against the current! Go against peer pressure. Go with God and His Word and your children will be taught by the Lord and know the peace of God.

What a mighty God we serve!

Heavenly Father, thank You for Your promise to guard my treasures. Please help me to firmly anchor to the Rock in all my relationships with my family.

April 14

Scripture: "Provoke not your children to wrath: but bring them up in the nurture and admonition of the Lord" (Ephesians 6:4, KJV).

Did you know that your home is bugged? Children have instruments of hearing—one in each ear. These magnificent "microphones" monitor the sounds of their surroundings. What messages are the sounds of your home sending?

Parenting is not for weaklings or wimps. Parenting takes skill, sincerity, and a stick-to-it determination. Often in today's society parenting is done by one. This creates an even greater responsibility. Separation, divorce, or death may have taken one parent out of the home. What is already an awesome responsibility becomes an even greater challenge as the single parent struggles to keep up with the whirlwind of job, budget, conflicts, decisions, and discipline. Often a single parent has found courage in the fact that other singles have made it; a support group can provide strength and friendship. One fact stands out clearly: God has promised to be there in our times of distress!

God designed the family. It is His will that we be fulfilled in our parenting relationships. That fulfillment will come in our total dependence upon God's guidance and our dedication.

Good parenting skills include . . .

> HUMOR
> HONESTY
> HUMILITY.

Parenting priorities should also include . . .

> COMMUNICATION
> CREATIVITY
> COMMITMENT
> CONSISTENCY.

Becoming a good parent just doesn't happen. It takes a great deal of energy to be a good parent. It also takes time! Parameters must be set, sometimes with great resistance from the children.

Good parents are involved with their children. Careers and other duties demand our attention, but nothing is more important than time spent with our children. Even a short amount of time can be fully focused quality time. Nurturing must be a priority! Provide a safe place for a child to fail or fall. A soothing touch gives a child security. Mix all of this with a great deal of love and respect. Positive results will follow. All of us respond to love!

Dear Jesus, thank You for the awesome privilege to be a parent. May my words be encouragement and my actions reflective of Your grace in my life.

April 15

Scripture: "Suffering produces perseverance; perseverance, character; and character, hope" (Romans 5:3, 4, *NIV*).

Wouldn't it be wonderful if growth was a painless process! Growth, however, brings struggles, stretching, and storms. One of those storms hit full force in the early days of our ministry. Our town was hit by a deluge of the flu virus. Being the caring and compassionate pastor he was, Walter continued to care for his sheep to the point of complete exhaustion from the ordeal and stress. He developed pneumonia and literally collapsed in the pulpit on a Sunday night. For 10 weeks he was unable to preach or fulfill his pastoral duties.

As a mother of young children, employed part-time in a legal firm, with increased church duties and a sick husband on top of it all, my world seemed to crumble around me!

When he collapsed, there was a message in tongues and interpretation that instructed him: "You are like a child in My hands and I am going to heal you step-by-step, not many steps at a time. Do not trust any other source nor look at symptoms."

We learned daily lessons in trust. We learned to lean hard on God, family, and friends. God is faithful! Ten weeks seemed like 10 months! Sleepless nights, endless days, darkness of spirit, and at times serious doubt all became a part of my life. But just as God promised, the healing gradually came. I will never forget the day that Walter stepped back into the church and walked to the pulpit. Oh, he was weak, pale, and very thin; but he had been delivered by the hand of God! And without any medical assistance. We had climbed our mountain with full assurance that in the midst of it all we had learned to trust the Peace Speaker to bring us out of our storm and into the sunshine!

Hope replaced doubt. Hope kept us going when everything looked uncertain. Hope gave us confidence as we exercised total dependence upon our faithful God. Storms will come. But the winds of adversity do not defeat a child of the King. They only cause our roots to grow deeper and our hold on God more tenacious.

Heavenly Father, thank You for the assurance to take us victoriously through all the storms that come our way. Please forgive us for desiring the painless path. We are assured that wherever You lead, You will sustain us and bring us to a place of peace.

April 16

Scripture: "Remind the people . . . to be obedient, to be ready to do whatever is good" (Titus 3:1, *NIV*).

"Ready, set, go!" These are childish words that we all remember. We may have spoken them at a game of tag, hide-and-seek, or any number of challenges we enjoyed.

Life is a lot like the childish phrase. The birth, growth, and nurturing process all prepare us for "ready, set, go." Endless hours of leisure, playtime, and daydreaming are suddenly shoved aside as responsibilities, demands, schedules, and a myriad of other adult challenges appear.

We are faced with questions such as "Where are you headed with your life?" or "What are you going to do when you arrive?" Questions with no easy answers! No longer can we rest, relax, and rely on the decision of our parents, teachers, or friends. We have to face up to the demands.

My face-up challenge came when Walter accepted his first pastorate several hundred miles from both our parents. We had enjoyed a safe cocoon during the college years. My secretarial position and his part-time employment gave us enough financial security for him to remain in school even after we married. Life seemed ordered, routine, secure for the moment, and fun as we enjoyed fellowship with other young college couples.

Now, an unknown loomed ahead—an opportunity to pastor a congregation that was totally strange to us . . . a parsonage we had never seen. Did I dare drag my feet and become a block of discouragement for my husband? Could I perhaps persuade him to wait for another opportunity? It was not an easy decision for me. Our apartment was small but neat. My job was challenging but enjoyable. My friends were close and comfortable.

Ready, pack, and go we did, but not without tears. That was over 37 years ago. From this side, I can look back and say, "I'm glad I faced up." Lifelong friendships were formed, faith grew stronger, and we saw firsthand the results of obedience.

Dear God, our responsibilities are so heavy at times. Please give us Your direction and divine guidance as we continue to strive to please and glorify You.

April 17

Scripture: "When you sow, you do not plant the body that will be . . . but God gives it a body as he has determined" (1 Corinthians 15:37, 38, *NIV*).

Have you ever had anyone tell you that you need to "make time count"? Make the most of every moment of life. Life is fleeting. Life is fragile. We must make time count.

The middle years of life remind us of the fall season and the ensuing harvest. Where did the yesterdays go? It seems just yesterday that I was in the spring season. Someone accurately said that a woman learns four things by the time she reaches her middle years: how to look like a girl, how to act like a lady, how to think like a man, and how to work like a dog!

Soon the warm summer rays give way to the crispness and coolness of fall. Gardeners check to see if there are perhaps a few tomatoes or green beans that can be salvaged from the exhausted plants that have so faithfully produced a bumper crop.

Just as nature produces a mature harvest, we plant seeds of faith, encouragement, and instruction in the lives of our family members. We can be certain of one thing: our children will follow our example more than they will follow our advice. We cannot be sure of the harvest that will be produced, but we do know that God sees our weakness and in Him we are made strong; He sees our imperfections and in Him we are made perfect. God uses the seeds we sow to produce spiritual maturity in the lives of those we touch.

Not only will our children inherit our material possessions, they will also inherit our values. Our lifestyle, character, and examples affect those who are following in our steps.

People in the fall season of life have come to the knowledge that life is real. Time is running out. We try to guide our children down the road we have walked. Careers are now in full swing and each day seems shorter, more crowded, but also more meaningful. It is time to make time count. We should eliminate the unnecessary; get rid of the trash in our lives; fine-tune our value system; look over our shoulder at the ones over whom we have influence. Then, we should take courage; consult God's Word; submit to His leadership; and align ourselves with Him. He will walk by our side through every season of life.

Thank You, God, for guiding my life through every season. Please help me exhibit Your personality and glorify Your name in my daily living.

April 18

Scripture: "When you go through deep waters and great trouble, I will be with you. When you go through rivers of difficulty, you will not drown! When you walk through the fire of oppression, you will not be burned up—the flames will not consume you. For I am the Lord your God, your Savior, the Holy One of Israel" (Isaiah 43:2, 3, *TLB*).

Life is full of misfortune, tragedies, distress, misery, and suffering. However, we have the glorious assurance that He, the Mighty Creator, the One altogether lovely, will walk every step with us and will not allow us to bear our troubles alone. "You are a shield around me, O Lord; you bestow glory on me and lift up my head" (Psalm 3:3, *NIV*). What encouraging words!

After examining 3-year-old Rhonda's eyes, the doctor announced: "By the time she is 6 years old, she will be legally blind with possibly only sufficient vision to make her way around a room."

What heartbreaking news! The lazy eye syndrome (amblyopia) was taking its toll on our youngest daughter. What horrible news to a young pastor and wife. "How could this happen again?" We had gone through a similar experience with our second daughter, Renea, who had positively responded to the specialist's treatment. Now we faced adversity again—glasses, eye patches, and the trauma that accompanies treating young children's eye diseases. Audible, sympathetic comments from people about the girls' appearance did not make things easier.

Sometimes we just have to advance with faith into adversity. Much prayer was made by family, friends, and congregation. And to the amazement of the eye specialist, Rhonda's eyes made a drastic improvement in just two weeks. Steadily and assuredly, God performed a wonderful healing upon her vision. When Rhonda took her exam for her driver's license at age 15, she passed the vision test without her glasses! Both daughters are now adults and blessed with good vision and gorgeous eyes! God is faithful!

Sometimes it is necessary to just go forward in faith in the midst of storms. Storms are not the time to retreat or withdraw from the battle. We are in spiritual warfare. It is time to advance and proceed by the grace of God!

Heavenly Father, how gratifying to know that You are strength in my weakness. You will make a way when there seems to be no way out. Help me to not take my focus from You.

April 19

Scripture: "Train a child in the way he should go, and when he is old he will not turn from it" (Proverbs 22:6, *NIV*).

The phone rang and our oldest daughter, Reita, who was away at college in another state, announced that she and Steve were coming to South Carolina to talk with us. Now, when a college student calls to say she is coming home in the middle of the week "just to talk," parents have a right to start worrying! Well, their talk was just the beginning of talks by Steve, Don, and Randy, who each wanted permission to marry one of our daughters. In much too short a span of time, all three daughters had "walked the aisle" in their own beautiful wedding and promised to love and honor their handsome young husbands. They left the nest to begin their own "nesting" process.

Years before, I read with little interest articles on the empty-nest syndrome. I was ill-prepared for how quickly this would happen to me. We had been so busily involved with our special little family that we didn't stop to consider how quickly time brings change. The years passed, and all too soon the girls were gone. One evening, Walter and I sat in our matching recliners attempting to focus on some television program. He remarked as he observed the three gold-framed portraits of each of our daughters at age 3, "I would give just about anything right about now to hear those little girls enjoying a good fight!" What he really was saying, "It is too quiet in this house!"

There is a positive side to the empty nest, however. No more middle-of-the-night feedings, or telephone calls, or rooms full of young, loud voices disturbing sleep. But in its own way, silence can be just as disturbing. No more interruptions at the dinner table to tell enthusiastic stories about some wonderful thing that happened at school. Quietly eating alone is not nearly as much fun!

Another positive side to the empty nest is that the daughters and their families come home and the house is again frequently noisy and cluttered.

Our goals have changed. Time is relished. Companionship deepens. Although we are not with our children on a daily basis, we can be with them in thoughts, prayers, and frequent visits both to their house and ours. Family holiday traditions have become very meaningful. Memories are made as young grandchildren learn to ride the horses, even though they can't reach the "pedals" (stirrups), as Taylor, age 3, observed.

Our roles have changed, but love for the children has not changed.

Our love for them demands our trust and our blessing. This is all a part of God's plan for the family.

Letting go doesn't mean loss. It is a step of faith. It is a journey into an unknown area.

Letting go means that I will not be judgmental.

Letting go means no guilt trips when children choose to establish their own holiday traditions.

Letting go means I will attempt to remain silent even when I may have a better idea.

Letting go means I will trust my training!

Dear Jesus, please encircle each family member with Your protective grace and mercy. I have committed them to Your care and provision.

April 20

Scripture: "Let us not become weary in doing good, for at the proper time we will reap a harvest if we do not give up" (Galatians 6:9, *NIV*).

It is regrettable that often we do not take the time to enjoy the many little pleasures that life has to offer. The fall season of life is a wonderful time to stop and be aware of the bountiful blessings we are privileged to share. This is a season to simply count our blessings. It is a time to rejoice about the many trials He has brought us through victoriously.

At this stage of life, one is more aware of the aroma of the cool frosty mornings, a pot of freshly brewed coffee, freckles on a child's grinning face, the spectacular colors of trees dressed up in their brightest hue, shiny red apples at a nearby orchard, glorious sunsets, brilliant orange pumpkins, and magnificent mums gracing flower gardens.

The days are shorter and darkness comes earlier. Autumn is a time for memories of the past summer and the knowledge that another season is ending. Farmers fill their storage barns with the yield from their crops. Without their diligence the world would suffer. Before a harvest can be reaped, there had to be preparation, planting, and perseverance.

The fall season of life is a wonderful time to reflect upon the harvest. What have you prepared? What have you planted? Are you persevering in spite of opposition and discouragement? This is the time to persist, keep at it, and press on! Reaping a glorious harvest requires honesty and loyalty in our relationships. Seeds of compassion and understanding and thoughtfulness must be sown. The autumn season should remind us of the grain of wheat that has to die, thus strengthening the commitment to die to our own desires and pleasures and to live to please God.

"He has shown kindness by giving you rain from heaven and crops in their seasons; he provides you with plenty of food and fills your hearts with joy" (Acts 14:17, *NIV*). God is faithful in every season of our lives!

Heavenly Father, help me to be a faithful and patient worker in Your harvest field. May my life produce fruit according to Your plan for my life.

April 21

Scripture: "For I am persuaded that neither death nor life, nor angels nor principalities nor powers, nor things present nor things to come, nor height nor depth, nor any other created thing, shall be able to separate us from the love of God which is in Christ Jesus our Lord" (Romans 8:38, 39, *NKJV*).

Midlife is a time of change physically, mentally, and sometimes spiritually. Someone has given this description of midlife: "an emotional trauma of crisis proportions." Webster defines *crisis* as "the turning point for better or worse in an acute disease; an attack of pain, distress, or disordered function; an emotionally significant event or radical change of status in a person's life."

Some feel depressed, lonely, worthless, hopeless, and that their best years are behind them. Wrong! It is time for a reality check! What has really changed? Well, age for one thing! Physical stamina has somewhat diminished. Forget things? Sure, but who hasn't forgotten something in every season of life!

You may identify with the observation my 4-year-old grandson, Taylor, made of me as we played basketball together. "You are just a misser, Mom-O," as he proudly sank another ball in his little boy-sized basketball goal. Often, I recall the truth of that statement when I can't seem to fit all the pieces together in a neat little package.

Midlife does not mean that we are "over the hill." On the contrary, it is a time to identify the problems we face. Perhaps it is the season of life to make new beginnings, to strengthen our relationships, rejuvenate old friendships, eliminate negative self-talk, rekindle the flame of the soul, and exercise our bodies and our minds. Make a new commitment to God.

Yes, the hair may begin to thin and gray. Even some new wrinkles will appear as the skin loses its elasticity. The weight gain seems more difficult to lose, and a glance in a full-length mirror prompts a quick straightening of the shoulders! However, I refuse to live in a perpetual pity party! I am a divine masterpiece and clearly aware that *vintage* means "enduring quality and importance." I have been created to glorify God, to sing His song, and to make a profound impact on others. So, this means I won't whine, wimp out, worry, or waste my time lamenting about what has been.

"The Lord is thy keeper: the Lord is thy shade upon thy right hand. The sun shall not smite thee by day, nor the moon by night. The Lord shall preserve thee from all evil: he shall preserve thy soul" (Psalm 121:5-7, KJV). Doesn't that sound great? Preserving power! Sustaining power! Overcoming power! Protection!

This too (midlife) shall pass! Stay in Him! "[You] are kept by the power of God" (1 Peter 1:5, KJV). There is not one phase of life in which our Creator will not be there. Concentrate on the finished product! You are a treasured masterpiece!

My Father, I am so grateful that You know me. You created all the wonderful phases of my life, and in each one I can be victorious by Your Spirit.

April 22

Scripture: "Come to me, all you who are weary and burdened, and I will give you rest. Take my yoke upon you and learn from me, for I am gentle and humble in heart, and you will find rest for your souls. For my yoke is easy and my burden is light" (Matthew 11:28-30, *NIV*).

It has been estimated that 70 percent of all Americans will be caregivers at some point in their lives. Reports reveal that the age group 85 and older is becoming the fastest-growing population in America.

Caregivers often find themselves physically drained and exhausted. We have been commanded to "love each other as I have loved you. Greater love has no one than this, that he lay down his life for his friends" (John 15:12, 13, *NIV*). However, this does not mean that a caregiver has to give to the point of burnout. Everyone has her own limits of physical and emotional stamina. It is important to remember that a person giving care to another requires support and loving care also.

Listed are suggestions for relieving the pressure brought on by the care of another.

Learn to spell RELIEF!

> **R** est and restore spirit by regular devotions.
> **E** liminate perfectionism from vocabulary.
> **L** et others share responsibility.
> **I** nclude frequent getaways.
> **E** mphatically nurture personal health.
> **F** ocus on the positive, not negative.

For the past 13 years my dad has made his home with Walter and me since my mom's death. Dad probably had to make the greatest adjustment from a life with Mom in their own home for nearly 50 years to a life with us in a parsonage. The transition has been easier because of the commitment of my husband to my dad and to my responsibilities. Four ingredients are present in our parent-child relationship:

Respect—by both parent and child.

Remember—to frequently share memories of the past.

Realistic responsibility—I have come to the realization that Dad doesn't expect perfection from me and that my inability to give him my total time doesn't lessen his love for me.

Refresh—physically, emotionally, and spiritually.

It is vital to keep in focus that instruments frequently need times of retuning—even caregiving instruments!

Dear God, I am grateful to You for the privilege You have given me to be a caregiver. Thank You for trusting me with this responsibility and for the source of strength I have because of Your grace.

April 23

Scripture: "It is good to give thanks to the Lord, and to sing praises to Your name, O Most High; to declare Your lovingkindness in the morning, and Your faithfulness every night" (Psalm 92:1, 2, *NKJV*).

A thankful spirit will bring healing to body, soul, and spirit. Life just goes better when you practice thankfulness. A grateful heart is a glad heart!

Philippians 4:8 clearly states that we have a choice: "Finally, brethren, whatever things are true, whatever things are noble, whatever things are just, whatever things are pure, whatever things are lovely, whatever things are of good report, if there is any virtue and if there is anything praiseworthy—meditate on these things" (*NKJV*).

Life takes on new meaning and new perspective when we count our blessings. Every season of life is filled with abundant blessings. How much time is wasted in failing to stop, look, listen, and count! Sunrise, sunset, storm clouds, rainbows, flowers, mountains, valleys, and all the beauties of creation should prompt thanksgiving. Add to that the daily provisions of grace, protection, mercy, and love which He provides. Family, friends, freedom of worship, and good health are excellent reasons to praise God.

I thank Him for every challenge He has helped me meet, for every struggle which He has given assistance, for every goal He has helped me achieve, for every sorrow in which He brought overcoming grace, and for catching me every time I fell!

Thanksgiving should be a part of every season of life, but the fall season seems such an appropriate time. A special day is set aside in November to stop and be thankful. However, at this point in life, every day is a marvelous opportunity to stop, reflect, and remember the gracious goodness of God!

O God, please receive my grateful thanks for all the past blessings. Thank You for daily benefits which You provide. Please help me to never take Your grace for granted.

April 24

Scripture: "He is like a tree planted by streams of water, which yields its fruit in season and whose leaf does not wither. Whatever he does prospers" (Psalm 1:3, *NIV*).

Someone aptly stated, "Don't worry what you could do if you lived your life over; get busy with what's left." Every day is prime time. Looking back may help one understand some things about life, but looking forward is what puts the "living" in life.

The term *winterizing* is often used at the end of the fall season as preparations are made for the winter months that lie ahead. Homes, cars, lawns, and even clothes closets all need special attention before the months of winter arrive. It is also necessary for people to winterize in preparation for the next season of life.

In anticipation of the winter season it is well to . . .

- Accept the challenges that lie ahead.
- Not waste any time mourning the wounds of yesterday. Acknowledge the fact that winter is a good season and that the journey will be enjoyable!
- Reevaluate financial security.
- Not let negative emotions mar your joy; manage your moods!
- Keep fellowship with God constant.
- Find places to minister; the hungry, sick, lonely, and aged are nearby.
- Advance into the winter season of your life with full confidence that the God who helped you throughout every day of your life to this point will faithfully walk with you through the next phase of life.

Fantastic days are ahead. Life is full of new beginnings and the winter season will be glorious. Someone made the following observation: "I do not see my way; I do not care to. But I know that He sees His way and that I see Him."

Dear God, I acknowledge my need of Your help. Please accept my grateful thanks and praise for Your unfailing love and grace throughout every step of my life's journey.

April 25

Scripture: "Do not forget my teaching, but keep my commands in your heart, for they will prolong your life many years and bring you prosperity. Let love and faithfulness never leave you; bind them around your neck, write them on the tablet of your heart. Then you will win favor and a good name in the sight of God and man" (Proverbs 3:1-4, *NIV*).

The winter season of life is a time of reflection, days to reminisce. Usually, it is a time of retirement and a slower pace of life. Sunrise and sunset are to be enjoyed. People in the winter season of life usually have acquired a great deal more understanding, patience, and forgiveness!

This is a time to walk leisurely with a grandchild and enjoy each detail that is pointed out along the path. There is time now to bake cookies or to spend time with a favorite craft. It is also a time of looking forward to the arrival of yet another grandchild and the beginning of a spring season again in that new life.

There is an art to retirement. One does not have to grow into this season with bitterness or regret. It can be a season of aspiration: "This is the day the Lord has made; let us rejoice and be glad in it" (Psalm 118:24, *NIV*). Look for ways to be of service and volunteer. Learn to be flexible and stretchable! One never gets too old to learn! Share yourself with others. Mentor someone! Sing! Life is easier when you sing! Pray for the ability to keep a sweet spirit and a right attitude. Learn to laugh at yourself. Determine that you will be a person other people enjoy being around.

Decide that you will not desert the ideals that have held you together all your life. Decide that you will still have faith, self-confidence, and hope.

Dear God, walk with me through each day. Help me to show forth Your love to all I meet. Give me wisdom and strength to face each obstacle that I encounter.

April 26

Scripture: "All the days ordained for me were written in your book before one of them came to be" (Psalm 139:16, *NIV*).

The winter season of life can be a winter wonderland! The Bible is filled with examples of people who effectively and positively made a difference in the lives of others during their golden years.

Miriam, the sister of Moses and Aaron, danced and sang a victory song (Exodus 15:20, 21). Here was a woman past 80 who made the decision to not be just "another little old lady." She was still useful, vibrant, and vivacious!

Reflecting upon the goodness of God, and having the assurance that God saves and the Spirit indwells, will provide us with the stamina to be a winner in winter! We can choose to be cheerful, or we can choose to be resentful. But cheerfulness is much more rewarding.

"I consider that our present sufferings are not worth comparing with the glory that will be revealed in us" (Romans 8:18, *NIV*). We can maintain our footing and fortitude during the winter season of life. In nature, the season of winter often speaks of gray clouds, barren branches, bitter cold, and frigid wind that turns the tip of our noses red. On the flip side of the coin, it is a season filled with holiday spirit and it gives opportunity for slowing down and reflecting on the goodness of God. There are moments to enjoy family traditions of celebration.

This is no time for depression. This is time for delight. In a season of nature that seems to abound with viruses, if we will sit at His feet, our devotions can be contagious! The high quality of charisma we possess can "infect" and enhance the lives of those whose paths we cross. Determine to be winsome in winter! When the cold winds blast, we can be warmed by and provide comfort to others through the warmth of His divine love.

Make a commitment to . . .

> **W** alk assuredly by His Spirit!
> **I** nvest in lives of others!
> **N** ip negativism in the bud!
> **T** rust God!
> **E** nter His courts with praise!
> **R** elish the season!

Heavenly Father, grant to me an adequate measure of strength. Help me to make this season of life truly a winter wonderland.

April 27

Scripture: "Now also when I am old and grayheaded, O God, forsake me not; until I have shewed thy strength unto this generation, and thy power to every one that is to come" (Psalm 71:18, KJV).

The literal meaning of the word *retire* means "to withdraw or to retreat." But retirement doesn't mean you are finished or through. Retirement can be a new freedom to enjoy things you haven't had time for previously. The fact is firm: aging is universal—but growing older certainly has many advantages and pleasures. It is up to an individual just how delightful retirement will be.

Dare to relish retirement and do not allow yesterday's regrets or tomorrow's fears to rob the joy of life. Learn to laugh more. Refuse to be a grumpy old person that no one enjoys being around. Delete faultfinding of others and yourself. Aspire to be agreeable and useful when you retire.

Lend a helping hand! Now you have more time to serve. Stretch the mind; read! Explore and be creative. You might just discover a hidden talent. Add a new dimension to your life. Inspire others by your example. Use every day to lift and encourage someone. Continue to practice good habits of grooming and dress tastefully. Do not hang on to those frumpy and well-worn articles of clothing.

Just as in any season of life, goals and objectives are essential. Adjustments require prayer! Prayer is our main source of strength and direction in every stage of life. Retirement certainly is not a time to stop praying. Praise and thanksgiving to God for all of His bountiful gifts and blessings will eliminate the "retirement blues."

Dear Jesus, Your name is to be glorified and exalted. Thank You for guidance and direction for my life. In this season of my life, You are my source of strength and my joy.

April 28

Scripture: "The righteous will flourish like a palm tree, they will grow like a cedar of Lebanon; planted in the house of the Lord, they will flourish in the courts of our God. They will still bear fruit in old age, they will stay fresh and green, proclaiming, "The Lord is upright; he is my Rock, and there is no wickedness in him" (Psalm 92:12-15, *NIV*).

They had been married 49 years. Those two had survived many trials and triumphs of life, encountered much illness, and raised their only child to serve the God they loved with all their hearts.

Now, my parents are separated by death. Shortly after midnight on a Sunday evening, Mom went home to be with the Lord. She and Dad had been to church earlier in the evening as they always did. He retired to bed, leaving Mom up to prepare a birthday card for a young neighbor boy. Dad found Mom sometime after midnight, sitting in her favorite chair in the living room, peaceful and quiet. Sometime in the interim she had slipped away to be with the Lord. Dad was left alone to face life without his friend, companion, and partner.

Life is complex. Life is loss. But God is faithful and just. Throughout the years that have followed since Mom's departure, I have sensed a deepening relationship between my dad and the Lord.

How do people survive the rocks and the ridges of this life without God? Loss is so familiar. Loss of friends, finances, and future security is all too real. But we can find security and safety in our God. He is a safe place. He provides a refuge from the storms that dash upon our shores.

Heavenly Father, thank You for being there in the midst of my storm. You are my peace. You are my security.

April 29

Scripture: "God is our refuge and strength, an ever-present help in trouble" (Psalm 46:1, *NIV*).

It has been noted that Americans are living longer than ever before. With increased life expectancy come increased health problems. Physical problems often take priority over all other retirement difficulties.

The condition of our health will be determined by heredity to a large extent, but the foundation we laid will be a large factor as to whether we enjoy or endure the senior years. Obviously, the hands of the clock cannot be reversed, but repairs and rebuilding can occur to deter further damage.

During the spring, summer, and even fall seasons of life, our bodies can tolerate a great deal of punishment. But the resilience diminishes in later years. That extra helping of a rich dessert will ultimately be paid for. Suffering is often a result of self-indulgence. A well-balanced diet is vital to good health. Often, seniors do not always eat well because they live alone or simply do not enjoy cooking for just one or two persons. The old adage "You are what you eat" has merit.

Don't we wish there were a fountain of youth! Aging is inevitable, but it can be enjoyable. Pain is a given! But old age does not automatically mean that one will be disabled or helpless. It is important to practice good health habits in every phase of life.

Mature, mellow, and magnificent can be the descriptive adjectives of a senior adult in the midst of failing strength. It is worth the effort and discipline to feel gloriously alive even in the winter season of life. The golden years can be the glorious years. Good health does not necessarily just automatically occur. But sometimes, with discipline, determination, and dedication to the Creator who formed our physical bodies in the first place, good health can be enhanced.

> You made all the delicate, inner parts of my body, and knit them together in my mother's womb. Thank you for making me so wonderfully complex! It is amazing to think about. Your workmanship is marvelous—and how well I know it. You were there while I was being formed in utter seclusion! You saw me before I was born and scheduled each day of my life before I began to breathe. Every day was recorded in your Book! (Psalm 139:13-16, TLB).

Heavenly Father, thank You for Your healing power. Your love for me will be my strength when I am weak.

April 30

Scripture: "I have fought the good fight, I have finished the race, I have kept the faith. Now there is in store for me the crown of righteousness, which the Lord, the righteous Judge, will award to me on that day— and not only to me, but also to all who have longed for his appearing" (2 Timothy 4:7, 8, *NIV*).

In verse 7 of our Scripture today, Paul reflected upon 30-plus years of labor and service as an apostle. He had, like an athlete in a contest, finished the race and was eligible for the winner's wreath.

What a reward awaits all those who have experienced salvation. In the race of life, Christ is that faithful companion who is ever near as a personal guide as His children navigate through each season of life.

Hebrews 4:15 tells us that "we do not have a high priest who is unable to sympathize with our weaknesses" (*NIV*). He has already been there and now reigns with power to guide us as a shepherd does his sheep—all the way home.

"Do not let your hearts be troubled. Trust in God; trust also in me. In my Father's house are many rooms; if it were not so, I would have told you. I am going there to prepare a place for you. And if I go and prepare a place for you, I will come back and take you to be with me that you also may be where I am" (John 14:1-3, *NIV*).

What a promise! What assurance! What a reward!

No suffering!

No pain!

No disappointments!

No death!

Just as in nature the season of winter will conclude in a glorious burst of spring, with all its beauty, freshness, and fulfillment, so for the child of God the end of the winter season is just the beginning of a glorious eternal springtime. So, relax and trust God. In a world of inconsistencies, you can rest assured that God is consistent. He is always with you and will always be there when you need Him.

As an athlete must finish the race to receive the winner's wreath, so must we! "Let us not lose heart in doing good, for in due time we shall reap if we do not grow weary" (Galatians 6:9, *NASB*).

Gracious Father, I am so grateful for Your sovereign power in my life. It is my desire to faithfully finish my course and hear You say, "Well done."

NOTES

NOTES

$\mathscr{M a y}$
Unconditional Love
Rebecca J. Jenkins

Rebecca J. Jenkins was appointed executive director of the Department of Ladies Ministries in 1992. Prior to coming to this office, she served as state Ladies Ministries president in Mississippi. She has also served as local and district Ladies Ministries president in Ohio and as executive secretary to members of the Executive Committee.

Rebecca also serves on the executive board of the Women's Commission for both the National Association of Evangelicals and the Pentecostal and Charismatic Churches of North America. She is a member of professional organizations related to her work as conference planner and editor of *Unique* magazine.

She is married to Dr. James D. Jenkins, who presently serves as a field representative for Church of God World Missions. They have one daughter and son-in-law, Dr. and Mrs. Russell S. Smith, and three grandchildren—Michael, Natalie, and Michelle.

May 1

Scripture: "Though I speak with the tongues of men and of angels, and have not charity, I am become as sounding brass, or a tinkling cymbal" (1 Corinthians 13:1).

Just what is so important about love? Almost anyone can be persuaded by a silver tongue. Who among us is not impressed when we turn on the radio and hear an announcer or a DJ with a deep, rich, melodic voice? And sometimes when we view a video vignette, we ask, "Who is the narrator?"

Recently while finalizing the script for our Ladies Ministries World Missions project video, I thought: *It would be nice to have a woman as narrator.* I didn't recall a video in which a woman's voice was used. While running a short errand, I tuned to the local religious station. A rich female voice filled my car. "That's the one!" I exclaimed. Interestingly, her name also caught my attention; she called herself "Becca." With the Lord's help, Rebecca's mellow voice has been heard all around the country introducing people to the street children in Brazil and the ladies' desire to build an orphanage there.

Ministers capture our attention if they have a pleasant voice and an eloquent manner. But how much more influential they are when their eloquence is accompanied with love. In today's society, many learn the right words to say for a particular occasion. Persuasiveness abounds in many circles; however, these words often are like a sounding brass or a tinkling cymbal.

In the first three verses of this chapter, the apostle Paul clearly communicates the unequivocal necessity of love in our lives, speech, and actions. Love defies definition, though there are many descriptions. One of the best descriptions is found in *The Pulpit Commentary:* "A generous moral sympathy for the race springing from love to the creator."

A life without love is often compared to a body without the five senses. The Word tells us that the mouth speaks what is in the heart. If love is present, our words will reflect that love. Love's origin is the nature of God, who is love. This love was manifest in the gift God gave to the world—His son, Jesus Christ. "For God so loved the world, that he gave his only begotten Son, that whosoever believeth in him should not perish, but have everlasting life" (John 3:16). Christ's entire earthly ministry defined love. His every action was motivated by love.

Love goes far beyond words, but words are effective when accompanied by love. They can uplift, encourage, minister, and glorify God. As we accept God's gift and invite Christ to be Lord of our lives, we can enjoy times of sitting at the feet of Jesus. Our words will no longer be as sounding brass. They will be effective!

Father, "Let the words of my mouth, and the meditation of my heart, be acceptable in thy sight, O Lord, my strength [rock], and my redeemer" (Psalm 19:14). Help me as I reflect upon the conversations of this day. Grant unto me a double portion of Your love.

May 2

Scripture: "Who shall separate us from the love of Christ? Shall tribulation, or distress, or persecution, or famine, or nakedness, or peril, or sword?" (Romans 8:35).

How shocked friends and relatives were when a supposed model mom decided to walk away and leave her two children and husband behind. No one could understand it then, and more than 25 years later it still remains a mystery. The family left behind managed to get through the crisis. Even this tragedy could not separate them from the love of Christ.

The mother must have felt this move would bring her the happiness for which she longed. Presumably, the past was put behind her. Excitement was present as children were born to a new union. As time passed, this was not enough either. The new family and new residence failed to give her the peace she was seeking. The restlessness mounted. Finally she walked away from this family too. Her departure, though painful and difficult, could not separate these children from the love of Christ.

They say the third time is the charm, so this woman tried it again and found herself with a third family. She seems to be coping with the responsibilities now. Her Christian heritage keeps prompting her to do what is right. Even neglecting her children, as unthinkable as that is, did not separate her from God's love. She might not have comprehended God's love, but God still loved her.

Society is intolerant of such behavior, and rightfully so. God is heartbroken by such actions, but He sees the deep recesses of the heart and mind. He honors the prayers of parents and grandparents and never withdraws His love.

The last I heard of this mother, her actions had improved tremendously, and there was considerable order in her life. "Behold, what manner of love the Father hath bestowed upon us, that we should be called the sons of God" (1 John 3:1).

Many children suffer neglect, hunger, and abuse. How will they know God's love? We become His hands extended in love. Let us remember that words, no matter how eloquent, without love are void and useless (1 Corinthians 13:1).

Mighty God of love, thank You for loving us when we are unlovely. If we appropriate Your love, nothing, no nothing, can separate us from Your divine and perfect love.

May 3

Scripture: "Charity [love] suffereth long, and is kind" (1 Corinthians 13:4).

Suffering long is called patience. When I think of patience, the word *mother* comes to mind. Who is more patient than a mother? God trusted her with a most important task—nurturing children.

During my daughter's teenage years, there were times when I didn't want the radio on while driving to the shopping center. Just about the time I was ready to say, "Please turn that off," my mother's example would come to mind.

My mother gave birth to 12 children. She must have read about Job often, for she certainly possessed some of his patience. During the 11 years of my life that she lived, she exercised patience on numerous occasions. One that stands out most vividly in my mind is when our family got a new upright piano. There were five children still at home at the time. We all wanted to "play" the piano.

She worked out a plan. We could each play the piano, back to back, for 30 minutes. This plan supplied her with two and one-half hours of "melodious" music per day. Can you imagine the stress of cooking three meals daily, keeping the laundry current, refereeing arguments, and doing all the things related to running a household, while five children who had never had music lessons played an upright piano? I do not recall her asking us to stop on any occasion.

God's love and the peace it brings will produce patience. We know His love more thoroughly and learn patience by sitting at His feet. Patience is a characteristic of love that we must continually strive for and practice. A patient, quiet spirit exemplifies the love of God to our children.

Children come to mind when the subject of patience comes up, but what about our testimony in the grocery line, at the bank teller's window, in traffic?

We are His image bearers. Will our action in these situations speak of the kind of love explained in 1 Corinthians 13? What about our patience with our husbands when they are late for dinner? Do we exercise patience with the mistakes made by fellow employees and friends?

Some things are painful, but love suffers long, or is patient. Was love seen in your life today through a patient, quiet spirit?

Heavenly Father, thank You for Your supreme example of patience. I am grateful for Your divine love which produces patience. Help me to glorify You as I develop more patience with family, friends, and the lost I am trying to win for You.

May 4

Scripture: "But the fruit of the Spirit is love, joy, peace, longsuffering, gentleness, goodness, faith, meekness, temperance: against such there is no law" (Galatians, 5:22, 23).

Notice that love is mentioned first among the fruit of the Spirit. That fact shows the importance of this characteristic.

Much emphasis is placed on the need for fresh fruit in our diets. It is proclaimed as a "perfect" food. We grew up with the saying "An apple a day keeps the doctor away." Fruit is beautiful, colorful, natural, sweet, and pleasant-tasting. There is great variety among fruit.

In our front yard is a peach tree. To date, the peaches serve very little purpose for food, but the grandchildren and neighbor children love to see how far they can throw them. Perhaps some day they can be used for their intended purpose.

We are to be like trees planted by the water. Strength should be evident in our lives. Christian maturity will evidence itself as fruit in our lives. More important than fruit is to the natural body, with its pleasant aroma and sweet taste, is the fruit of the Spirit in our lives. Fruit grows on live trees. If we have the first one—love—the others come more naturally.

When we receive Christ into our heart, we receive divine love. He then commands us to love one another. To bear the fruit of love in our lives, we must first love God and develop our relationship with Him. The more we sit at His feet and learn of Him, the more we will love and the easier it will become to love others.

> Ye have heard that it hath been said, Thou shalt love thy neighbour and hate thine enemy. But I say unto you, Love your enemies, bless them that curse you, do good to them that hate you, and pray for them which despitefully use you, and persecute you; that ye may be the children of your Father which is in heaven: for he maketh his sun to rise on the evil and on the good, and sendeth rain on the just and on the unjust. For if ye love them which love you, what reward have ye? do not even the publicans the same? (Matthew 5:43-46).

This kind of love calls for more than human love. We can attain this kind of love when we allow the love described in 1 Corinthians 13 to operate.

Lord and Master, You are the author of love. If I were choosing fruit of the Spirit, I could not think of any better than the fruit listed in Your Word. These are tremendous attributes. Help me to cultivate them in my life. May I love as You love.

May 5

Scripture: "Doth not behave itself unseemly, seeketh not her own" (1 Corinthians 13:5).

Unselfishness is a must in the life of a Christian. Christ was the epitome of unselfishness in His life on earth. "Greater love hath no man than this, that a man lay down his life for his friends" (John 15:13).

Selfishness and the term *Christian* are opposites. It is difficult to imagine that someone who has received Christ can be selfish.

As a teenager, my older brother Bob brought a bag of tangerines home and shared them with the other children. I can remember thinking, *Now I know he got saved.* Oddly enough, I can't remember any selfish deeds he did, but this act of generosity made a definite impression. Fruit was not plentiful at our house. Christmas was the time for fruit. As a minister whose salary was the offering paid into the church and who had many mouths to feed, my dad did well to provide the absolute necessities.

Joseph had some brothers who behaved themselves "unseemly." Can you imagine your brothers and sisters reacting in such a dramatic manner if you told them you dreamed they would bow down to you? On the other hand, I don't know many children who would be happy about that possibility.

No doubt their behavior haunted them all through the years as they watched their aging father, Isaac, grieve for his dear son. Little did they dream that the fulfillment of Joseph's dream was in their future.

Joseph could have behaved in an unseemly manner and been very selfish when he recognized his brothers who had come to buy grain. We are not told how tempted he was to "really make them pay for what they did to him"; nevertheless, if there was the slightest temptation in that direction, he did not act upon it.

Why should Joseph repay their wickedness when God Almighty had taken the evil they intended and turned it (through many difficult times) into good—good not only for Joseph but for his brothers and the entire family. If Joseph had chosen to return evil for evil, who knows what the final outcome would have been?

Let us keep this example in mind when we are tempted to "give someone as good as they have given." Love does not behave itself in that manner.

Lord, You know my weaknesses and temptations. You know that I was made from dust and without Your help I am weak. My human nature at times wants to be selfish and act toward those who have wronged me in a manner that would not glorify You. With Your help I can love enough to look beyond myself and see others' wants and sorrows.

May 6

Scripture: "Charity [love] suffereth long, and is kind" (1 Corinthians 13:4).

Some of the synonyms for the word *kind* are compassionate, considerate, generous, and gentle. These sound like the manifestations of love.

Are our lives too hurried to be kind? It does take time to show compassion, consideration, generosity, and gentleness, but the rewards are far greater than the investment.

Kindness should begin in the home. We should know that our family will not laugh at us when we make mistakes, though they might smile with us. As a young child, I was quite anxious to display my reading ability, so I read aloud a newspaper article to the entire family. My heart was touched by the article about an infant's death. As I read the account I said, "The little 'infect' was buried in the Lake City 'seminary.'" Of course the older children were amused, but they didn't criticize or make me afraid to read aloud.

Kindness is especially appreciated when we are ill. Most of us need reassurance when we are sick or in pain. At such times, children want their mother, for they can depend on her kindness. Women want their spouses. One May 6, after enjoying being with my grandchildren, I drove to Chattanooga to meet my husband who was returning from Zaire following a 10-day trip. It was nice to have him back home. Little did I know that within hours pain would be my partner, and I would be even more thankful he was home. He was very kind, but somewhat bewildered at seeing me in this condition. My high tolerance for pain had previously spared him much moaning and groaning, but he got a good taste of it that evening.

When we are at the mercy of others, kindness is especially welcome. After suffering all night Saturday and until noon on Sunday, I visited a walk-in medical clinic and subsequently made a trip to the emergency room at the hospital. Once in their care, you are at the mercy of strangers. They tell you what will happen next.

The first nurse was polite as she inserted the intravenous needle, but it seemed that her familiarity with the task diminished her compassion and empathy. Others along the way could be described in the same manner. Occasionally one would be different. With that person, it was obvious that this was more than a job. Compassion accompanied the kindness. She could smile pleasantly when she told me I was allowed nothing to eat or drink until the infection was gone and the gallbladder surgery was history.

I won't forget the nurse who had been there each day and was preparing me to go home. She wanted me to take one more walk around the hall before I left. In gathering the stand, pump, and cords connected with the intravenous needle, the tubing came loose near my hand and blood gushed. She did not have rubber gloves, but she immediately responded to stop the bleeding. At that moment, her compassion and training kicked in. She cared more about stopping the bleeding than she did about protecting herself. My heart was filled with compassion for her, for she didn't know me and didn't know whether or not she was in danger.

It is heartwarming to know that in a world filled with danger and disease, kindness can still be found.

Lord, may Your love be manifest through the kindness I show to others. It is not always easy or convenient to be kind, but by Your grace we can avail ourselves of opportunities to share Your love with others.

May 7

Scripture: "Jesus answered and said unto him, if a man love me, he will keep my words: and my Father will love him, and we will come unto him, and make our abode with him" (John 14:23).

As parents, we understand the importance of children keeping our words. We get frustrated when children disobey something that is spelled out for them clearly. For children to obey our words (rules), they must be communicated. If these regulations are unheeded, we cannot blame the children if our regulations have not been conveyed. Once these have been conveyed, however, the responsibility to obey lies with the child.

As a child I was bothered by the idea of displeasing my parents. Most of the time I endeavored to keep their words. But at times, I felt so strongly about something that I took a chance.

Some of my dad's rules were stricter than my mother's. He felt that a young lady's legs should not be bare in public regardless of her age. As a result, we left home with long cotton stockings and ended up at school with big rolls around the ankles. I am glad there are no pictures of that scene.

Another thing he objected to was cutting my hair. While he was away preaching at times, my mother would give me a good trim. I recall one day he came home unexpectedly, just after I had gotten a shorter trim than usual. He never did say what he thought about my keeping my hair in curlers the entire weekend. I'm sure he guessed what had happened and just didn't want to confront me. Parents generally aren't just waiting to "smack" their children at every occasion.

God's Word has been given to us. It is our responsibility to read it often and keep His commandments. God says we will keep His words if we love Him.

Have you told the heavenly Father lately that you love Him? How easily we can believe we are abiding by His instructions if we do not reread them and examine our actions.

Is there a lack of communion? Perhaps we are not keeping His words as we should, for He will come and live with us when we are fulfilling this duty.

As parents we like to be with our children and have fellowship with them. It is much more enjoyable when they are obedient and have a desire to do what is right.

"But whoso keepeth his word, in him verily is the love of God perfected: hereby know we that we are in him" (1 John 2:5).

Dear Lord, I want to prove my love to You. Help me to hide Your Word in my heart that I might not sin against You.

May 8

Scripture: "Behold, children are a heritage from the Lord, The fruit of the womb is His reward" (Psalm 127:3).

God loves us enough to give us rewards. Our heritage from the Lord involves a tremendous miracle—the birth of a child.

One might think that the months prior to my birth couldn't have been very exciting for my parents. My mother and dad had enough children, and the children had plenty of brothers and sisters.

Though very little outward affection was shown, I felt loved by the entire family. Never once as a child did the thought enter my mind that I wasn't wanted. Interestingly enough, I wasn't just another number nor was I treated as if I were just like all the rest. I was accepted as an individual.

Needless to say, having nine living children and being a pastor's wife kept my mother pretty busy. My dad took a special interest in my spiritual welfare. He noticed my love of music and wanted to see that nurtured. Before my third birthday he took me to the radio station and held me in his arms while I sang for the radio audience. On occasions before his death I heard him lament the fact that he did not have a tape recording of that "beautiful" (to his ear) singing. He would demonstrate how I sounded while singing "Take Your Burden to the Lord and Leave It There." That song is a real inspiration to me today; its message still serves me well.

He recalls that I was asked to sing at a district rally. Being the proud dad that he was, this delighted him. He took me to the stage and stood me there. No sound could be heard from that little girl. Instead of getting frustrated or angry, he tried to determine the difficulty. Suddenly he remembered that at the radio station he had held me in his arms. When I felt his strong arms pick me up, the song began to flow. At that young age, I didn't comprehend the love my dad was showing, but it affected my life.

Another time he exhibited his love in quite a different way. I learned that he had bought me a doll for Christmas and begged to see it ahead of time. After much time elapsed, I asked if I could see it for just one minute. He agreed. After exactly one minute the doll was taken. It was hard for me to see that taking the doll back in the agreed time meant that he loved me. Only later did I fully understand that he was teaching me to watch my words and never to misuse the truth. He believed the words found in the Bible, "Let your 'Yes' be 'Yes' and your 'No' be 'No'" (Matthew 5:37, NKJV). I'm glad he loved me enough to teach me that lesson. Of course, I am still guilty of saying, "I'll be back in a minute," but immediately I realize I should be more realistic.

When I see the Bible a radio listener sent me when I was 4 years old, my heart is grateful for my dad's interest in my spiritual welfare and his encouragement to develop my musical talent.

Heavenly Father, thank You for giving me an earthly father who realized that I was a gift from His Father God. Thank You that he loved me enough to teach me about You, Your love, and Your precepts. Help me to pass along this heritage to future generations.

May 9

Scripture: "Delight yourself also in the Lord, and He shall give you the desires of your heart" (Psalm 37:4).

We can see God's hand and His special love in so many areas of our lives. He grants the desires of our heart—at times even desires of which we are unaware. When I was 11 years old, I had one of those very rare evenings alone with my mother. As a matter of fact, it is the only time I remember having her all to myself. She played the piano and we sang. Then she showed me fabric for dresses she planned to make. She cut out some pillowcases to be sewn the next day. Before the rest of the family got home, she heated a blanket on top of a gas heater and placed it over my shivering body as I went to bed in the cold bedroom. She assured me that I would be all right and would get warm soon.

In approximately four hours, my dad awakened me, my brothers, and sisters and told us our mother was sick. She did not know any of us, and our living room was filled with church people praying and begging God not to take her. Since it was her time to go, I'm thankful God granted her wish and let her go quickly. Those hours I was privileged to spend alone with my mother will always be treasured. When thanking God for his special blessings, this is on my list.

Life was different for our family following that night. Yet God granted the desires of my heart on many occasions during the ensuing years. He gave me friends and relatives who cared deeply for me. We moved many miles away when I was a teenager, and it was there I met my husband at a church picnic. God has blessed our ministry. His blessings to me through my husband are too numerous to include in this devotion. His love for me is reassuring and gives me confidence.

My dad outlived my mother by 34 years and one week. He lived hours away from all the children, but each one visited him at every opportunity, especially after he was diagnosed with cancer. After a second surgery, the daughters took turns going to stay for a week to help our stepmother care for him. My older sister left on Friday, and I arrived on Sunday. My dad was sent home from the hospital on Monday and seemed to be doing well. I was privileged to get his prescriptions filled and to make some banana pudding, which he seemed to enjoy. After dinner on Tuesday evening, I invited him to join me in singing "Follow Me." He told me he couldn't sing, but he would like to hear me sing. He was so inspired by the words that he found strength to join in and sing most of it with me.

Soon it was time for his medicine which had to be taken with food. He wanted banana pudding to "wash down his medicine." He took the medicine, asked me to raise the head of his hospital bed higher, and in a brief moment he was gone. In reflecting on how privileged I was to be with him at that last moment, I realized that spending the evening and singing with both of my parents on their last nights on earth—34 years apart—was my very special blessing, a blessing only God could give.

165

Lord, You love to grant the desires of Your children's hearts. I do not take Your blessings for granted. Just as earthly parents love to do nice things for their children, You enjoy sending blessings our way. Help me to use my blessings to bless others.

May 10

Scripture: "Let your conversation be without covetousness; and be content with such things as ye have: for he hath said, I will never leave thee, nor forsake thee" (Hebrews 13:5).

From the time I can remember, we sang these words of a song:

I know the Lord will make a way for me.
I know the Lord will make a way for me.
If I live a holy life, shun the wrong and do the right,
I know the Lord will make a way for me.

Then we would sing:

I know the Lord has laid His hand on me.
I know the Lord has laid His hand on me.
If I live a holy life, shun the wrong and do the right,
I know the Lord has laid His hand on me.

I think I felt the reality of this song even before I accepted the Lord as my personal Savior at the age of 6. I believe He caused the lady standing beside me to notice that little girl who was putting one foot out and bringing it back as they gave the invitation. His Spirit was drawing me, and I have never doubted my experience since that day. I wish I could say that I had never failed Him, but I can tell you with certainty that He has never failed me. Just as He promised, He does not leave us.

During a short period of my adult life, I was having difficulty seeing God's hand and the direction He was leading. A Ladies Ministries seminar was conducted nearby. At the end of one of the workshops, the leader said, "Let's sing 'I Know the Lord Will Make a Way For Me.'" When we got to the words, "I know the Lord has laid His hand on me," I was reassured that He had been with me all of my life and that He was directing my steps.

He manifests Himself to us in unexpected and unusual ways. Knowing His hand is upon my life keeps me going through both good and difficult times. I believe His promise that He will never leave us nor forsake us. This is another assurance of His love.

Father, forgive me for those times my faith has wavered. I know that my steps are ordered by You. Help me to slow down and not get ahead of Your direction. I want to sit at Your feet more often and allow You to direct me at all times.

May 11

Scripture: "There is no fear in love; but perfect love casteth out fear: because fear hath torment. He that feareth is not made perfect in love" (1 John 4:18).

The closer our daughter, Janet, got to 11, the more I lay awake at night fearing that I would die and leave her without a mother. I was 11 when my mother died of a heart attack.

Though I was young when she was born, my baby daughter was the joy of my life. I was blessed with an easy delivery and couldn't wait for the five-day required hospital stay to end. I wanted to brush her thick black hair (the nurses didn't get the part straight). Her dad took one look at her and forgot that he had said for nine months that he wanted a boy. In those days we didn't find out ahead of time whether we were having a boy or a girl, and I'm not sure I would have wanted to know.

We enjoyed her so much. Yes, we spoiled her, but I often said the spoiling didn't take. She was an unselfish little girl and loved to share. She has never given us any trouble.

Slowly the worry began. I didn't want her to spend the rest of her life without her mother as I had. I wasn't sick and didn't expect to die, but I worried. This continued for several months.

When a friend of mine died unexpectedly and left a young son and daughter, I was quite concerned for the children and wanted to do everything I could for them. In my concern for my friend's children, suddenly I realized that the Lord would provide someone just as concerned for my child if He saw fit to call me home before she was grown. The fear subsided.

My worry was in vain. Thank God He allowed me to see my little girl grow into a lovely, unselfish adult with a wonderful husband. As a bonus, I now enjoy my three grandchildren.

We worry about many things. Usually the worry has no foundation. Worry serves no useful purpose, and it can be extremely harmful.

Why should we worry? My husband preaches a sermon on worry. He reads in God's Word that God never slumbers nor sleeps, and he says that he sees no reason for both of them to stay awake. So he leaves everything with God and goes to sleep shortly after his head is on the pillow.

Let's leave the unknown with God. We don't know the future, but we know the One who holds tomorrow. God loves us and is directing our steps. He does all things well.

"He that feareth is not made perfect in love."

Thank You, Father, for that peace which passeth all understanding. Fear does not come from You. Help us to release our fear and trust Your love.

May 12

Scripture: "That their hearts might be comforted, being knit together in love" (Colossians 2:2).

When I think of hearts being knit together, I think of David and Jonathan in the Bible, and then I think of twins.

May 12 is the birthday of my twin sisters, Rita and Cleta, who are four years older than I. Twins have an indescribable bond. Often if one is sick, the other one is too. Frequently one knows what the other is thinking. As we were growing up, my sisters were always "partners in crime" when it came to getting their younger sister to do what they wanted. At times when the three of us shared one bed, they wouldn't let me in bed until I brought them a drink of water. There was never a doubt about the special love they enjoyed, even when their words claimed "I'll be glad when I never have to see you again." Now that they are grown and have children and grandchildren, they cannot imagine feeling that way for even a moment.

Today that bond is stronger than ever before. Recently the twins, our older sister, and I went on a vacation together. This was the first time we had an opportunity like this. We had a great time. My oldest sister and I teased about being only a "sister," not a twin. The fact that the twins have this bond is understood. Neither Ruth nor I feel neglected when the twins think of each others' needs before thinking of their sisters' needs.

Through the common bond of Christ Jesus, sisters in the Lord should enjoy a similar relationship. We should hurt when our sister hurts and rejoice when she rejoices. When we think of ourselves, we will find ourselves thinking of her.

Just as a parent is disappointed and frustrated when children quarrel and are unkind to each other, our heavenly Father is not pleased when we treat one another unkindly.

We have a beautiful example of friendship in the story of David and Jonathan. Can you imagine being the daughter of a king, entitled to certain privileges? Would you be happy for another young lady if she instead of you were designated to receive the benefits and blessings that should be yours? Could you bring yourself to help her come to the throne?

Jonathan did this and more. He exemplified a love that is rarely seen between friends or even siblings.

I am blessed to have three wonderful sisters. My sisters in the Lord are also a tremendous blessing. I want to be the kind of friend whose heart can be knit together with the sisters God has given me.

Lord and Master, thank You for Your love which affects our relationships. By Your help, we can love others with the kind of love that pleases You. Help me to be as unselfish as Jonathan was and, in turn, bless the lives of friends.

May 13

Scripture: "Look at the birds of the air, for they neither sow nor reap nor gather into barns; yet your heavenly Father feeds them. Are you not of more value than they?" (Matthew 6:26, *NKJV*).

Watching the animal kingdom astonishes most humans. With what great thoughtfulness the Maker designed these animals! And His word tells us He cares even more for us.

During one of the more difficult times in my life, I noticed some robins had built a nest in our shrubbery. Each day when I arrived home from work, I looked inside and watched the eggs. It was exciting to see the little birds hatch and to observe the way the mother cared for them.

A mother is a partner with God. He entrusts her with one of earth's most important tasks—caring for her children to whom God has given life through her.

Children grow up and usually are the ones to leave us, but for my husband and me this scene was reversed. It was difficult to move to another state just months after our only daughter got married. But we all adjusted, and life was normal for them in Ohio and for us in Tennessee. Four years later when I learned she was expecting her first child, my deep desire was to be there when my first grandchild was born. Of course I knew the distance and the uncertainty of an arrival date were against me, but I still felt in my heart that I would be there.

When I spoke to her all was well, she said, so I decided to stay longer at work and complete any tasks that were on the "must do" list. However, when I got home on that cold Friday in January, the desire to go to Ohio became stronger. You guessed it! My flight arrived in Cincinnati on Saturday evening, and on Sunday morning we were on the way to the hospital. A beautiful baby boy was born on that Super Bowl Sunday evening. Only a grandmother can know how I felt when I first saw little Michael (well, if you call 9 pounds, 4 ounces "little"). In addition to the joy of being a grandmother, my heart was filled with gratitude to my heavenly Father for affording me this special privilege. It wasn't many months before our daughter's family moved closer.

Five years later, we received the call from Knoxville, Tennessee, that it appeared we would be celebrating two birthdays on the same day. Our granddaughter, Natalie, was born on Michael's fifth birthday, and the entire family was in the birthing room when she arrived. As I watched my daughter, there were times when I wondered if being in the birthing room was a blessing for me. I would gladly have traded places with her to help her bear the pain. But when the baby came, I knew it was a special privilege to have been there. Once again I felt God's special love. In 1989 Michelle, our third grandchild, was born. We made the trip from Jackson, Mississippi, to Cleveland, Tennessee, in time for her birth.

The birds of the air are a testimony of God's love and provision. On Mother's Day, I saw each of the baby robins fly from the nest. For me, this was a special gift from God and a reminder of His love for me. My desire is to enjoy good health and long life and see my three grandchildren grown, gifted, and guided by the Lord.

We are the objects of His special love, and He does direct our steps.

Lord, thank You for the assurance that we are more important than the birds of the air. I want to trust You and Your direction. Thank You for Your special love and Your many wonderful blessings—blessings that money cannot buy. I know You will meet my needs just as You care for the birds.

May 14

Scripture: "And the bow shall be in the cloud; and I will look upon it, that I may remember the everlasting covenant between God and every living creature of all flesh that is upon the earth" (Genesis 9:16).

God manifested His love by giving a promise to Noah that He will never again destroy the earth by flood. He chose the beautiful rainbow as a reminder of this covenant.

What comes to mind when you see a rainbow? It reminds me of God's love, His promises, and special blessings which are sometimes referred to as "handfuls on purpose." What a rare treat to see a rainbow!

Since I became an adult, I recall three distinct occasions when I was awed by the sight of a rainbow. Several years ago we were privileged to attend a conference in San Juan, Puerto Rico. A friend and I got away for a few minutes to walk on the beach. We shared about our common love of seeing the waves come to shore and how the water glistens in the sun. As we talked about various things, suddenly she looked up and saw a rainbow around the sun. We were both as thrilled as an excited child to see the rainbow. We learned that our fascination with rainbows was another thing we had in common. We couldn't look at it very long because of the brightness of the sun, but that beautiful rainbow is etched in my memory. Reflecting on God's promises and special blessings brings forth gratitude.

Years later, I stepped onto the front porch. It was rainy, and the sun wasn't shining too brightly inside me either. I had been talking to the Lord about a matter with which we needed His help. As I looked into the distance, there was a beautiful rainbow which seemed to begin and end on each side of our house. The tears began to roll. Was this God's way of telling me He loved me and knew the circumstances? The rainbow was there for anyone to see, but I could have missed it! I was grateful for this special blessing.

Last summer we were at the ballpark watching our grandson play ball. He made us proud as he hit a home run. As we watched him, our hearts were grateful for a healthy, talented young man. Our need of God's direction in dealing with this teenager was also recognized. Like other parents and grandparents, we remind the Lord of our need and ask for His hand to be upon our children and protect them from the snares of the devil. On that day God had another huge rainbow prepared.

Each new day as we open our eyes, we can praise God that His promises are true and are for us. We don't have to see rainbows to be assured of this fact, but when we do, there is a unique sense of gratitude and a touch of excitement. The rainbow most often accompanies those times when fears could arise because of the storm. Without the rainbow, Noah's descendants might have been very fearful, but the storm brought the rainbow and God's special promise. An interesting fact is that it takes the sunshine as well as the rain to produce a rainbow. When the rays of the sun fall on the moisture-filled cloud, the rainbow is produced.

I feel an assurance of His special love for His children. The sunshine is there along with the clouds.

The words of a very old song convey the message well:

> God put a rainbow in the cloud,
> God put a rainbow in the cloud;
> When it looked like the sun wouldn't shine any more,
> God put a rainbow in the cloud.

If you wonder whether or not the sun will ever shine again in your life, visualize a rainbow; remember His promises are true and that He loves and cares for you.

Another beautiful thought about the rainbow is recorded in Revelation 4:3: "And he that sat was to look upon like a jasper and a sardine stone: and there was a rainbow round about the throne, in sight like unto an emerald."

Father God, thank You for the beautiful rainbow full of color and promise. Make our lives a rainbow to the lives of those who have suffered much rain. Help us to communicate Your love.

May 15

Scripture: "Owe no man any thing, but to love one another; for he that loveth another hath fulfilled the law" (Romans 13:8).

It is difficult to imagine the time when we will owe no one anything. We long for the day when our car loan is paid in full, only to discover that we need a new one by then. The mortgage on our house seems to be for an eternity. Even if these things are paid in full, each month we owe the utility bill, and our homeowners and auto insurance premiums come due too frequently.

At first we ask ourselves how love and law are related. The law is associated with authority, and love relates to the heart. This verse tells us that if we love one another we have fulfilled the law. If our actions are truly motivated by love for God and others, we will have no need of the law to keep us in line. When we love others, we think of their welfare as if it were our own. Certainly we will never intentionally harm them when this is the case. If we truly love our neighbor, we will not covet his property, steal from him, take his wife, or kill him. We won't tell untruths about him. When we consider those things, we understand how the law is fulfilled through love.

Why do we do things for people to whom we owe nothing? God's love motivates us to show kindness to others. We want good things for them.

Several years ago my husband made his first trip to Seoul, Korea. We had been told of the bargains to be found in Etawon. Those friends who expressed they would like something brought back for them were given the opportunity to make a list of the items they wanted. We encouraged them by telling them the items that were the best bargains. Some sent money, and others were prepared to pay when he returned.

Before the day of his departure, we realized that our concern for others had gotten us into a much larger situation than expected. I was still trying to organize all the purchases according to item, color and size as he drove to the airport. He spent much of his free time shopping for other people and then packing the merchandise in boxes for shipment back to the States.

What was in it for him? Only the joy of seeing excited friends when they received their jackets, leather goods, brass items, shoes, and so forth. We didn't owe these people anything, and they owed us nothing.

Yes, we know if the Lord tarries our mortgage will be paid in full. There is a debt, however, that will never be paid. We owe our lives to the Lord, and we can never repay His love to us. Salvation is a gift from God, but our love motivates us to work toward repaying our Lord. The debt of love is not a heavy burden.

Lord, help us to work toward owing no man except to love him. Debt can be bondage, and we want to be free to share Your love with others.

May 16

Scripture: "For he shall give his angels charge over thee, to keep thee in all thy ways" (Psalm 91:11).

Many people are fascinated by angels. Others find it difficult to believe there are angels watching over us even though there are scriptures like Psalm 91:11 and Psalm 34:7, which say, "The angel of the Lord encampeth round about them that fear him, and delivereth them."

These verses do not give us a license to act carelessly. Satan tried to tempt Jesus: "If thou be the Son of God, cast thyself down: for it is written, He shall give his angels charge concerning thee: and in their hands they shall bear thee up, lest at any time thou dash thy foot against a stone" (Matthew 4:6). But Jesus responded, "It is written again, Thou shalt not tempt the Lord thy God" (v. 7).

Believers and nonbelievers find themselves attracted to beautiful angel figurines. Ladies collect them, wear them on their lapels, wrap gifts in angel paper, send angel cards, and use angel letterhead. Friends gave me a beautiful angel figurine for Christmas last year. This year I received another. I enjoy their beauty because they remind me of God's love for me.

Angels delivered Lot from Sodom, Daniel from the lion's den, and Peter and the apostles from prison. They were there at the Savior's birth and at various other stages of His life. They will be involved in His second coming. As we reflect on these facts and the love of God, it is easier to believe that He gives His angels charge over us. What a comforting thought! Angels are God's messengers and are at His service. Both mercies and judgments are dispersed by them. Those of us who fear God are kept from many evils which would come our way.

This is another beautiful way God manifests His love for us. Reflect on His love. Sing the lovely words of the old song "The Love of God."

We are told the last verse was penned by an individual who was thought to be mentally deranged. As you sing those words, you can sense the depth of the knowledge of God's love. May we know His love in the manner experienced by composer F.M. Lehman.

Once again, Lord, my heart overflows with gratitude for Your love and care. I don't know how people face each day without You. Forgive me for the times I have failed to express my love. Thank You for giving Your angels charge over me.

May 17

Scripture: "He saith unto him the third time, Simon, son of Jonas, lovest thou me?" (John 21:17).

Should Peter wonder that the Lord asked him this question the third time? Peter had denied the Lord three times. Yet the second portion of this verse tells us Peter was grieved because the Lord asked him this question the third time.

Is Christ asking us that question today? Can we pretend to love Him if we have little knowledge of Him? How can we love someone we don't know? Our knowledge must start with the fact that Christ is the Son of God and that He was born of a virgin, crucified for our sins, and resurrected. We must believe John 3:16: "For God so loved the world, that he gave his only begotten Son, that whosoever believeth in him should not perish, but have everlasting life." A song I have sung since childhood is:

> I love Him, I love Him,
> Because He first loved me;
> And purchased my salvation on Calvary.

The knowledge of His love for us should invoke our love for Him. How do we show our love for Him? We will talk about Him and His goodness. We will want to know more about Him. Reading His Word will be a vital part of our lifestyle. We will make time to sit at His feet and spend time in prayer. Sharing Christ's love will be a natural outcome of our love for God.

Jesus tells us, "If ye love me, keep my commandments" (John 14:15). What are His commandments? We should look at them one by one. To some we can readily respond, "Of course, I keep that one!" But how about some of the others? Read the twentieth chapter of Exodus and see how many you can really whiz through. On the surface they seem easy, but looked at in depth, it might be another story.

If the Lord asked me today, "Do you love me," I would immediately say, "You know I do, Lord." But if He asked for proof, what would the confirmation be? I tell Him often how much I love Him, but if He still asks me this question, perhaps He is saying "Your actions aren't consistent with your words." In 1 John 3:18 we read, "My little children, let us not love in word, neither in tongue; but in deed and in truth."

My daughter heard our oldest granddaughter, Natalie, praying. She said, "Jesus, I love you [she paused trying to find a word to communicate how much and then said] to the end of numbers." Let's count the ways we love and put action to our words today.

Heavenly Father, I realize how empty words alone can be. Examine me, Lord, and help me to see my shortcomings. I want to show You more than ever before that I love You with all my heart and that my love has no ending . . . to the end of numbers.

May 18

Scripture: "The Lord is my shepherd; I shall not want" (Psalm 23:1).

Many of us learned the Twenty-third Psalm as small children. Some recited the entire psalm both in Sunday school and at public school. It is one of the sweetest and most often quoted psalms, and it shows that David was keenly aware of God's love.

To have the assurance that Almighty God is our shepherd makes us feel secure. With Him as our Shepherd, all our needs will be supplied. David knew about the care of a shepherd. This statement reveals a depth of experience and knowledge. God brought David from the responsibility of caring for the flock to that of being king of Israel. What an awesome elevation! Imagine . . . the Lord is *my* shepherd! This knowledge will free us from many fears.

As sheep, we would no doubt wander aimlessly about were it not for the guidance of the Good Shepherd. In today's stress-filled world, it is comforting to know that "He maketh me to lie down in green pastures: he leadeth me beside the still waters" (Psalm 23:2). Even these words have a calming effect. Imagine sitting beside a large body of water with waves rolling in and the sunshine beaming down. For me, there is something tranquil and majestic about that scene. He *still* leads us beside still waters and makes us lie down in green pastures. Just one touch from the Master will soothe a weary, anxious soul as nothing else can. He restores our weary souls.

People can overcome many fears, but the fear of death haunts so many—even Christians. David tells us, "Yea, though I walk through the valley of the shadow of death, I will fear no evil: for thou art with me; thy rod and thy staff they comfort me" (v. 4). We have never experienced death, but we have enjoyed His presence. He will be with us all the days of our lives and will be there when our work on earth is finished. The last verse of this psalm tells us that surely (for a certainty) goodness and mercy will follow us all the days of our lives. Let's reflect upon His goodness and mercy in the past and the present. Those same blessings will be ours in the future. When this life is over, we have the assurance of dwelling in the house of the Lord, the Great Shepherd, forever.

Let us rejoice because He is our shepherd and His love and care are ours.

How humbling it is, Lord, to know that You are my shepherd. Make me more aware of this wonderful fact. Help me to travel beside the still waters with You and lie down in Your green pastures. Thank You for the assurance of Your hand upon my life today.

May 19

Scripture: "And thou shalt love the Lord thy God with all thy heart, and with all thy soul, and with all thy mind, and with all thy strength: this is the first commandment. And the second is like, namely this, Thou shalt love thy neighbor as thyself. There is none other commandment greater than these" (Mark 12:30, 31).

Love my neighbor as myself? How can this be? In today's world many people don't even know their neighbor's name. How can they love him as this verse commands? It is examination time again. We must search our hearts. If we want God's love and His blessings, not only must we love Him with all our heart, soul, mind, and strength, but we must also love our neighbor as ourselves.

We certainly don't wish our neighbors any harm. We are considerate of them when we plan our work. We don't mow our lawn too early in the morning in case they are sleeping. Talking loudly on a warm, summer evening when we are outside late also is something we considerately refrain from doing. We do show neighborly regard for them, but what do we do *for* them?

These reminders are needed more in the '90s than ever before. Have we taken the time to see if there is a need at our neighbor's house? Do we know if he has accepted the Lord as his personal Savior?

Ann Kiemel, a noted author and speaker, uses some unique ways to witness to her neighbors. She tells of baking chocolate chip cookies and taking them to her neighbors. She felt foolish after she got back to her apartment and asked the Lord to forgive her. But this action paid off. Those neighbors wanted to talk to her about her Lord.

What do you have that can be used to share God's love with a neighbor? Smiles are wonderful. Mowing lawns and watching out for a neighbor's house while they are away are great. But do they know why you are so nice? Have you talked with them about God's love for them?

We sponsor missionaries to take the gospel around the world, but who will take the good news to our neighborhood? There are some things that we must do.

How about today? Have you shared God's love with your neighbors?

This is one I need Your help on, Lord. I must slow down and realize my responsibility to my neighbors. Help me to do better. I do care and want to share Your love.

May 20

Scripture: "Charity [love] suffereth long, and is kind" (1 Corinthians 13:4).

Hearts for Rent was a title on the cover of an airline magazine that caught my attention. It was an advertisement for a comedy production. The "hearts for rent" attitude of today's couples, however, is not humorous. Too many rent their hearts to one today and in a short while rent it to another person.

Marriage is a lifetime investment. We would much rather invest in a home than pay rent. If we like a home enough to buy it, we will invest our energies to make it better.

Relationships also require investments. They often begin with romantic love, which is a self-serving kind of affection. It is not based on enduring values; it is a part of our biological makeup. We try hard to keep a touch of this love all the days of our marriage; however, its basis is usually in the realm of Cinderella. While we are trying on the glass slipper, gazing into our handsome prince's eyes, or opening elaborate gifts, it is difficult to comprehend that our future will include bills to pay and sick children to care for. As wonderful as romantic love is, it is very fragile.

Later, especially after marriage, fact overrides fantasy. We must look for deeper love. Friendship love is an important type of love. Friendship love must be cultivated through caring and sharing. You can look at some couples and know immediately that they are best friends. How encouraging and challenging! This can happen only when we are willing to invest ourselves in each other's lives. It comes about through genuine concern for our mate and what is happening in his life.

Before becoming best friends, we must be real. When we are real, we are vulnerable. We say to the other person, "I know you love me for who I am, and I have nothing to hide from you." In this day of counterfeit jewelry, clothing, handbags, and many other things, it is difficult for the untrained eye to detect the difference. We must carefully guard our marriages from falling into the counterfeit category. We can easily master the art of smiling and saying the right things in public while hiding the fact there is trouble at home.

Spending time together is a must if we are to become and remain best friends. Finding time is becoming increasingly difficult. Spending time together doesn't require spending a lot of money, though the relationship is worth a financial investment. But if money is not available for expensive gifts or getaways, other activities can be just as satisfying and effective. These might include taking a walk and sharing the day's activities or driving around town or to a nearby town while leaving the power off on the cellular telephone. You might enjoy a snack while you watch a favorite program on television and laugh together. Make your time together quality time. Just as we designate a specific time of day for our personal time with the Lord, we should devote a time to be with each other. Without setting aside a designated time, the busyness of today's hectic lifestyles leaves no time for quiet togetherness.

Time spent together does wonders for a relationship, but we must also communicate—share joys and sorrows with the assurance that confidences will never be betrayed.

A selfish marriage—one with two takers and no giver—creates serious problems. Marriages need unselfish, self-giving love. This is the type of love Christ has for us. That kind of love is described for us in 1 Corinthians 13. Genuine love . . .

> is long-suffering (patient)
> is kind
> is not jealous
> is not boastful .
> is not arrogant
> is not rude
> is not selfish
> is not resentful
> does not think evil
> rejoices in truth
> bears all things
> believes all things
> hopes all things
> endures all things.

How many of these qualities can be found in your love? This kind of love is far superior to romantic love or friendship love. The possessor of this kind of love will almost certainly be loved in return.

Start doing specific things for each other every day. Remember the things that caused you to love in the first place, if you find your love is decreasing. Doing so can help you to love again. Self-giving love is pure love. It is born out of God's love. It involves one person placing the welfare of another before his own.

Recently I was told of Siamese twins who were undergoing surgery. The parents had to make a crucial decision—which one would get two of the three legs? I asked myself what my decision would be if a choice involving a limb for my spouse or myself were required.

Let's do a self test to be sure we are committed to enhancing our relationship and love for our spouse. Remove any signs indicating "hearts for rent." The investment of our love must be for a lifetime.

Lord, I realize my family is very important. Thank You for giving me a loving, caring spouse. Help me not to give my husband the leftovers of my life. I want to show genuine love that is kind and suffers long, if necessary.

May 21

Scripture: "But you, beloved, building yourselves up on your most holy faith, praying in the Holy Spirit, keep yourselves in the love of God, looking for the mercy of our Lord Jesus Christ unto eternal life" (Jude 20, 21, *NKJV*).

These words direct our thoughts to the great theme of the Bible—God is love. We are instructed to keep ourselves in the love of God. Jude describes us as "beloved." We are the children of God and can rest in His love. His love is our greatest treasure.

The knowledge of our parents' love keeps us during good and difficult times. How much more will we be kept by God's love!

If we travel the path of disobedience or decide to do things our way, we don't enjoy the atmosphere of His love. We soon realize that something is wrong.

To be kept in His love involves a life of obedience. As a child, did you wonder if your mother and dad still loved you when you disobeyed and they punished you? As adults, we know this is not the case. Good parents discipline because of the very fact that they do love. Children cannot comprehend the depth of their parents' affection while undergoing unpleasant discipline. It's only later that both understanding and gratitude come. How often we react as a child. We think God is not with us, when, in fact, we have removed ourselves from the atmosphere of His love, through straying down our own paths, disobedience, or sometimes active rebellion.

The admonition found in Jude is for a close walk with our Lord. We sing these words:

> Just a closer walk with Thee,
> Grant it Jesus is my plea;
> Daily walking close to Thee,
> Let it be, dear Lord, let it be.

He is pleased when we desire a closer walk with Him and are willing to invest the time it requires. We cannot allow the influences of this world to deter us. We must keep ourselves in the love of God and maintain an intimate relationship with Him.

We are to build ourselves up in our most holy faith and pray in the Holy Spirit. When fears and cares weigh us down, we need to let the Holy Spirit lift us. By His Spirit we are drawn into His presence. "Likewise the Spirit also helpeth our infirmities: for we know not what we should pray for as we ought: but the Spirit itself maketh intercession for us with groanings which cannot be uttered" (Romans 8:26).

Worried about tomorrow? Keep yourself in the love of God. Nothing can separate us from the love of God (Romans 8:38, 39).

Father, help me to desire a closer walk with You that I may keep myself in Your love. Thank You for loving me enough to send Your Son that I might abide in Your love.

May 22

Scripture: "I have shewed you all things, how that so labouring ye ought to support the weak, and to remember the words of the Lord Jesus, how he said, It is more blessed to give than to receive" (Acts 20:35).

To our human nature this seems impossible. But love makes giving a joy. This does not mean it is not also a joy to receive. We all like to receive and should do so graciously.

God gave His Son for us, and Jesus willingly laid down His life for us. God is always sending His blessings. He is a giving God. We cannot reflect upon His blessings without sensing His love for us. If we are to be like Him, we will be blessed by giving.

When we give, our thoughts turn away from ourselves and our problems to others and their needs. We must share ourselves, as well as our possessions.

When this spirit is prevalent in the home, difficulties will be minimal. Can you imagine how pleasant life would be if both parents and children lived by this principle? Can our children learn this principle unless we teach them? Many marriages are filled with argument because at least one spouse refuses to give. What a different atmosphere will be in the home when both partners find it more blessed to give than to receive.

Friendship must also be a giving situation. We hear people say, "They are your friends as long as they need you." One-way streets are confusing. They are dangerous if you are traveling the wrong direction. In relationships or friendships, I don't like one-way streets, even if they are coming my direction. I cannot be a receiver only. On the other hand, everything going the other direction doesn't bring abundant happiness either.

Giving is the right attitude in the workplace also. Too many want to receive the vacation days, holidays, the highest pay possible, and all the benefits; but they want to give as little as they can manage in return. We will not give our best if our attitude is "What's in it for me."

A lot of things can be given. We often think of gifts or money, but strength and encouragement are important gifts too. Just as we like to receive encouragement, so do our friends and family.

My grandmother lived with us during the last few years of her life. During that time my dad learned she had always wanted a strand of pearls. He couldn't afford that gift, but he found great joy in sacrificing to buy them for his mother though she had such a short time left on earth.

Truly, it is more blessed to give than to receive. I want to give in many ways and especially those things of eternal value.

Your example of giving, heavenly Father, is one I want to emulate. Help me to see the opportunities You are giving me to prove Your love by giving.

May 23

Scripture: "For God so loved the world, that he gave his only begotten Son, that whosoever believeth in him should not perish, but have everlasting life" (John 3:16).

Occasionally we meet couples who feel their love is the most perfect love in the world. They can't comprehend a love greater than theirs. Whether or not we can comprehend it, there is a love beyond comparison or duplication.

God loved us supremely and so He sent His only begotten Son; and the Son loved us so deeply that He willingly laid down His life. God so loved. Often we say, I love you so much. Our "so" can't compare with His. Tough love was exemplified long before we read about it in books. God actually forsook His own Son for a time because of His love for us. No, we can't understand this—it is divine love. We understand it only enough to be awed by it and to want to respond to this marvelous love.

I haven't observed it often, but occasionally there are friends who seem to admire one another so much that they love with a higher, more unselfish love than is usual. When I am the receiver of that special kind of love, I certainly can't explain why. I can only thank God for using me in a manner that blessed that individual and made them appreciate my life.

God's divine love was directed at the entire world—not just one person. I'm so glad that "whosoever" included me. Thank God that this love was revealed to me as a young child. Of course I didn't understand it, but I received it. It continues to make a difference in my life every day.

God's Son cried out in agony "My God, my God, why hast thou forsaken me?" (Matthew 27:46). Imagine your child in this or even a much less serious situation. Divine love is too deep and too wonderful for us to comprehend.

As we read God's Word and apply it to our lives, we will come closer to understanding this marvelous love God has for us. Thank God for His love to mankind and for the everlasting life that love provided.

Father God, I realize how unworthy I am. Thank You for giving Your love freely. Mankind can never deserve Your love, but we are grateful for it. Help us to pass it on.

May 24

Scripture: "And Jesus answered and said unto her, Martha, Martha, thou art anxious and troubled about many things: But one thing is needful: and Mary hath chosen that good part, which shall not be taken away from her" (Luke 10: 41, 42).

Bible students are very familiar with this passage and with Mary's special love for her Lord. Mary, with her sister, Martha, and brother, Lazarus, were the Lord's friends and enjoyed a unique relationship with Him, and He loved them very much.

These sisters' personalities were as different as siblings' personalities often are today, but the Lord loved them both, accepting each for herself; but when questioned by Martha, He pointed out that Mary had chosen the good part.

Martha loved Jesus too. She wanted everything to be right for Him—just as someone must prepare food when company comes to our homes for dinner. She was expressing her love in a different way. She desired to serve Him and to please Him.

We don't know what Mary did prior to Jesus' arrival. She could have helped in the duties around the house, but once Jesus arrived, she couldn't think of anything but sitting at His feet.

Do we sit still long enough to realize Jesus has come and wants us to choose the good part? Recall the last time you sat at His feet when you had things that seemed to be screaming at you to do.

Recently, our general overseer called our denomination to Solemn Assembly. We were asked to come to church at 7 p.m. and remain all evening for prayer. At noon that day, the International Offices were closed, and we were asked to fast and pray in preparation for the Solemn Assembly. When I got home that afternoon, for a brief moment the temptation to do something around the house hovered in my mind. I reminded myself that though no one else would know, we were given that time to fast, to pray, to prepare. Reading God's Word and praying the entire afternoon helped prepare me for the all-night gathering. Words cannot express the blessing of sitting at His feet—even in the midst of household tasks that needed attention.

There's nothing wrong with taking care of matters in the home, but how much smoother life is when we set these aside at times and dedicate ourselves completely to sitting at His feet. The things of this earth will pass away, but when we choose the good part, it will endure. His Word will never pass away.

Sitting at Your feet, heavenly Father, is a privilege I so often take for granted. Forgive me and help me to find more time to devote entirely to You and Your work, regardless of other demands on my time. Thank You, Lord, for visiting my home and for the love You extend to me.

May 25

Scripture: "And whosoever will be chief among you, let him be your servant: Even as the Son of Man came not to be ministered unto, but to minister and to give his life a ransom for many" (Matthew 20:27, 28).

To many children, the chief person in the home is their mother. This doesn't diminish the man's status as head of the home. But the mother has a willingness to serve her family in a unique manner.

Though the purpose of Jesus' coming to earth was to minister rather than be ministered to, He also took time to get alone and to visit the home of friends.

Nothing speaks of love quite like a desire to serve another simply because you want to. Servers at a restaurant may serve you without having any emotional ties. The impetus for their service is to make a living and get an extra token of appreciation from you. We respond well to those servers who give us extra attention and appear to enjoy serving us. The server benefits by receiving a nice gratuity.

A mother gets little in return for her service until her children are grown. She is pleased to receive small rewards from time to time. Seldom do children realize the unselfish service of their mother. They don't understand why they are drawn to her and want her when they are ill or facing a difficulty.

Serving others is a wonderful attitude toward life not only to our children but to others. It is rewarding to be privileged to serve. God's Word plainly lets us know that the Lord takes notice of our service to others. He considers our acts of kindness as personal acts to Himself. He tells us that even if we give a cup of cold water in His name, we will not lose our reward.

We are not superhuman or made of steel. We must find time to sit at His feet and regain our strength. It is necessary to go back to our source many times.

Recently a major Convention and Visitors Bureau brought a group of convention planners and their spouses to their city to see the hotels and the attractions in the area. One of the things they had us do was visit an attraction where we were given a power pack and a laser gun to shoot the enemy and defend our fort. Now this isn't something I would choose for entertainment, but I decided to be a good sport. When we had been shot often or had used up our power to shoot the enemy, we had to go back to the power station for a recharge. That was just a game, but there is a vital lesson to be learned.

How much more we need the power of the Holy Spirit. Rheinhard Bonnke tells us there is a flame for every head and that this is our individual power station.

We wouldn't put our lamps on the table and fail to plug them in. We know it takes power to produce light. If our oven isn't working, we don't mix cornbread. It takes the power of the oven to transform this mixture into delicious bread.

Some of us would rather serve at church than at home. Our homes should not be neglected as a result of our overinvolvement at church. When determining what jobs to accept at the church or in the community, Kay Arthur says in a book titled *Can a Busy Christian Develop Her Spiritual Life?*: "We must remember that husbands and children are eternal beings who not only need to hear the gospel, but need to be nurtured in it through exposure to a consecrated life born out of genuine intimacy with the Father."

We want to follow the Lord's example and serve others as we remember the importance of taking time to commune with Him and minister to our families.

Father, thank You for the wonderful examples we find in Your Word. I want to have a servant's heart and bless others for Your glory. If I can help others along the way, my living will be useful and not in vain. I realize this service is not by might, nor by power, but by Your Spirit.

May 26

Scripture: "But Ruth replied, 'Don't urge me to leave you or to turn back from you. Where you go I will go, and where you stay I will stay. Your people will be my people and your God my God. Where you die I will die, and there I will be buried. May the Lord deal with me, be it ever so severely, if anything but death separates you and me'" (Ruth 1:16, 17, *NIV*).

These beautiful words are often quoted or sung during a wedding ceremony. They very appropriately describe our relationship with our spouse. However, most of us have difficulty thinking that we could feel that way about other relatives, perhaps especially about a mother-in-law. People prefer to tell jokes about their mothers-in-law.

My mother-in-law went to be with the Lord approximately six months after Don and I married. She was a precious saint of God but was in poor health the entire time I knew her. Our relationship was a very short one.

Now, I'm a mother-in-law. I have a wonderful son-in-law. Even if I had a daughter-in-law, I can't imagine that she would say these words.

Why did Ruth feel so strongly about going with Naomi? It certainly wasn't for material security. Naomi was desolate and destitute. That's when many spouses and friends turn away. The commitment ceases when there are financial difficulties.

Naomi gave Ruth the freedom to go back to her people. This was decision time for Ruth, but her mind was made up. In every relationship there will come times of decision which reveal the depth of commitment.

Ruth said Naomi's God would be her God. Naomi's character was rooted in religion. Ruth loved Naomi and the character she exemplified.

Is God's love so evident in my life that someone wants to be near me? Am I setting an example that others want to emulate? When I was a child, we had no television to occupy our time. Almost anytime friends came over, we played church. What began as play generally turned into reality. In fact, one child was baptized in the Holy Spirit during a time that started out as playing church.

What made us play church? Church was modeled for us and was an intricate part of our lives. My dear dad read the Bible during almost every spare moment He had. After retirement, many hours each day were spent in the Word. He didn't have to study for sermons now that he was retired; he just had a genuine love of God's Word. Where have such role models gone? Who are our children emulating?

May we be challenged to live a life so full of God's love that our spouse, children, and friends will want our people to be their people and our God their God.

Ruth's faithfulness was rewarded far beyond her expectations. God is "no respecter of persons"!

Father, help me to be so committed to You that others will accept You as their personal Savior. Bless the home of each person who reflects on this scripture today.

May 27

Scripture: Ye have heard that it hath been said, An eye for an eye, and a tooth for a tooth: But I say unto you, That ye resist not evil [him that is evil]: but whosoever shall smite thee on thy right cheek, turn to him the other also. And if any man will sue thee at the law, and take away thy coat, let him have thy cloke also. And whosoever shall compel thee to go a mile, go with him twain. Give to him that asketh thee, and from him that would borrow of thee turn not thou away" (Matthew 5:38-42).

Wow! Can a human being actually live up to these words? Well, I might be capable of doing these things for family.

These verses are included in the Sermon on the Mount. Jesus talked about what His listeners had heard before, but then He added, "But I say unto you." He is the final authority. It doesn't matter what they had heard before. We know that Jesus lived by these principles. We also know that only through His strength can we begin to measure up. This is the same Jesus who gave the supreme sacrifice. After praying "If it be possible, let this cup pass from me," He continued, "Nevertheless not my will, but thine, be done" (Matthew 26:39; Luke 22:42). He renounced His own life for us.

We must decrease as He increases. Only then can we show this kind of love. We must die to self and allow the Lord to live through us. He went the second mile for us; therefore, His instructions to us to go the second mile are justified. Sometimes our philosophy is "She might do me wrong once, but she will not get the chance to do it again." What if

Jesus would not give us a second chance—did He not go that second mile with us?

As we contemplate the love and mercy He has extended to us, we realize that we are hypocritical to accept His forgiveness and love but in turn be unwilling to give someone else a second chance. As we extend His love to those who have done us wrong, their lives can be changed and they will want what we have. We are to forgive "until seventy times seven" (Matthew 18:22). His Word plainly tells us that if we do not forgive those who wrong us, He will not forgive our trespasses.

A lot of people are walking for their physical health these days. Try going the second mile. It is a wonderful spiritual exercise which is very good for your heart!

Lord, I'm not always good about going the second mile. Teach me to die to self and live for You in such a manner that I can turn the other cheek and go the second mile.

May 28

Scripture: "And I give unto them eternal life; and they shall never perish, neither shall any man pluck them out of my hand" (John 10:28).

What woman or man doesn't like a bargain or a gift? Women seem to get more excited than men about free offers in the mail or a real bargain on a dress.

It is a delight to get free tickets through the airlines' frequent flyer program. Our entire family has been privileged to make some trips by getting these tickets. I was in the gate area in Washington recently when my name was called. Having no idea why I was being paged, I walked to the desk to learn that they were upgrading my ticket to first class. No one had purchased a first-class ticket for that flight, and they needed some passengers to sit in front. This was a benefit of being committed to flying with one specific airline every time their schedule worked for me. This commitment earned me Gold Medallion status, and that is why my name was called. A free flight is over in a short while. Our bargains will soon wear out or go out of style. Any of our material goods can be stolen, but God's gift of eternal life cannot be taken away. Neither can we be plucked out of His hand.

When we find a good sale, we tell friends and family. We want them to share in this good fortune. Think of the excitement you experience when you go to the store just to look and find something 75 percent off the regular price. When someone tells us the dress is pretty, our first impulse is to tell them what a bargain we got. Are we that excited about the most wonderful gift ever given or received?

How long has it been since we shared this good news? People are dying without the knowledge of His love and His free gift of eternal life. If we had the cure for cancer or AIDS, we would want to spread the word so all would know. We have the cure for the worst disease ever known to man—sin. We must share the news of the best bargain yet—eternal life.

Years ago we sang these words:

> I traded my sins for salvation,
> I traded my load for relief;
> I got peace for my condemnation
>   and the joy of the Lord for my grief.
> I traded a life that was wasted, a temple
>   to dwell in God made.
> I got so much more than I had before,
>   I sure got the best of the trade.

Father, thank You for trading peace for my condemnation and joy for my grief. Your love and forgiveness are the best bargains I have ever received. Help me to share the good news so others will receive this wonderful gift.

May 29

Scripture: "Then said his wife unto him, Dost thou still retain thine integrity? curse God, and die. But he said unto her, Thou speakest as one of the foolish women speaketh. What? shall we receive good at the hand of God, and shall we not receive evil? In all this did not Job sin with his lips" (Job 2:9, 10).

What does suffering have to do with love? In Job we see love for God, love for his wife, and love for friends even in the midst of suffering. Weak love would never have survived this terrible trial. This was a time for tough love, and Job possessed it.

How do we handle suffering? Do we accept God's good gifts and refuse things that are painful? Some people want to curse God, turn their backs upon Him, and feel He has failed them if disappointing things come their way.

Our children think we don't love them when we exercise tough love. Yet we know what is best for them, and many times it is not what they want at the moment. We think we know how to love our children and give them good things. How much more our heavenly Father knows what is best for us.

Not one person I have ever known has suffered the losses that Job suffered. When we experience the loss of a loved one, good health, or finances, we find ourselves asking why. These times demand a determined love for our Lord and Master. We know His eyes are beholding the scene, and if we keep the right attitude, He will bring us through. When we get to the mountaintop and look back, it will be evident that there were lessons to be learned in that valley. Those lessons should be sufficient for us to travel on and enjoy the good life.

Can we say with Job, "Though he slay me, yet will I trust in him"? (Job 13:15). We all like to enjoy the good times; however, we need a love that is strong enough to stand fast during the difficult times and help us keep our trust in Almighty God.

Lord, help me to trust You in all circumstances of life. I know that every good and perfect gift comes from You. Thank You for Your love and care.

May 30

Scripture: "Train up a child in the way he should go: and when he is old, he will not depart from it" (Proverbs 22:6).

There are many difficult tasks in life. Training a child in the proper manner is one of the most difficult but rewarding responsibilities we will ever have. To invest this much time and effort requires a deep love for that child.

Can you imagine how much excitement there must have been the day I was born? On August 23, the tenth child was born to my parents. They already had five boys and three girls. Why would they be overjoyed with another one? Perhaps some of the younger children were a little excited. Maybe even my mom and dad were thrilled, but honestly it is hard for me to imagine that I would have been delighted if I had been my mother or dad.

If there was a lack of joy, however, I certainly never knew it. Love was always felt at my house. My mother kept busy most of the time keeping up with the cooking, washing, ironing, and sewing. She didn't have time to lavish much attention on anyone, but her beautiful spirit and faith in God spoke volumes to me.

My dad seemed to take a special interest in my spiritual welfare as I'm sure he had the other children. I can't remember a time that I did not love the Lord, but I do remember the night I went to the altar and asked Him to come into my heart. I was 6 years old. Even at this young age I felt the Holy Spirit drawing me.

My dad took me to the radio station with him. When I was 3 years old, he would hold me in his arms while I sang "Leave It There." When he visited other churches, I went with him.

He took the time to teach us that we must watch our words and always speak the truth. He wasn't fond of exaggeration and would punish us quicker for not telling the truth than for almost anything else we did. If he promised punishment, he followed through. He was a man of his word and expected the same of us. He taught us lessons about not taking things that did not belong to us and not saying anything if we couldn't say something good.

Thank God for parents today who love their children enough to invest the time to train them. With work outside the home, financial demands, and stresses of life, the temptation is to take the easy way out and ignore some of the things children do. It is easier to let the television be the baby-sitter than to spend quality time with the children.

Nevertheless, the investment is well worth it. Pass on the heritage that was given to you so it will continue to be passed from generation to generation.

Lord, You are so good to me. Thank You for godly parents who took the time to teach us about You. You helped us train our daughter. Help me to be found faithful in doing my part to train my grandchildren. Your Word is a lamp unto our feet. Thank You for Your Word.

May 31

Scripture: "Having loved his own which were in the world, he loved them unto the end" (John 13:1).

Jesus' public ministry was over, and He was with those He was depending on to continue His ministry. He wanted them to be ready for His departure. He loved them to the end. As a token of His abiding love, He washed their feet. Everything He had done during His ministry spoke of love, and now at the end of His ministry His love was still evident.

These men were not perfect, but Jesus loved them. That is comforting to us. Jesus loves us even with our faults. Even when we are selfish and ambitious, He loves us. He loved even to the end of His earthly life. He will love until the end of our lives and to the end of time. His love has no limit.

If someone stops loving us, generally we can make ourselves "fall out of love with them." However, Jesus loves even when our love has failed.

If we have His love, what else do we require? There are times we cannot comprehend His love. Why does He send some things we don't want and withhold those we desire greatly? Some answers we may never receive in this life.

As we look at the children of Israel and the provisions made for them in spite of their many mistakes and much complaining, we see a portrait of God's love. God is love.

We know some spouses who suddenly decide they no longer love their husband or wife and they leave to seek new adventure. Friends will sometimes decide they no longer have anything in common with a friend, totally ignoring the fact that they have been through many joys and heartaches together. Children will occasionally determine they don't need parents. There is no need to question God's love. He will love us to the end of our lives and to the end of time.

In our world of constant change, it is comforting to know that God is love and His love will never fail. He will be our shepherd and lead us by still waters. He will restore our souls and be with us when we walk through the valley of the shadow of death.

In response to this kind of love, how can we keep quiet about our heavenly Father? We should love to tell the story of His love. Regardless of today's circumstances, thank Him for His love, and rest assured that He loves you to the end.

Dear Lord, help me to never doubt Your love, even during those times when I cannot feel Your presence or see that You are handling the circumstances. I know You care and that I need to remain steadfast regardless of circumstances. Thank You for Your love—my unspeakable treasure.

NOTES

June
Visions of Hope
Shelby Aycock Harvell

Shelby Aycock Harvell from Millen, Georgia, is married to the Reverend Kenneth T. Harvell. They have three children: Kenneth Duane, of Lawrenceville, Georgia; Karen Denise, of Lilburn, Georgia; and Dana Kaye, of Hagerstown, Maryland. They have seven grandchildren: Talon, Kyle, Brent, Parker, Randi, Kali, and Kelsey.

Shelby has a bachelor of science degree from Lee College in elementary education K-9. She taught kindergarten for eight years with the Cleveland City School System. She and her husband have pastored in Tennessee and Georgia and worked in administration in Tennessee, Arizona, Maryland, Delaware, D.C., and Kentucky. Presently they are back in Cleveland, where her husband, Kenneth, serves as general director of Publications for the Church of God Publishing House.

June 1

Scripture: "For you have been my hope, O Sovereign Lord, my confidence since my youth" (Psalm 71:5).*

Every time we pray, sing praise, or murmur a blessing for good, we acknowledge the goodness and generosity of our loving heavenly Father. He gives us life. But He gives us one blessing, the value of which we cannot even comprehend—hope!

One definition of *hope* is "confidence in the future." However, it is so much more! The Hebrew word translated "hope" is *tiqvah,* which means to be "twisted or tied together like a cord." Psalm 71:5 assures us that the Lord is our hope and our trust. Hope is a cord that binds us to God.

Even in great tribulation or disaster when we sometimes almost lose hope . . . hope does not lose us! That cord is never cut. God's never-failing love (the unbroken cord) holds us. Because of hope, we too can wait for healing, wait for the morning, wait for the future that God has promised us.

My prayer for you as you read this month's devotions on hope is that you will feel this unbroken cord—the gift of hope that binds you to God. May He be your companion and guide and bring you the joy and confidence you need to face each new day.

June 2

Scripture: "My hope is in You" (Psalm 39:7, *NKJV*).

One thing our thoughts automatically turn to in June is new brides. Back before my time, brides had hope chests. They gathered things to be put away for that new home they were preparing to live in with their new husband. I remember when I received my white oak Lane cedar chest for my 16th Christmas. I, too, put a few things into it for my future home. It mostly contained keepsakes that I didn't want to lose. It still holds my children's wedding gowns and other valuables.

We can apply the "hope-chest" principle to our spiritual lives. How? By adding daily the things that cross our paths that help build us, mold us, and make us fit candidates for true servants of God. If we add daily to this "spiritual hope chest," we will be sensitive to His leading and His will for our lives. To accomplish our goal, we have to be found sitting at His feet. We must turn our eyes toward our final home—the one for which we have been filling our "hope chest."

*The Scripture references used for this month's devotions are from the *New International Version* unless otherwise indicated.

194

Lord, help us to lift these empty hope chests to You. If there are rags of fear, inertia, or depression in them, pull them out and help us fill our chests with the "white robes and raiment" that will be pleasing in Your sight.

June 3

Scripture: "But as for me, I will always have hope" (Psalm 71:14).

When I was 2 or 3 years old, my dad walked into my grandmother's kitchen just in time to see me cut the vinyl tablecloth with a pair of scissors. Immediately he asked, "Shelby, who cut the tablecloth?"

My answer was, "Dot-tee." Dot was my older sister. At that age, I never would take the blame for my actions. It was always "Dot-tee" who was responsible, even if she were in school at the time.

From the accounts I have heard concerning these episodes, I was never allowed to get away with dodging the blame, but it seems I never gave up hope. I still tried over and over again.

Our hope in Christ should be just as devout. We need to keep trying to please Him and do those things pleasing to Him. Even if the actions don't always turn out the way we want them to, we can't stop trying. We can't always see the good that results when we try. It is the lifetime of commitment that counts, and we can never afford to stop trying.

Lord, let us renew our commitment to You each day and keep You ever in mind in our actions.

June 4

Scripture: "Put your hope in God" (Psalm 42:5).

When my young brother was around 6 years old, he had terrible headaches. I remember one night he came to Mom's bed sobbing and holding his ear. She asked if he wanted her to pray for him. He nodded yes. Mom was desperate that night and gave Jay and his headaches to God. She knew it was out of her hands. In just a few minutes his headache eased off, and it never returned.

We try to hold on to things in our lives and never realize that they are completely out of our hands. Instead, we need to hold on to God and trust Him to sort things out for us. We make so many mistakes, but we can depend on Him to always make the right decision. We may not think so at the time. Later when we look back and can see the whole picture, then we can finally admit, "God, You made the right choice."

Father, help us to know when it is time to let go and wait for You to work out the problems in our life. Thank You for letting us sit at Your feet today.

June 5

Scripture: "Hope deferred makes the heart sick" (Proverbs 13:12).

We rode the school bus to school, since our home was out in the country. When the bus left the school, it intersected with the highway. It turned right to go to our house. Then it made a circle around and came out on the same highway about two miles from where it entered to begin the route.

We were the first to be picked up in the early morning (7 a.m.). In the afternoon we were the first off the bus. We had a little first grader who was the last to be picked up in the morning and she wanted to be the first off in the afternoon. When her feet hit the top step of the bus, she'd start begging, "Please, Mr. Charlie, take me home first." She refused to sit down unless it was on the floor right beside him, and she would never let up on her begging.

The driver became so exasperated with her. Sometimes he would tell her he would take her to the end of the road to her house and she could walk the two miles home. She would never agree to this until he started to turn in the opposite direction, and then she'd agree. This incident did not happen just occasionally, but every day.

We have to be tenacious in our hold on God like this little girl that hated to ride around the long bus route. Yes, there will be trials and tribulations, but there will also be joy, peace, and a few mountaintop experiences.

How firm is our hold on God concerning our lost loved ones? Can we truly say that we "pray without ceasing"? If not, then we need to pull ourselves up and realize that one of these days we are going to a new home in heaven. If we ever want to see our precious ones again, we must make every effort to see that they are ready to meet their God.

Lord, help us remember our lost loved ones in prayer this day, and to keep them ever lifted up to You.

June 6

Scripture: "Dreaming instead of doing is foolishness" (Ecclesiastes 5:7, *TLB*).

Have you ever watched a child mimic someone sing, cook, or play the piano? When I was a child, my younger sister and brother and I mimicked in our play on a daily basis. We played church, and could I ever play a make-believe piano! I could sing, pray, preach, pray for the sick, and drag those sinners to the altar!

Children will try to do the things they see going on around them. Adults often wish they could do the same.

Sometimes we procrastinate doing things we really could do. We just keep putting it off . . . tomorrow we will have more time . . . tomorrow the sun will be shining . . . tomorrow the rain will stop, and so forth.

We need to stop dreaming of the things we cannot do and do those things we can—read that book we have been saving, visit that friend who is so ill, read to that grandchild, or just take time to smell the roses!

It is great to have dreams, but we have to do the doable. What could you do right now, today, to fulfill one of your dreams? Determine to do it before this day passes.

Lord, give us the active faith of a little child.

June 7

Scripture: "And now abide faith, hope, love, these three . . . " (1 Corinthians 13:13, *NKJV*).

Faith, hope, love—the three permanents of our Christian walk with God. Do you pray for more hope? Have you ever thought about what scientists are discovering about the value of hope? Elizabeth Sherrill reports in *Daily Guideposts* (1993, p. 38) about psychologist Charles Snyder, of the University of Kansas, who tested thousands of college freshmen on a "hope scale." He found the level of hope a more accurate predictor of future grades than SAT scores.

In this same article, Timothy Elliott, psychologist at Virginia Commonwealth University, reports that spinal-injury patients with high hope have a much better recovery record than those with identical injuries and low hope. Dr. Aaron Beck of the University of Pennsylvania has developed a lack-of-hope scale to identify high-risk mental patients.

The dictionary says that hope is an "expectation of good." Vaclav Havel of Czechoslovakia was imprisoned by the Communist regime and still he was able to write, "I carry hope in my heart. Hope is a feeling that life and work have meaning despite the state of the world around you. Life without hope is an empty, boring, and useless life. It is as big a gift as life itself."

Should we pray for more hope in our lives? It is a definite "yes" for me. Hope touches all parts of our lives, and our hope in Jesus Christ is the mainstay of our Christianity.

Lord, renew our hope today. Give us a positive attitude even when we face impossible circumstances.

June 8

Scripture: "Having been justified by his grace, we . . . become heirs having the hope of eternal life" (Titus 3:7).

To the writers of the New Testament, hope meant first of all the hope of heaven, the expectation of eternity filled with joy in the presence of God. Do we hope . . . long for . . . eagerly long for heaven?

My dad had a paralyzing stroke one year before his death. He would beg God to release him from his prison on earth and take him to his eternal home. He had lost his hope for things of this world; his only hope was for that home above. This was the promise he had lived for, worked for, anticipated! His funeral was a celebration! Of course we missed him. We still do, but we know where he is and how happy he is in the presence of God.

Just before Mary Stuart, Queen of Scots, was put to death, she penned this in her prison cell:

> O Master and Maker! my hope is in Thee.
> My Jesus, dear Saviour! now set my soul free.
> From this my prison, my spirit uprisen,
> soars upward to Thee.

Father, help us to realize and understand that our eternal hope is all we really have that is dependable. Our wealth, health, even life itself, are not dependable—only our hope in You.

June 9

Scripture: "But this I call to mind, and therefore I have hope: the steadfast love of the Lord never ceases" (Lamentations 3:21, 22, *NRSV*).

Have you ever noticed the way your mom would turn her house plants away from the sun? The plant will start leaning toward the light, and it will be one-sided if never turned. This persistence in plants is called *heliotropism*—"turning toward the sun."

There is a word that can be used for this same quality in human life—the ever-repeated turning to God—no matter what traumas come our way. This word is *hope*.

The poet John Milton felt this hope when he lost his sight. Totally blind, dependent on others not only to set down his words but for the simplest acts of living, he could say in Sonnet XXII:

> . . .Yet I argue not
> Against Heaven's Hand, or Will, nor bate one jot
> Of Heart or Hope; but still bear up, and steer
> Right onward. . . .

Father, no matter the hardships, please let us continually seek the warmth of Your Son and keep turning our faces toward You.

June 10

Scripture: "We have this hope as an anchor for the soul, firm and secure" (Hebrews 6:19).

Hope is often represented in Christian art as an anchor. An anchor weighs down, holds in place. Our position in God is a stable one in which hope, as an anchor, keeps us steady through the changes and chances of daily life.

The foundation of our hope—God's love, God's provision, God's power—is not always visible. But His love is real. When our hope is fastened to Him, then passing events—a job layoff, surgery, death of a loved one—cannot dislodge us from our solid place in Him.

Our anchor will hold us steady and will help us keep our perspective so we can press on toward the goals God has given us. He will help us hold that hope close to our hearts—not swaying to the right or to the left. Then at the end of our earthly journey, we can be considered faithful when we enter that heavenly gate.

Father, make the anchor strong that holds me fast to You today.

June 11

Scripture: "Therefore, since we are surrounded by such a great cloud of witnesses . . ." (Hebrews 12:1).

Sometime during the week that my maternal grandmother was killed in a car accident, my father had a dream. He dreamed he saw his mother, who had been dead for several years, leaning over a balcony beckoning someone very joyously. He was very upset and never mentioned the dream to anyone because he thought he was the one she was welcoming to heaven. When Mom called him home from work and broke the news about her mother's accident, he told Mom, "So that was who she was welcoming." He then told her about his dream.

The hope we have of finally reaching our eternal home is what keeps us going in spite of the hard times the devil may throw in our paths. We can have that assurance of seeing and being with our departed loved ones again. Will your family circle be complete? It will be if we will sit daily at the feet of Jesus and keep our petitions for their salvation ever before Him.

Father, keep us where we can touch You at all times. Help us never lose the faith and hope of seeing all our loved ones with us in heaven.

June 12

Scripture: "But the eyes of the Lord are on those who fear him, on those whose hope is in his unfailing love" (Psalm 33:18).

My husband and I had just finished building our retirement home on family property in south Georgia. A bulldozer had been working all morning clearing the yard around the house. My mom came up to see our finished work. We were in the front yard, and she asked where the long-ago, unused roadbed was located. It was only a few feet in front of us, and as I walked to the old roadbed, I glanced down to the ground. What I saw stopped me dead in my tracks! The largest diamondback rattler I have ever seen was diagonally stretched across the old roadbed. The snake was about six inches wide. The black diamond stripes on its back were about an inch wide.

Now when I think back, the snake was beautiful with its deep, gold skin and black diamond stripes. However, at the time, it appeared to me as only dangerous and evil, and I couldn't get away fast enough. It was so serene lying there, so still that my mom wanted to move closer to see if it was dead.

Since then people have told me that when a rattler stretches out in a still position it is getting ready to strike. If I had not glanced down directly in front of me, I would have stepped on that snake. It would be hard to convince me that God wasn't in that swift glance. I didn't know the danger was there, but He did! I didn't know anything was in front of me, but He did! I didn't know that only about four feet kept me from being snakebitten, but He did!

We don't ever know when we will need God's protective hand to cover us. That is why it is so urgent for us to sit at His feet at all times so that we can rest in the assurance of His protection.

Lord, keep Your protective hand upon us this day. Be our go-before God and push the rocks and stubble out of our paths as we walk toward You.

June 13

Scripture: "You are my refuge and my shield" (Psalm 119:114).

One rainy afternoon my family left my sister's house in north Georgia heading back to our pastorate in Savannah. We were on a two-lane country road. As we descended a long hill, an 18-wheeler gas tanker came around a curve facing us. As the driver started to straighten his truck out of the curve, it jackknifed. The tanker trailer was coming down the hill beside the cab of the truck. The truck's back wheels were off the road on our side. Just before we got to the truck, my husband never braked but turned down into a deep ravine on wet grass. Then he came right back up as we went around the truck. As we reached the blacktop, I noticed a concrete culvert about six feet from where our car came back up.

Talk about God being our refuge and our shield! It was a long time later that day before either my husband or I regained our strength. We can lean on the Lord when we can't lean on each other. We can lean on Him when the pavement is swept away from under us. He is our rock. He is our source. He is our strength.

Whatever is in your path today that you just can't handle—He can and will handle it if you will just let Him. Why not give Him the opportunity to be your rock, your source, your strength.

Jesus, thank You for letting us sit at Your feet today and give all our problems to You.

June 14

Scripture: ". . . a still small voice" (1 Kings 19:12, KJV).

When my baby daughter was born, she was allergic to milk fat. We almost lost her when she was six weeks old. She lived on soybean milk. Just before her second birthday we were visiting my mom for Thanksgiving. Without thinking, someone gave Dana a buttered biscuit. When Sunday came around we had not had one night's sleep.

My husband particularly wanted me in church that Sunday night. He suggested someone keep Dana in the nursery because you could hear her breathing in the next room. We had a wonderful service that night. Right in the middle of his message, my husband stopped and gave an opportunity for a healing line. I went up and asked them to pray for Dana. I did not know that the lady keeping her in the nursery had her right behind me.

It was close to midnight when we finally got home that night.

Kenneth asked me if I wanted him to fix the vaporizer for Dana. That "still small voice" whispered in my ear, "Are you going to trust Me?"

I didn't answer my husband, so he didn't fix the vaporizer. For the first time in days, we got a good night's sleep! After this healing, Dana's favorite snack was butter and bread.

God will lead us and will speak to us in the "still small voice" if we will just heed His call. After talking to Him, unloading your burdens and petitions, give Him praise. Then it is time to be still and listen for that "still small voice" as you sit at His feet today.

Father, let us find the time today in our busy schedule to sit at Your feet and listen to Your "still small voice."

June 15

Scripture: "He always lives to make intercession for them" (Hebrews 7:25, *NKJV*).

When my daughter went into labor with her daughter, I was visiting with my mom about 300 miles away. Her husband called us at 8 that morning and said she was about 30 minutes away from delivery and for us to stay put until he called us back.

At 10:30 he still had not called, so Mom started preparing lunch for us. About 10:50 I missed Mother and went to look for her. She had slipped into another room and was standing looking out the window with tears streaming down her face. She said something told her to pray for Denise and pray right now! Fifteen minutes later the call came that I had a new granddaughter.

When we reached the hospital I was relating this incident to Denise and Roger when he said, "What time did you say?" I told him and he started stammering and telling me what was happening at that exact time. The cord was wrapped around the baby's neck. The doctor had to cut the cord before the baby could be delivered. All the time she was in labor the cord was pulling tighter. The baby was so blue that Roger thought she was dead. He literally turned sick.

Today she is a healthy 6-year-old and will be entering first grade in a few days. My mom was interceding for her when she needed it. We didn't know the circumstances, but God did. Christ is enthroned at the right hand of the Father interceding for us. He is the royal Intercessor, and that is exactly the role He has chosen for us. He loves us so much He desires us to intercede with Him as He intercedes with the Father.

If you ever have a special urge to pray for someone, please don't hesitate. Intercede for them at that moment. You have no idea what the person is facing.

Father, help us to follow Your urging and not fail to intercede for the people of this world.

June 16

Scripture: "Hope does not disappoint us, because God has poured out his love into our hearts" (Romans 5:5).

Kathy and Dan Blackburn, missionaries to Haiti, said they became involved in a children's orphanage when an old grandmother, almost dead with disease, brought a tiny newborn and insisted they take her. Though she could hardly walk, she walked for three hours to bring the child to them. Her daughter had died giving birth to the baby, and there was no one else left who could care for it. Despite her frailty, hope was alive and guided her forward. What good would it do the old woman, or the baby, if the Balckburns had just told her about God's love and then sent them away?

To keep hope shining in the eyes of those less fortunate than we are, we have to not only share the story of God's love, we have to also show God's love operating in our own lives. We have to be concerned with the unfortunate ones God sends across our paths. True, they need our prayers, but often they need so much more. And usually there is something else the Lord wants us to do along with offering to pray for them.

My dad almost carried this principle to the extreme. At least most of his family thought so. I would dare say, you could count on one hand the times he failed to help when called upon, providing he had the means. That is a lot to say for an 81-year-old man. If he was chided, he responded with something like this: "The Lord gave it to me, and He will replace it."

Jesus, I pray that You will give us more compassion and love for one another. Enable us to keep hope shining in others' eyes as we sit at Your feet today.

June 17

Scripture: "Listen and hear my voice; pay attention and hear what I say" (Isaiah 28:23).

Several years ago in our adult Sunday school class, our teacher was challenging us to witness to the people who worked with us. Since I was a kindergarten schoolteacher, I automatically pushed it aside, saying to myself, *Those professionals don't want to change their minds about God.*

It still bothered me, so I started praying that God would make me sensitive to any opportunities that came my way to witness for Him. Suddenly, it seemed that during my planning period, someone would just drop in to chat and start sharing a problem. I also noticed that parents picking up their children from school would share a problem. I had been missing these opportunities because my ears were not tuned to God's voice. I wasn't sensitive to the needs and hurts around me because I was too busy!

Did you know that ministers' wives can be too busy doing God's work for God's people to keep their own relationship with God where it ought to be? We can be so busy making sure everyone else's children are living a good Christian life that we push our own children in the background. Who will make sure they make it?

I once told my husband that if we spent our whole lives helping others' children make it to heaven and neglected just one of our own, we would have failed to fulfill our first responsibility to God as Christian parents. Think about it. If you have been so busy, even with church affairs, that you have neglected to devote enough time to one of your little ones, stop today. Do as much as you can, but save time for your own children and keep that hope of eternal life shining in their eyes.

Father, help us to take stock of our lives today and make sure we do all that we can to help those around us—especially our own little children You have given us to bless and nurture.

June 18

Scripture: "Let us hold fast the confession of our hope without wavering, for He who promised is faithful" (Hebrews 10:23, *NKJV*).

My daddy was called into the ministry when he was very young, but my grandmother would not consent for him to go to Bible school to prepare himself. Eventually he became so discouraged that he went back on the Lord when I was a small child. When I was in high school, it was just Mom, the smaller children, and I who attended church. Dad was in and out.

It was all planned that I attend Lee College in the fall. During the summer I could not get away from the feeling that I just could not leave Mom alone! Every Sunday when he was at home, I would beg Dad to go to church with us. With tears in his eyes, he refused. I got so desperate that I felt maybe it would take my death for my dad to be saved.

He and Mom brought me to Lee College and helped get me settled in my dormitory. Sunday night before they were to go home the next morning, Dad agreed to go to North Cleveland Church with us. When the pastor gave the altar call, he all but called my dad's name. Finally, Dad stumbled out of his seat and gave his heart back to God.

From that time on he did everything he could to make up for those "lost years" when God did not direct his life. We never gave up hope; we kept pressing; we kept believing; we kept trusting God that He would bring him back to us and to Himself. And He was faithful!

Does it seem like you are fighting a losing battle? Do you feel all alone and that no one cares? Don't give up hope; keep pressing; keep believing. God is faithful! One of my favorite choruses we sing in church is:

> But "I know whom I have believed,
> And am persuaded that He is able
> To keep that which I've committed
> Unto Him against that day."

Father, I pray that You will give encouragement where it is needed today so that Your children will have the strength to keep believing for that miracle.

June 19

Scripture: "But I have prayed for you, that your faith should not fail" (Luke 22:32, *NKJV*).

A wise man once said, "The chief glory of man is not that he never fails but that he arises from each failure." Whatever failures or whatever sins we may have committed, God offers us the chance to begin again. There is the hope of another chance for those who have failed.

During the Great Depression many, many people lost all of their material possessions. My mom told us many stories of how destitute they were and how a man would plow behind a mule from daylight to dark for just 25 cents. Many people just couldn't live with the hopelessness that existed. Instead they ended their lives. So many days and even years went by that they couldn't see a light at the end of the tunnel.

Unless you have personally lived through such a time, it is hard to imagine how bad it really was. I do know if we will place our hope and our trust in the one living God, He will sustain and keep us. This does not mean we will not go through the valleys or that our paths will not be as hard as others.' It does mean He will never leave us nor forsake us, and we can have joy and peace in our hearts despite the circumstances around us. Remember the hard places in Jesus' life—He had to face a cross on a hill. Are our troubles that bad?

Let me repeat: There is nothing that affords us greater hope than the fact that life gives to all of us the glory of another chance.

Lord, give us this day our daily bread; lead us not into temptation, but lead us ever toward You. Let us use our failures as "stepping stones" and "ladders" that will help us reach Your side.

June 20

Scripture: "I can do all things through Christ who strengthens me" (Philippians 4:13, *NKJV*).

All of us meet disappointments at one time or another. Some feel that life is one tarnished dream on top of another and become utterly discouraged. If only we could realize that every person who has accomplished anything worthwhile has had to meet and overcome reverses.

God called Moses to lead His people out of bondage, but Moses had to pass through 80 years of preparation before this hope could be realized. He had to spend 40 years in Midian before he could even start on his goal. Then he had to deal with Pharaoh. Later he had to deal with his own people who were often suspicious, critical, unappreciative, and prone to forget God.

I read a statement that said, "middle age is the period of life when people build a pigsty out of the materials which in their youth they had gathered to build a temple to the stars." Most of us start with high ideals and dreams, but along the way we let our house of dreams be destroyed by the persistent gnawing away of the termites of life. Why do we let our dreams vanish like a puff of wind? Were they foolish to begin with? Were we just spoiled children instead of adults? Were our ideals deserted because we were not taught to stick with a task until it was finished? Was our attention span too narrow? Or, are we like the man who said, "I am working on my second million; the first one is too hard to get"?

Some of us have the idea that if a thing is difficult or unpleasant, it isn't worthwhile. Life was not always pleasant for Nancy Hanks Lincoln, but she inspired her young son Abe to be somebody. Life was not easy for John Bunyan, but while imprisoned in Bedford Jail, he wrote *Pilgrim's Progress*. Susanna Wesley must have found life hard at times, but she did not give up hope. She did not desert her 17 children.

She inspired them to change their world. Someone has said of Beethoven who was deaf that he "beat out upon the anvil of his own soul symphonies that have thrilled the heart of the world."

It cost Jesus something to become the world's Savior. He could not do it through ease. He could not just step off the pinnacle of the Temple. He could not do it by a miracle. He could not do it through world domination. He had to go the way of struggle, disappointment, sorrow, Gethsemane, Golgotha, the tomb.

It may cost us something—struggle, hardships, pain, even death—to accomplish those goals and dreams set before us. God gives us the strength to accomplish those dreams in the hope of eternal life with Him in heaven. We can do all things through Him who strengthens us.

Lord, make us stronger and more determined today than ever before to be all that You would have us to be.

June 21

Scripture: "Put your trust in the Lord your God, and you will be established" (2 Chronicles 20:20, *NASB*).

Even though I was raised on the farm, I never was comfortable around farm animals. My brothers and sisters rode horses all the time, but not me. When I was in high school, my younger brother and sister rode the horse over to our grandparents' house. I walked. When we started home, those two rascals persuaded me to ride. They were supposed to lead the horse. When I was on the horse's back, instead of leading him, they slapped him on the rump. He didn't stop running until he got home.

I had placed my hope and trust in Jay and Jo, but they let me down! Have you ever been let down by someone you trusted? Did you know that God is the only One we can put our hope and trust in and know without a shadow of a doubt that He will never leave us nor forsake us but will go with us all the way?

Aren't you ready to lay that heavy burden at His feet today? Make a new commitment and give it all to Him.

Lord, if there is one who reads this devotional that does not have complete faith and trust in You, please give her new faith and new trust. Make her more determined than ever to give all her burdens to You.

June 22

Scripture: "He will give His angels charge concerning You; and on their hands they will bear You up, lest You strike Your foot against a stone" (Matthew 4:6, *NASB*).

When I was very small, I was very daring in that I loved to walk on narrow places—like on the outside of the banister around the porch. One day my aunt came into the room and I was balancing on the arm of the rocking chair. She was afraid I'd fall before she got to me, so she was talking to keep me calm. She said, "Shelby, aren't you afraid you will fall?" But I replied, "You're watching out for me, ain't you?"

Though I was very young, I knew that she was interested in my welfare and if I did fall, she would be there to catch me. I felt secure! Do you have a feeling of security in your daily walk? Do you walk through life with joy and peace, or are you one who is always afraid something bad is going to happen? That is not the way God wants us to live. We can overcome those fears if we will only depend on the One who will always catch us. This reminds me of the poem of the two birds:

Overheard in an Orchard

Said the robin to the sparrow:
"I should really like to know
Why these anxious human beings
Rush about and worry so."
Said the sparrow to the robin:
"Friend, I think that it must be
That they have no heavenly
Father
Such as cares for you and me."
—Elizabeth Cheney

(The Treasure Chest: Harper & Row, p. 138.)

Father, give us the peace and joy needed in our lives this day, we pray.

June 23

Scripture: "For He will give His angels charge concerning you, to guard you in all your ways" (Psalm 91:11, *NASB*).

When I was 5 years old, my dad had an emergency appendectomy and was in the hospital. We lived 10 miles in the country with the closest neighbor about a mile away. We had a kerosene refrigerator, and Mom had put fuel in it before going to bed. We had all finally settled down for the night.

About midnight, someone called my mom's name, "Exie." She was tired and so she only grunted. The voice called again, but this time louder, "Exie." She sat up in bed and answered. Then the kerosene refrigerator exploded in the dining room. In just a few minutes the flames were out the front windows of the house. My mom, grandma, and all four children escaped without harm. Someone was looking out for us, protecting us from harm and danger that night.

Have you ever been to the place where you did all you could do and then said, "OK, God, it's out of my hands. I give it to You"? He knows what we are facing and what we need Him to do for us, but He wants us to talk to Him and ask Him for His help. He will give it!

Lord, guide and protect us this day and increase our faith and dependency upon You. Be our go-before God today.

June 24

Scripture: "Call to me and I will answer you" (Jeremiah 33:3).

Daddy was killing and processing hogs for the winter the year my sister was 2 years old. She was out by the barn playing with one of the sticks used to hang the butchered hog. The stick was sharp on the end and Dot fell on the stick. The pointed edge went in under her chin and came out in her mouth. Daddy grabbed her, took her to Mama on the porch, and then jerked the stick out. When he did, blood began to spurt from the hole with each heartbeat. Mama and Daddy were both paralyzed with fear when Aunt Myrtle, Daddy's sister, came on the porch and saw what was happening. She immediately began to spin round and round, speaking in tongues. The blood stopped immediately. Later they carried Dot the 10 miles to town for the hole to be stitched.

That was indeed one of the miracles in my family. That small child would never have made it 10 miles in a horse and buggy. But when the Holy Spirit hit Aunt Myrtle, He was right there, and He was in time.

Sometimes we don't have but a split second to invoke His mercy when a catastrophe hits. You may just have time to say, "Jesus." He'll be there!

Father, we thank You that we can call on You, and it doesn't take an hour or a week or a year for You to be there. You are there even as we speak. Keep us this day.

June 25

Scripture: "Martha was distracted with all her preparations; and she came up to Him, and said, 'Lord, do You not care that my sister has left me to do all the serving alone?'" (Luke 10:40, *NASB*).

We were visiting my sister's family during the Christmas my son was 2. My nephews had received football outfits for Christmas, and they dressed Duane up in their outfits. We were in the bedroom admiring the new baby girl when Duane came in all dressed out and said, "Look, Mom, I'm a peetball payer." The words all ran together and we were all distracted by the baby, so we couldn't understand Duane's speech. He got so excited and furious as he speedily repeated his very important announcement that no one could understand.

Have you ever had a time in your life when you were so pleased with yourself and no one—I mean, no one—even noticed your accomplishments? Or have you really struggled to make a program go over the top, and someone else got all the recognition? Did you feel somewhat like that small "peetball payer"?

What we have to stop and realize and take to heart is the same message Jesus gave to Martha: "You are cumbered with so many things but there is only one thing that counts—sitting at His feet and doing His will" (see v. 41).

Duane's hope of recognition in his new outfit was just as frustrating as Martha in her hope that Jesus would command Mary to help in the kitchen. Are you too busy doing "things" so that you are letting the really important things slip by you? Just take a few minutes and analyze your life, and ask Jesus to help you get things in the right perspective.

Jesus, help us keep You at the top of our agenda this day.

June 26

Scripture: "The Lord is near to all who call upon Him, to all who call upon Him in truth" (Psalm 145:18, *NKJV*).

When my sister and her family were pastoring in Savannah, Georgia, their son Keith had misbehaved and was sent to his room to pray. Later his dad went to ask if he had made everything right with the Lord, to which Keith answered: "That's just the trouble, Dad. I've tried, but I just can't get in touch with Him."

Sometimes it seems that we can't get in touch with God. We feel just like Keith felt—we've tried, but just can't get in touch with Him. Could it be that we know we are asking amiss? Even though you know you shouldn't be asking, you want it anyway!

It is true that we can't see all the particulars that are ahead in our lives, and we may be praying for something that would ultimately end in failure. That is why it is always good to end such petitions with

"Father, not my will but Thine be done." He sees the future, and He knows what is best for us. Can you end your prayer this way today?

Father, let Your will be done in our lives today, and lead us in Your way. Keep us in the palm of Your hand.

June 27

Scripture: "My grace is sufficient for you" (2 Corinthians 12:9, *NKJV*).

When we suffer from a hard blow, our immediate reaction is likely to be one of incredulity. "It isn't so! This can't happen to me!" We think we must be dreaming, and we react in a daze. Gradually the shock subsides, and the chilly winds of pain and grief press upon us the realization of our situation. We realize that tragedy has overtaken us and we are indeed in the situation that denies or destroys our previous lifestyle.

For most people a relatively short time is required to bring them to the realization of their changed situation. Then begins a much longer process of adjustment—the first step of which is acceptance. This acceptance involves emotional and spiritual responses that are at the very core of our being. We may have an outward response and action, but underneath may be resentments, protests, and escapes that will dangerously distort and twist us.

There was a widow who kept setting a place at the table for her late husband, and a mother who would not part with the wardrobe of a daughter who had died. I've heard of parents who locked up their departed child's room and refused to let it even be entered. My dad has been dead three years, but one of my brothers gets very upset every time we try to put Dad's things away. Pretense seldom accomplishes the purpose for which it is assumed. It keeps a person from the hope she might have if she adjusted and found her potential in her present situation.

Many people, when confronted with tragedy, resent their misfortune as unjust. They rail against fate and curse God. They argue that life should have turned out differently for them, and they develop bitterness in their heart. Disappointment is understandable, but resentment is deplorable. Maybe life should have turned out differently and the current frustration is a heavy burden. Yet, now that it has happened, our only hope lies in preventing bitterness from standing between the tragic present and a possible future. Resentment itself is a dead-end street!

Religious faith can lead us to a solid hope only if we begin by acknowledging our predicament. To resent the actual and wish the factors were changed is not constructive. We have to begin where we are. We have to accept our situation, then we can sit at Jesus' feet and He will give us the hope and faith we need to make a new start.

My prayer for you today is that if you are knocked down and are at the very bottom, you will turn your thoughts and put your trust in that higher power that is able to deliver you.

June 28

Scripture: "Fear not, little flock; for it is your Father's good pleasure to give you the kingdom" (Luke 12:32, KJV).

What a marvelous promise! What rich hope it brings! Jesus points us beyond Himself to a Presence at the heart of the universe who is waiting to pour out blessings upon those who are rooted and grounded in Him. This is the secret of the hope Christian faith can bring, for Jesus reveals a God who is an infinite source of wisdom, power, goodness, and love.

Martin Luther said, "Everything that is done in the world is done by hope. No husbandman would sow one grain of corn if he hopes not it would grow and become seed; no bachelor would marry a wife if he hoped not to have children; no merchant or tradesman would set himself to work if he did not hope to reap benefit thereby."

After visiting the Farmer's Market, I observed to my husband how long it took the farmers to collect and pick their produce offered for sale. Since I was raised on the farm, I knew what was involved—timewise and moneywise. We may not be farmers, but whatever the job, we still doggedly try to do our best day after day. If we don't have hope in the future, what can we do? We all have the same blind hope which grows out of ordinary experiences.

Most of us operate on this basis. The woman working at a job she does not enjoy, the couple maintaining a marriage for which they are not suited, the person living with the discomfort of asthma or arthritis—all are people who exist from day to day and year to year in a rugged faithfulness to a pattern of performance, alleviated only by the blind hope that some day some new and surprising turn will bring relief. We have this basic impulse to move on toward tomorrow. If we have our faith and trust in Jesus Christ, we have a hope that far exceeds this basic, instinctual hope. We have hope of eternal life with our Lord.

"Fondly do we hope," said Abraham Lincoln in his second inaugural address, as in the midst of conflict he looked forward to the end of the scourge of war. Whatever may be the burden that weighs heavily upon us, we do look forward. Fondly do we hope! The Creator in His wisdom made us so that we are not easily defeated. Alexander Pope said, "Hope springs eternal in the human breast." We are so glad this is part of our makeup, but our hope of eternal life keeps us keeping on.

Father, we are so glad that the hope placed within us glows brightly and the hope of seeing You never diminishes.

June 29

Scripture: "In My Father's house are many dwelling places; if it were not so, I would have told you; for I go to prepare a place for you. . . . I will come again, and receive you to Myself; that where I am, there you may be also" (John 14:2, 3, *NASB*).

We had always lived in the house with my grandmother, but she wanted a house of her own. So Dad built her a little three-room, green-shingled house next door to her daughter. She was living there when she had her first stroke and was never able to live by herself again, but she never reconciled herself to this situation. Whether she was at our house or her daughter's, if it was at all possible, she would slip away and go to her house. We would find her trying to cook on a stove that had been disconnected. She wanted to go home!

Sister Evie was in her 90s and had been serving the Lord for more than 60 years when she was hospitalized for the last time. For three or four days before she died, she would hold her hand out toward the door in intensive care and beckon someone to enter. She'd say, "Come on in, Jesus; I've been waiting on You and I'm ready to go." She welcomed her Lord and her homegoing.

We never know when Jesus will be coming to take us home. Are you as anxious as Granny Aycock and Sister Evie were to go home? Can you truly say that all is well with your soul and in any split second you would be ready to be "caught up together with Him in the clouds"? If not, please take a few moments now and make things right between your soul and your Savior.

Father, give us the courage and the hunger to make all the wrinkles smooth in our garments today. Let us anticipate and long for Your coming.

June 30

Scripture: "Blessed is he whose help is the God of Jacob, whose hope is in the Lord his God" (Psalm 146:5).

When the 1900s were still in their teens, Luther B. Bridgers was a popular songwriter and singing evangelist who traveled the revival camp-meeting circuit. One of his songs, "He Keeps Me Singing," was being sung in churches and religious meetings from coast to coast. In its original form it had four verses and a chorus:

> There's within my heart a melody,
> Jesus whispers sweet and low;
> "Fear not, I am with thee, peace, be still,"
> In all of life's ebb and flow.

> All my life was wrecked by sin and strife,
> Discord filled my heart with pain;
> Jesus swept across the broken strings,
> Stirred the slumb'ring chords again.

> Feasting on the riches of His grace,
> Resting 'neath His shelt'ring wing;
> Always looking on His smiling face,
> That is why I shout and sing.

> Soon He's coming back to welcome me,
> Far beyond the starry sky;
> I shall wing my flight to worlds unknown,
> I shall reign with Him on high.

> Chorus

> Jesus, Jesus, Jesus,
> Sweetest name I know;
> Fills my every longing,
> Keeps me singing as I go.

The fifth verse was written six years after the song was first published and made popular. But it is the final verse (now listed as verse 4 in most hymnals) that shows the real meaning of the song that Jesus gives and the depth of character that plumbed the soul of L.B. Bridgers.

Returning to his home in Kansas after a weeklong meeting, he noticed from the train window that a fire was burning fiercely in his city. He paused a moment to offer prayer for the people involved in that tragedy.

Stepping into a carriage that would take him to his house, he noticed the fire was in his section of town. Getting closer, the fire seemed to be on his street, and as he turned the last corner, he realized it was his house that was ablaze.

Leaping from the carriage, he was restrained by the neighbors. One of them said, "It's over. There's nothing you can do. You've lost everything."

"What do you mean . . . everything?" he asked. Slowly and softly the neighbor answered, "Everything . . . your house, your possessions, your wife, and your two children. Everything."

Bridgers sat alone on a stump in his front yard in stunned silence, the smoke still rising from the embers of what had been his home . . . even his life. Then, without getting up, he took some paper from his pocket and wrote these words for his favorite song:

Though sometimes He leads thru waters deep,
Trials fall across the way;
Though sometimes the path seems rough and steep,
See His footprints all the way.

Now that is what I call hope!

Father, I pray that our hope and faith in You have grown stronger and that our anchor has been made more secure in You during this month of devotions. Keep us ever near You is our prayer.

NOTES

July
Daily Challenges
Beverly Simmons Richardson

Beverly Simmons Richardson was born and reared in Canton, Ohio, where she was converted to Christ as a teenager in the Canton Church of God. Her college education included Lee College, where she was elected by her classmates as Miss Lee College. Two additional years of college training were experienced at the Ohio State University in Columbus and at the University of South Florida in Tampa.

Beverly and her husband, Carl, evangelized in 30 states and ministered in many foreign countries prior to their first church pastorate in Ashland, Ohio. Through their pastorates in Ohio, Chicago, Illinois, and Lakeland, Florida, she served as leader of local Ladies Ministries. She was a regular on the nationally syndicated *Power Unlimited* telecast and *Forward in Faith* radio broadcast aired in all 50 states and 87 foreign countries.

Beverly has written three books and has created a popular cassette tape album especially for women, titled *Women of the Word*. She regularly teaches in overseas crusade ministries, sponsored by Carl Richardson Ministries. She and Carl are the parents of four children: Paul, Juanelle, Christi, and Jonathan; and four grandsons.

July 1

Scripture: "Thou hast set all the borders of the earth: thou hast made summer and winter" (Psalm 74:17).

It's the middle of summer now—when the livin' is easy.

Looking out at the grass and shrubs growing at an alarming rate, it's almost hard to remember how I longed for the spring. But I do remember seeing the earth repent of its icy hold on nature and melt with contrition as it welcomed the sun to restore it.

Trees that seemed by every look and action to be dead began, very slowly, to feel a surge of life moving in them again. And seemingly as momentum gathered, this new life touched every limb of the trees and they broke forth in joyous beauty.

And now as I look out the open window, I realize how much I love it. I have waited through the long, dark winter for springtime and summertime. I enjoyed watching the trees take on newness of life. Clumps of green that I either never noticed or thought were useless weeds suddenly displayed their loveliest bloom because they had been restored and revived. I must admit that around February every year I long for the dying of winter . . . and the arrival of summer.

There comes a wintertime to most every heart. Finney said that periodically he had to come to a time of renewal and breakthrough.

Christmas Evans once became aware of a cold heart and went into a secluded spot for prayer. While there, he received this renewal . . . a revival within about which he later wrote in his journal: "That prayer was like the breaking up of a cold, hard winter."

If there is life in you, you have felt like that—like God needed to revive you . . . the breath and life were gone. Where was the joy?

The routine of living from day to day takes its toll, and we become satisfied to just do each day's accomplishments routinely . . . to do less and less each day. We lose our drive. Perhaps the daily cares block our sight of the great goal. And whether we face it or not, we become cold, lifeless.

But the Son has the power and willingness to breathe the summertime of love into the wintered soul.

Dear God, thank You for the warmth of Your love which can melt the coldness of my heart. Let it be summertime in my heart today.

July 2

Scripture: "And after six days Jesus taketh Peter, James, and John his brother, and bringeth them up into an high mountain apart" (Matthew 17:1).

"I miss the mountains."

It was one of the family commenting again after we moved from Tennessee to Florida. But I understood. As much as I love Florida, I had to admit it was flat—no mountain peaks, no summits.

It seems that everyone loves the summit, the mountaintop. As Christians we all have had those occasions or times in our lives when we have been on the summit. Victory is ours and we say, "God is blessing," as though only mountaintop experiences are assurances that God favors and loves us.

Everything is going great. Perhaps there is prosperity, fame, or success. It's often easy to feel like prosperity or success is God's stamp of approval. Anything less smacks of lack of faith.

The summits are intoxicating. The higher we go, the more intoxicating they become. We can easily lose our perspective.

Peter got carried away . . . absolutely engrossed on the Mount of Transfiguration. So Peter did what we are tempted to do at the time of great mountaintop experiences. He became so confident within himself and felt so elated spiritually he decided to let Jesus know what would be good to do next!

I too have been carried away with schemes that seem great and full of faith, when in actuality they are the headiness of ideas on the mountaintop! However, the mountaintop is really a place to listen to the voice of the Lord. Moses listened while God spoke on the mountain. And God said in effect to those on the Mount of Transfiguration, "Be still and know that I am God." Listen to God while He is speaking. Those glorious times on the mountaintop are precious. Allow Him to teach you and talk to you as you face today's challenges.

But the mountaintop is only for visiting. As much as we would love to live in this lofty realm, we must always come down from the mountain. God called people to the mountaintops for special times of instruction and inspiration, but He always sent them down in the valleys to minister afterward.

I would love to stay here on this spiritual summit, but I realize Moses didn't, David didn't, Elijah didn't, Peter didn't, Jesus didn't, and you and I won't.

Dear God, help me to listen and learn of You while on these spiritual summits so that I may be able to walk confidently through the valleys and face the daily challenges.

July 3

Scripture: "And he [Jesus] said unto them, Come ye yourselves apart into a desert place, and rest a while" (Mark 6:31).

As a kid, *vacation* was a word filled with magic. It was that long-awaited time in the middle of summer when Dad actually took some time off to go to Canada fishing. It wasn't always every year. Sometimes it was two years before we knew the bliss of loading up the Nash Rambler with fishing gear and six kids and heading north from Ohio. It all seemed so exciting, yet so peaceful and "together."

If anything unpleasant happened, it has long ago been extinguished in my mind by the fire of glowing memories. But as a parent, vacation took on a whole new meaning. Oh, we always planned for it to be a wonderful time of family togetherness. Usually there was the big choice—where to go. Of course, our choices were pretty easy. It was wherever Carl was preaching camp meeting or wherever the General Assembly was convening.

With that settled, it was on to bigger decisions, like what to take to wear (which was everything in everyone's closet, since we were also going to camp meeting or General Assembly).

Finally the day would come. All the suitcases, boxes, cans, and cartons were loaded into the car, along with four energetic children. Heading out from Tennessee, about an hour from home, I knew it was going to be a long trip to the Montana camp meeting!

Time has mellowed those memories, until all I remember now are the exciting places we visited . . . the joy of fishing in Yellowstone . . . the thrill of seeing the animals roaming the plains and the mountains of the West . . . the serenity of the cool, star-filled evenings. I remember just getting away . . . resting . . . calming down . . . thinking . . . meditating . . . watching the children enjoy life. Even though there were challenging days, there were also days of rest.

The monotony of everyday living can become a heavy burden. This is especially true for the laboring man or woman in the busy day. The tedious chores, the repetitious movements, the routines often stifle and choke the inner man.

A good vacation rejuvenates the mind, renews the spirit, relaxes the body. Take your example from Christ and "get away and rest."

Dear God, You know that we are human and must have the renewing of heart and mind and spirit that only You can give.

July 4

Scripture: "By one sacrifice he has made perfect forever those who are being made holy" (Hebrews 10:14, *NIV*).

Fifty-six men gathered in a small room in Philadelphia and boldly signed their names to the parchment. It was called the Declaration of Independence. These 56 men were committed, at the price of death, to sign the pledge.

History tells us what happened to these committed men:

Robert Morris, owner of 200 ships, lost everything in the war. He was imprisoned for debt and died in poverty.

Richard Stockton had donated the land for Princeton University. Imprisoned, he was made to live on a thief's diet of bread and water. He died shortly after his release.

Nine of these original 56 died of wounds or wartime hardships. Five were captured by the British and subjected to brutal and inhuman treatment. The homes of 23 were burned, and 17 lost everything they had. Everything. The wives, sons, daughters, even the fathers and mothers of many were killed, jailed, or tortured. All but two men were offered immunity, freedom, restoration of their property, and the lives of their loved ones if they would break their pledge.

But they were all committed.

These were prestigious and wealthy men who knew what this pledge would cost them. They considered liberty important enough to pledge their lives . . . their fortunes . . . their sacred honor.

And they fulfilled their pledge. They paid the price. Marching behind them throughout history are men and women, young and old, who have accepted the challenge and not allowed liberty's torch to fall.

Freedom's torch, held high, has lighted the way through . . .

The snows of Valley Forge.

The fires of Harper's Ferry.

The darkness of the days of a slain president.

It has shone to distant lands across oceans where a million and more of our countrymen have also paid the price for freedom.

But there was One who paid the full price for our freedom. Even since that fountain of cleansing blood was opened at Calvary, millions have received forgiveness and pardon in its life-giving flow. On Calvary's ground we all become the same size in God's eyes. Forgiveness is available. Spiritual freedom is given to all who come.

America offers freedom for a lifetime; Christ offers freedom for eternity!

Father God, I thank You for the spiritual freedom we receive when we choose to live for You.

July 5

Scripture: "And God shall wipe away all tears from their eyes; and there shall be no more death, neither sorrow, nor crying, neither shall there be any more pain: for the former things are passed away" (Revelation 21:4).

I watched a little boy trying hard to be brave. One big tear escaped and rolled down his cheek as the nurse gave him a shot.

"Good boy! You didn't cry," she smiled.

We try not to cry from wounds of the flesh. "It's not adult . . . not mature." It makes us appear too sentimental and weak.

But wounds of the heart . . . that's different. Just as there is a time for laughter, there is a time for tears. So dramatic was the emotion that Jesus felt at the death of Lazarus that only two words were used to describe it: "Jesus wept."

As a child I learned this verse in Sunday school because it was the shortest verse in the Bible. But the impact and implication were lost. Jesus actually shed tears.

- When David realized the depth of his sin, there were tears.
- When David heard of the death of his son, Absalom, there were tears.
- When Jeremiah spoke of the judgment to come to Judah and tried to warn the people, there were tears.
- When a father came to Jesus with his dying son, there were tears.
- When Mary saw Jesus suffering on the cross, there were tears.
- And along with the sufferings of Job and Hosea and Paul, there were the tears.

Tears wash our eyes and help us see clearly. The tears of our own sorrow and bereavement help us see more clearly the sorrow of others.

A life that feels no hurting tears is a life that can offer no healing touch. Tears, for whatever reason, are only for this world. In the next life, we are promised that God shall wipe away all tears.

Dear Father, You gave us the capacity and the emotions to shed tears. May we use the sorrow we have felt to help those who are now in the midst of sorrow.

July 6

Scripture: "That which is born of the flesh is flesh; and that which is born of the Spirit is spirit" (John 3:6).

While looking through some old photos, our daughter found a picture taken when she was just the age of her son, Tory.

"Look at the similarities . . . the same shape head . . . the nose, the eyes, the smile." It was the first time she really noticed how much her child looked like her.

It's one of those little gifts God gave us. Before He stepped back from His role as Creator, He gave the command for everything to reproduce after its own kind.

Birds were to reproduce birds and were to look and act like birds; cows were to look and function as cows. He gave order to everything. Whatever family they were born into would determine how they would look and act. God established this pattern of reproduction.

The world was made aware of sad circumstances a few years ago when a family discovered the little girl they had reared as their own was the daughter of another couple. Their babies had been switched at birth in a small Florida hospital.

Their natural child, now a teenager, has never recovered from the startling revelation. I saw her on television meeting her birth mother and family. What could not be denied was the resemblance to the other children in the family. Even though she was reared far away in very different circumstances, it was easy to see that this was her family. Those innate characteristics were born in her.

I wonder . . . *Could someone look at me and tell what family I was born into? Could I be observed by others and categorized as Christian by how I look, talk, and act?*

Of course the secret of a Christlike life is the miracle of reproduction. Christ is not imitated in our lives, He is reproduced. We do not try to be like Christ so much as we allow Christ to become manifest in us.

Dear God, fill my life with Your Spirit so that others may know I belong to You.

July 7

Scripture: "But when Jesus saw it, he was much displeased, and said unto them, Suffer the little children to come unto me, and forbid them not: for of such is the kingdom of God" (Mark 10:14).

Across the yard she ran as fast as the legs of a 2-year-old could run.

"For you," she said as she pressed into my hands a fistful of broken dandelions. A bouquet of spring flowers for her mom. It was her way of saying, "I love you."

Memories are photographs taken by the heart. We all have precious ones tucked away.

The most vivid memories of childhood are usually not the big things that happened, but memories of little happenings when Dad or Mom gave their special time. Maybe it was time to teach us to ride our bicycles, time to play ball, or time to take us fishing. It may be just sitting in a swing on a summer's evening and listening.

It doesn't take extravagant wealth—just time. This is what you remember. It takes time to make memories, but how can we effectively convey love without giving something precious? Giving of our time speaks volumes.

Days which passed so slowly in our own childhood now pass before us in much too rapid succession. We are all busy, and there will always be things to do. But time given to a family member on a lazy summer day is time invested that will reap rich rewards.

I can only wonder if our family would be as close as it is today had we not shared joy, laughter, pleasant experiences—along with painful challenges.

Sharing is a lifetime of experiences. Christ, the greatest life with the greatest commission in life, had time for individuals, including little children.

Our heavenly Father, help us remember to take the time for the really important things in life—like sitting at Your feet.

July 8

Scripture: "Praise be to the God and Father of our Lord Jesus Christ, the Father of compassion and the God of all comfort, who comforts us in all our troubles, so that we can comfort those in any trouble with the comfort we ourselves have received from God" (2 Corinthians 1:3, 4, *NIV*).

Bent and stooped, she came to Christ. Walking was extremely painful to her, yet so anxious was she to see Jesus that the burden of her affliction and the pangs shooting through her feeble body with every movement of her limbs did not stop her from going to the synagogue that fateful day.

For many years she had been unable to stand erect and lift her head. Her vision was limited and it encompassed only those things she could see by looking down . . .

- The dirt on the skirt of her long garment as it brushed the road.
- The shuffling feet of the crowd.
- The dusty Galilean road.
- The earthy.
- The mundane.

But love touched this woman and with its transforming power changed her whole view. She was never the same!

Lifting her head, she was able to see things differently and was struck by the uncommon beauty of common scenes—beautifully colored birds circling in the blue sky overhead, swaying green branches of the palm trees, rich golden fields of grain swaying in the wind, snow-topped mountains in the distance.

The sheer wonder of the scenes overwhelmed her. But they had been there all the time! She just could not see beyond herself. Oh, yes, the dirt was still clinging to her garment, but she didn't dwell on that now. Now, she could see others. She could see their faces. They too had pain, heartache, and disappointment.

Tragically, we often find ourselves bowed down, turned inward, concerned only with ourselves and our own daily challenges.

God often touches us with His love and expands our vision so that we may see clearly those around us who are bowed down, perhaps waiting for our loving touch.

Dear God, help me today to be aware of those I meet who may need just a loving touch.

July 9

Scripture: "Search me, O God, and know my heart: try me, and know my thoughts" (Psalm 139:23).

Several years ago, Ethel Barrett wrote a book titled *Will the Real Phony Please Stand Up?*

The truth is, most of us feel like phonies at some time or other. We are troubled by the standards we have set for others that we can't live by ourselves. We are ashamed of our own imperfections—our anger, our resentment, our hurts, our suspicions . . . all the emotions we feel a "good" Christian just shouldn't have.

We love to talk about our mountaintop experiences, but when the everyday challenges of life set in, reality crashes in with a thud. Usually, mountains and valleys are just our way of describing the difference between what we believe and how we behave.

Sincere is actually a Latin word, meaning "without wax." In ancient times there was a very fine porcelain which was very expensive. Often when fired, tiny cracks would appear. Dishonest merchants would cover these cracks with a white wax and pass them for true porcelain. Honest dealers marked their flawless vases *sine cera*—"without wax."

Genuine sincerity means no hypocrisy or sham, no cracks hidden or covered over. Some people become so good at covering their true selves—at being a phony—they almost convince themselves. The truth is, we can be honest with others and with ourselves.

But it's not easy. In fact, being honest with everyone at all times is one of our most difficult challenges. And being honest with ourselves sometimes seems almost impossible. Sometimes we wonder if the real phony stood up, would there be anyone left sitting?

Search me, O God, and know my thoughts and ways. Keep me honest with others and honest with myself.

July 10

Scripture: "Be ye angry, and sin not" (Ephesians 4:26).

He was outraged and He didn't care who knew it! What's more, He did something about it!

How dare they undermine and destroy the sanctity of His Father's house! So there He was—in the Temple, overturning the tables of the money changers and driving out the offenders with their animals.

Yes, Christ displayed outrage, but He had good reasons. The issue was very important.

How dare we sit passively by while other people and outside forces invade our homes, captivate our minds, and destroy the sanctity of our house!

With sickening regularity, we see manifestations of the "new morality" everywhere. Now, prime-time television has programs for "mature adults only" which are shown nightly. Even the commercials for them are too vivid for children to view.

We seem almost to have lost the ability to sense what is happening. If we do feel any sense of inner rage, we quickly squelch it lest we appear "not with it" or unsophisticated or, even worse, as if we belong to one of those fringe fanatical religious groups!

We don't know exactly how or when it happened, but it did. That cold clammy hand of indifference has our souls in its grasp. What we thought would be temporary moral numbness has grown into a large dead spot inside us. Somewhere along the road to broad-mindedness and permissiveness, the last remains of innocence got stomped to death.

This is where Christ comes in and shouts, "Be angry and sin not." Those words imply that God wants us to use our God-given temper for Him, that some things are worth getting angry about.

Outrage demands action. One thing that distinguishes a spiritual woman is her attitude toward sin. It is time to take action in our homes . . . in our churches . . . in our communities.

Someone has said, "There are situations in life in which the absence of anger would be the essence of evil."

Dear Father, allow the spiritual blindness to fall from our eyes as we sit at Your feet. Help us to arm ourselves with Your Spirit and Your Word to fight for our families and our nation.

July 11

Scripture: "Charge them that are rich in this age, that they be not highminded, nor trust in uncertain riches, but in the living God, who giveth us richly all things to enjoy" (1 Timothy 6:17).

The year 1929 was bleak and dark. In was an ominous year in our nation's history. Some people did not survive. Many lost everything. Some took their own lives.

The story is told that Eddie Canton, hearing of the suicide of several bankrupt moneymen, added a new joke to his routine, in which a hotel reservations clerk asks a guest: "Do you want the room for sleeping or for jumping?"

Yes, some took their lives even though they still had their health, the love of their families, and their keen minds. In fact, they still had everything except their money.

They hadn't lost their real wealth. All they had lost was their money. But sometimes money seems to outweigh everything on the scale of life.

Luke describes a man sincerely desiring true life from the Master. He obeyed the Scriptures, was a good person, and loved people. In fact, everything in his life was fine, but the love of his money held him back. He sadly turned and committed spiritual suicide (18:18).

Christ was saddened by his response. He saw beyond this short span of humanity into the riches of God and knew the young man was actually giving up true wealth.

Christians must get their priorities straight about money. Perhaps this is why Christ spoke so frequently about it. Whether you have a little or a lot, money is not really the important factor. What you do with what you have is the challenge.

Getting your priorities straight can sometimes alleviate financial struggles. Being content with "such things as ye have" is as healthy for the pocketbook as it is for the soul.

Of course, money is important. We have to have it to live. But think of the most important things in the world to you. Could money buy them?

The lack of money can never deprive you of the really important things in life, and an abundance of money can never buy them.

Heavenly Father, thank You for all the riches You have given us. They are beyond wealth and cannot be measured.

July 12

Scripture: "And they shall be mine, saith the Lord of hosts, in that day when I make up my jewels" (Malachi 3:17).

He was on *Good Morning America* with his prized gem worth thousands of dollars. Polished, cut, and displayed under just the right lighting, its value was evident. But it wasn't that way when he found it.

The young boy was doing what has become a fad with thousands—panning for gems. He brought to the owners of the digging lands what appeared to be a muddy lump of stone. Upon closer examination by professionals, it was discovered to be the most valuable gem ever to be found in amateur digs.

God planned and planted originality and individuality in all His creation, but nowhere is it more evident than in man. Through the ordering of Providence, we are born with varying characteristics and gifts. Sometimes the gifts are evident, like a shining diamond, cut and polished. But more often our gifts and abilities are covered with layers of humanity—undiscovered, undeveloped, unmined treasures. People who accomplish extraordinary feats are only "ordinary people" to their friends and neighbors.

After losing many elections, Abraham Lincoln may have appeared to most of his friends little more than a born loser. He lacked the looks and charisma of a leader. He seemed so ordinary. But many ordinary men and women achieve true greatness.

Fear of failure and ridicule, pressures from society, and years of daily challenges sometimes bury originality in all of us. But whether buried, hidden, forgotten, or neglected, our unmined treasures are lost to the world. God cannot use a buried talent, but He can take a life, polish it, and make it shine like a jewel.

Dear God, You know what I have to offer is very ordinary. Polish my life so I may shine for Your glory.

July 13

Scripture: "I write not these things to shame you, but as my beloved sons I warn you" (1 Corinthians 4:14).

As I scanned the clouds, I knew the storm clouds were gathering. The fierce, energy-driven storms, generated from the heat of the Florida sun, frequent the late afternoons in July. The storms come quickly. Often from a seemingly bright, sunny day, they gather their fury.

Carl and I picked such a day a few years ago to go fishing with some good friends. The day was just a little breezy as we rounded the bend going out into the open gulf waters. As we were heading out into the gulf, the storm-warning flags were flying, alerting small boats and amateurs that the waters were getting rough . . . they needed to go back to shore. But we were already out past the flags. Their message was lost to us.

I am not a good swimmer. In fact, I can barely stay afloat in a swimming pool. So as we crossed the choppy waters of the open gulf, my fingernails buried deeper and deeper in Carl's arm. I listened to the voice of the friend who tried to sound calm and reassuring, "It is just choppy in this channel. It will get better when we cross over into the deep."

I wanted to turn back immediately. This challenge was not for a coward like me on the water. So we listened to what we thought was the voice of experience repeating, "It will get better."

The further we went, the worse it became. Finally, our friend acknowledged that we had better make a run for it straight to the shore. By this time we were far out into the channel and had to cross those same choppy waters to get back.

Each huge wave seemed destined to be the one to swamp the boat and destroy us all. We prayed, and I clung to Carl so tightly that my fingernails made permanent indentations in his arm.

We were never more relieved to see the shore than on that stormy day. As we rounded the bend toward home, we could see the warning flags flying stiffly in the breeze. They were posted to warn people just like us not to foolishly go out into the gulf that day. We missed their message.

Have you ever had little flags go up when you started to do something? That gnawing little voice telling you, "Heed the warning!" Today's scripture says, "I write not these things to shame you, but . . . [to] warn you."

Warnings are a sign of love. Christ promised He would lead and guide us; however, He does not push and shove us into His will. We must be sensitive to His voice . . . read the signs . . . heed the warnings . . . know His Word . . . ask His advice. He loves to guide us through the rough spots.

As you set sail for another day, watch for the warning flags!

Heavenly Father, may I heed those loving warnings You give daily.

July 14

Scripture: "But grow in grace, and in the knowledge of our Lord and Saviour, Jesus Christ" (2 Peter 3:18).

All the health experts agree on one thing—we should eat at least five servings of fruits and vegetables daily to help ward off several potentially fatal diseases.

To me there is nothing more satisfying than a fresh-picked McIntosh apple. Growing up in Johnny Appleseed country (northern Ohio), apple trees grew everywhere. Their blossoms adorn hillsides in the spring, and their wonderful fruit supplies a tasty treat in the early fall.

Have you ever waited in the summertime for apples to ripen? When you are a child, it is a long process. One summer it was just too long a wait, so I picked the green apple before it was quite ready. I expected a juicy bite (maybe a little on the tart side), but what I got was a sour disappointment. It didn't even taste like an apple. But that didn't mean it wasn't an apple . . . or even a good apple.

My first thought was, *This tree has bad apples on it; they are no good.* But the truth is, the apple had not been allowed to grow. As long as the fruit remains connected to its source of life, it will grow and mature.

I saw the same tree go through terrible storms, high winds, drought, hot sun, but the little fruit just hung there with nothing under it holding it up. It was attached to the limb.

Growth is such a difficult process. Ask the little toddler. Ask the teenager. Ask the new mother. Ask the mother whose last child just left home. Ask the widow who lost her husband.

How we would like to be instant possessors of all the wonderful graces found in Galatians 5. We would love to skip the growth which brings them into fruition. These qualities may be the fruit of the Spirit who lives within us, but such fruit does not suddenly appear fully mature in our lives.

Are we still growing as Christians? It took a lifetime for Simon, the son of Jonas, to grow into the apostle Peter. It took years before Saul of

Tarsus became the spiritual giant Paul. They too faced challenges and weathered storms, high winds, and drought. They had knocks and falls, failures and disappointments.

God is still working on us. Don't allow Satan to torment you because you don't seem to be the perfect Christian you desire to be. If you are growing with Christ, you may be green and sour, but you are still valuable fruit!

Our heavenly Father, only by sitting at Your feet and staying connected to You can we grow spiritually. Keep us clinging to the Vine.

July 15

Scripture: "How long halt ye between two opinions?" (1 Kings 18:21).

I am standing in the aisle of the department store trying to make up my mind. My daughter has already gone on to another counter. She has learned the tragic truth . . . her mother is indecisive.

It is not that I don't know what I want. I just have to weigh all the possibilities: Will I be able to find this dress somewhere else cheaper? Will I like it once I get it home? Will we have to come all the way back to town to exchange it? Do I really want to even take my time and try it on? Others are waiting for me. I think I'll just wait until later.

I suppose this kind of indecision is permissible. Many women fall prey to it. It may be because there are so many choices!

Spiritual decisions, however, are not like that. There are only two choices.

See Elijah standing so magnificently on the side of God, truth, and right that day on Mount Carmel. Consider the odds. On one side is the king with the priests of Baal and all the uncounted multitude of people. On the other side stands one man, Elijah, with one huge challenge.

All day long the priests of Baal screamed and cried and wailed and cut themselves with knives in self-torture in a futile effort to induce Baal to let the fire fall. No fire fell, and in late afternoon the 850 priests lay in an exhausted heap of defeat and despair.

Earlier that day, Elijah had stepped forward to address the multitude of people assembled on Mount Carmel: "How long halt ye between two opinions? if the Lord be God, follow him: but if Baal, then follow him" (1 Kings 18:21).

The people on Mount Carmel had two choices—only two. God calls for a decision. His call is clear: "Choose you this day whom ye will serve" (Joshua 24:15).

Like it or not, we all have a decision to make. We dare not neglect it. We dare not ignore it. Indecision paralyzes the present and causes inaction. To refuse to take a stand for the right is to end on the side of wrong.

I may be indecisive in the clothing store, but I want to be 100 percent decided for Christ!

Dear God, I am so thankful that many years ago You called for me to make a decision and I stepped out for You.

July 16

Scripture: "I can do all things through Christ who strengthens me" (Philippians 4:13, *NKJV*).

I can see my grandfather sitting on the front porch in his swing, making the statement and punctuating it with his thin finger: "There will never be a man on the moon."

He was a mathematician and a lover of history, especially anything to do with Abraham Lincoln. Although he was an intelligent and learned man, he thought it couldn't be done.

On July 20, 1969, Neil Armstrong planted his left foot on the surface of the moon, taking "one small step for man, one giant leap for mankind." My grandfather never lived to see that day; but when I saw the televised picture of Neil Armstrong on the moon, I thought of him.

In 1926 the man whose invention would ultimately produce the television tube made an interesting statement: "Television is an impossibility, commercially and financially. It's not worth our dreaming."

In 1945 a naval officer said, "The thing will never go off. It's the biggest fool mistake we've ever made. The atomic bomb will not explode. I ought to know, because I'm an expert in explosives." On August 6, 1945, an atomic bomb destroyed Hiroshima, Japan.

The ship set sail on its maiden voyage and never reached its destination. The *Titanic,* the ship even God couldn't possibly sink, rests 13,000 feet below the surface of the Atlantic Ocean.

In 1948 the Roper Poll stopped taking polls. "There is no need for further survey. We already have a winner." George Gallup continued to take polls, but he agreed with Roper, "Thomas E. Dewey is the next president of the United States." The idea that Dewey could lose was so impossible that at least one newspaper printed the morning edition with the banner headline: "Dewey Elected President." Yet Harry S. Truman occupied the White House for the next four years.

Life is filled with "impossibilities." Fortunately most of us don't believe them. We look at an obstacle and say, "I can do it; I can succeed—through Jesus." Far too many people look at His demands and say, "I can't; there just isn't any way!"

They forget that the Christian church is made up of individuals who have had the impossible accomplished in their lives. Sins for which they could not forgive themselves were forgiven by God. Lifestyles were conquered by a personal faith in a life-changing Christ. Emptiness was filled with the love of Christ and overflowed into the lives of others.

Impossible? Not if the name you trust is Jesus.

Heavenly Father, this day I can do all things through Christ who strengthens me.

July 17

Scripture: "Study to shew thyself approved unto God, a workman that needeth not to be ashamed, rightly dividing the word of truth" (2 Timothy 2:15).

Almost every family has a clutterer—one who can't stand to throw anything away and can never organize all the stuff. But even if you have one in your family, that individual can't be as bad as Kathleen Nelson Coley. She was the millionaire daughter of an Illinois banking family. The policemen who investigated her death called her "Garbage Mary."

Mary lived in a cheap, two-room efficiency apartment. It was a pack rat's delight. It was also full of smelly garbage, rotting food, and moldy clothing. The detective said the odor permeating Coley's apartment was ghastly. There was garbage in the refrigerator, the stove, the sink, the cabinets, and the bathtub. When the policemen searched the apartment they made an astonishing discovery. Scattered among the trash they found Mobil Oil stock, worth almost a half million dollars. There were other stocks in major companies like U.S. Steel, Uniroyal, and Squibb. In addition, they found valuable oil-drilling rights and passbooks to eight large bank accounts.

Garbage Mary died in abject poverty, surrounded by incredible wealth. Hearing about Garbage Mary, most of us shake our heads and think, *How sad.* And yet how like most Christians she is, surrounded by wealth and living in poverty. The bankbooks which we leave unopened number not eight but 66. They begin with Genesis and end with Revelation.

Our lives are too cluttered. Even though they may be worthwhile, there are too many activities and people and things. Good things can clutter our lives until we have no room for the valuables.

The Bible is always a best-seller. Yet according to pollster George Gallup, Jr., Americans are trying to do the impossible, "being Christians without the Bible." Mr. Gallup told editors at the Evangelical Press Association's meeting, "We revere the Bible, but we don't read it."

This book is a wealth of information on everything from family living to life everlasting. It even introduces personal stories of real families who suffered pain, sadness, disappointment, discouragement, and all the gamut of experiences and daily challenges we face. This how-to manual is not afraid to set definite responsibilities, privileges, guidelines, and goals. For it was written by the One who knows just how the family should function. Yes, this book is more precious than gold!

Don't be like Garbage Mary. Don't live in poverty while surrounded by wealth.

Thank You, Lord, for this wealth You have given to us all. Let it become a living Word in my life.

July 18

Scripture: "The tongue can no man tame; it is an unruly evil, full of deadly poison" (James 3:8).

I heard the bickering coming from the bedroom and knew it was our twin grandsons. Although Josh and Jon love each other dearly, they have the normal malady common to all twins, or so it seems, of wanting what the other has.

"What is it this time?" I said, although I knew exactly what to expect. Sure enough, each was tugging at some unknown object and claiming it for his own. One of them angrily asserted: "He has that piece of string, and I had it first."

I couldn't help but laugh out loud. Here were two 8-year-old boys standing in the middle of the floor filled with toys, fighting over a piece of string. Even they saw the humor in the situation. This, however, is no more amazing than how we as rational adults sometimes act.

While evangelizing, Carl and I have had the misfortune to be around people who bickered and fought with each other over trivial matters. How uncomfortable it is to be caught in the situation where there is open hostility.

But what is even more damaging are the behind-the-back

whisperers—the gossipers. The gossiper's tongue is unruly—an unruly evil. We somehow have the idea that a word spoken is gone, but the words we speak in gossip linger to wound, sometimes for a lifetime.

Not all gossip is intentionally malicious. Some people are unknowing rumormongers—talebearers rather than burden-bearers.

It is true. By what I say, I can create or destroy an atmosphere for those around me. By my words, I can make life brighter or darker for them and for me. My words can spread a pall of misery, or my words can create a garland of peace. I must never forget that my words are creators of good or evil. What I say—what you say—is immeasurably important. We must guard against spreading gloom and doom. I must not divulge privileged information. Now and then we must have a silent thought. Candor is not a license for slander.

If you drop a pebble into a pool, even unintentionally, ripples are sent out to every part of the pool, and the most distant rim feels the disturbance.

You've heard the childhood saying: "Sticks and stones may break my bones, but words can never hurt me." It just isn't true. Words can hurt you and those you love. Words can be devastating in the damage they cause and in the pain they inflict.

Gossip is a killer, a murderer. A friend of mine wrote about it:

> I crucified a soul today.
> I murdered it with words, you see;
> Void now is one testimony.
> My tongue did nail it to a tree.

> —A. Child

Beware of hearing, beware of spreading, and beware of uttering "They say."

> "They say" is the writer of anonymous letters.
> "They say" is the killer of sterling character.
> "They say" is the assassin of good reputation.

Lord, help me this day to guard my speech. Let my mind and heart be filled with Your goodness as I sit at Your feet.

July 19

Scripture: "But when he was yet a great way off, his father saw him . . . and ran [to him]" (Luke 15:20).

See the little house in the valley with the smoke curling up through the forest of trees? Peaceful and warm, it's like a scene from a Rockwell painting. But look closer. Close enough to see the aged face behind the newspaper. Close enough to see the eyes that stray from the reading to the long road that winds down the valley. Close enough to hear the old man sigh because the road is empty. His son is not coming home again . . . again. Together we see the sadness of a father's heart, a sadness no time can erase, a sadness that lurks in the shadows even when he smiles, a sadness beyond words.

Christ painted the word picture to His followers. It is a picture of a heavenly Father sad at a child wandering farther and farther from home. Sad at a son losing his inheritance and wasting more and more opportunities.

Only those who understand love can appreciate fully the loneliness of a father's heart when a child is missing. Loneliness is a vacuum nothing can fill.

In the portrait of the waiting father, we see patience. The father never gives up on his son. He is patiently waiting. Always waiting!

We see love and hope in this portrait.

Some people today see no hope. They see only pain, frustration, darkness, and death. In fact, man without hope is dead while he yet breathes. Without hope, man doesn't get up. Without hope, prodigal sons and daughters die in the pigpen.

As long as God the Father is alive, there is great hope. When the child returns, there is great joy.

There stands the son . . . amazed . . . beholding the transformation taking place in himself . . . tears flowing . . . heart filling . . . overwhelmed and overcome by the Father's grace and love.

I wish it were possible for every runaway to see the beautiful picture of the Father waiting with arms outstretched.

Dear God, perhaps there is someone today that I will meet who needs to be shown the way home. May I point others to Your waiting, outstretched arms.

July 20

Scripture: "Thus saith the Lord, thy redeemer, and he that formed thee from the womb, I am the Lord that maketh all things" (Isaiah 44:24).

It is a very hot July day. As we drive down the highway, the heat is causing a mirage on the road. A mirage is an optical illusion caused by the reflection of light through layers of air with different temperatures. A mirage is seeing what doesn't exist. There are tales of stranded mariners seeing ships on the horizon of the ocean—phantom ships, illusory ships.

A far more destructive mirage, however, is the mirage of inferiority. Too many of us, young and old alike, see ourselves in a false light. Rather than the real, we see the illusion created by what others expect of us and by what we have come to expect of ourselves. We see a false image of self, an unreal image. Quite often it is this feeling of inferiority that shackles and binds us and hinders us from being the success God wants us to be.

While teaching third grade many years ago, I saw children who suffered from deep feelings of inferiority. These feelings stem from many sources: looks, talents, family background, education—even one's state of health. The point is that such feelings have little or no basis in reality. God doesn't want you and me to be handicapped by our own feelings. He doesn't want our vision fixed on a mirage.

Some people haven't let the miraculous truth sink in that God made them. Along with the physical body—or the physical "temple," as God calls it—there is also your eternal soul, the life principle which was created at your birth. We call it the breath of God. God made you. God formed you. God gave you birth. God gives you breath right now.

Not only has God made you, but God has given you certain talents. In the ordering of Providence, we are born with varying characteristics and gifts, distinctive and individual. In the parable of the talents, the talents were not distributed evenly, but each person received at least one. God has excluded no one. It is in this area, more than any other, that most of us tend to feel inferior and insecure. I have met many pastors' wives who have tried to pattern their lives after another individual they greatly admired. They tried to be a carbon copy of some ideal they had seen or heard. Tragically many women go through life with their self-worth linked to some pseudoself they are trying to project.

We are sometimes so uncertain of ourselves in so many areas that we glance around to see what others are doing before we know the accepted code.

But when you decide to be yourself, when you give up pretense and lay aside all efforts to be what someone else wants or expects you to be, that's when your own personal talent will begin to blossom.

There is no one exactly like you. God makes no off-the-rack Christians. We are all originals, designed and crafted under His supervision.

Dear Lord, thank You for the care and love with which you have created us. Guide me this day so that I may use for Your glory the talents You have loaned to me here on earth.

July 21

Scripture: "She looketh well to the ways of her household, and eateth not the bread of idleness. Her children arise up, and call her blessed" (Proverbs 31:27, 28).

"I am woman . . . I am invincible . . . I am tired!"

These words had to come from a mother.

"If life is a battle, I know where it is being fought . . . in my mind and spirit." Other words were pouring forth, not from a tormented psychotic but from a young Christian mother trying to sort through the myriad of feelings which had trampled through her life and left her emotionally drained and bewildered.

As Christian mothers, it strikes a familiar chord in the melody of many of our own lives. Listening to the rhetoric, we become confused. We are simultaneously admonished to find our place of fulfillment in the home and outside the home, as if the *place* were the absolute answer.

In Christian service we are all, or should be, on the same side. And yet, there are forces that seem determined to split us into opposing factions and demand that we choose sides.

It is sometimes difficult for life to seem meaningful when you live the life most mothers live—life as the sole ringmaster in a three-ring circus being invaded by a caravan of monkeys and still trying to carry on.

It is not uncommon for a mother to feel completely overwhelmed by the complexity of her life. She is not *just* a mother! She is the head of her family's department of health, education, and welfare. She is not only the department head, she is the administrator, bookkeeper, nurse, janitor, and sometimes the only worker.

If you are a stay-at-home mom, you become just that. You no longer have a name. You are just somebody's mom. Most of the child-raising is left to you. Until a few years ago, the role of fathers was a bit part. For the most part, he came in and tossed the children up until they were either crying or throwing up, tickled and wrestled them until they lay in convulsive heaps, then walked off with that satisfied look, muttering about "the joys of having children."

But a mother's responsibilities extend far beyond her children. She still has obligations to her husband, her church, her relatives, her friends, and sometimes her employer. As she is pulled by every one of these areas, there is little, if any, time for herself.

It is not fair to paint a picture of the ideal mother as if mothers are perfect. We are not. We are reminded of this fact daily. And if you have a youngster in the house, you are probably reminded even more often. And if you have a teen, you are probably reminded hourly!

Each Christian mother must sift through the volume of values and find the golden priorities for her life. We often have to turn deaf ears to demands or criticisms that pull us from our first obligations. Leaving off some of the good things, we make room for those of greater value.

Mothers sometimes get little encouragement . . . no one seems to notice. It is wonderful that they have a day called Mother's Day. It is a shame, however, that a law had to be enacted setting aside a certain day of each year so that some people would be reminded to honor their mother.

She may be a queen or she may be a homeless pauper; but if she is a mother, she will step from the throne or the gutter and give her all to her child.

May I be aware this day, dear God, of the privilege of being a mother.

July 22

Scripture: "As for me and my house, we will serve the Lord" (Joshua 24:15).

"Robin Hood in Reverse" was the headline in the newspaper. The front-page story was about five youths who snatched the purse of a poor woman and her husband. Inside the purse was the couple's life savings. They were on their way with their $33,000 in cash to buy their "dream home," a new double-wide mobile home.

"The youths, ages 15 to 18, were all from wealthy, respected homes and were just out looking for something to do," the story continued. I turned the page to continue reading the story, and my eyes fell on the full-color pictures of the five boys. In horror, I realized that two of them were the sons of our neighbors.

How could this happen in this home? The mother was a teacher at the junior high, the father a respected businessman. They lived in a nice home in a nice neighborhood. They all drove nice cars. They were nice people!

Sadly, even the best of homes are often plagued with disaster. A drinking problem, immorality, a drug problem, a child caught cheating or stealing, violence—problems that invade the sanctity of the strongest Christian homes.

Paul admonished us to speak "the truth in love." Many families are breaking apart under the burden of pretense. Under the guise of "holiness" we try to perpetuate the image of the perfect family even when deep problems exist. Healing comes slowly, or not at all, to a wound that is ignored.

Christian families are not perfect families. Many face the same challenges and problems, but they know where to seek solutions. Victory comes by being strong enough to face the issue no matter how painful it is. The process may be slow, but when you begin with the truth administered with love, you can look into the heart of another and hear his or her cry for help.

The home should be a sanctuary, a fortress from the hurts and insults of the world. The strength of our words and actions must be tempered with the sensitivity of our love. The wisdom of God allows us to know when to be tough and when to be tender.

Being sensitive requires thoughtfulness. We must be aware of others, aware of their thoughts and feelings, listening with hearts of love to the special messages they are sending and the cues and clues they give.

Be sensitive to the child who wants you to listen to his "important stuff."

Be sensitive to the husband who wishes you wouldn't criticize him in public.

Being sensitive may mean "bending" a little in things that are not really so important. How many times have we alienated some of our family members because we insist they live, act, dress, and think like we do?

A Christian lady, mourning the death of her son, tearfully remarked, "I wish I hadn't been so interested in how he looked and acted around others and been more interested in *him*."

Dear Lord, I thank You for the most precious gift here on earth, a family. Help me to live the Golden Rule in my home.

July 23

Scripture: "What meanest thou, O sleeper? arise, call upon thy God" (Jonah 1:6).

It's great when school is out and the household can sleep past 6:30. There is something comforting about our God-given ability to sleep. In *Macbeth,* Shakespeare described sleep thus:

> Sleep that knits up the ravell'd sleave of care,
> The death of each day's life, sore labour's bath,
> Balm of hurt minds, great nature's second course,

Chief nourisher in life's feast.

But slumber also has its dark side. There can be a danger in drowsiness. We are not keenly aware of our surroundings. We are vulnerable. We are easy prey when we are sleeping.

Jonah was a man who slumbered. Jonah was a good man, a preacher—a man God called to do a specific job. But he ran from God and found himself on board a ship sailing away from the will of God. While on board ship he fell asleep.

Jonah wrestled with himself about his decision, and now that he had decided to run from God, an eerie drowsiness made his eyelids heavy with sleep. Even though the battle with his conscience was lost, he was able at last to sleep. But God was not through dealing with Jonah. Mercifully, God sent a storm after Jonah. While Jonah slept, the storm raged, the wind howled, and the sea whipped into a frothing, foaming mass. But Jonah slept on . . .

He slept while others around him were working.

He slept while the ship was sinking.

He slept while God was moving—that's right—while God was moving.

Finally Jonah was awakened out of sleep. Although the road back to God was rough and challenging, he took the first step in the right direction. He awoke out of sleep.

While we were taking a pleasant snooze, did it happen to us? Did the things that are important to the world become important to us? Did the philosophies of the world become our philosophies? Have the ideas and ideals of the Bible become a little "old foggie"?

The world would like to take over our media, our schools, our government, and our families. The enemy of our souls will try to spiritually anesthetize us and cause us to become numb to what is happening.

Before we can ever expect to save our communities, our churches, our homes, we must first wake up!

Awaken my soul, dear Lord. Help us, as Christians, not to become numb to the tactics of Satan.

July 24

Scripture: "Therefore shall a man leave his father and his mother, and shall cleave unto his wife: and they shall be one flesh" (Genesis 2:24).

Did you ever consider how wonderful it is to be able to love? Why did God give us this great capability? He could have created us as Spock-like creatures with great minds and lives, ruled only by logic . . . no emotion. Or we could have been designed with instincts like animals. We could learn to respond and obey and just follow our instincts for the rest.

One of the reasons, of course, is that we couldn't really know God without emotions, for the Bible tells us that God is love. God gave humanity part of divinity when He gave us the capacity to love.

Another reason is, it is so wonderful! God delights in giving good things to us . . . things we enjoy . . . things that make us happy . . . things such as love. Who but God could create something so wonderful as love and marriage?

We sometimes equate love with the things that come out of Hollywood. Someone has said, "One of the tragedies of American life is that love is being defined by those who experience so little of it."

But through the Scriptures, the example of the love of a husband and wife are used as a type of God's love to us. On what a high plain this places marriage! Perhaps this is one of the reasons we see such an attack on marriage and the home today. Satan desires to pervert one of the greatest ideas of God—to pull it out of the spiritual world and bring it down to the cheap and mundane. But it is still in such a lofty position in the Word and plan of God that He refers to His church as the Bride, and our time of great communion with Him as the Marriage Supper of the Lamb.

But love, like most intangible, illusive qualities, must be preserved through some very concrete, tangible actions. Love can be a never-ending circle of giving and receiving. Or it can cut off at either end and die like the lovely fruit cut from the vine.

Love seeks only the best for its mate with no thought of competition or outshining the other. One may speak of life as a stage, but marriage is not. There are no stars in a marriage. But there is a leading man and a leading woman each uplifting the other so that the marriage is a hit.

So give . . . give, so completely in love that you forget to ask yourself whether or not you are loved in return. For the circle of love to be complete you must also learn to receive. Though love is often cut off by a mate who will not give in, it is also frequently killed by a mate who will not consent to be served.

When Christ stepped forth and began to wash the disciples' feet, Peter shrank back and declared, "Lord, not me. You will not serve me!"

He seemed to miss completely the message Jesus was trying to teach— that the ministry of servanthood demands not only servants but also people willing to be served. Peter was denying Christ the joy of serving.

You probably know people who will never let you do anything for them. They take the joy out of spontaneous giving.

Blessed are those who can give without remembering and can receive without forgetting.

Blessed is a marriage when a wife can say, "I love you. Thank you for looking into my heart, passing over all my faults, pushing aside my weaknesses, and bringing into the light the beauty that no one else looked far enough to see."

Dear Lord, I am thankful for this wonderful communion of marriage which You established.

July 25

Scripture: "He who continually goes forth weeping, bearing seed for sowing, shall doubtless come again with rejoicing, bringing his sheaves with him" (Psalm 126:6, *NKJV*).

In her autobiography, *The Woman Within*, Ellen Glasgow, Pulitzer Prize winner, wrote of her father: "He was entirely unselfish, and in his long life he never committed a pleasure."

Joy is a characteristic of the Christian life. When Paul listed the Christian graces known as the fruit of the Holy Spirit, he listed *joy* second. When Jesus performed His first miracle, it was a miracle of joy—He attended a wedding and turned water into wine.

Christian joy does not exclude sorrow or weeping. The psalmist declared, "May those who sow in tears reap with shouts of joy" (126:5, *NRSV*).

I remember clearly the little brown-skinned lady we met that rainy day in Mahaica, Guyana, South America. It was a dismal, gloomy day with rains thundering down when we drove through the dense jungle to the little settlement.

They opened the large iron gates and let us in because we were with the Scottish missionary who had ministered there for years. You see, Mahaica was a leper colony.

We walked down those long, gray halls and said "Good morning" to a young man who was dragging himself along in a cardboard box. His legs had been eaten away by the dreaded disease.

We entered the large room and proceeded to a tiny sectioned-off portion, which contained a bed and a little dresser, to visit Dorcas. Her "home" consisted of this tiny space; her possessions consisted of her Bible, a few clothes, and some personal effects. This was her world—the confines of a leprosarium.

I can't express how I felt as I looked at the 77-year-old woman, her sightless eyes almost beaming as she hobbled down the corridor on crutches. She had been only 11 years old when she came to Mahaica. Her family discovered a small spot on her back. When it was found to be leprosy, her family had brought her to this colony in the middle of the jungle, left her, and never had any further contact with her. In this particular section of the country, lepers were treated as outcasts. Their families disowned them. They all changed their names and are known only as John or Mary or Dorcas, the leper.

As a teenage girl she was there alone, disowned by her family, when a missionary led her to the Lord. Her world ended, but her life began. Since her conversion, she had led over 60 of the patients and 20 of the nurses and doctors to the Lord by her consistent life and godly testimony.

Her testimony rang with joy: "I am happy, happy, happy."

Joy is not a requirement of Christian living; it is a result of it. Joy is what happens when we live in obedience to God.

Thank You, dear Lord, for the joy of the Christian life.

July 26

Scripture: "Do ye look on things after the outward appearance?" (2 Corinthians 10:7).

It was really just a neighborhood carnival, but when it came to town we couldn't resist it. We loaded up the grandkids, fought the traffic, inched through what had been a vacant lot, and found a parking place.

We bustled along the grounds to the beat of the recorded calliope music, stopping for the few "kiddie" rides, the usual games, and some of the food from the good ladies of the local Catholic church. It was a rather ordinary affair, but the kids loved it.

One thing caught my eye. It was the house of mirrors. We all laughed at the distorted images each mirror projected. "Look at this one," one of the boys shouted. We all looked and saw four short, squatty bodies with enlarged heads.

As they raced on, I looked in the next mirror. I couldn't believe my eyes. Staring back was a thin image! I looked again, turning to see all sides. Yes, there it was . . . that slim body, those long, thin legs, those firm upper arms. What weeks of dieting and fretting couldn't do, this wonderful mirror could do in an instant. It was just an illusion, a false image, but who cared? I wanted that mirror!

A Pharisee of Jesus' day must have looked one day in his distorted mirror and proclaimed, "Just perfect." With that image fixed in his mind, he arrived at the Temple. Nobody was more religious than he, and it showed.

First of all, he looked the part. Dressed in the most accepted religious garb of the day, he came in carrying his large leather-bound scrolls.

Then, too, he talked the part perfectly. When he spoke, it was with just the right "tune" and just the right sprinkling of "thee" and "thou." He was fluently versed in the newest translation of the ancient scrolls. And could he ever pray! The Bible says he prayed to himself. But never mind, the prayer was only for those around him anyway.

Also, he acted the part. He attended all three services on Sunday, early-morning prayer meeting on Tuesday, Wednesday-night fellowship service (where he served as an usher), even made a brief appearance at the ladies monthly matzo-ball supper. He had read all the latest religious periodicals, had watched religious shows, had given tithes, and had even given, with much ado, to the poor beggar outside the Temple.

Yes, as he arrived at the Temple, the view of himself in the distorted mirror this morning was firmly fixed in his mind. Sadly, this man never saw himself as God saw him. He never saw himself as he truly was.

We are so concerned with the outside . . . how we appear to others. And it is true that how we appear often affects how we are thought of in man's eyes. But not to God. "For the Lord seeth not as man seeth; for man looketh on the outward appearance, but the Lord looketh on the heart" (1 Samuel 16:7).

Our heavenly Father, may our hearts be so filled with Your image, that our lives will reflect it to others.

July 27

Scripture: "He maketh the storm a calm, so that the waves thereof are still" (Psalm 107:29).

Middle Florida always has something growing. "U-pick" is big business here—U-pick strawberries, oranges, tomatoes, beans, and so forth.

I made the horrible mistake years ago of taking our four children, then ages 3, 5, 6, and 8 to pick strawberries. What a challenge! The heat must have gotten to me that particular day because I reasoned, "This will be a fun learning experience for us all." And I suppose it would have been except for the scorching heat, the backbreaking work, and the children.

As I look back now I wonder what ever possessed me to take four children to a berry patch and expect them to all stay together with their mother and pick berries. We weren't even finished listening to the instructions from the supervisor in the field, who said, "Please pick only in the rows assigned to you," when I looked around for my little berry pickers.

Dashing through plants with little reverence, the 5-year-old was almost out of sight. Carrying the 3-year-old and pulling the 6-year-old along, I headed after her while the 8-year-old kept clanging, "Mom, can I pick here? Mom, can I pick here?"

My neat little picture of a wonderful day with the children suddenly crumbled. We get disturbed when our plans are thwarted. In the midst of our perfect plans we look around and exclaim, "How did I get in this mess?" We may have the ideal day planned, but we have to live with reality. A similar thing happened to Jesus and His disciples (Matthew 14:13-33).

Perhaps that is how the disciples felt that day. Here they were taking a relaxing time off with the Lord. I am sure Peter pictured it differently than it turned out.

He may have wondered, *How did it happen? How did we get in such a mess?* First of all, the spiritually hungry crowd that followed them essentially ruined their chance of a quiet time. After a full day of ministering to the people and feeding them from a small lad's lunch, Jesus constrained the disciples to get into the ship and go out on the sea.

Does this mean Jesus didn't realize how dangerous this was going to be?

So here were the disciples out on the sea—their "fun" day messed up by the crowd and a storm and feeling very much alone. I can remember being in the midst of storms and feeling that no one was there to help and that even God was somewhere on the shore out of the reach of the storm.

Peter probably felt that way. Then he had renewed hope in verse 29: He saw Christ there on the waters. He heard His voice say, "Come." Without hesitation, he got out of the boat. He did what he thought was right—what Jesus wanted. As he valiantly began to walk by faith, he became so overwhelmed by the boisterous wind and seas . . . so overcome by reality that faith fled and fear took hold. I can hear his mind telling his body, "Another fine mess you've gotten us into!"

Peter did what we do so often when our best-laid plans go astray and we are sinking in the storm waters—he cried out to the Lord. And Jesus was right there with His hand reaching, ready to lift him up and out.

When your plans have all gone wrong and the boat rocks with daily challenges, remember where you are and who is with you. Just call upon the Master. He is still on the seas with His hand outstretched to you.

Dear God, may I always be aware who is walking with me through the storms.

July 28

Scripture: "And the Word was made flesh, and dwelt among us" (John 1:14).

Lovingly Carl cut the piece of pie and set before our daughter who was about 3 years old at the time.

"Not that much," the child replied.

So Carl took the piece back, cut off a small section and set down the reduced piece in front of her.

"Not that much," she repeated more emphatically.

Dutifully Carl took the plate of pie and once more cut off a small section and handed it back. By this time the slice was just a sliver.

Frustrated by her lack of ability to communicate exactly what she wanted, she tried one last time: "Dad, not that much. I want more!"

She had tried to tell us exactly what she wanted. To her "Not that much" meant "Give me more." To us it was the exact opposite: "Not that much" meant "Give me less."

Children have a special way of communicating. That first smile of a young child is a heralded experience. And from there the English language goes to pieces. New one-syllable words joined together with hyphens appear daily. Parents who were former professors at universities now coo "ba-ba" (for bottle) and "da-da, mom-mom, bye-bye." Eventually "no-no" creeps into the vocabulary, but all smart babies know they have a grace period of months before restriction begins. They take full advantage of it, too.

But days will pass, along with innocence, and gone will be the days of dandelion bouquets from young hands. Also gone is that special communication between child and parent. Sometimes there develops within that close-knit unit what has been termed a "communication gap."

A *gap* has several definitions. It can be "an opening made by a break or a parting; a break in continuity." A *gap* can also be "a blank space," such as a gap where a baby tooth had been. That gap is merely an evidence of healthy growth. It is a signal that all is well and the child is growing. But the words "communication gap" convey a negative feeling—a signal that all is not well and that a relationship may be dying.

Difficulties arise when there is a gap. It's hard to touch across a gap. We reach out with our hands, but are never quite able to touch the one on the other side. It's hard to talk quietly across a gap. In desperation our whisper of love may become a shout of anger.

There was a time when a gap existed between a Father and His children. It was difficult to touch the children, to speak to the children. They seemed not to be able to hear His voice or to be interested in anything He said. The communication had been broken. The Father realized what had happened and longed to restore the fellowship which once existed.

Then God looked down from heaven and knew the time had come to build a bridge to His children. The voice of God, which in times past had spoken in the power of Creation, spoke again in love.

"And the Word was made flesh."

And His Word of love spoke to His children as nothing else could. His love reached through time and generations and still speaks to us today.

What a glorious privilege He has freely given to mortals . . . the ability to commune with God!

Thank You, our heavenly Father, that through Christ we are able to commune with You.

July 29

Scripture: "Use hospitality one to another without grudging" (1 Peter 4:9).

Hospitality seems to be a lost art. Or at least it got shoved back in the corner by two-career families and fast-food restaurants.

During the years when Carl and I evangelized, I learned many lessons about hospitality. How well I remember driving our Nash Rambler from Baltimore to Florida and arriving at the parsonage of what I thought was the most beautiful setting in the world for a church.

We were packed! We looked like the children of Israel leaving Egypt. To complicate everything, we were neophyte parents with a 3-month-old baby. Unloading the car became embarrassing. There was the portable crib/playpen, a small chest of drawers, a baby bath, clothes, a huge supply of diapers and a diaper pail (this was before disposables). There waiting to meet us with a gracious smile was the Byrd family, making us feel like we belonged, like we were family, hands already outstretched for the crying, colicky baby. In those weeks we lived with that family, I learned about hospitality. The Scriptures tell us we should be "given to hospitality" (Romans 12:13).

Hospitality is just showing God's love to others. It is the Golden Rule living in a heart.

There are so many examples of hospitality in the Bible.

Elisha learned about hospitality from a Shunammite woman and her family who prepared a little room for him. The woman and her husband furnished the room with a bed, a table, a stool, and a lampstand and had it ready when Elisha passed by again. But she was later rewarded with the life of her son.

Jesus was often the recipient of hospitality. Mary and Martha opened their home to Him on many occasions. They, too, received someone back from the dead.

Even a tax collector entertained Jesus. He was rewarded with the knowledge of how to receive life everlasting.

You don't have to have a mansion furnished with all the fineries of life to show hospitality. Jesus said, "And whosoever shall give to drink unto one of these little ones a cup of cold water only in the name of a disciple, verily I say unto you, he shall in no wise lose his reward" (Matthew 10:42).

Help me to be given to hospitality, dear Lord.

July 30

Scripture: "And he said, Draw not nigh hither: put off thy shoes from off thy feet, for the place whereon thou standest is holy ground" (Exodus 3:5).

The wind blows across the hot desert hillside. The lone figure braces against the wind and heat, his garment blowing about him. Desolate and alone in a barren spot with his flock of sheep, he stops to survey the land. Something catches his eye. It is a strange sight. As he ventures close, he realizes it is a small fire.

Then Moses becomes aware that there is something unusual about this fire. The bush is burning, but it is not being consumed! *This is not an ordinary bush,* thought Moses, and he turned to walk closer to witness the great sight. But Moses was stopped by the voice of God: "Draw not nigh hither: put off thy shoes from off thy feet, for the place whereon thou standest is holy ground."

Holy ground? Here? This desolate place?

Look around you, Moses. How can this desolate, barren spot be holy ground? There is no one around here . . . no beauty . . . no adornment . . . no beautiful temple. This is desert, not a beautiful place of worship.

Where is the action? Where are the people? Where is the applause?

But God is meeting a man here today, and the spot is made sacred and holy because here God is touching a life.

What about your corner of life? Is it filled with so many challenges that there is no meaning?

We can live through just about anything if it is meaningful. But what is your idea of a meaningful life, and where does the idea really come from? Does society dictate it? Does your environment create it? Does the church or some other organization mandate it?

Is something meaningful only as long as everyone knows about it?

Is it meaningful if it's the biggest, the best, the most?

Is it meaningful because the people who know about it applaud it?

It may be in a small place you find yourself. Perhaps barren, ugly, and seemingly unfruitful and lonely. No one around to applaud you in your corner of life. No elaborate spotlight. No beautiful position where God has led you.

Take another look around and listen for the voice. If God is there, take off your shoes. You're on holy ground.

Dear God, open my eyes so that I can see the holiness of the place where I labor for You.

July 31

Scripture: "And Joseph remembered the dreams which he dreamed" (Genesis 42:9).

What ever became of your dreams? Were they pushed back by the busyness of life? Have you let the changes you have encountered in life rob them? Has the thrill and anticipation of some great achievement for God been thwarted?

Are they tucked away in a safe place in the back of your mind, waiting like some fragile glass figurine to be taken out and displayed?

Abraham must have lost all hope of ever having a child by Sarah after he became an old man. But God is not subject to Eastern Standard Time . . . or any standard time. John was what we would call an old man. Here he was, exiled to the isle of Patmos and living in a cave, a man who had already lived through crisis experiences again and again. Could this person still be used of God . . . where he was?

Yes, even there, he was given the greatest unfolding of events past, present, and future. It was so great we simply call it "Revelation."

Recently I saw a sign which read, "If things get better with age, then I'm approaching magnificent!"

Grandma Moses took up painting seriously at the age of 77. At the age of 88 she was awarded the Women's National Press Club award for "outstanding contribution to contemporary thought and achievement."

Clara Barton, founder of the American Red Cross, lived actively until the age of 91.

Oliver Wendell Holmes started writing *Over the Teacups* at age 79.

Dr. Lillian Martin, famous for her work in old-age clinics around the country, learned to type at 65. She learned to drive a car in her 70s. At 75 she went alone to Russia. At 81 she toured Mexico alone in her car. At 88 she made a tour of South America, including a journey up the Amazon. At 89 she managed a 64-acre farm (at a profit) with four 64-year-old helpers.

Whoever you are, wherever you are, or whatever has happened to you, you can dream a dream. Dreams are not for those who have achieved but for those who want to achieve. Dreams lift us, inspire us, put new zest into our lives, motivate us, and move us ahead. They help us to reach higher than ever before. So with God's help *live* until you die, tackle those challenges, and rekindle those dreams.

Dear God, awaken within me those dreams which have been buried by time and the grind of daily challenges.

NOTES

August

Hearing Hearts
Pat Bradbury

Pat Bradbury was born in Rome, Georgia, and graduated from Pershing High School in Omaha, Nebraska. She also graduated from Christian Booksellers Association Management and Marketing Institute.

Pat served on the CBA Board of Directors for one term and was an area consultant for CBA. She is listed in *Who's Who of Outstanding Business Women of America* and presently serves as sales coordinator for Pathway Press. In addition, Pat is a teacher, speaker, merchandise consultant, and a member of the Pathway Credit Union Board of Directors. Pat and her husband, Richard, live in Cleveland, Tennessee. They have two daughters and six grandchildren. Pat and Richard attend the Mount Olive Church of God.

August 1

Scripture: "Turning your ear to wisdom and applying your heart to understanding" (Proverbs 2:2, *NIV*).*

Books, sermons, stories, commercials, cards, valentines, and cupids carry a similar message—hearts! Millions of dollars are spent each year on hearts. I did not realize until I was assigned the devotional topic "Hearing Hearts" just how many times the word *heart* is a part of our language and culture. We say it so often as part of our daily lives, but I wonder if we stop to think what it really means.

Let's consider two kinds of hearts—the physical heart and the spiritual heart. The physical heart is the body's most vital organ. It pumps the blood supply to every fiber of our body to keep it working properly. When the heart quits working, everything else quits. But what about the other heart, that spiritual part of us that is the core of our existence?

The spiritual heart is dependent on the true source of life, the broken heart and shed blood of Jesus Christ. Only by having His redeeming blood applied to our heart can we take all the "stuff" life throws our way, and bear the heavy burdens in spite of the circumstances. Why? Because the hearing heart listens to its life source. It is replenished and nourished by our prayer life and the daily application of His Word. There isn't a heartbeat or pulse that assures us this spiritual heart is still ticking. It's by faith that we turn our ears to wisdom and apply our hearts to His understanding.

On this first day of August, let's give our hearts to Christ anew. Let's sit at His feet and ask Him for wisdom and understanding. I want to hear what He has to say to me this month. How about you?

Thank You, Father, for Your love. Thank You for sending Your Son whose bleeding heart made it possible for us to have hearing hearts.

August 2

Scripture: "Trust in the Lord with all your heart and lean not on your own understanding" (Proverbs 3:5).

The date was July 1987—one of the worst memories of my life. I was facing the stark reality of letting go and closing a chapter in my life I desperately wanted to hold on to. My heart was breaking, my emotions filled with depression, worry, and anger. I could not imagine coping with all the pain. My husband was so supportive and reassuring. He

*The Scripture references used for this month's devotions are from the *New International Version* unless otherwise indicated.

understood my feelings of grief for the loss of the ministry I felt God had given me. One of my last duties was to attend the Christian Booksellers Convention in Anaheim, California. Off I went to the conference to teach a workshop, serve on a committee, and say goodbye to colleagues and friends.

The large convention floor was the size of two football fields. It was covered with hundreds of exhibitors and thousands of noisy people mingling in the bright colors and light. I walked in the midst of all this, teary-eyed and sad. As I passed one section of booths, my eyes made contact with a dear friend, Chuck Colson. He had already heard the news that I was saying goodbye to this phase of my life. He also knew how the loss was affecting me. Surrounded by reporters and dozens of people, he motioned for me. As I poured out my dilemma, the floodgates opened and the tears flowed. And he listened.

After a few minutes of listening, he quietly started talking. I still find this difficult to explain except to say it was one of those hearing-heart experiences. With all the noise and confusion around us, I wasn't aware of anything except what he was saying to me about God and His faithfulness. It was as though God put me in a cocoon so He could show me that although one door was closing, He was opening another one. He chose that place, time, and person to minister to me.

Chuck gave me a hug. As I turned to leave, it occurred to me that something extraordinary had happened. There were still lots of details to work through, details which would take months; but at the time of my greatest despair, God reminded me through a friend that He is absolute. There is no shadow of turning in Him. He was, He is, and forever will be faithful to His Word, and to me. No more wallowing in the sea of self-pity and discouragement. I had to get back to listening with my heart.

Thank You, Father, for sending special friends with listening hearts who remind me of Your faithfulness. Help me to be sensitive when my friends are going through similar circumstances.

August 3

Scripture: "But if a widow has children or grandchildren, these should learn first of all to put their religion into practice by caring for their own family and so repaying their parents and grandparents, for this is pleasing to God" (1 Timothy 5:4).

One of life's greatest treasures is found in those endearing creatures we call grandchildren. They bring so much joy and pleasure to all of us middle-agers. Actually they make silly creatures of us.

Their acceptance is so free, their love so unconditional. My grandchildren love me just because I'm "Memom," not because I'm the prettiest, thinnest, or smartest person in their lives. They don't judge me by the standards of society. They enjoy telling me about camp, soccer, swimming lessons, and school. If energy could be bottled, I think it would look like my grandchildren. Those little "genies" never walk when they can run. They never sit still more than two minutes at a time, and they love to stay up late when they spend the night with me.

I have those wistful moments when I'm watching them, wishing they could stay young and innocent—untouched by sin and life's ugliness. But it is not to be. They will grow up. Instead of camp it will be dating, instead of swimming lessons it will be cars, and school will turn into college. It's the natural evolution of growing up and getting on with life.

Their Papaw and I feel so blessed their moms gave us six wonderful grandchildren. We are constantly reminded that God uses even those things that are priceless possessions to us, like our grandchildren, to keep us listening to Him with hearing hearts.

When any one of these little ones snuggles up to me and whispers in my ear, "Memom, I love you," it is just another way I hear God saying, "Pat, I love you, too."

Thank You, Father, for my six precious grandchildren who mirror Your love to me and remind me that children are a heritage from You.

August 4

Scripture: "They that wait upon the Lord shall renew their strength" (Isaiah 40:31, KJV).

Follow me for a day. I am always in a rush—rushing to the dry cleaners, stopping at the bank, driving to an appointment, meeting with a committee, planning a big event, tearing down *after* that big event. My life is in a constant state of busyness. I'm always saying, "When I get time," or "If I had more time."

Stop! Let's rewind this tape. Follow me again. (We're both tired now.) Let's face it. My day is no different from yours. It has 24 hours—no more, no less. But how I choose to use those 24 hours is up to me. That's what makes it different from yours.

Those who work with computers get uptight when they have downtime. Hey, there are some days I long for "downtime." Clear out. Give me peace and quiet. Then I'm ready to go again. In reality, I believe I thrive on the pressure of juggling hectic schedules and meeting impossible deadlines.

What I have to remember in all this is that every day is a gift from God. He has entrusted me with these 24-hour segments. I can't waste today worrying about yesterday or fretting about tomorrow. Today is what is important. Jesus says, "Do not worry about tomorrow, for tomorrow will worry about itself. Each day has enough trouble of its own" (Matthew 6:34). Where does my heavenly Father fit in all this busy routine of mine?

First and foremost, He is the essence of who I am. As I go through my frantic and hurried days, I take time to keep my heart tuned to Him, listening intently for His guidance. His presence calms my spirit and helps me fit in my priorities: my husband, children, grandchildren, and my church. With every tick of the clock, I am aware that He is helping me, sustaining me, and turning my busyness into productivity. He keeps me going!

Thank you, Father, for the gift of each day. May I always keep my heart open to hear You, even in my busy pace.

August 5

Scripture: "Nevertheless, listen to what I have to say in your hearing" (Jeremiah 28:7).

Some of the most pleasurable times in my life are those rare Saturdays when my calendar says, "Free." My kitchen becomes the haven of Chef Bradbury. With a pantry and freezer full of raw and frozen ingredients, I bake, marinate, saute, and put together dishes and casseroles of all descriptions. As I stir, chop, and mix, I am at peace with the world. I can also listen and hear with my heart.

My husband cannot understand this at all. "How can working so hard make you so happy?" he asks. It's because cooking is therapy for me. I forget about work schedules as I mix ingredients to make all these different elements come together into a wonderful and tasty dish. Usually I give all the food away because my meat-and-potatoes husband can't believe anyone actually eats broccoli casserole or sweet potato pie. Forget about incense and simmering potpourri; I'll take the aroma of food sizzling, boiling, and baking any time. The wonderful fragrance permeates the whole house.

As I putter in the kitchen I often think, *God must see us in a similar way.* Just as it takes different ingredients to make a recipe into an elegant, tasty dish, He blends our unique personalities, interests, and creative decisions. Through His redemptive process this human mixture becomes the body of Christ—not yet finished, but forgiven.

This must be a wonderful aroma to the heavenly Father. My heart is blessed as I put away the food, clean my kitchen, and pause to reflect on the goodness of God. The food I've prepared will be quickly gone, but His blend of redemptive creations is eternal.

Lord, thank You for all the special blends of people in Your family. My heart rejoices at the wonder of Your eternal creation.

August 6

Scripture: "Jesus called the crowd to him and said, 'Listen and understand'" (Matthew 15:10).

Remember the old song that says, "I'll be somewhere listening, I'll be somewhere listening, I'll be somewhere listening for my name"?

It's confession time. Listening is not my strongest attribute. Yet, God constantly places me in situations where He teaches me important lessons in listening and understanding with my heart.

One of my dearest friends suffered a tragic and humiliating breakup of a long-term marriage. She was devastated! The shock of finding out about the lies and betrayal overwhelmed her. I could not personally identify with her pain and grief, but she was my friend, and she needed me.

Driving to her house I prayed, "Lord, give me the right words to say." But the Lord spoke to my heart and said, "Just listen, Pat. Listen with your heart."

Some people are natural listeners; but for extroverts, like me and many of you, listening is not our first instinct. We want to jump right in and say the right words—we want to be "instant fixers." Listening requires concentration and discipline. There will be a time to speak, but first we must listen and understand.

All night and the next day I stayed with my friend. I said very little. I was just there to support her and pray with her. Later she told me this was just what she needed at the time. To have someone who was there just for her, someone who would listen, meant more than all the fancy words and phrases I could have offered.

Jesus said in our scripture today, "Listen and understand." If I'm talking, I can't listen. And to understand I must first listen. My dictionary explains *listening* this way: "to be alert to catch an expected sound." If I am talking, I certainly cannot catch a sound, but my heart can.

The Lord taught me a valuable lesson through this incident. A sensitive, hearing heart can benefit not only my friend who is hurting, but me as well. The Holy Spirit, our Comforter, is there, preparing and consoling. He can use us to be there listening for hurting friends and family—if we are sensitive to Him with hearing hearts.

Lord, may my heart always be listening to You so that I will know when to listen and when to speak.

August 7

Scripture: "This calls for patient endurance and faithfulness on the part of the saints" (Revelation 13:10).

The hour is 6 p.m., and I'm just leaving work on this August afternoon. The sun is still beaming hot right into my car. About the time I get home, the car is just beginning to feel comfortable, but not really cool like my house.

Opening the door I am greeted, not with the usual kick-off-your-shoes-and-relax atmosphere, but with a hot, humid house turned inferno. Anger and panic kick in at the same time. Tennessee is in its worst heat wave in 60 years, the temperature is over 100 degrees, and my air conditioner is not working!

Frantically I reach for the phone book to call a repairman when my husband walks in. He is as surprised as I am that the air conditioner is not working, but he calmly tells me to put down the phone book until he checks it out. In order words, be patient.

Oh, great! I'm hot, tired, and now irritable. And what is he? Calm and patient. I don't want to be calm or patient. I want to be cool. Dialing for a repairman with one hand and fanning with the other, I hear the hum of the air conditioner click on. My grinning husband walks up the stairs with a satisfied look of "I told you so."

Something as simple as a tripped breaker in the fuse box had caused the air conditioner to go off. With the flip of a switch my husband spared us a costly repairman and hours of being hot and inconvenienced. Most of all, he taught me patience.

In reflecting on this, I thought, *How often we allow the little things to trip us up in our daily walk with God!* We make situations more difficult because we worry, fret, and fail to be patient. Wouldn't it be much easier to let the Holy Spirit whisper in our hearts the reassurance that He is always working on our behalf—calming, soothing, and even cooling our temperaments.

Help me, Lord, to stay focused and hear with my heart the Holy Spirit speaking to me to "stay cool."

August 8

Scripture: "Listen to me; be silent, and I will teach you wisdom" (Job 33:33).

There are times when God seems silent. I cannot hear His voice. I cannot feel His direction in my life. My heart feels cold and devoid of joy. I cry out to God, "Why?"

During these periods of silence, we learn to walk by faith. We must stay in His Word and know that God's silence is not like our human silence. He has a purpose!

In her book *His Imprint, My Expression*, Kay Arthur says, "[God] may be silent because He has spoken and we have not responded—so He waits. Or He may have spoken and we have said 'no'—so He gives us time to see the consequences of our disobedience. Or he may want to speak, but we are so busy that we are not giving Him the silence needed to hear 'His still small voice' in the recesses of our hearts. Or God may be silent because it is His time to be silent." Whatever the reason, we can still trust Him with our hearts.

The apostle Paul poses the questions of a troubled heart in Romans 8:35: "Who shall separate us from the love of Christ? shall tribulation, or distress, or persecution, or famine, or nakedness, or peril, or sword?" The answer resounds in the next few verses that nothing, not even silence, can "separate us from the love of God, which is in Christ Jesus our Lord" (v. 39, KJV).

One of the world's greatest composers, Ludwig van Beethoven, was unable to hear his own music for much of his adult life. His ears could not hear the joyful melodies, but his heart could. He could join with the psalmist in declaring: "You have filled my heart with greater joy than when their grain and new wine abound" (4:7). One of the most beautiful pieces of music ever composed is Beethoven's Ninth Symphony. It concludes with a choral rendition of the German poet Friedrich von Schiller's "Ode to Joy,"—the kind of joy that comes from the heart.

Even when all I hear is silence, help me Father to trust Your Word and know that You are still there, working in my behalf, and ultimately for my good. Thank You for joy during those times of silence.

August 9

Scripture: "Teach me your way, O Lord, and I will walk in your truth; give me an undivided heart, that I may fear your name" (Psalm 86:11).

We have all identified with the "Gloom, despair, and misery" song on the TV program *Hee Haw*, because we've all experienced these feelings. Recently I heard Kay Arthur talking about "Satan's Five Deadly D's." My first thought was *only five?* But when I heard the five, I knew these are the things that set a trap for me and divide my heart:

- Disappointment
- Discouragement
- Dejection
- Despair
- Demoralization

I am not a psychologist, but I can see a domino effect, beginning with the first D—disappointment. If we fail to deal with disappointment, discouragement quickly takes over. We then identify with the Cowardly Lion in needing courage—courage to stop the process. If not, the deadly D of dejection traps us until we sink in the quicksand of despair. The deadly D's are downward and demoralizing.

The key to victory is first of all to recognize Satan's cunning scheme. We cannot avoid disappointment, but we can stop the downward spiral. We can enter into spiritual warfare, sending Praise to the front lines. If we praise God in the disappointment, the D can be changed to an H, and we have "His appointment." His appointment is to sit at His feet and hear these words of encouragement:

"Be strong and take heart, all you who hope in the Lord" (Psalm 31:24).

"Be strong and courageous. Do not be afraid or terrified because of them, for the Lord your God goes with you; he will never leave you nor forsake you" (Deuteronomy 31:6).

Take the first step. He'll meet you there!

Thank You, Heavenly Father, for Your promise to never leave us. Give us undivided hearts set on You and Your Word.

August 10

Scripture: "Above all else, guard your heart, for it is the wellspring of life" (Proverbs 4:23).

During a recent windstorm, the giant maple tree that stood in the heart of our neighborhood fell. It was a landmark of sorts with a homemade swing that was the favorite thrill of the children. But now it was on the ground with its once-sturdy branches spreading awkwardly across the sidewalk.

Upon closer examination I discovered that my favorite maple didn't just give in to the gusty winds. It had some kind of disease that had been at work for a long time. Deep within the core of the maple tree, erosion had been eating away the strong fibers. This decay may have been going on for years, but no one could see it. The external bark looked strong and healthy, while the interior deteriorated. It just took one big puff to blow it down. Luckily no one was injured in the fall.

Within a short time the city came with their heavy equipment to clear away the limbs, leaves, and debris of the fallen tree. Newcomers to the neighborhood would not miss the lovely structure. They would not know anything unusual had happened.

What was an easy matter to clean up after a fallen tree is not true with a fallen life.

The sin that infects our lives eats at the very heart of our being, eroding our character, destroying our influence little by little. Then when the big temptation comes, there is a sudden collapse.

That's the way it is with sin. It's erosion could be at work even though the bark looks healthy and the fruit tastes sweet. Slowly and methodically, the will gives in, the compromise begins. And the fall is great!

Guard your heart. It is the wellspring of life!

We know that "man looks at the outward appearance, but the Lord looks at the heart" (1 Samuel 16:7). Keep our hearts pure, Lord, cleansed of the dreaded disease of sin.

August 11

Scripture: "I praise you because I am fearfully and wonderfully made; your works are wonderful, I know that full well" (Psalm 139:14).

Our hearts have over 100,000 miles of veins and arteries running throughout our bodies. This miracle pump transports the blood throughout the 100,000-mile course many times per day.

When the heart stops pumping blood, we've lost our source of life.

Each of us is infinitely valuable! As the psalmist said, we are "fearfully and wonderfully made."

This scripture became so real and significant to us when our granddaughter Brittany was born. When she was only two days old, the physician informed her parents that Brittany had a dangerous problem with her blood. In order for her to survive, all her blood would have to be transfused with other blood. Brittany was less than 6 pounds, tiny and frail, and the ordeal she would have to go through was a terrifying thought to us. The doctors assured us it would be harder on her parents and grandparents than it would be on the baby. As we looked at her through barriers of windows, she looked so helpless connected to tubes and machines. I remember thinking that as precious and valuable as she is to all of us, her family, how much more valuable and precious she is to God, for she is "fearfully and wonderfully made."

We cried and prayed and put Brittany in God's hands. She came through with flying colors, within hours was off the tubes and machinery, and in 48 hours went home with a relieved and happy family.

Today, eight years later Brittany is a healthy, happy child with more energy than any of us can imagine. Every life has value and meaning and a reason for being. Jesus gave His life so that we could have abundant life. As Brittany grows up, I want her to know how fragile her life was and how God touched her. I want her to know Him as Savior and Lord and listen with her heart to His guidance throughout her life.

As I write this, Father, my heart is filled with joy and thanksgiving remembering how good You are. Thank You for giving Your Son so that we might have eternal life.

August 12

Scripture: "Love the Lord your God with all your heart and with all your soul and with all your mind and with all your strength" (Mark 12:30).

Technology. Gadgets. Silicon Valley keeps dangling the latest electronic toys for us to bite and run with. As someone declared, it has made dentistry painless, bicycles chainless, carriages horseless, laws enforceless, cooking fireless, telegraphy wireless, coffee caffeineless, childbearing painless, oranges seedless, putting greens weedless, roads dustless, steel rustless, tennis courts sodless—and, in so doing, our lives godless.

Given a toehold in our hearts, sin quickly spreads not only across our own personal landscape, but also into the hearts of those around us. Sin is never isolated. Its consequences leave scars and pain. Sin not only has devastating effects on the one whose life it invades, but it also causes heartache and suffering to family and friends.

One of the worst effects of sin is that it can only reproduce rebellion, anger, bitterness, and hatred. On the other hand, love can only reproduce itself. If you sow love, you will reap love. It's impossible for love to reproduce anything less. Obedience, faith, and forgiveness can only be done in love. Galatians 5:19-25 makes this very clear. Sin wants to render us a godless society, our lives empty and useless. Thank God, we have the power through Christ to denounce sin, its cause, and its effect.

Today we choose to walk in love and its attributes. We refuse to be cold and heartless. We choose to listen with hearing hearts to the Holy Spirit so we can walk in love with the only true source of love, Jesus.

Father of love, forgive us our sins. Wash us pure, and give us hearts that seek to know You more intimately each day.

August 13

Scripture: "Be careful, or your hearts will be weighed down" (Luke 21:34).

God is interested in your care. As Paul wrote to his friends in Corinth, our lives are like letters people can read.

Someone has said, "Guard your heart, for out of your heart will flow your life story." Guard means to protect from danger by watchful attention, like protecting your infant. What's in our heart today and tomorrow will someday tell the story of who we really are.

Life flows from the heart. Gary Rosberg stated in his book *Guard Your Heart*: "The heart is where our life meets our environment. It's the gateway to our emotions and our relationships. It's where we feel deep joy. It's where we experience deep pain."

It boils down to this: We need to have a plan for constructing strong boundaries around our hearts to keep them tuned to the heart of God and protect them from invasion, contamination, and destruction. But the best laid plans can be attacked by the Enemy if we are not constantly on the alert. It can come out of nowhere. Just when everything appears to be going along fine, suddenly we are faced with a situation that brings unspeakable pain.

A few years ago my husband and I were surprised by the actions of someone very close to us. When the phone call came, we were devastated. I thought I would die from a broken heart. I don't believe anyone has actually died from a broken heart, but the anguish was so overwhelming I thought I could.

When the pain subsided briefly and we were able to be more focused, the Word of God that we believed and lived by became real and paramount at the time we needed it most. Proverbs 3:5, 6 became our theme: "Trust in the Lord with all your heart, and lean not on your own understanding; In all your ways acknowledge Him, and He shall direct your paths."

Only through a relationship with the Father and having hearing hearts which can hear Him speak, can we be overcomers through difficult circumstances. In the process, unbearable pain can become joy.

I know. I've been there. I've experienced it and can honestly say I am who I am in Christ because of His grace.

Gracious Father, open our eyes and hearts to Your Word. Only then can we trust You more.

August 14

Scripture: "We are God's workmanship, created in Christ Jesus to do good works, which God prepared in advance for us to do" (Ephesians 2:10).

We all seek significance—a need to love and be loved—a need to be accepted, not for what we do but for who we are. Success is fleeting, but personal significance is forever. Because of who we are in Jesus Christ we can take an inside look and say, "I have meaning. I am of value."

Our heart is really the issue. If it's open and willing, God can touch our lives and give us meaning and direction. However, if it is hardened or closed, we can expect a continual search for meaning and success. The bottom-line question is not who we are, but whose we are. Who do we trust with all our heart? We don't have to perform to be accepted. He accepts us with our flaws, our imperfections, our humanness.

Life would be wonderful if others accepted us as God does. I have a needlepoint phrase hanging in my kitchen that says, "I know I'm somebody because God doesn't make any junk."

At times I remind myself of that when I try to live up to the image and standards set by everyone else instead of God. Television, movies, magazines, and models bombard us constantly with their ideas of how we should dress, what car we should drive, what hairstyle we should have, what food we should eat, and even what places we should visit for fun and recreation. They want us to believe that these things make us feel accepted and worthy.

I've struggled for years with a weight problem and have tried every diet, fad, and book that came out that guaranteed me I would lose weight. None of these magic cures have been successful. They want me to believe that by just becoming thin I will be successful, happy, and accepted. What they don't know is that I'm already all of these. My happiness and self-worth are not directly related to what the scales say, what car I drive, or which clothes I wear. My self-worth is based on my relationship with Jesus. He gives me acceptance, worth, meaning, and direction for my life. Even when I fail, He constantly reassures my heart of His love. Because of who Jesus is and because I am His, I know who I am. My life has value and meaning. I mature spiritually as I listen with a hearing heart.

Open my heart, Lord, and fill it with Your divine love. Thank You for giving meaning to my life.

August 15

Scripture: "Put on a heart of compassion, kindness, humility, gentleness and patience" (Colossians 3:12, *NASB*).

Do you see a contrast between praying, "Lord, get me through the week; help me find a good parking place," and praying, "God give me power to speak Your Word with boldness"?

God's power fills the heart that wants only to see the Kingdom advanced. You may need to pray alone or you may be able to gather a core of right-hearted believers; but find a place, create the time, fall before God in the discipline of waiting. Do not procrastinate . . . because the stirring in your heart right now is a signal to pray without ceasing.

When you read the biographies of great saints of God like John Wesley, who so touched England's heart that its compassion was awakened to adopt 30,000 homeless children of London, you know his heart was open to the needs around him.

Charles Finney's heart was open to a fresh anointing. He was the major voice describing a second experience he called "the baptism in the Holy Spirit."

Women whose hearts the Lord has touched are not ordinary. They are extraordinary. They are powerful. Several observations have been made about those whose hearts have been touched by God:

- They are consistent in spending time in the Word.
- They have a joyful and contented attitude.
- They have a vibrant prayer life.
- They have a worshipful spirit.

Pray this prayer with me today:

Father, touch my heart and make it a heart of compassion, kindness, humility, gentleness, and patience so that I become an extension of You.

August 16

Scripture: "There is therefore now no condemnation to them which are in Christ Jesus, who walk not after the flesh, but after the spirit" (Romans 8:1, KJV).

The audience is anxiously waiting. Out walks the first-chair violinist to tune the instruments. For the next few minutes the notes sound chaotic as everyone tunes to the pitch of the violin. Once the process is finished, the conductor begins the concert. Glorious harmony pours forth. Every instrument is in tune, performing with perfection the orchestral symphonies. The audience responds with applause and encores.

Our lives, too, become chaotic when the things we use every day—our car, appliances, the watch we wear for correct time, the computer we work at for hours—are not maintained and kept tuned. Even our television sets and stereo systems have controls that will fine-tune the sound and color. When any of these things are not working properly, we get out of sync and life becomes complicated. But when they are right, life flows much easier.

What about the really important issue in our lives—keeping our hearts in tune with God? When our hearts are fine-tuned to God's Word, everything works better for us:

- We see problems and circumstances in a different light.
- We can live without condemnation.
- Our faith is renewed.
- We have confidence that our prayers will be answered.

Our scripture today says, "There is therefore now no condemnation to them which are in Christ Jesus, who walk not after the flesh, but after the spirit." This can only be accomplished with a heart tuned to God, listening for His instruction and guidance.

When we get "out of tune" because we neglect our priority time with God, it takes an adjustment to get our hearts once again in tune with the Father. Keeping God's Word in our hearts enables us to go about the Father's business, performing as the fine-tuned creations He designed us to be. The Enemy cannot take this away.

Fine-tune our hearts, Lord, so that we can build Your kingdom in glorious harmony.

August 17

Scripture: "For you did not receive a spirit that makes you a slave again to fear, but you received the Spirit of sonship. And by him we cry, 'Abba, Father'" (Romans 8:15).

It came from nowhere.

My husband was in Manila, Philippines, teaching Bible at their camp meeting; I was catering my daughter's Junior-Senior Prom and coordinating a major personal appearance for Chuck Colson in the bookstore. Without warning, a dark cloud settled over me, and I was depressed. Anxiety and fear gripped me with a paralyzing force.

I was terrified. Nothing like this had ever happened to me before. I didn't sleep, could barely eat, cried constantly, and rarely talked to anyone. I thought I was losing my mind. The more anxious I became, the more symptoms I experienced.

Looking back, I don't know how, except by the grace of God, I managed to get through all my commitments. When my husband came home, he knew immediately something was terribly wrong with me. I could not put into words how I felt because I didn't know what was wrong.

A visit to the doctor was the next step for me. I dreaded his diagnosis, thinking I certainly couldn't handle it. However, the doctor told me my problems were normal hormonal changes. Normal? Not for me. Not on this planet.

What he could not diagnose was the abnormal fear I had allowed to envelope me. Sure, a certain amount of reactive fear (fear of water or some other phobia) is a part of who we are. But the fear I was experiencing was rendering me useless. I could hardly function.

Thank God for a husband who is sensitive to the Holy Spirit. He recognized what a medical doctor could not. I certainly had some medical problems, but my fear was of a spiritual nature, which only the Word of God could combat.

We went to the Word. My well-worn *Amplified Bible* became my sword: "For the weapons of our warfare are not carnal, but mighty through God to the pulling down of strong holds" (2 Corinthians 10:4, KJV). Daily I let the Word penetrate the depression and gloom, and the clouds began to lift. My joy returned. Fear was replaced with peace.

This saga is much longer and more detailed than space would permit to tell, but in a matter of weeks the old Pat was back. The fear and depression were gone.

I'm so grateful for a hearing heart that was embedded with the Word of God. When I needed it most, my heart, mind, and spirit embraced the Word and received victory over fear.

Thank You, most gracious Father, for Your Word that pulls down the strongholds of fear and depression.

August 18

Scripture: "In everything I did, I showed you that by this kind of hard work we must help the weak, remembering the words the Lord Jesus himself said: 'It is more blessed to give than to receive'" (Acts 20:35).

Jesus himself said it is more blessed to give than to receive. My sister Peggie is one of those genuine individuals who not only believes this motto—she lives it every day. She and her husband, Dennis, believe that giving is a scriptural principle. Many times they have given out of their own need and have never been surprised when God comes through for them.

There is an old saying, "If you have much, give of your wealth. If you have little, give of your heart." Peggie listens with her heart instead of her reason, knowing if God is speaking to her heart, she must obey. She is not concerned with storing up material treasures here in this life. By their obedience, she and Dennis are a living legacy to their children, grandchildren, family, and friends. Their example of giving—often sacrificial giving—even in physical pain and difficulty is honored by God.

They have been an inspiration to people all over this country. They never ask for credit or recognition—that belongs to God. They never give with the expectation of receiving something in return. That, too, is up to God.

I have been amazed over the years as I watched God honor their giving. Peggie keeps a "Blessing Book." In it she records every time anyone gives to them, prays for them, or ministers to them in any way. How wonderful it is to see God's faithfulness. Even in times when finances are very limited, Peggie and Dennis open their bank account, their home, and their hearts. As a result many, many lives are touched and blessed.

God also keeps a record of our obedience. His blessings "are new every morning: great is [His] faithfulness" (Lamentations 3:23, KJV).

Respond to God's Word with a heart that blesses others. You too will be blessed!

Faithful Father, we honor Your Word; we respond with giving hearts knowing that every good and perfect gift comes from above.

August 19

Scripture: "Create in me a pure heart, O God, and renew a steadfast spirit within me" (Psalm 51:10).

Turn your eyes of understanding to your heart—the place where the King comes to reign like a brilliant pearl from the treasures of the Far East. Many who seek to grow in faith take their eyes off the Lord. Instead, they try to imitate the example of others.

I read that one of Alexander the Great's soldiers, who also happened to be named Alexander, needed disciplining for bad behavior. The soldier was brought before the great conqueror. After the soldier confessed his sinful deeds, Alexander turned to his namesake and made one simple statement: "Soldier, either change your conduct or change your name!"

Could the same admonition apply to those of us who bear the name of Christ?

Following the spiritual path without getting sidetracked is not as easy as it seems. But when we purpose to be women after God's own heart, we seek the following spiritual virtues:

1. An attitude of heart that peacefully rests in God, receiving from His good hands, so that we may have joy in Him in spite of our circumstances (Philippians 4:4-8).
2. The ability to let God reveal and put to death the things in us that seek esteem and power over others, so that we can freely love God and affectionately serve others in meekness (1 John 2:16).
3. Faith enough to trust and let go of our earthly securities, whether possessions or people, and trust only in our Lord, whose kingdom is eternal (John 18:36).

You may be thinking, *Wow, that's a big assignment!* I agree. But if we are willing to seek this kind of Christian maturity, He provides spiritual nourishment and renews a steadfast spirit within us.

Let's make Him proud to call us His namesakes!

Thank You, gracious Father, for adopting us as daughters. Create in us a pure heart that always follows You.

August 20

Scripture: "He heals the brokenhearted and binds up their wounds— curing their pains and sorrows" (Psalm 147:3, *Amp*).

There are so many wonderful attributes of God it is difficult to single out just one. Our scripture today says that He heals those who have a broken heart and binds up their wounds. He also cures their pains and sorrows. What more could we desire?

If ever anyone suffered a broken heart, it was David. Did he spend time feeling sorry for himself? No. Because his heart was right, David pressed on, seeking the heart of God for healing and restoration.

Over the years it has been amazing to me how God has made it possible through time and the healing balm of the Holy Spirit to heal bad memories and experiences. Even when the event was devastating, God, the Word, and time worked together to dull the painful ache, allowing us to get on with life and put the painful memories behind us.

Psalm 126:5 assures us, "They who sow in tears shall reap in joy and singing" (*Amp*). There isn't a physician, therapy, or medication on the market that can come close to this promise. If we can just remember when we are in the midst of our grief, God has already made provision for the healing process to begin. We do not have to live emotionally and spiritually crippled from painful memories of yesterday. As Christians we can believe God's Word and let time do the rest.

In Chuck Swindoll's book *The Finishing Touch*, he describes how to respond when struck by one of life's arrows: "Don't waste time licking your wounds or wondering why. Make a decision to do what you were doing even better than ever. Life's arrows are nothing more than momentary setbacks that help us regroup, renew, and reload."

I'm not suggesting this is easy. It's tough. These momentary setbacks can seem more like months, or even years. But the hope, peace, and joy Christ gives will overcome bad memories. Listen closely with your hearing heart. Hear the Father caring for His hurting child, speaking healing and comfort.

For all the times You comfort and heal our wounded hearts, thank You, Father. Help us listen more closely and receive healing and comfort.

August 21

Scripture: "I applied my heart to what I observed and learned a lesson from what I saw" (Proverbs 24:32).

I suppose one of the advantages of getting older is being able to look back over our lives and reflect on the people and events that helped shape and mold us. I must be getting older because I now reflect with a grateful heart and remember so many people who believed in me and opened doors of opportunities for me.

E.C. Thomas, who gave me my first job with Pathway and later gave me a managerial position, stands out as one of these memorable persons. In the early '60s when it wasn't very popular to hire a woman for any position, Brother Thomas changed my life. Over the years he and his wife, Alice, became dear and special friends. They ministered to my family in so many ways. My husband is still using golf clubs that were given to him by Brother Thomas.

H. Bernard Dixon took the time and effort to teach, train, and encourage me when I started with Pathway. Under his guidance I learned about marketing, sales techniques, and other skills that aren't taught in any classroom or textbook. By his example I saw how integrity in any business transaction is the only way to go. He is a man of Christian character who has proven that you can be Christian and still be very successful.

Debbie Massengale Tucker who worked with me for over 20 years taught me that beauty, design, and color have a place in marketing and the kingdom of God. She is an artist who sees God's handiwork in almost everything. She can turn the mediocre into something beautiful and spectacular for the glory of God. I'm proud to call her friend.

Haskel and Elizabeth Holloway became our family and have a place in my memory hall of fame. When we moved to Tennessee, they gave us a place to stay and became surrogate grandparents to our girls. For more than 30 years they have been a special part of our lives.

Jerry and Pat McNabb, Gerald and Sue Holloway, and all the couples in the Young Companions Class and the Liberty Class allowed Richard and me to have a ministry with them and were instrumental in our spiritual development.

Others too numerous to mention have inspired, ministered, and positively impacted my life. My heart is filled with gratitude to God for allowing these godly friends and coworkers to intersect my life at just the right time and place.

Father God, I want to thank You again for my friends—those who mentored me and helped me in my life's pursuits. I pray special blessings on them and their children.

August 22

Scripture: "If your heart is wise, then my heart will be glad" (Proverbs 23:15).

Recently I was rushing to Chattanooga to keep an appointment. Driving too fast, talking even faster on my car phone, and trying to remember a dozen things I needed to do that day when I arrived at my appointment would register about 8.5 on the stress-level Richter scale.

No matter how organized I think I am, there never seems to be enough hours in the day to handle all I want to accomplish. As I settled down to reality, I remembered something I recently read by Warren Weirsbe. He said, "God isn't in a hurry." I wondered, *Then why am I?*

I'm always rushing to finish one project, have several more simmering on the back burner, and constantly feel frustrated because I can't do more. So what is wrong with this scenario? Weirsbe also said, "A weary body is usually a sign of a foggy mind."

Wait a minute! A foggy mind? Not me (I don't think).

At this time in my life I'm not sure how to make life less stressful. If I could just shift out of overdrive into a lower gear—without losing productivity—life would be smoother for me and those around me.

Then my hearing heart whispers: "Pat, you know what will help you cope. Pause long enough to listen and respond to the Holy Spirit." Of course, I know. What about the many times in the past when He spoke peace in the midst of chaos and patiently reminded me that the Word of God is my stress release.

God's timing is always perfect. His Word is sure, His grace abundant, His mercy available, His peace constant, and His love enduring. And best of all, He never changes. Who God is, is now and forever absolute. So everything I need has been provided by God through the Holy Spirit—not just to serve my carnal desires, but to teach me to use my time wisely.

The scripture today says, "If [my] heart is wise, then [His] heart will be glad."

My hurried lifestyle may not change to a peaceful, calm, slow existence, but my hearing heart is never too busy to recognize His voice speaking in the midst of all the stress.

Thank You, Holy Spirit, for every time You whisper to me, "Slow down; I'll help you cope."

August 23

Scripture: "May he give you the desire of your heart and make all your plans succeed" (Psalm 20:4).

Recently I took my two 11-year-old granddaughters shopping. They were so excited, especially since they know I am such a soft touch when it comes to giving them the desires of their hearts.

They quickly educated me on the right backpack, Air Nikes, and starter jackets. One shopping spree and I was up-to-date on what's cool and what's not.

As my energy level waned, I dropped to low gear, but they stayed in high gear (maybe overdrive). Even though I was enjoying spending quality time with my grandchildren, was I ever getting tired! At each store there was something they just could not live without—that is until we got to next store. That "just perfect" item was quickly replaced with, "This is exactly what I've been looking for!"

Finally, after a very long day, they decided on the jackets, shoes, and hats that would make them feel cool. They were so happy. And I was delighted that I could indulge my granddaughters in things that pleased them. Their thanks and hugs of appreciation were like receiving the greatest prize in the whole world.

Yet I realize that as my husband and I love, affirm, and bless our grandchildren, an even greater prize is in store for us who love the Lord with all our hearts. The *Living Bible* reads like this in Philippians 3:13-14: "I am still not all I should be but I am bringing all my energies to bear on this one thing: Forgetting the past and looking forward to what lies ahead, I strain to reach the end of the race and receive the prize for which God is calling us up to heaven because of what Christ Jesus did for us."

What a blessing! As my grandchildren tire of their toys and gadgets, change styles of jackets, and outgrow their Air Nikes, I pray a special prayer each day that they will realize that these "prizes" are temporal. The only thing that has eternal value is giving their hearts to Jesus as Lord and Savior.

May I always respond as the Holy Spirit speaks to my heart to nurture, love, and pray for these prize grandchildren, my spiritual gifts from God.

Father, as much as we love to give gifts to our children and grandchildren, how much more do You delight in giving good gifts to us, Your children! Help us to keep reaching for the eternal prize.

August 24

Scripture: "My son, do not forget my teaching, but keep my commands in your heart" (Proverbs 3:1).

All of us at some time in our lives have heard these words: "It's time we had a heart-to-heart talk." This could apply to a boss and employee discussing a problem; a husband and wife needing to talk about the budget, relocating, or some major decision; a friend wanting to discuss a crisis or problem; a member of the church family wanting to minister or give counsel; and of course, the big one—between parent and child.

We who are parents can never forget those infamous heart-to-heart talks with our adolescents and teenagers. Some were direct and painful, some life-changing; others made no difference at all. Yet someone at some time felt the need for an intimate talk.

While our two daughters were still at home, these heart-to-heart chats were often accompanied with consequences like "You're grounded." We even used the approach from Ephesians 6: "Children, obey your parents . . . that you may live long on the earth" (vv. 1, 3).

Our girls did not think this was funny at all. Every time we used this one they would roll their eyes and moan as if.to say, "Oh, no, not the obey-your-parents-thing again."

Seriously, I remember heart-to-heart talks over the years with family and friends that were for my benefit. I've been ministered to, and I've made significant changes because someone cared enough to have a heart-to-heart talk with me.

There have also been those times when God would tell me it's time to have that talk with someone. I've seen hard hearts softened, pent-up tears released, pain and grief eased, and forgiveness manifested. Then I ask myself, "Am I this sensitive and open to hear from the Holy Spirit on a heart-to-heart basis?" I hope so. After all, only He can mold our character to make us conform to the image of Christ; only He can break bad habits and reverse wrong attitudes; only He can change rebellion to obedience and make us spiritually healthy.

This kind of heart-to-heart encounter comes with this warning: "Permanent, life-changing effects!"

Thank You, Holy Spirit, for all the times You have spoken to my heart while sitting at your feet.

August 25

Scripture: "When he arrived and saw the evidence of the grace of God, he was glad and encouraged them all to remain true to the Lord with all their hearts" (Acts 11:23).

Bob Hope's famous theme song, "Thanks for the Memories," could also be my theme song. My husband and I love to travel. The joy of experiencing beautiful scenery, meeting new people, making new friends, and of course enjoying great food combine to make travel one of our favorite pastimes. I store these wonderful memories in my heart. From time to time, Richard and I reminisce about how blessed we are to have these reflections. There are still many places we would like to visit, but we have the same dilemma as many others—not enough time and money.

Some of the more memorable experiences include these:

- The trip to the Holy Land and the touching communion service by the Garden Tomb led by Bob Sustar and Paul Henson.
- Two weeks in the Philippines with our good friends Gerald and Sue Holloway who made us part of their conference, in addition to the times of laughter, talking, and sharing as only old friends can.
- Hong Kong, where we spent several days with Lovell and Ginny Cary, going to all the right shops, seeing the beautiful scenery, and eating truly memorable meals at McDonalds.
- A much-needed time of rest and relaxation at the Royal Hawaiian Hotel in Hawaii that included incredibly beautiful weather, exquisite food, and walks on the beach.

We have visited so many places in the States which have provided wonderful memories, but one place and event holds a particularly warm place in my heart. Richard and I were in San Francisco—one of our favorite spots. One morning we left our hotel while it was still dark, walked to Fisherman's Wharf, got us a steaming cup of coffee, sat at the edge of the water, and watched the sun come up over the bay. It was an unforgettable experience! Just being together in quiet solitude, talking about the magnificence of God's creation encouraged us to remain true to the Lord with all our hearts.

How blessed we are to personally know the Creator and experience His grace. These memories touch my heart as much today as the day we made them.

We thank You, Father, for every opportunity we have to visit faraway places and enjoy Your creation. Thank You for the memories.

August 26

Scripture: "Let those who love the Lord hate evil, for he guards the lives of his faithful ones and delivers them from the hand of the wicked" (Psalm 97:10).

We were terrified as we rushed through traffic to the emergency room of Children's Hospital. Our 3-year-old daughter, Linn, was very sick—almost delirious with a high fever, screaming, "My head is hurting!"

After what seemed to be an eternity of excruciating tests, they informed us Linn had spinal meningitis. I nearly fainted with fear as the doctor explained the complications that could occur and the isolation that would be necessary. I could hear Linn crying for her Mommy and Daddy, but we could not go to her. (Remember this was 1960 and the hospitals and technology were not as advanced as they are today.)

To further complicate matters, I was in labor with our second child. Afraid I was going to deliver there, the staff at Children's Hospital kept trying to rush me out the door, but I was reluctant to leave Linn. I agreed to leave only if I could see her. It was one of the most heart-wrenching scenes: looking through thick glass at my child encased in a large crib with her arms outstretched for Mommy and Daddy. She cried so hard her voice became hoarse.

Leaving Linn in the care of our pastor and my sister, we raced across town to Methodist Hospital. Two hours later Kelley was born.

Richard ran back and forth from Children's Hospital to Methodist

Hospital to check on Linn and the new baby and me. Because of complications I was hospitalized for seven days. The day Kelley and I left the hospital, Linn was well enough to leave Children's Hospital. After all the prayers, Linn was completely healed of meningitis and has never had any problems from the illness.

Never have I been so grateful for my personal relationship with Jesus and my church family. My heart is still moved, even after 38 years, at the faithfulness of God. The scary events of that day are still as vivid as if they occurred yesterday. Thinking back, I wonder how we ever got through it. Then I realize it was only the grace of God that sustained us.

Father, I am amazed at the many times You undergird us when we feel overwhelmed. Thank You for Your faithfulness.

August 27

Scripture: "You yourselves are our letter, written on our hearts, known and read by everybody" (2 Corinthians 3:2).

It's a lazy, autumn Saturday afternoon, and Richard and I are in the den having one of life's greatest pleasures, a cup of Starbuchs coffee. He is watching football and I am reading. I glance over at him and think how fortunate I am. We have been married 39 wonderful years, and it has been quite a journey.

Of course we've had peaks and valleys, sicknesses and surgeries. There have been times of plenty and times of want. We've been hit with some of life's unexpected crises; we've raised two children, ministered in several churches, and made great memories together. We have been through thick and thin together literally, and still I want nothing more than to grow old with this man I married.

We're so different—he's a procrastinator; I'm impulsive. He's a thinker; I rush to judge. He's an introvert; I'm an extrovert. He likes to go to bed early, and I'm a night owl. He likes to save; I like to spend. He is a meat-and-potatoes man; I'll eat almost anything.

With all these differences you'd think life would be difficult, but not so with us. It has made life more interesting. We can now finish each other's sentences, and anticipate each other's moods, likes, and dislikes. I love being with him, laughing, talking, and sharing our hopes and dreams. And he has a great shoulder to cry on.

Richard is my husband, lover, best friend, model Daddy, and Papaw. Even with his faults, he is still the man I have unquestionable confidence in as a Christian. I have never known him to compromise his integrity or character. He still makes my heart sing, and I'm proud to be his wife. God has taken two opposite personalities and blended together a strong relationship, a solid marriage, and a beautiful life.

Through the years, I've listened as the Holy Spirit spoke to my heart about every phase of my life. When it came to Richard and our marriage, I'm so glad I listened. Richard is the best thing that has ever happened to me.

I praise You each day, Father, for giving me a godly husband, father to our girls and grandfather to our grandchildren.

August 28

Scripture: "Bear with each other and forgive whatever grievances you may have against one another. Forgive as the Lord forgave you" (Colossians 3:13).

It's not hard for me to say, "I'm sorry," or "Forgive me," because I've had lots of practice. In my heart I would never hurt someone intentionally, but it still happens through periods of indifference, wrong attitudes, or sudden anger. Sometimes it's a matter of just proving I'm right. Not long ago I hurt a coworker's feelings very badly. It was not intentional, but when I realized how hurt and devastated she was, I was crushed. The last thing I would ever want to do is be a source of pain for her.

We have worked together for many years and not only have a good working relationship but also a close friendship as well. Yet in this situation I had hurt her deeply and brought her to tears. I not only needed to apologize and ask her forgiveness, but I also needed to be forgiven. With tears in my eyes I apologized and asked for her forgiveness. Being the person and Christian she is, the incident was put behind us and the relationship grows stronger.

I've had to apologize to my husband, children, family, friends, coworkers, and even customers. I don't take it lightly or apologize with words only. I truly want to be repentant and sorry if I have been the means of any pain, misunderstanding, or confusion. With my outgoing, extroverted, and opinionated personality, I've hurt people without even realizing it. I occasionally remind myself that not everyone agrees with my views or even wants to hear them.

Our hearts must be right with God before we can relate to others with love and forgiveness. I'm very grateful for a hearing heart that is sensitive to the leading of the Holy Spirit—one that is always ready to say, "I'm sorry. Forgive me." After all, this is only possible through the Spirit, not human efforts. His Word tells us in Colossians 3:13 to "bear with each other and forgive whatever grievances you may have against one another. Forgive as the Lord forgave you."

Remind us, dear Lord, that we are to forgive others as You forgive us. Keep our hearts sensitive to Your Spirit so that we can hear and respond.

August 29

Scripture: "He is like a tree planted by streams of water, which yields its fruit in season and whose leaf does not wither. Whatever he does prospers" (Psalm 1:3).

In my yard stand seven huge, majestic maple trees. In the fall they burst into blazing, glorious colors. In spring and summer we enjoy their beautiful green leaves and cool, refreshing shade.

Even in the winter their tall, bare limbs frame our home, just waiting to produce beautiful foliage again come spring. I'm amazed at how sturdy these trees are year after year. They have weathered the test of time through rain, snow, wind, and heat. With very little care, they keep giving us the shade and beauty we've come to expect.

Sitting on my patio with newspaper and coffee in hand, I relish not only the security and beauty of these mighty maple trees but also all the picnics, parties, Easter egg hunts, and cookouts we have shared together. Richard and I have clocked many hours sitting in the swing— talking, planning, and reminiscing. The grandchildren play ball, ride bikes, run and play, never giving a thought about the shade or protection these trees give.

Hanging in the tree right outside our bedroom are wind chimes that delight my heart with each new song of melodic praise rustling through the trees. I've told my husband I would live in this house just because I love the trees. He shares my feelings except in late fall when he has to rake leaves from seven maples. Yes, they have weathered the test of time through rain, snow, wind, and heat; and they continue to amaze me with their durability and beauty.

I want my life to resemble the things I see in these trees:

- I want to stand firm and unbending when the storms of life hit.
- I want to produce the fruit of the Spirit over and over again.
- I want the beauty of Christ to be manifested in my life so that others can see God in me.
- I want the wind of the Holy Spirit to sweep through my heart with cleansing power so that I will always be faithful to God and His kingdom.

Father God, creator of all things in heaven and on earth, we bless You today for who You are. We exalt Your name and worship Your majesty.

August 30

Scripture: "I will restore to you the years that the locust hath eaten" (Joel 2:25, KJV).

A few years ago I delivered the eulogy at the funeral of a young man 34 years old who had died a tragic death. He and his family have been close friends for more than 25 years. He was gifted in music, but somewhere along the road to success he lost his way. The pleasures of sin had taken their course and now had taken his life.

Through his illness and death, I watched his Spirit-filled mother stand by him with a steadfast faith, believing God to restore him. Raised in a loving, Christian home could not save him. Death was a devastating blow to this family, yet his mother never wavered in her belief that he would come back to the Lord before he died.

A few days before he went into a coma and died, he told his mother, "Everything is all right between me and God. It is well with my soul." These were the sweetest, most assuring words she had ever heard. As he lay in a coma, hours from death, his family surrounded his bedside, singing the Christian songs he had sung growing up. Only minutes before death as his family sang "Peace, peace, wonderful peace," he joined them in singing, in perfect harmony. This was his glorious entry into the presence of the One he was singing about.

A few days after his burial, his mother wrote me a note and said the Lord had given her this scripture in Joel 2:25. "I will restore to you the years the locusts have eaten." To her, this was the Lord's way of telling her what sin had stolen from him is now restored. What a beautiful testimony!

In the six years since her son died, death has taken her 14-year-old granddaughter, her mother-in-law, and her husband of more than 40 years. She has cancer, yet she has never asked, "Why me?" Her trust in the Lord is stronger than ever, never questioning God. Through the years I've heard her sing, "It Is Well With My Soul" and "Great Is Thy Faithfulness." These were not mere words to her. She lived them! And God sustained and strengthened her through the difficult circumstances.

I can never read the following passages of scripture without thinking of my friend. For our prayer today, join me in praying Habakkuk 3:17-19:

Though the fig tree does not blossom, and there be no fruit on the vines; [though] the product of the olive fail, and the fields yield no food; though the flock be cut off from the fold, and there be no cattle in the stalls; yet I will rejoice in the Lord, I will exult in the [victorious] God of my salvation! [see Romans 8:37]. The Lord God is my strength, my personal bravery and my invincible army; He makes my feet like hinds' feet, and will make me to walk [not to stand still in terror, but to walk] and make [spiritual] progress upon my high places [of trouble, suffering or responsibility]! (Amp.).

August 31

Scripture: "But Mary treasured up all these things and pondered them in her heart" (Luke 2:19).

What are you pondering in your heart today? If the word *pondering* is an out-of-date term, let's replace it with the word *focus*. What is my focus? A real giveaway is, What *words* am I speaking?

Christ did not ignore this topic. He spoke with clarity in Matthew 12:37: "For by thy words thou shalt be justified, and by thy words thou shalt be condemned." Why our words? Because the words we speak reveal the things on which our hearts are focused.

Joseph Stowell said in his book *Shepherding the Church Into the 21st Century*: "In a sense, words tattle on our hearts. Words betray a confidence regarding the real me. And wouldn't this mean as well that words are a reflection of our relationship to Him? If He indeed is the treasure of our hearts, if our hearts are rooted in walking in ways to please Him, then our words will reflect that. If, however, all we have is a religion that is simply a habitual, professional, well-practiced ritual, then ultimately it's our words that will unmask the fact that our hearts are far from Him."

I can hear you saying: "But, Pat, what about those who know just the right words to say. How can you *really* tell what's in their hearts?"

The Pharisees had the right words down pat, but Christ said they were defiled within. That mask eventually dissipates, and the issues of the heart—like our dreams, desires, and decisions—come through loud and clear.

What's the answer? The hymn writer Charles A. Tindley says it best:

> Nothing between my soul and the Savior,
> So that His blessed face may be seen;
> Nothing preventing the least of His favor.
> Keep the way clear! let nothing between.

Father, You know our hearts. You know our motives. Help us keep out all the clutter so that nothing comes between us and Your favor.

$\mathscr{September}$

Listening Ears
Pat Delk Daugherty

Pat Delk Daugherty grew up in southern Georgia. Her parents, the late John Paul Delk and Grace Delk, ministered in the Church of God for over 40 years. While at Lee College she met and married Robert E. Daugherty of Chattanooga, Tennessee. They have four children who are actively involved in some facet of local church ministry.

Pat's talents and creativity are utilized in every aspect of church ministry including music, evangelism, Ladies Ministries, teaching, drama, administration, entertainment, and creative writing. Pat's ministry is mainly one of sharing. Whether it be a play, skit, Sunday school lesson, or a seminar, you can be sure the message is one from the heart. She currently serves as state Ladies Ministries president in South Carolina and is a member of the International Ladies Board of Directors of the Church of God. Pat's motto for living is "I can do all things through Christ who strengthens me" (Philippians 4:13, *NKJV*).

September 1

Scripture: "See then that ye walk circumspectly, not as fools, but as wise, redeeming the time" (Ephesians 5:15, 16).

"September's Song" used a couple of words in its lyrics that I want to borrow—"dwindle down." September is the month that indeed the days do begin to dwindle down, grow shorter. We begin counting down the days until the end of the year. The chill of air that blankets September announces our descent into fall. The definition of *dwindle* is "to make or become smaller and smaller."

The headline on the front page of *The Greenville News* caught my attention: "Some Think Age Issue Can Hurt Thurmond, but He's Not One of Them." South Carolina senior senator, Strom Thurmond, at 92 is gearing up for another election bid next year! Is the fountain of youth somewhere here in South Carolina?

Thurmond responded to the article like this: "There are very few people who at 92 years of age are in as good a shape as I'm in. Ordinarily when you think of a person of 92, you think of a person that's beyond the age of activity. I'm not. I took 50 minutes of exercise this morning; I swim twice a week. I don't plan to run but one more time." Then he chuckled, "I hope to still be serving at age 100 . . . can you imagine that?" Pretty impressive, wouldn't you say?

Caleb, the centenarian, impressed me by taking on mountain climbing at 100! The facts are, the days of Thurmond, as well as ours, will *dwindle down*. Many cancer patients face the reality of such days. We know we will have thousands of years to sit at His feet in eternity, but what about today? Do I have time to *sit at His feet* this year . . . this day . . . this moment?

Listen closely and see if you can hear what I hear in Ephesians 5:15, 16: "See then that ye walk circumspectly, not as fools, but as wise, redeeming the time." The Lord is saying, "Buy up opportunities to serve Me."

Assuming we live out our allotted "threescore and ten years," take five years off for being a baby, and one-third of our time spent sleeping, and it quickly drops to 43. Subtract other life segments and it leaves so little time allocated to serving Him. Do we let the day *dwindle down* without spending some time sitting at His feet? He gives us strength to get up on our feet, and remain on our feet, and He sends us on errands of service for Him!

I have had days I allowed to *dwindle down*. It was a day crammed full, yet at the end of that day, I asked myself, "What did I accomplish of worth today?" At the end of our days, how horrible it would be to discover that we let the days *dwindle down*! We could have redeemed (saved) or used them more wisely. September is a great month to begin saving dwindling days!

Father, at the beginning of this month I pray that You would open our ears. Clear out all the distractions that hinder us from sitting at Your feet and listening to You.

September 2

Scripture: "Sing the Lord's song" (Psalm 137:4).

Another Sunday . . . I dreaded it. After having been a pastor's wife for 28 years, I had come to understand Sundays are a BIG DEAL! But my new attitude in my new circumstances was expressed in the song title, "Never on Sunday."

Bob had really settled into his new assignment as the evangelism director of South Georgia. But for me . . . I missed our fashionable church in Jesup, Georgia, where I taught a Sunday school class and played the organ on Sundays. For several Sundays now I had accompanied Bob in organizing new churches. Today we pulled out at 7:30 a.m. for this Sunday's appointment. We were driving along one of those long stretches of South Georgia country road flanked by tall sapling pines.

Suddenly that lonely, lost, what-am-I-doing-here feeling crept over me. I reached for the knob on the radio and turned it down. "Bob," I said. "I don't want to hurt your feelings about your sermon today, but do you know what I think would help me the most?" That will rattle any preacher. Jumping right on it, he asked, "No, what?"

"A choir," I answered. "I haven't heard a choir sing in months!" Then he began to fill in details he had neglected to tell me earlier. First of all, we would not be meeting in a church, but a trailer. Second, this was the first Sunday for the people to worship in the trailer. I drew my own bleak conclusion. Forget the choir!

A group of 15 to 20 people and a wonderful black lady pastor greeted us. The group was excited over officially coming into the Church of God. This was a day of celebration!

The service began. The pastor said, "Our sanctuary choir is coming to open our worship." Looking around, I saw no evidence of a choir. A teenage boy went to the piano, the back door opened, and in came three beautifully robed black sisters. They were singing and clapping their hands as they marched down the short trailer aisle. To this day, I have never heard anything like it. Neither Solomon's Singers nor the Brooklyn Tabernacle Choir could have had better harmony or melody.

Tears streamed down my face. Then I felt that familiar nudging in my heart—a word from the Lord: "You asked for a choir today, didn't you? How's that?" When my eyes met Bob's, he winked at me! It was confirmation. God sent me a choir! I have found if I will have a listening ear, God will sing to me. He sings to me in the rustling of the trees, the crackle of a fire, or the song of a bird. I have awakened many mornings with a song.

God gives songs in the night! (Job 35:10).

Dear Father, You wrote the original score; You are the song! When other things distract us, help us listen for Your song.

September 3

Scripture: "O taste and see that the Lord is good" (Psalm 34:8).

On the car radio Dr. Tony Evans was waxing eloquent in his sermon on the moral vices of sin when he exclaimed, "You are going to hell if you keep on partying." My daughter, Robin, and her son, Anthony, then age 5, were the only ones in the car. Both heard it clearly and distinctively, but it made no great impression . . . it seemed.

After a few moments we heard an instant replay! "Mom, why would you go to hell for having a birthday party?" Anthony asked. Robin explained, "He is not talking about birthday parties, Anthony. Sometimes when people get older they drink beer and liquor. That's wrong, so don't ever do that." Being the smart boy he is, he seemed to understand her explanation. After a few moments, suddenly he bolted up on edge of the seat to confess, "Mom, I've drank some root beer, but I have never messed with that licorice!"

Licorice . . . I love it by the cords! My children have always thought I was truly weird, so it was no problem for them to save me all the black jelly beans. It's the clear choice for me in candy shops. How delighted I was recently to discover that this leguminous plant from Europe and Asia with its sweet taste is good for me. Its dried root, or an extract made from it, is used in many medicines, as well as confections. Just what my listening ears wanted to hear—it's good, and good for me!

When I sit at Jesus' feet, I hear words that lift my heart. I cannot imagine sitting at Jesus' feet with my heart all bent out of shape! It might have been broken when I first came into His presence, but not for long. Proverbs 17:22 tells me that "a merry heart doeth good like a medicine."

I like three words beneath Charles Swindoll's book title *Laugh Again.* They say, *Experience Outrageous Joy.*

Dr. Evans spoke truth. People about us are on their road to hell. Other travelers, like ourselves, are taking the scenic, higher route and experiencing outrageous joy on the journey.

Why live a life that is bound? Lazarus was all bound up, but he was dead! Jesus said, "Loose him." Teens put it this way: "Loosen up, man." I would say, "Lazarus, have some licorice!"

There are times when I need healing inside—a spoonful of medicine. Jesus always knows how to put a little sweetness in the pain. I join with the psalmist in offering you some "licorice."

"O taste and see that the Lord is good!"

Father, for joy and laughter, we give You thanks. We offer You a sweet-smelling fragrance of joyful praise today!

September 4

Scripture: "The sheep follow him: for they know his voice" (John 10:4).

He is dashingly handsome with his gorgeous deep-brown eyes. His gray hair, tipped with white edges, makes him look distinguished! He is my backyard squirrel.

He first visited my patio area with a bunch of his wild friends. I had tamed squirrels before in my Charlotte home. Upon seeing them playing around my patio here in Greenville, I made a few sounds and talked to them as I threw out a handful of South Georgia peanuts— straight from Jimmy Carter country! They all reminded me of Ray Steven's squirrel. They went berserk! After going back into the house, I noticed they were back, enjoying the treats.

Day by day, I noticed this one particular little fuzzy fellow. He perched himself on a burnt wooden Daugherty sign nailed to a tree in the patio area. When I would see him there, I would get some peanuts for him. At first, I had to throw him a peanut to talk to him. Then I began noticing . . . I could begin talking to him, throwing him a peanut now and again. He would jump down, get another peanut, and I could continue talking while he listened and munched away. He was becoming familiar with my voice. He was sitting closer to my feet than he had ever been before.

I know a few things about this squirrel. He likes peanuts. What he doesn't know about me is that I have lots of South Georgia pecans in my freezer that he'd like even better. I have enough peanuts that I could give him treats all winter. There is only one thing I want from him—to recognize my voice and respond to it. I have other good things to share with him. I know he has a fondness for leftover peanut brittle.

Does my heavenly Father want less than this from me? He has dropped far more than peanuts into my life to draw me close to Him. He gives handfuls on purpose to me. While I am enjoying them, He reminds me from whence my blessings have come.

What does He want? Voice recognition and activation! "The sheep follow him: for they know his voice" (John 10:4). The voice of God activated creation. When *God said* . . . waters moved, lights came on, land shifted into place. Forget the yellow Caterpillars!

Voice prints can be strong evidence in court. I have a small GE recorder that responds to my voice! Moses knew the voice of God. One day Moses asked God for far more than peanuts. He asked to see His glory! Something no one had ever asked of Him. God granted it to him by tucking him inside a rock while His glory passed in review. God told him to listen for His voice. How would Moses know it was God and not an angel? The voice would identify God. We have family voice recognition. God wants us to personally recognize His voice. Are we satisfied with peanuts? Follow His voice. It belongs to the Good Shepherd!

How can we follow, Father, if we don't hear Your voice? We accept Your best, not second best, because that's what You have provided for Your children.

September 5

Scripture: "Come unto me, all ye that labour and are heavy laden, and I will give you rest" (Matthew 11:28).

Rest. What is that? The clock said 7 a.m. I finally got up, rolled out of bed—tired, exhausted, sleepy, and grumpy. I just spent my first night in the flight path of USAir! I was not a happy camper. As a matter of fact, you couldn't convince me that the parsonage was not actually on the runway. Those are not what I call "friendly skies"!

I remember my prayer in devotions that morning very well. I said, "Lord, I can work for You here, but You know I will need my rest." Having said that, I hit Eckerds and bought two sets of ear plugs, sponges, cotton, and a sound blocker (a machine built to make the soothing sound of waterfalls). Mine sounded like NIAGARA!

Men have this need to get the facts, which is what Bob did. Somehow it helps to know what you are dealing with. He came home with a "Caleb" and "Joshua" report: "There are 157 flights per hour from USAir's hub at Charlotte's Douglas Airport, but we are well able to take it!"

Weeks of nights wrestling to sleep turned into months. Then came

Operation Desert Storm. What couldn't get worse just did. I fought (in bed) my way through the Persian Gulf War. Each one of those big German cargo planes heaved as it struggled to lift itself over my house. The house vibrated and shook as the planes became airborne.

The sleep deprivation was taking its toll. Fatigue was wearing me down. In south Georgia jargon, I was waking up dog-tired. Because of the constant noise bombardment and the high decibel of noise that kept my waking and sleeping cycle interrupted, I was sleeping, but not resting. I know how Garfield feels: "I don't do mornings, either."

Oh, the joy of moving into a quiet new home. My first morning there, I couldn't believe the difference one night of rest made. Eight hours of rest felt great! Real birds (not planes) overhead were praising the Lord, and so was I.

Is this the way life operates? The world is noisy and unsettling. Simple basic pleasure seems to elude us. It's natural for working men and women to become tired and weary. We are heavily laden with the stress of living. Where do we take all this? To Him! He invites us, "Come unto me." Where He is, there is quietness and true rest! The first Monday in September is Labor Day! So rest!

Dear God, thank You for those precious moments of rest and quiet.

September 6

Scripture: "Speak; for thy servant heareth" (1 Samuel 3:10).

Do you remember when CB radios were all the rage? I remember driving to the General Assembly after we bought one. What fun the men and boys were having with their toys! Over all the static, you would hear somebody break in with "Got your ears on, good Buddy?" It was so neat and so cool! An acknowledgment came back: "That's a 10-4, or 2 x 4." Whatever! Who cared? We were really into the big C word—communications. At least we had the basics down—talking and listening.

Can you go back even farther and remember the dog sitting beside the RCA Victrola in *Life* magazine? The dog has moved. Now he sits with his ear cocked beside a satellite dish! But his message is still the same . . . *I'm into listening. I'm near the source!*

Seems like everybody's into listening. We wear pagers, have car phones, and carry cellular phones in our purses. We would not think of leaving home without them! We want to be in touch wherever we are.

Alexander Graham Bell hired a young assistant. His job was to be a good listener. Can you imagine day in and day out the many times

Thomas Watson tinkered with those wires? How many times Bell told his young assistant to be ready because soon speech would be transmitted. Can you imagine how many times he picked up a dead receiver? We will never know.

Can you also imagine the day he heard the ringing of a telephone and picked it up to hear Mr. Bell say, "Watson, come here; I want you." We can only speculate that he answered, "Right away, sir." He had heard the voice of Mr. Bell over the wireless! The world would never be the same. He was a witness. He had truly heard it.

What did Jesus say to His disciples in Matthew 11:4? "Go and shew John again those things which ye do hear and see."

Things have not changed with God. He wants more than idle listeners. He wants hearers! Perhaps if we haven't heard God speak to us lately, it just might be we are doing too much of the talking. There is a big, big difference!

Listening is difficult for me, Father. But today, I want to listen—not ask You for anything—just to listen to what You are saying to me.

September 7

Scripture: "O foolish people . . . which have ears, and hear not" (Jeremiah 5:21).

It has been said, "Things are not always what they seem." Might I add, "nor what one hears"!

My dad was quite unique. He had a great sense of wit and humor that we shared together. We both liked to laugh, even when the laugh was on us. Several years before his passing, he began experiencing a loss of hearing. We first began to notice it when we called and talked with him. The calls took longer and cost more because we had to repeat things several times for him to understand. Looking back, if I could I would call more often and talk longer.

I remember when he was fitted with hearing aids. It really was great for him and us. It was fun to watch him tinker and fiddle around with his new *gadgets*, not to mention the squealing and ringing pitches he could get out of them.

One evening while visiting with Mom and Dad, we all were in the den watching the 6 o'clock evening news. The news commentator announced, "The president has declared war on couch potatoes." He explained that we Americans are overweight and underexercised.

First of all, Dad would not have picked up on the trendy phrase "couch potatoes," because he was not your lie-on-the-couch person. He was a very active yard-and-garden man.

Second, it's possible he didn't even hear the word *couch* because of the rise and fall of the commentator's voice. Low pitches were hard to snare. We do know, part of the message to him got bleeped out. Shortly thereafter, he got up from his favorite brown tweed chair and started toward the kitchen. He stopped right in the middle of the den and you could tell his blue Irish eyes were bothered by what he'd heard. To all of us he said, "Well, what in the world is going to happen next? I don't see how having a few hills of Arsh [Irish] potatoes out there in the garden could hurt anybody." It was funny! When we explained to him what a couch potato was, he enjoyed the humor, too.

Today as I replay this scene, I am reminded of the little drummer boy's question, "Do you hear what I hear?" Sometimes, we don't. We fail to get the full message.

Do I listen to others with just my ears or with my feelings as well? Jeremiah described us as "foolish people . . . which have ears, and hear not" (5:21).

Lord, help me today to truly listen with my heart—not just to the words, but to the message and feeling being spoken!

September 8

Scripture: "And if we know that he hear us, whatsoever we ask, we know that we have the petitions that we desired of him" (1 John 5:15).

"Complete voice rest," said the doctor. A nurse posted a sign on the foot of Bob's hospital bed that read, "Patient cannot speak." While pastoring in Hazlehurst, Georgia, Bob noticed a persistent hoarseness in his voice. A trip to a throat specialist revealed a nodule on his vocal cords that required surgery.

Communicating with him was difficult. We had to ask questions that could be answered yes or no. Most of the time he just nodded his head. On his notepad he wrote a personal note to me: "You need to be here when people visit to talk to them!" It was a quiet recovery.

Meanwhile back at our busy church, the hospital was filled with sick church folk. After a few days at home he felt well enough to do his hospital visitation, providing "Aaron" would accompany "Moses." I was to do the talking. Those of you who know me are already laughing! Here is how it came down. Together, we'd enter the room and I would explain, "Brother D. can't speak yet, but he wanted to come by and visit with you and have prayer."

A pattern began to emerge in each scenario. First, the folks began directing their conversation to me. After all—excuse me, dear, if you read this devotion—I had a *dummy* by my side. Second, because he couldn't and didn't speak to them, they inevitably would say, "Tell Brother Daugherty so and so." They assumed he could not hear! Oh, he heard, all right. After leaving one room he whispered a sweet nothing in my ear, "Do you have to talk and pray so long at each place?"

Now let's play "Can you top this?" A charter member of the church died during this recovery period. Bob decided the only thing he could do was to write out his sermon and have me read it. We both remember it well. He is not sure I read it as he wrote it, and I didn't gain many friends nor influence many people with my first and last "officiating" at a funeral. We split hairs over who should get the credit on his ministerial report!

I felt that a little shock therapy might speed up his recovery and said to him one day, "I am so tired of having to do all the talking for me and you. I'll be so glad when you can do your own talking." He whispered, "Not nearly as glad as I will."

I am so thankful Jesus has a listening ear. He cuts through the verbal minutia and reads the sincerity of my heart. He overlooks faults and faulty prayers. He responds with such compassion. What a wonderful assurance we have in 1 John 5:15: "And if we know that he hear us, whatsoever we ask, we know that we have the petitions that we desired of him."

Having a listening ear is hard work! It requires patience!

Thank You, Father, for being so patient with us and hearing us when we pray.

September 9

Scripture: "She hath washed my feet with tears, and wiped them with the hairs of her head" (Luke 7:44).

BHD stands for bad hair day! It makes you appreciate a GHD—good hair day. We've all had them both!

Some of you may have seen my "Hair" monologue in which I flip about 25 wigs in 15 minutes. You have no trouble drawing a mental picture of what I am looking like at 6 a.m. (the time I'm writing this devotion to share with you). I'm thankful, this page is not a mirror. The hair monologue has been a great blessing in my life. On a BHD people might have thought, *Maybe she's going to do her HAIR THING, so she didn't put much effort into it!* On the contrary, women put a lot of effort into this HAIR THING.

Do you remember the era when we stacked our hair up "Somewhere Over the Rainbow . . . way up high"? A lady in our church during that time had a standing hair appointment on Wednesday nights (during

FTH). I could sympathize with her in her plight (not every beautician could do a COG hair stack). Her problem curled my hair! I had to ask myself, "Is this lady's hair appointment more important to her than worship?" After all, doesn't the "paraphrased" version of Luke 15:4 say: "What woman of you, having a head full of hair, would not leave the ninety and nine (FTH attendance) and go find a hairdresser?"

Is this devotion going to have a practicable application? I hope so. Today I just reread the story of the sinful woman in Luke 7:44: "She hath washed my feet with tears, and wiped them with the hairs of her head." Tears and hair. Notice how they seem to go together? I've been to church when my hair looked so pitiful I wanted to cry! Whether she was having a good or bad hair day is not important, but her hair was very much in place. She would be accepted letting her hair down in the presence of Jesus.

If she were a normal Jewish gal, she would have given much attention to her hair, taking great care to protect it during certain seasons of the year. She would have worn a headdress to protect it from the sun. Ruth wore a headdress in the field. Maybe her mother-in-law decided that if she was going to wear a hair covering, she didn't need to look like Yasser Arafat. I'll bet Naomi told Ruth to put on a brightly colored wrap. In other words, "Ruth, do something with your hair!"

Jesus was a guest in the house of Simon, a Pharisee. This sinful woman in our text came to Simon's house with a gift for the Lord. She brought an alabaster box of ointment and tenderly began anointing, kissing, and bathing the feet of Jesus with her tears. She did what a *proper* woman would never have done in public—she let her hair down. She used it as a servant's towel to dry the feet of the Savior. She was lost in adoration to Jesus. What did her listening ear hear that day? She heard Jesus as He rebuked Simon for his judgmental and proud attitude. To her, Jesus said, "Your sins have been forgiven . . . go in peace" (see v. 48).

Her act of devotion involved using and giving her best (her glory, her hair) to rightfully adore the Lord of Glory! Maybe you won't get every hair in place today, but you can take your hair to the right place. At Jesus' feet you will hear His words of acceptance.

Thank You, dear Lord, for accepting me just as I am.

September 10

Scripture: "Therefore we ought to give the more earnest heed to the things which we have heard, lest at any time we should let them slip" (Hebrews 2:1).

"Stop that right now," is what you would like to say to the cricket who invades the privacy of your bedroom. After retiring and it's just about *lights out* for you, then you hear him. Jiminy Cricket, or one of his cousins, is somewhere in this room, doing aerobics—rubbing his legs together. It is getting on your nerves. The harder you try not to listen, the more irritating the sound becomes. Your ears are so sensitive they feel like rabbit ears. This bug is in your ear!

A bug can literally get in your ear. It happened after a Sunday evening service shortly after moving to Gainesville, Georgia. We were fellowshipping in the church vestibule when, for some strange reason, a bug made a beeline right into Bob's ear. ZAP! Robin came to me and said, "Daddy's got a bug in his ear." When I got to him, I knew he was in pain. Several of us gathered around him, trying to figure out what to do. Someone came up with the idea of shining a flashlight in his ear to lure it out. That did not work. Bob was in absolute torture. We had no choice but to get him to the emergency room.

It wasn't funny at the time, but since then we have had a few good laughs. Can you imagine this grown man, local pastor, daddy of four, sitting in the waiting room among all the trauma cases—having a bug in his ear?

A pediatrician on call was told the nature of Bob's emergency. Coming over to him he said, "I can't treat you here. I know you're in pain, so if you will go over to my office I can help you." Bob was willing to go with anybody, anywhere.

On a tiny tot's table, the doctor retrieved the bug—alive. They both analyzed him thoroughly. His wingspan was so large that when he nose-dived into Bob's ear, it wedged him in so tightly he could only flutter. The fluttering and scratching sent horrible vibrations down the ear canal to the eardrum, thus the pain and discomfort. It was an experience we all remember—the night Daddy got a bug in his ear.

An ear that listens to God is susceptible to being bugged by Satan. He uses the airways, too! We tend to air things that bug us. Bugs of a negative and critical spirit sometimes fly right into your ear. Some folks are so negative that the only way to not hear them is break out the earmuffs! Listen to the advice in Hebrews 2:1: "Therefore we ought to give the more earnest heed to the things which we have heard, lest at any time we should let them slip."

Today seems like a good day to put a bug in someone's ear about the goodness and greatness of our God!

Almighty God, we acknowledge Your lordship in our lives. May we never forget those things we have heard and lessons we have learned from serving You.

September 11

Scripture: "He touched his ear, and healed him" (Luke 22:51).

Can you think of a better example of "listening ears" than those of a mother? They have listening ears. It's their survival kit! They can pick up unrecognizable language—that is, if they have little boys!

Mothers can read the sounds of cooing or crying. Mothers can hear what is not spoken. They can hear the sounds of greatness in a young musician who is hitting every note but the right one.

When our son Robert was small, he was the one most often plagued with earaches. Father does know best, but you could not convince our children of that. Their dad was always saying to them as they dashed out on a cold windy day, "Put on your hats." They hated hats, so his advice often went unheeded.

Anywhere between 1 and 5 a.m. was prime time for the earache to hit. An earache with its stabbing throbs is painful. As you well know, a person with an earache is not a gracious person. Robert fit this characterization. If I did not hear him trashing about in his bed, he would get up and slip into our bedroom. He would always come to my side of the bed. To the top of his lungs (it seemed), he would announce, "Mama, my ear hurts." Talk about getting your adrenaline going; that will do it! Naturally, I was startled after being so abruptly awakened. It was life-threatening—I almost had a coronary. I had tried to explain to him several times, "Son, when you come to wake me, please either shake me or whisper. Don't shout right into my ear. Even though I am asleep, I can hear you."

I would do for him what you have done for a kid with an earache. I would warm drops and put into his ear. I tried to calm him. I did everything I knew to get him to stop the pacing back and forth. I tried to talk him through the pain. We prayed together.

Is our Father any different? He is our Father with a mother's ear for listening. He hears the cries of His children. Unlike me, He never sleeps. How often I have come to my Father and shouted into His ear, "I'm in pain. My ear hurts. I've heard shattering news! I hurt. Can You hear me? I cannot be still. I am restless." What can God do for a hurting ear? What did He do for the hurting ear of the servant Malchus? He picked up the severed ear and healed him. Luke, the physician, recorded the healing and the tenderness with which Jesus healed him.

Healing his ear was more than a cosmetic need. Can you imagine the pain that ripped through the young servant? He needed help. Jesus knew the pain in his ear. Jesus understands when the pain of a circumstance makes you scream out to Him. Jesus himself, from the cross, cried out in a loud voice to His Father. He knows when the pain is unbearable. He knows how to talk us through the pain. He knows the pain when we have heard the words *cancer, failure, betrayal, rejection,* and other painful penetrating words. As tenderly as a mother listens, He applies a touch of healing. He restores what was severed from us.

Today if you feel you have been cut off from words of encouragement, go to your garden of prayer and ask Jesus to make it better!

Thank You, Jesus, for bearing the stripes and receiving the wounds that provided healing for us. You are our redeemer, our healer, and our soon-coming King!

September 12

Scripture: "Can a maid forget her ornaments, or a bride her attire? yet my people have forgotten me days without number" (Jeremiah 2:32).

"Going to the Chapel," the song says. I really will go to the chapel today along with many other ladies in our area for our six-month Bible study each Tuesday until February. We are having our study in our newly refurbished South Carolina Chapel.

A Southern Gospel group sings a song that asks the question, "Is That Wedding Music I Hear?" Today in the chapel I will hear ladies' voices practicing wedding music. Like you, over the years, I have heard all sorts of wedding music. I have heard some rather strange tunes sung at weddings. I have also heard some strange happy-anniversary commemorative songs. Not too long ago, we visited a church in which they sang "Happy Anniversary" to the couple celebrating their day. At the end of "Happy Anniversary," the congregation, without a cue from any source, broke into "And when the battle's over, we shall wear a crown." I kid you not. I looked at Bob and he said, "They may know this couple better than we do!"

I remember the sweet sounds of "Whither Thou Goest," "I Love You, Truly," and "The Lord's Prayer," which were sung at my own wedding, but especially "The Bridal March." I remember the music at each of our children's weddings and the beauty of my daughters and daughters-in-law as they stepped into the aisle for "The Bridal March." I have also had the wonderful and exciting joy few daughters have had. I was my mother's matron of honor. After the death of my dad, the music in her life stopped. On July 17, 1994, in a full-blown church wedding, complete with a limousine (compliments of dear friends of hers), she stepped into the aisle after me. She was 75, but I cannot say I have ever seen a lovelier bride! I have seen much younger, but lovelier . . . never!

While "The Bridal March" played, she made her way to the altar to join a wonderful Christian gentleman of 82! The wedding music sounded as if it came from heaven. Why would it sound any other way? Where does love come from? God is love!

The purpose stated in the song for going to the chapel was to get married! Actually, I do have a wedding on my mind today. I am involved in making wedding plans. I am preparing myself daily. I have the word of my beloved Bridegroom deep within my heart. He promised He would come for me. I am seeing signs that let me know He has not changed His mind. I am going to the chapel today to join my Christian friends who will make up my wedding party.

In the chapel today, I will continue adorning my inner life as a bride. Today, September 12, could be my wedding day. Today, I might hear the trump of God. If so, you will hear it too. I might add, I am marrying quite well off—I am marrying into royalty. The bridal march of which I speak will play for the wedding of the ages. By the way, the invitations have already been sent out. Thank you for the invitation to your wedding.

RSVP: I plan to attend your wedding. I'll be there!

Dear Jesus, each time I attend a wedding and hear the wedding march, I am reminded that You are preparing a wedding feast for me and all Your children. Help us to be ready to meet You.

September 13

Scripture: "Before the cock crow, thou shalt deny me thrice" (Matthew 26:75).

"Listen for the bird, Peter" is how Jesus could have said it.

Brent, our grandson, had come for his first solo visit with us. We ended his first day by taking him to a restaurant near the Charlotte Speedway called the Sandwich Construction Company. A race car is perched on the roof, and race-car drivers are known to frequent the place. We were trying to make his first visit with us special.

At bedtime I thought he might be afraid to sleep upstairs by himself. He liked the idea of sleeping on a hide-a-bed in the den just outside our bedroom. We all bunked down and for me it was "lights out."

About 20 minutes later, Brent came to the doorway and said, "I can't go to sleep." I assured him he was just tired and to go lie down and rest. About an hour later he was up again. From the doorway I heard him say, "Nanny Pat, I'm scared." We assured him Papa and I were right there. I tucked him in again. (We were beginning to think we had a case of the dreaded childhood disease—homesickness.)

At 4 a.m. he appeared in the doorway again, crying, "Nanny Pat, your house makes squeaky noises and something is going BONG, BONG, BONG." (He banged on the door frame to illustrate the sound.) Getting into bed with him, I snuggled him close and promised I would listen for the squeaky noises in my house.

I listened and I heard them. There were four clocks ticking—none of them synchronized. Upstairs, the ticking pendulum of a schoolhouse wall clock was in motion. Children on a merry-go-round began dancing on a cuckoo clock. This was followed by a cuckoo bird with laryngitis (he has been at it for several years now). The door barely clicked on his heels, when a musical chime went off on the mantle anniversary clock. Then came the big finale as the grandfather clock played a rendition of Westminster chimes and followed it with a BONG, BONG, BONG, BONG! I felt Brent sort of cringe, but he didn't awaken. Detective Columbo would have been proud of me. I had a pretty good idea of the squeaky noises in my house. I slipped out of bed and stopped the thing that was going BONG, BONG, BONG!

Jesus told Peter to listen for the bird. "Before the cock crow, thou shalt deny me thrice" (Matthew 26:75). He heard more than a cuckoo bird that daybreak. Three short cock-a-doodle-dos delivered a special message from a friend. We give our friends information that we withhold from others. Peter was included in that inner circle of friends. Peter now remembered the time he sat at the feet of Jesus. It was there he heard Him say, "I call you not servants . . . but I have called you friends" (John 15:15). Is this where we got the saying "A little birdie told me"? The "friend who sticks closer than a brother" just might be trying to send a special message to us. Do we have listening ears today?

Father, open our ears, but most of all, open our hearts to receive what You want to say to us today.

September 14

Scripture: "He that planted the ear, shall he not hear?" (Psalm 94:9).

Ear specialists have special training in the anatomy of the human ear. They tell us it is one grand piece of architecture. Why do we make this comparison? The ear has arches, walls, floors, canals, aqueducts, galleries, intricacies, convolutions, and machinery of the most delicate nature.

"Planted" is a good description of how God tucked away three ears on each side of our head: the external ear, the middle ear, and the inner ear. A telegraph system connects them to each other.

How do we hear? We have the hammer, which strikes the sound.

Sound that is sent strikes the anvil. The stirrup (like the stirrup of the saddle) is how we mount the steed of sound. The sound is beaten out on a set of drums. God is great in mechanics! Beltone advertises a new smaller ear device that is nearly undetectable. Their marketing line is "You will not believe your eyes, but you will believe your ears."

God filled our middle ear with air, the inner ear with fluid, and the external ear with wax. Agh, what did you say? Yet it all works so perfectly that we can sort out the sound of jet planes or the hum of bees. The question we should ask ourselves is this: "If God created such a marvelous instrument just so we could hear, shouldn't we be more selective in our listening?" According to Mark 4:24, the answer is *yes*! "Take heed what ye hear."

Also in Romans 10:17 we are instructed, "So then faith cometh by hearing, and hearing by the word of God." Some people must depend on their ears to compensate for the loss of their sight. Their very life depends on their listening ears. Our spiritual life is the same!

The psalmist asks, in effect, a comforting question. "Shall our God who gave us such an intricate hearing apparatus not use His ears to hear us?" (Psalm 94:9). Shall a God who allows us to hear a rippling waterfall, the whistle of quail, the rustle of wind in the trees, and the chirp of a cricket not use His ears for listening to His children? He is not just a casual listener. David said, "He hath inclined his ear unto me" (Psalm 116:2). Isaiah implied "ditto" in 65:24: "Before they call, I will answer; and while they are yet speaking, I will hear." He listens intently and deliberately.

The Holy Spirit came *down* with a sound, and we are going up with a sound. Perhaps that's why the Lord's return will be announced with the fanfare of the trumpet of God. Not only will every eye see Him, but every ear shall open to hear the great symphony of sound. All mankind will experience the sights and sounds of His return!

Father, let hosannas run down the corridors of our ears today and alert us to the approach of the blessed One who comes in the name of the Lord!

September 15

Scripture: "Thine ears shall hear a word behind thee, saying, This is the way, walk ye in it" (Isaiah 30:21).

Not every word you hear behind you is from the Lord. Some voices are saying, "Get outta my way." At a ball game the mother of a young son on a Little League ball team would be wise to be careful in her cheerleading antics. Why? Because the mother of a son on an opposing team might be sitting in front of or behind her.

Being a state president, all of us try to choose themes for brunches, luncheons, or ladies days we feel will fit the need of our women. We choose themes about which we have strong feelings. Two years ago in Western North Carolina, I chose the theme "Angels on Assignment." I had just written a minidrama that I felt was inspired of the Lord. As the time drew nearer to camp meeting, I saw the themes of others and thought maybe I should have chosen something else. I needed confirmation.

I went to south Georgia to be with my mom on Memorial Day—the day my dad had died one year before. As the sun was coming up, I walked out on the back stoop patio. In the backyard there is a toolshed my dad built. It really was a multipurpose building (FLC—Family Life Center). Although I told you it was a toolshed, it has a steeple and a belfry on it. I kid you not. This was his early-morning place of prayer—our family's life source.

As I looked at his handiwork, I remembered this scripture: "Their works [and prayers] do follow them" (Revelation 14:13). I heard a word drop into my heart and spirit. The Lord said to me, "Now you know what the angels' assignment was a year ago. They came to Tifton, Georgia, to pick up a prophet and take him home. But they have not forgotten the little widow they left here. They stood watch over her day and night and kept her safe from harm."

As I praised the Lord, it seemed the Lord put a P.S. on it: "Now about the camp meeting drama—right on!" I knew I had been directed by Him and whatever would happen would be for His glory.

Father, thank You for giving us wisdom, guidance, and that extra reassurance when we need it.

September 16

Scripture: "The joy of the Lord is your strength" (Nehemiah 8:10).

Dad, I'm writing this devotional in memory of you. You could tell some of the funniest stories. I'm glad I had listening ears. I might have heard them several times, but they were still funny each time because you enjoyed telling them so much. Also, I knew you wanted to make me laugh. Funny stories that happened to us were our gifts to each other!

You were a great after-dinner speaker. Mom gave me your banquet cue cards. I cannot make heads or tails out of some of them. Here's one you used:

A man said when he married his wife she looked like a slender birch. Now she looks like a knotty pine.

Two-word clues gave your memory a jog, but they leave mine in a *fog*!

Laughing at the hard knocks in life was something I admired in you. Thanks for telling me your boyhood stories. I will share two of them with my friends today.

At age 9, you worked an entire summer on a farm breaking up new ground (south Georgia lingo). At the end of that summer when it was time to receive your pay, the man told you he didn't have any money to pay you, so he handed you one pair of new overalls. It hurt because you needed the money to buy school clothes and help your widowed mother. Thanks for always adding a footnote to the story. You said, "That's the year I became a man. At least I could wear one less pair of homemade pants."

I like the story of your relatives from the North sending your family boxes of clothes that always contained girls' shoes. Your mother sent you off to school with a little black patent-leather pair of shoes. You always stressed that they even had bows on the toes. You were a sport when you told how you waded through the branch on your way to school and those shoes slipped right off and washed down the creek. When you got home and told your mother about losing them, she said, "Paul, you are the roughest boy on shoes I've ever seen." The next year, they would send more. Your life wasn't easy, but you made it sound like fun!

Dad, you have been gone five years now. Maybe one of the angels will bring the love contained in this little devotional to you. I've enclosed a little thank-you note to my heavenly Father.

Father, thanks for making my Christian life fun. In the tough times, You have often pointed out "funnies" to lift my spirits. I cannot recall the times You have broken into my writing with a funny punch line or a good zinger. (You may be thinking this is a good spot right here.) Humor has kept me well emotionally. Humor is a treasured gift from You. Once I was having writer's block and whining to You because I had not had a creative spurt in a while. I will never forget what You said to me. "If you want to be more creative, spend more time with the Creator." Thanks for every creative idea and thought (serious and humorous) You have given me. I know "the joy of the Lord is my strength." I have found out in living life that tears and laughter are not really that far apart. Thanks for both!

September 17

Scripture: "The steps of a good man [or woman] are ordered by the Lord" (Psalm 37:23).

September is back-to-school month. Your kids may have just dashed

301

out the door. How you hope they will have listening ears during this school term. Remember the book titled *Everything I Need to Know I Learned in Kindergarten*? Today I am sharing stuff I have learned while sitting at Jesus' feet.

1. I can't see the stuff behind His back.

You may be having a cup of coffee and wondering, *Where do I start cleaning up all this stuff I can and cannot see?* There is stuff behind God's back I don't want to see. Hezekiah said to God: "Thou hast cast all my sins behind thy back" (Isaiah 38:17). What's more . . . He forgets the stuff behind His back (Isaiah 43:25)! There! That may be your answer: Forget it! Forget the stuff but not the Forgiver!

Do you remember that ambitious mother in Scripture who thought sitting at Jesus' feet was too lowly a position for her sons? They were head-of-the-class material. They were not "footstool" boys. Can we, like her, feel a need to unload a lot of junky stuff today at Jesus' feet?

2. At His feet . . . I can see His lovely face.

The look on your kid's face today probably told you stuff you needed to know. Jesus reads stuff on His kids' faces. He read Cain's. Rachel's smile sent Jacob out to work seven years for her. By the way, did you smile at your family today before they went out to school or into the workplace? The smile of Jesus makes working for Him a pleasure. As an artist looks at the model to produce a facsimile of the original, so we look upon the shining, lovely face of Jesus. The face of Moses shone after being with Him.

3. At His feet . . . I'm not lonely.

Loneliness is one of the world's greatest problems. There is a difference in being lonely and being alone. To be alone is to be by oneself. To be lonely is to feel isolated by one's solitude. Being an only child, Sunday afternoons were lonely for me. After our Sunday dinner Mom and Dad would take their weekly nap. Although we were in the house together, I felt lonely. I promised myself that when I had kids, I would never sleep on Sunday afternoons. (Promise kept—except the occasional lapses into Rip Van Winkle territory while reading the Sunday paper.) Jesus never sleeps, in or out of my presence. You can be home alone, but you don't have to be lonely. Hebrews 13:5 promises, "I will never leave thee, nor forsake thee."

4. At His feet . . . I'm not lost.

Being a woman has its privileges. When you are lost, you do something a man will not do—*stop and ask for directions*. I've had to say to the Lord, "I'm lost—I can't find me." I've discovered the way to find me is to find Him! I once played a party game where each husband had to match up his wife's shoes with her feet. If I can just find Jesus' feet, I know where I am. He said, "I am the way" (John 14:6). His tiny footprints were recorded in Bethlehem's courthouse (well, maybe not). But from the moment His tiny feet were wrapped in swaddling cloths until the moment they were wrapped for burial, His steps were ordered by His Father. So are mine. "The steps of a good man [or woman] are ordered by the Lord" (Psalm 37:23).

Today you might be trying to work your way through the stuff. See what kind of stuff you can learn sitting at His feet.

Thank You, Jesus, for reserving us a spot to sit at Your feet and learn from You.

September 18

Scripture: "She had a sister called Mary, who sat at the Lord's feet listening to what he said" (Luke 10:39, *NIV*).

Listening ears may mean hearing things that are good for you, but not necessarily things you want to hear. Sometimes God speaks through mothers!

It has been just over a year ago that we felt the nudging of the Lord to leave our comfort zone in Charlotte and move to South Carolina. We agreed that upon arriving at the General Assembly we would make our feelings known to the Executive Committee for reassignment and accept whatever they decided as God's will for us. On Saturday morning at the General Assembly, we were told we would be moving. The where had not been determined, but the committee member assured us we would be told by that afternoon.

After hearing this, I knew I needed to call my mom back home in Georgia. I did not want to hit her broadside, or have someone else tell her about it. (Let me give you some background knowledge that will set this up for you: My mom had heard of the recent moral failures of some ministers and the breakup of their homes. She was concerned and disturbed over them. She has no degrees in marriage counseling. She loves Bob—her one and only son-in-law—dearly, and would take his side over mine in any dispute.) Sorry, I left you holding on the phone. When she answered, and after a little small talk, I said, "Mother, we are going to be moving. I'm supposed to know where this afternoon and I'll call you back then." This was her response: "Well, I feel this is the will of the Lord for you. I want you to promise me that when you get wherever you're going, you will stop running all over the country trying to make other people laugh. I want you to stay home and make your husband laugh [and she added for emphasis] for a change! Bob is not so old but what somebody wouldn't love to have him."

Whoa! I heard that! I also read a lot of stuff between the lines. I understood she was speaking from a heart that had lost her husband through death. In looking back, she treasured each moment they had spent together. She was saying in her wise reprimand of love, "Guard your home and its interests. Care for the one you love. Give your best to your family. Make your home a happy place."

Did I really listen to her admonition? I have since tried to curtail some activity or take Bob along with me. (I'm afraid he'll call her and tell her "she's gone.") Every so often I ask him, "Are you having fun yet? Why aren't you laughing?"

Mother's advice comes from Proverbs 7:18, 19: "Come, let us take our fill of love . . . for the goodman is not at home, he is gone [on] a long journey." You will recognize that was advice against wicked women. The principal message is for good men or good women.

Do something today to make your spouse feel warm. Remember, the most important things in your home are not material things—not the Precious Moments, Llardos, or Hummels. The most precious things in your home are the relationships within it. Guard them carefully!

Father, help us be like Mary and listen as we sit at Your feet.

September 19

Scripture: "And the cares of this world, and the deceitfulness of riches, and the lusts of other things entering in, choke the word, and it becometh unfruitful" (Mark 4:19).

This past May I spoke at a mother-daughter banquet. I arrived early enough to mingle among the ladies as they gathered. I went over to a table of older ladies and visited with them. They were friendly and pleasant except for this one little lady who seemed to be obviously upset. I spoke to her several times. She was unresponsive. Finally, she just got up and walked away. The group did not seem upset over her behavior, so I figured neither should I be.

I moved to another table and started talking to those ladies when the little lady from the first table came over to me. She took me by the hand, and drawing me away, said, "Could we walk over into that corner?" (motioning toward it). I was thinking, Oh, no, she's unhappy with something in her church . . . or upset with her pastor . . . or, to use Burger King's line, not "having it her way." I was wrong on all counts.

She said to me, "Honey, I wear hearing aids in both ears, and when I get in this kind of noise, it makes me so nervous. I hear so much noise I cannot understand anything. I have never had an overseer's wife speak to me before, and I wanted to hear what you said to me."

She touched me. I understood where she was coming from. We

pulled up a couple of chairs like old timers and had the most pleasant visit, just the two of us. While we were talking, I tried to listen to what her ears must be hearing. The cacophony of sound (her term *noise* is more descriptive) was terrible, even for a normal ear. See if you can hear it as I describe what was going on in the background. There were at least 250 ladies laughing and talking loudly in a concrete gym; a PA set was blaring out what was supposed to be background music; a group of teens preparing for a skit was banging and hammering around on a stage, setting up props; the kitchen crew was rattling pots and pans madly; the servers were rattling dishes, glasses, and silverware on the tables; at least five baby daughters, if not more, were unhappy at being dragged off to this affair and were doing vocal maneuvers in varying stages of intensity. Now magnify all of the above!

The thought zipped through my mind: *In a few moments you will get to speak over all this! I also thought, Sweetie, you are fortunate. You have the wherewithal to turn off all this commotion.*

No wonder when I was speaking to her, she could not distinguish what I was saying. The message was being drowned out. Jesus spoke to us about such a problem. In the parable of the sower, did He not address the condition of the hearer? He said the hearer receives the message but it cannot penetrate his heart because it is too crowded. My friend heard my sound, but the other sounds were crowding out the message she wanted to hear.

Is it possible God is speaking and we are striving to hear, but the Word can't get through all the other things that are choking and blocking the sounds from our hearts?

Lord, You are speaking to me today. Help me receive the Word, not only in my ears but in my heart as well!

September 20

Scripture: "Take heed, and be quiet" (Isaiah 7:4).

Cities are noisy. The combined noises of traffic and the hustlings of the crowds are sounds we become accustomed to. As a child I remember visiting my grandmother's farm at Piney Grove, Georgia. It was so quiet there. We lived in Savannah near an Army base and that, plus the regular city noise, made it a busy and noisy place. It was in the evenings at my grandmother's house I noticed it most. We would sit on her porch and as the older people talked, the quietness of the evening settled around us. You could hear the crickets, frogs in nearby ponds, and the distant sound of a train 10 miles away passing through the little town of Odum, Georgia.

I had a similar experience while living in western North Carolina. We had the use of a hideaway place in the beautiful Great Smoky Mountains. It was there, going to bed at night with no hum of an air conditioner, that the night quietness magnified the sounds of nature. It seems the night creatures have their own symphony of praise. It seems you can sleep with your ears open. You can hear the stillness admonished in Isaiah 7:4: "Take heed, and be quiet." What is God saying? Be quiet and listen up! The voice that sounds like mighty waters often desires to speak in a still small voice.

Isn't this how God speaks through nature? He sends quiet messages in many ways. He has been known to send a quiet message by a rainbow to establish covenant. He used a quiet pillar of salt for admonition against looking back. He used an ax head quietly taking a swim to tell us of His guidance and concern for us. He used the quiet rustling leaves of the fig tree to prophesy of His second coming. He said even the strong, silent type—the rocks—could take voice to praise Him if He so chose.

Where can we go to get away from the hustle and noise of life? You might not escape it whether you live in the city or the country. There is only one place, according to Job 34:29: "He giveth quietness." At Jesus' feet is the getaway place. It is a place where the heart can be quiet.

Is it expensive to get there? Yes, but it's worth the trip. According to 1 Peter 3:4, "A meek and quiet spirit . . . is in the sight of God of great price." God knows how much it will cost you to pull off the fast track today to spend some time at His feet. The quieting of a troubled heart and calming of a restless spirit is without price. It feels so good!

Father, You know our hearts. Give us rest in You today.

September 21

Scripture: "In the same way, the Spirit helps us in our weakness. We do not know what we ought to pray for, but the Spirit himself intercedes for us with groans that words cannot express" (Romans 8:26, *NIV*).

On a recent trip by air, I picked up Delta's *Sky Magazine*. There was a full-page ad on learning foreign languages. The headline drew me in, and I began to read the "rest of the story." The headline read "Learning Foreign Languages . . . Incredibly Fast!" It stated in the article that you could learn languages as stresslessly as your child does, providing you ordered their audiocassettes. This was of particular interest to me because we were flying to the Southwest Indian Camp Meeting, where Bob would be preaching with a Navajo interpreter. (Actually, it wasn't his preaching on my mind as much as the length of his sermon and its interpretation.) I thought how much shorter the sermons would be if only he could speak their language!

It was almost ironic that seated directly behind us was a bilingual mother and her young daughter. They were speaking in a foreign language to each other. They would change, back into English when speaking to the flight attendant and others around them.

After about an hour of hearing them, Bob said to me, "I think whining is the same in any language." I agreed. We had listened to them long enough to distinguish that much. We were both amazed at the ease with which this preschool toddler was bilingual. She had acquired her language skills simply by listening to her parents speak the language. She never had to pay 300 bucks and spend hours listening to a tape.

If this devotion still seems "up in the air," it is. It was right then and there I suddenly realized that I am bilingual! I learned it simply from hearing my Father speak the language. He speaks to me in my understanding, but also in the language of heaven. I have become quite comfortable speaking to Him in the Holy Ghost and having Him speak back to me in tongues and interpretation in services. Like the ad promised, you can learn to speak "incredibly fast."

I'm sure it happened to you the same as it did to me. We all had one initial lesson! It was at the time of our initial infilling of the Holy Spirit. It happened that way for the receivers in Acts 2:2, 4: "There came a sound from heaven, as of a rushing mighty wind . . . and they were all filled with the Holy Spirit and began to speak with other tongues, as the Spirit gave them utterance" (*NKJV*).

Just as the little girl learned by having a listening ear, so do we! When we allow our prayer language to lift our praises and petitions on the wings of praise, our Father responds to us. And just like the child, I have been known to whine! Haven't you? Even then, the Spirit intercedes for us with "groanings which cannot be uttered" (Romans 8:26, *NIV*).

Aren't you thankful the Father speaks our language? Aren't you thankful we can speak the Father's language? I am. The Holy Spirit is a wonderful teacher and communicator—from me to the Father and from the Father to me!

Thank You, heavenly Father, for speaking our language. Help us not to whine, but to look to You for our help.

September 22

Scripture: "Faith cometh by hearing, and hearing by the word of God" (Romans 10:17).

"Consider the source," is what my mother always told me. Remember the song "I Heard It Through the Grapevine"? It was sung by those little purple California Raisins with the cool sunglasses and zany hats.

How often do we refer to information, often misinformation, that we hear on the church grapevine?

We know grapevine news is not always trustworthy or accurate, but still we have listening ears for what comes to us via the grapevine. What's new? Seems I can recall the Old Testament grapevine episode (Numbers 13) that sounds a lot like today. It was over the grapevine that talk was picked up by the Israelites: "We can't take the Promised Land because the Canaanite men over there look like giants and we look like grasshoppers." (See vv. 31-33.) Ten out of 12 spies sent that message down the Israelite grapevine and it was believed by the men to the extent that it caused great confusion. They did not consider the source!

Two guys in the scouting party, Joshua and Caleb, did not believe the rumor put out on the grapevine. These two had faith. They didn't have listening ears for the grapevine but for what God said in Romans 10:17: "Faith cometh by hearing, and hearing by the word of God." They considered the source! The source made them boldly declare that we are well able to possess the land. It was this one act of not believing the grapevine talk that wrote their names in the pages of Scripture. They had their own conviction concerning the circumstances. While they were in the land of Canaan, where the grapevine was, they picked one single cluster of grapes. What Del Monte would give to have the rights to grapevines like that! The cluster of grapes was so grand it dragged to the ground when suspended between the shoulders of two of the scouts. What a source! What a resource!

Grapevine reports often bring discouragement, disillusionment, and dismay. Could it be that we need to have listening ears for the grapevine rumors, and when we hear them, take action? Isn't that what Jesus did? The grapevine talk at the wedding was that they had run out of wine. Jesus simply took control . . . and turned water into wine. Consider the Source!

The report that the majority of the spies sent down through the grapevine was referred to in Scripture as "an evil report." (Numbers 13:32). Have you heard the latest report from the Lord? It's found in Philippians 4:8: Think (reflect) on things that are of "good report."

The grapevine *can* be useful. Send a word of encouragement to someone today who needs it! He or she will consider the source and call you friend!

Thank You for Your Word—the "grapevine" that delivers good news!

September 23

Scripture: "And [one of the lepers] fell down on his face at his feet, giving him thanks: and he was a Samaritan" (Luke 17:16).

Thankful people find a place to sit at His feet. In our scripture for today, only one leper returned to give the Lord thanks. Ten men made up the group of lepers who hollered out to Jesus, "Heal us!"

Remember the bumper sticker that reads, "Have you hugged your kid today?" These 10 men had not had any hugs for many days. No one could touch them, much less hug them. Jesus had compassion and made them touchable and huggable. As they ran to the priest for their health permits, all 10 discovered they had been healed.

All 10 of them heard Jesus say, "Go shew yourselves unto the priests" (v. 14). The lone Samaritan brought his gift of gratitude and laid it at the feet of Jesus. The picture in my mind is of a man clinging to and hugging the feet of Jesus. Jesus knew the count of the ungrateful. We can almost hear the disappointment in His voice as He asked, "Were there not ten cleansed? but where are the nine?" (v. 17). There should have been 10 men hugging and clinging to the feet of Jesus, their healer! Although He healed 10, Jesus knew them individually. In Dr. Charles Stanley's book *How to Listen to God,* he said, "God doesn't hug two people at a time; He hugs us one at a time." To get a hug from God, you have to be near Him.

Recently while sitting in a doctor's office in Greenville, I initiated a conversation with the lady sitting by me. She got around to asking what my husband did for a living. I told her he was a minister. She then asked me, "What church?" I told her. Then I gave her the locations of several of our area churches. She said she lived near the Tremont church. I intended to give her an invitation, but she volunteered that she had visited there with a friend of hers during a revival. "How did you enjoy the service?" I asked.

"Oh, it was wonderful," she said. "They had a healing line and I went up for prayer. God healed an infection on my leg." We talked a good while about healing. Then she said, "You know, I really need to go back over there because I have got a lot more things wrong with me now." It would be funny if it wasn't so sad, and so typical of us humans. God waits for our response to what He has already done for us.

Perhaps our problem is that we keep looking for spectacular answers or manifestations of God's presence. Are you waiting for God to speak to you out of a burning bush like He did for Moses? Are you asking

Him to collapse walls like He did for Joshua? But He is constantly speaking to us, not out of a burning bush or through walls of cities falling down flat. He speaks to us quietly—every day—if only we have our spiritual ears attuned to hear.

Lord Jesus, help us to listen with all our heart for Your gentle voice. Let it speak peace and healing to our troubled soul. And may we return to You with a grateful heart and give You praise.

September 24

Scripture: "Serve the Lord with gladness: come before his presence with singing" (Psalm 100:2).

Today's devotion is similar to the one I shared with you on September 8, in which I told you about the time Bob had to have complete voice rest. You have heard it said that perhaps that is why God gave us two ears and only one mouth. He wants us to listen twice as much as we talk.

I have a dear friend, and though I don't see her that often, I like to call her and just chat. Upon returning home after having been gone for several days, I decided I needed to call her. I was really excited and looked forward to hearing her voice. When the receiver was picked up on the other end, her husband answered and we chatted a minute. Then I asked to speak to Jerri. He said, "Jerri can't talk."

"What do you mean, Jerri can't talk?" I asked.

"The doctor has ordered her not to talk for two weeks!"

"Get her on the phone and let me talk to her," I said. After a moment of silently transferring the receiver, I asked, "Jerri, if you are there, tap on the phone." I heard her faintly whisper, "Hi, Pat." As I talked to her, my heart almost broke because she couldn't speak back. It was best for her voice not to speak; I understood that. As I began to pray for her, I mentioned to the Lord she was a preacher's wife and needed to talk!

Preachers and preachers' wives need their voices. They also need times to have listening ears. I thought of an occasion in Scripture (Luke 2) when a preacher was ordered to have complete voice rest. God knew it was best for Zacharias not to speak. What timing God had! Here was Elizabeth expecting their child, and the preacher can't talk. She got in her 25,000 words per day and then some! God allowed an angel to impose a silence upon him for the entire nine months! Why? Because he had expressed doubt instead of faith. Would he have said things to discourage Elizabeth for nine long months? If he expressed doubt and discouragement to God's messenger, he might have sent poor Elizabeth over the edge! Gabriel was sent to him to deliver the announcement of the child, and he asked for a sign. In fact, Gabriel had to say, "I am Gabriel, that stand in the presence of God" (Luke 2:19). In other words, "What more do you want, Zacharias?" Perhaps Zacharias might have said to his wife, "Hon, do you really want to eat all that?" "Aren't you gaining a bit too much weight?" "Let's name our baby, Zacharias II." Humor aside, it was only after the birth of the baby, and after Zacharias called for a writing table and wrote the name John, that the Lord gave him permission to speak. And he did much more. He sang a great hymn that he composed during his abstinence from speech. His song is recorded in Luke 1:68-79.

What kind of song will you sing when you have come through the dark place? A gloom-and-doom song like we hear on *Hee Haw*, or a song like "Song, Sung Blue—Everybody Knows One"? In the tough times, how gracious God is to drop a song into our heart. It is the Lord's song! Israel decided, "We will not sing the Lord's song in a strange land. We will be silent and so will our harps" (see Psalm 137:1-4). God had disappointed them and they were pouting and sulking. Their silence hurt no one but themselves. They had forgotten they were not singing for the people; They were singing for God. A listening ear can hear the Lord's song way down in the heart even when times are tough.

Psalm 100:2 says, "Serve the Lord with gladness: come before his presence with singing." Today if you can't talk and you don't have a word to speak, maybe you have a song. The Lord loves it when we sing to Him!

With glad hearts we give You our songs of praise today.

September 25

Scripture: "Rest in the Lord; wait patiently for Him to act" (Psalm 37:7, *TLB*).

Having listening ears in prayer is perhaps one of the hardest but most important parts of prayer. We pray to *tell* God our personal requests, petition Him for others, intercede, and offer praises. But most of the time, it is difficult for us to wait to hear His voice or get into listening.

Matter of fact, it's hard on us to listen for any instructions, especially recorded messages. Recently our state office initiated an automatic answering-machine system. The caller is answered with the recorded voice of our receptionist, who pleasantly says, "You've reached the South Carolina State Office. If you know the extension of the person to whom you wish to speak, you may enter it now. If not, to reach the state overseer, press 2; to reach the LM office, press 6. If you need assistance, please stay on the line and the receptionist will be right with you." Now, isn't that a nice, kind offer? The initial response of folks to this newfangled idea was resistance. It all boils down to the human nature in us. Nobody wants to be told what to do by a recording!

It occurred to me that this carries over into our prayer lives. We want God to speak to us and personally thunder out His answer from heaven. Why should He? He has already left recorded messages in His Word. We simply do not want to take the time to listen to them.

I have found that developing a listening ear in prayer takes patience. Patience is hard on folks. For me it means I cannot dash in, blurt out my want list, and sprint off into the day. That's His whole point. He wants me to relax, cease from my anxiety—let it go and let God speak. That's the same thing I want—but in a hurry.

Why did David leave a recorded message for me? "Rest in the Lord; wait patiently for him to act. . . . Don't fret and worry. . . . All who humble themselves before the Lord shall be given every blessing, and shall have wonderful peace" (Psalm 37:7, 8, 11, *TLB*). What did David know about prayer? He knew a lot. He learned patience. Matter of fact, he said in another recorded message, in Psalm 25:5, "On thee do I wait all the day." ALL DAY! Have you ever said to the Lord what I have, at least in your heart, if not verbally? "Lord, speak to me, but hurry—I don't have all day!" Come on, fess up!

David also left another recorded message for me about when I should pray. In Psalm 63:1 he said, "Early will I seek thee." Do you have time today to listen to one last recorded message? If you truly want to reach the Father today, listen to the instructions given in Matthew 6:33: "Seek ye first the kingdom of God, and his righteousness; and all these things shall be added unto you."

Lord, we give You this day. Our first priority is to seek You first, and everything else will fall into place.

September 26

Scripture: "Weeping may endure for a night, but joy cometh in the morning" (Psalm 30:5).

"I hear him; he's crying," I said. That memory is fresh in my mind today on the birthday of our oldest son, Andric. Well, it should be, because he was the first child born to me that I heard cry. His two older sisters were born while I was under a medically induced sleep. Both of them were brought into my room washed and blanketed.

But that day, with Andric, was different. I was awake. I was really there. I heard his 10½ pounds give a lusty top-of-his-lungs cry! I listened to him cry over all the fuss the doctor and nurses were making over this big guy. When they finally snuggled his cheek up to mine, his snubbing stopped. Mine went on for a while. They were tears of joy!

At age 8, one afternoon he walked into the kitchen where I was, with one arm dangling down by his side. At first glance, I knew it was broken. We were in revival; I quickly got the evangelist to drive us to the emergency room. We had to cross a very rough section of railroad track. With him in my arms, we started over that bumpy track and he said, "Mamma, hold me." I knew what he meant—"Hold me tighter; I can feel the vibration and it hurts." We were both crying tears of hurt. We were hurting together!

He had a beautiful wedding to Rhonda, the girl of his dreams. While they were standing for a song near the unity candle, I saw him brush a tear of his own and then flip one with his index finger from the cheek of his bride. I shed a tear (*tears* may be more accurate) for his happiness! We were both happy!

He was walking down the hospital corridor taking giant steps toward his dad, Twyla, and me. He was holding a bundle of love in blue. He was a father. As we gazed into his arms at Brent, our first grandchild, we all shed tears of unity. We are family!

Baby Moses cried at the prompting of God and it took him all the way to Pharaoh's throne room. I'm so thankful we have a God who hears the sound of a single teardrop. He hears us when we cry. The vehicle of tears can take us all the way to His throne—no matter if it's tears of new life as in John 3:7, "Ye must be born again," or tears of pain as in Psalm 30:5, "Weeping may endure for a night, but joy cometh in the morning." There are tears of unity and togetherness. John 10:30 tells us, "I and my Father are one."

Today, reflect back on the spiritual day of your birth. Let's light a candle and celebrate. We are family. Happy Birthday!

We do celebrate the family today. It's Your plan, Father, and we thank You for every member.

September 27

Scripture: "Come, ye children, hearken unto me: I will teach you the fear of the Lord" (Psalm 34:11).

What we hear has a powerful influence upon us, especially children. We are told that a child who lives with praise develops self-esteem. If the child is fed negatives, he or she lives down to that evaluation.

I waited 27 days to figure out how to work a grandmother's story into a devotional. Now, what kind of grandmother would I be if I didn't seize this moment to share a grandmother's testimony?

This summer we had the privilege of having all three grandsons with us for the 7- to 12-year-old age group South Carolina Youth Camp. Jonathan is only 4, so he did not go to the camp except at night with Papa and me. It was Anthony's first camp while Brent was a seasoned camper at age 9.

The guest speaker for the camp was Ginger Brown. She is quite a gifted ventriloquist. Each evening in the service, she introduced various characters to the kids. Two were instant hits with the boys—a lion and a pig. Brent liked Linus the lion because he always used the line "I ain't lying!" The lion taught the memory verse each evening. In a deep, gruff voice and in broken sentences he would attempt the memory verse: "For I am not ashamed of the gos-spell. . . ."

When Anthony got back home to Houston, he was going to recite the memory verse for his dad. He went into an imitation of how the lion had said it. My son-in-law had no clue as to how it had been taught. He asked Robin, "What's wrong with him, talking like that?" She explained that's how the lion talked.

When Jonathan got home, Twyla was trying to get him to take his bath, and he squealed out, "Noo, me too tired." The pig was Jonathan's favorite character. His favorite line was "Noo, me too tired"—in a lazy, high-pitched voice. She understood his response when we told her he had used the pig's line. I had thought they were fidgeting around too much in the service to get much out of it, but then what did I know? Somehow their listening ears grabbed an impression of what they had heard.

In Psalm 34:11 we read, "Come, ye children, hearken unto me: I will teach you the fear of the Lord." Several places in Scripture instruct us to be like children. One is the way we listen and learn; the other is in how we forgive. Health freaks, doctors, and nutritionists tell us we are a product of what we eat. Don't you think we ought to include that we are products of what we hear?

As we sit at Your feet today, teach us as Your children. We come with listening ears.

September 28

Scripture: "I cried unto God with my voice, even unto God with my voice; and he gave ear unto me" (Psalm 77:1).

Today I stood in a worship service and sang the chorus "I Love You, Lord," along with 500 other worshipers. The line we were singing jumped out at me. The petition we were asking of God was that our worship of Him might be a sweet sound in His ear.

The sound of a telephone can be a sweet sound if you know it is a loved one calling. When Bob is away on a trip, he tells me he will call at a certain time. That ring-a-ling lets me know it will be a sweet experience.

The ring of the phone was not always sweet at one church we pastored. One lady did nothing all day but sit by the phone and call folks. Naturally, at the top of her list was the parsonage. My time for her call was 10 a.m. This was her pattern and mine for four and a half years. It was always the same. I would answer and she would say, "Sister Daugherty, please pray for my lost loved ones." I would answer, "Sister X, we will pray for your lost loved ones today." That's all it took. (By the way, her children were mean as snakes and needed the prayer.)

Sometimes when I was having devotions or busy with other things, the ringing of the phone would get on my nerves. One day when the phone rang at 10 a.m., I knew who it was, and in my impatience I decided to get the call over with even quicker today. I picked up the receiver and said, "Sister X, we are praying for your lost loved ones today."

"Sister Daugherty," she said, "that's not why I called today." (The nerve of her! That was the first and only time in four and one-half years she had not given me that same line!) I then had to listen to a 10-minute prayer request!

That flashback made me ask myself: "Does the listening ear of the Lord tire of my repetitious prayers? Do I sound like a broken record to Him? When does God stop listening?" According to His Word, He will not hear a vain heart, a heart with iniquity in it, the prayers of a husband and wife in discord, or the prayer of a mocker in the day of calamity.

What sweet sound does the Lord love to hear? The prayers of the lost, the prayers of His servants, and the praises of the saints. He loves the sounds of His children who are happy and walking in truth. The psalmist said, "I cried unto God with my voice, even unto God with my voice; and he gave ear unto me" (Psalm 77:1).

God always has listening ears.

Father, today we pray that the sounds we send to Your listening ears will be pleasant and sweet ones!

September 29

Scripture: "Mary . . . sat at Jesus' feet, and heard his word" (Luke 10:39).

The second verse of "Mary Had a Little Lamb" says the lamb followed her to school one day. In this verse we can reverse that: Mary followed the Lamb to school!

When Mary sat at Jesus' feet, she assumed the learner's position. Jesus is the Chancellor, the headmaster of all knowledge! Paul, in referring to his educational background in Acts 22:3, said he studied at the feet of Gamaliel.

Has someone ever asked you where you went to school? A good answer would be "At the feet of Jesus!" Kind and gentle words of affirmation can be heard at Jesus' feet. Little children often were found sitting at His feet. He is the Principal in the grammar school! He always has a place at His feet (in His school) for children. He said, "Let the little children come to me, and do not hinder them, for the kingdom of God belongs to such as these" (Mark 10:14, *NIV*).

Many times He picked them up and set them on His lap as He demonstrated a lesson of truth. They heard kind words of instruction from the *principal* Teacher.

Jesus is the Chief Physician in the school of medicine. The sick were never turned away from His school. The Scripture says in Matthew 15:30, "Those that were lame, blind, dumb, maimed, and many others" were laid at His feet. They heard healing words of wholeness!

In law school, Jesus is the Great Advocate. We can never forget the picture given to us in John 8:1-11. Early in the morning, Jesus had just seated Himself and began His teaching. Suddenly the crowd was shoved aside by the Pharisees, keepers of the law. A disheveled woman of ill repute was brought into His courtroom. We call her what they called her, an adulteress. The law of Moses demanded on-the-spot stoning.

Jesus arose and wrote a legal brief on the blackboard of sand. The accusers all slowly walked away. When Jesus faced the poor woman standing in her embarrassment and shame, He tenderly asked, "Has anyone brought charges against you?" She answered, "No one, Lord." Jesus said to her, "Neither do I condemn you: go and sin no more." She heard gracious words of forgiveness and acceptance.

School will soon be out and it will be graduation day. Soon the bells of heaven will ring. Jesus will be sitting upon His throne. We will take our position at His feet again. Final exams will all be over. We will be given a crown to cast at His feet (Revelation 4:10). We will hear wonderful words of commendation: "Well done, thou good and faithful servant: thou hast been faithful over a few things . . . enter thou into the joy of thy lord" (Matthew 25:21).

Father, today we hear and receive Your words of forgiveness and acceptance, just like the woman who was thrown at Your feet. Thank You for not giving up on us.

September 30

Scripture: "Be still, and know that I am God" (Psalm 46:10).

Today is the last day of September and my last day to share with you. I have been ministered to as I put my thoughts on paper. It has been what I needed. Sitting at Jesus' feet has helped me develop listening ears. I will continue to work to improve my listening ears!

When Wanda Griffith sent me my month's assignment, "Listening Ears," I thought, *This is a joke, right?* Of all my friends writing in this book, I probably have a harder time than any of them. I scanned the list and felt I could do a better job on one of the other topics. Today, I am very sure this was definitely the assignment God meant for me. Thanks, Wanda, for your sensitivity to the impression of the Holy Spirit.

You see, God had been dealing with me about listening, but I would not *listen!* Let me explain. We moved to South Carolina in August. I quickly jumped into gap-filler jobs that one of South Carolina's beloved first ladies, Kohatha Culpepper, had spoken about. The ball was ready for kickoff when I got here. There was no time for me to learn the game plan or develop a new one. It was just, "Sadie, get the ball and run with it." I took off like greased lightning!

I planned a bus trip to the "Making the Pieces Fit" conference in March. Pulling off for Mobile, I took a tumble in the bus, my left leg taking the hardest blow. It was hurting, but I determined it was not broken. The healing process took months. I was just thankful, it was not broken. I have a couple of souvenir scars from the trip.

Shortly after that, in the spring, I decided my yard would be gorgeous in a few weeks, and I donned the straw hat and hit the yards. In tidying up, I introduced myself to poison oak along my backyard fence. It took me a month and $250 to get rid of it. By this time, I was feeling like Calamity Jane.

In devotions one morning, I said to the Lord, "Lord, why am I having so much bad luck? Why is all this stuff happening to me?" As you know, the Lord deals with me with humor. It seemed I could almost see a grin on His face as He dropped this into my spirit: "Dear, I have almost had to break your leg and give you a case of the seven-year itch just to slow you down and hope you would listen to Me." Actually, He didn't say it just like that. He directed me to the scripture I found in Psalm 46:10, "*Be still*, and *know* that I am God" (emphasis mine).

God was right. I needed to slow down, pull aside, and allow Him to speak to me. Do you know what? For these 30 days, mostly mornings, we have had some of the sweetest moments together. Tomorrow we will continue our walk in the Word with Jackie Walker into October. Remember, if the turbulent waves of the sea would listen to God when He spoke, saying, "Peace, be still" (Mark 4:39), maybe there is hope for you and me to have listening ears!

Thank You, Father, for each person who has read these devotions. Help them, I pray, to have listening ears to hear what You have to say to them personally.

NOTES

NOTES

October

Remembering
Jackie Touchstone Walker

Jackie Touchstone Walker has been actively involved alongside her husband in varied ministry roles for 36 years: as state secretary-treasurer in Indiana, Michigan, and Northern Ohio; state Ladies Ministries president in North and South Dakota; and development director at Northwest Bible College. She has also served as executive secretary to both the president of the School of Theology and the International Department of Ladies Ministries, as well as being on that board. She presently serves as state Ladies Ministries president of Tennessee and on a task force under Operation Compassion (Department of Benevolence). Recently she created strategic programs of ministry focusing on widows and fatherless children. The "Bless A Widow" program was launched January 1995 in Tennessee, and the "Bless A Child" program will be launched in 1996.

Jackie and her husband, Dr. Donald M. Walker (state overseer of Tennessee), live in Chattanooga. They have two daughters, Donna, who is married to Brad Scoggins, and Denise, who lives in Atlanta, Georgia. Her two grandchildren, Preston and Jordan Scoggins, make Jackie a proud grandmother.

October 1

Scripture: "To every thing there is a season, and a time to every purpose" (Ecclesiastes 3:1). "And [she] shall be like a tree planted by the rivers of water, that bringeth forth [her] fruit in [her] season" (Psalm 1:3).

Can it possibly be October? Where did spring and summer go? Many things I planned to do have not yet been done. How did the weeks pass so quickly?

Spring made her colorful entry as the early showers caused bulbs to explode into fragrant flowers; budded trees became dense with leaves giving new shape where birds, as well as other creatures, could find shelter and make their music. Spring covered the earth with plush carpets of unexplored green paths, and there was a full awareness of the birth of new life.

Then Summer pushed Spring away, bringing long periods of high energy, growth, and frantic activities. Sometimes it was uncomfortable, often hot and dry; nevertheless, it was a maturing time. This was such a busy time—the days even lengthened to allow for everything to be accomplished.

Autumn now makes her arrival and slows things down a bit. Nature makes plans for her long nap. Not to be outdone, Autumn paints the trees and shrubs in such brilliant colors that Spring's gentler hues cannot compete. Artists gather to capture the myriad colors of Autumn on canvas. She is admired and photographed so that this late-life beauty can be remembered. She walks on the wind and rustles her leaves with sounds of taffeta. Her influence is such that she even commands time to be set back an hour. The crispness in her mornings and evenings perk up the spirits of those she touches. She takes the hands of those nearest her and finds a warm, comfortable spot for a time of reflection and forewarnings of things to come. Old Man Winter is soon to change her drastically.

Scriptures admonish us that our lives should bear fruit—not just seasonally but every day: love, joy, and peace; long-suffering, gentleness (kindness), and goodness; faith (faithfulness), meekness, and temperance (self-control).

For the next four weeks I want to share with you some personal glimpses of my own life-walk through the spring, summer and now these early days of autumn.

All yesterdays are memories. Admittedly, sometimes it's difficult to be fruitful when life is overwhelming. I believe things happen for a reason. At the time, we can see no good in negative experiences, but later we find we can draw from them to help influence others.

As I reflect over these 50-plus years, my focus will be on the . . .

- Power of promises
- Power of people
- Power of persistence
- Power of performance.

No matter what season you are in, God gives you a tomorrow!

He whispers to you, "Guess what! Tomorrow is a new day." Then He gently prepares you. Your tomorrow may hold sorrow, hurt, or loneliness; and Satan, or an enemy, will try to destroy you. But God knows all about it, and He is watching over you.

You have a choice: You can accept His gifts or you can turn away from them. He loves you! He has always loved you. One day when all our seasons are behind us, we will see Him face-to-face. And when we see Him, we will be changed into His likeness. Hold on to that wonderful thought!

O God, let this be a time when we realize our dependence upon the Holy Spirit for every day—every season. We know we cannot escape the raw realities of life, but we know they can build our faith.

October 2

Scripture: "I . . . meditate on your promises. . . . The Lord is faithful to all his promises" (Psalm 119:148; 145:13, *NIV*).

The world of marketing is often deceitful. If the product sounds too good to be true, it likely is! From the wrinkle-removing miracle cream to the latest electronic gadget—the advertised image is often a major disappointment. God never advertises more than He delivers! He does not deceive us. He has never made a promise that was too good to be true. He keeps His promises . . .

- On His terms
- By His methods
- In His time.

The promises of God are the heart of the Bible. *His terms, like many warranties, are good only if you do not violate the agreement.* That certainly was the case in the Garden of Eden. Eve could have enjoyed life there forever, but she broke the rules and suffered the penalty of death (see Genesis 2:16, 17).

Some of His promises are conditional: *if* we obey. Other promises are unconditional—nothing will stop them. He is faithful to His Word—He cannot deny Himself (see 2 Timothy 2:13).

God promised Noah He would never send another worldwide flood. God promised Abraham a son—a nation of descendants. David was assured his royal line would last forever. God promised to restore the nation of Israel. Jesus promised that when He ascended, He would send the Holy Spirit. He promised that the forces of Satan will never destroy the church. He promised to save, keep, and resurrect to eternal life all who trust in Him. God has promised that His Son would return to earth and reward the righteous and punish the evil.

His methods are often unfathomable to us: "His ways are not our ways" (see Isaiah 55:8, 9). He surprises us! When God told Pharaoh He was going to send frogs—He did! When He told David his son would build a temple—Solomon did! When God promised a Messiah—He came! Jesus said the Temple would be destroyed—it happened! Jesus promised to build the church—it's growing. Jesus promised to send the Holy Spirit—the Day of Pentecost came. The Bible is filled with promises.

His time is not our time. Like the tangled threads on the back of a tapestry, the events of our lives often seem to us to have no pattern. We cannot see the design from God's vantage point. We must have faith like Abraham's. He packed his bags not knowing where he was going. The lives of the Old Testament prophets were filled with immediate blessings and delayed fulfillment. Hebrews 10:23 admonishes us to "hold fast . . . for he is faithful." If we adopt the philosophy of the old hymn "Standing on the Promises," we can be sure we are on solid footing.

Even though I conscientiously believe His promises, there were times I struggled with His terms, His methods, and His timing. There were times when I felt God must have changed His address and didn't receive my prayers . . . times I simply walked by blind faith—certainly not by feeling. There were times I felt very much alone and a voice would whisper in my soul, "Lo, I am with you always"; times when I was frightened of the immediate future and, like a warm, soothing oil, I was comforted by the words "Be not afraid"; times when I felt betrayed and abandoned but I clung to His promise "I will never leave you nor forsake you"; times of challenges when I dared to leap into unknown arenas and I stepped out, assured that if I kept my focus in the right direction I would not make the wrong turns. Matthew 6:34 taught me I should "not worry about tomorrow, for tomorrow will worry about itself" (*NIV*). Each day has enough trouble of its own.

I remind myself that it was not raining when Noah began building the ark. He heard from God, believed in his heart, and obeyed in spite of the ridicule. His God was faithful. My God has been faithful to me. How about yours?

Some promises are conditional: *if* we trust . . . *if* we obey . . . *if* we follow not after our own selfish ambitions and desires but seek His will and His purpose.

324

It's only when we genuinely become as little children and follow Him with complete trust that we can accept the *terms*, the *methods*, and the *timing* of His promises.

Dear Lord, I really do believe Your promises are for me. Make me aware that those conditions I must meet in order for Your Word to be fulfilled in my life must not be taken lightly. I bow my heart before You. I am standing on Your promises. I trust You completely with my today and my tomorrows.

October 3

Scripture: "I am not ashamed of the gospel of Christ, for it is the power of God to salvation for everyone who believes"(Romans 1:16, *NKJV*). "For I know the plans I have for you . . . plans to prosper you and not to harm you, plans to give you hope and a future" (Jeremiah 29:11, *NIV*).

Billy Graham explained the way of salvation. Under the huge tent, I was only one of hundreds who went forward. I was 12 years old, and this was my first public expression of a faith in Jesus Christ. It was a decision of the head and the heart. My newfound faith received no nourishment at home, as my family did not attend church. Two years later, prompted by curiosity, I visited the Hemphill Avenue Church of God (now Mount Paran). What were "Holy Rollers" anyhow? The large church was renowned for its spirited Southern Gospel music. It was a good time for me to visit because the church was having revival. I took some of my friends.

April 22, 1953, is recorded as the most phenomenal date in my life. God made the appointment, but I did not know it. As soon as we entered the church, "something got hold of me." It seemed everything the minister said was just for me. When the invitation was given, a precious gray-haired lady took me by the hand and invited me to go forward. (Was she an angel sent by God?)

I knelt at the altar and accepted Christ as my Lord. When those who were praying with me encouraged me to accept the gift of the Holy Spirit, I did not know what they were referring to. I had never even seen anyone kneel and pray at a church altar. I had certainly never seen anyone seek the Holy Spirit. I had been baptized in the name of the Father and the Son and the Holy Ghost, but I had never heard of anyone being "filled with the Holy Spirit." I had never heard anyone "speak in tongues." But if there was more, I wanted it. Instantly, I received the baptism of the Holy Spirit with the evidence of speaking in tongues. When I stood, I felt like a new person! I could not explain what had happened to me.

The first 14 years of my life had been insecure. My parents divorced when I was very young. Preschool years were spent with my divorced working mother, but my parenting came from day care, boarding school women, and our maids. I didn't realize my life was bad or sad. It was normal for me.

There was a Pentecostal woman who kept children in her home. When Mother would *forget* to pick me up on Fridays, she would take me to church. She invested in my life. She prayed, "God, please keep your hand on Jackie." When she found me crying into a pillow, she reminded me, "Jesus loves you, and He knows right where you are. You are never alone. He will *always* know where you are." Those were promises I pulled deep inside me. They never have been broken. Even though home life was not ideal those early years, God placed influential people in my life. He was *watching over me* all along!

Mother remarried when I was in the fourth grade, and we moved to another Atlanta neighborhood. Two children (a boy and then a girl) were born to this marriage. I loved them dearly, but the marriage was an unhappy one.

During my early years I had to assume too much responsibility. Later I realized I was cheated out of my childhood. Yet God had known me from my mother's womb! Could He possibly take all the negatives and make good things happen? Is it possible that even though things happened I could neither prevent or dodge that *joy* was never lost, *hope* was never killed, and *dreams* never died? An emphatic YES!

God gripped my hand early in life. I purposed that no matter what, I would keep a positive mind-set for the pursuit of happiness. Philippians 4:8 taught me to think on good things.

Are you nursing wounds of yesterdays? Don't allow yourself to get stuck in the pain of the past. Self-pity is like smog that obscures the light of the Son. Lean into the promise of the future!

The scriptures we have read today speak forcefully to us. First of all, we must know Christ as our Savior. Then we need to adopt His Word as our bread of life. Our relationship with Him must be a personal one. We must talk to Him often, listen to Him intently. This is a good day to sit at His feet and remember the power of His promises.

Dear Lord Jesus, sometimes I feel ashamed when I allow self-pity and resentment of past experiences to surface. Today I forgive those who have wronged me. I acknowledge anew that You have a design for me, and You are not finished with me yet! Remind me again that You can take bad things and make them into glad things. No matter what happens today, I refuse to surrender my joy, my hope, and my dreams. I feel Your hand in mine, leading me along.

October 4

Scripture: "I will remember the covenant I made with you in the days of your youth" (Ezekiel 16:60, *NIV*). "Remember those earlier days after you had received the light, when you stood your ground in a great contest in the face of suffering" (Hebrews 10:32).

When I was asked to prepare devotionals for this month using the theme "Remembering" and to reflect on my own personal experiences, I agreed. Now I am wondering *why* I agreed. I feel my mind is on rewind. As I traveled back in time, I wiped tears, I giggled, I ached, and I reexamined my own history. Eleanor Roosevelt said, "In the long run, we shape our lives, and we shape ourselves. The process never ends until we die. The choices we make are ultimately our own responsibility."

I came from a dysfunctional home. I remember the police coming to my house more than once because of the violent arguments. Yes, there was alcohol abuse. (Today we label it a "sickness," and we label abusers "chemically dependent.") Once addicted, they are trapped, and they are sad people. They not only inflict suffering on themselves but also on those around them. It's evil. It's sin.

I remember as a child (and later as a teenager) how hurt and embarrassed I was by having an alcoholic stepfather and a mother who was not a good woman. Seldom did I ever have friends come to visit. Weekends were the worst. There were times I had to wait in the car when my stepfather would drive to a run-down old house and purchase "moonshine." I hated it then, and I hate it now! When he would go hunting or fishing with his friends, he always came home drunk. Then there would be quarreling. It was indescribable torment. Sometimes I would slip into the kitchen and pour the liquor down the sink. Often no one even noticed. Still today the very smell of alcohol arouses unpleasant memories. When I see drunkenness in someone's eyes, I have mental flashbacks of scenes of yesteryear. This I learned: Drinking is dangerous, debilitating, and depressing. I have never had one drink of alcohol to my lips.

My own father was only a check each month and a gift on special occasions. I saw very little of him in my childhood. He remarried when I was an adolescent. His wife never really accepted me. They did not live in Atlanta, and I was never invited to visit in their home in south Georgia.

My mother worked full-time and we had a maid. She was like family and I loved her dearly. She later became my first "convert."

When I became a Christian, my mother and stepfather were vehemently opposed to what they called my fanatical religious experience. At first I was forbidden to go back to church. Even though I was young, deep in my heart I knew something very unusual had happened to me. I spent hours reading the Bible and learning. It seemed to come alive in my spirit. Mother would come into my bedroom, take my Bible from me, and sling it across the room, demanding I stop reading it. She finally took me to a psychologist. (This was long before seeing a counselor was the *in* thing. I was humiliated!) Much to her dismay, he encouraged her to simply leave me alone. He felt this religion thing would "run its course." That was 43 years ago! My experience is just as real today as it was then.

I really tried to honor my father and my mother. I read and internalized Ecclesiastes 12:1: "Remember now thy Creator in the days of thy youth." I begged God to save my family!

In preparing this section, I brought from its secret place the only little Bible I had. Many of its pages are tearstained. Numbers of scriptures are marked; I adopted them as specifically written for me. The power of those promises kept me on track. I never realized how many scriptures had to do with God being *my* Father.

Unless your background is similar, you will not understand. I have difficulty expressing on paper just how meaningful it was that God became my heavenly Father. In my simple, childlike way, He became the father image I had never known. From my inner soul I could spend long periods of time just talking to Him about everything. Can you understand when I say that in the quietness of those times I felt the sacred embrace of His love and assurance that He would always be with me—as close as my breath? Can you understand when I say that mysteriously He spoke to my spirit and a strange, warm presence came into my room?

The Father took an insignificant young girl with little promise of a good future, lifted her out, and set her feet on a new path. It's been an exciting journey!

Even if your background was quite the opposite of mine, God still wants to be your heavenly Father. Will you forsake all to follow Him?

Father, here I am again, just needing to thank You for Your rich blessings to me. Thank You for making of yesteryear's experiences memories that light the corner of my mind and colors that decorate my life today. Please speak to others the same words of encouragement and promise!

October 5

Scripture: "Be not afraid, only believe" (Mark 5:36). "Jesus went about . . . teaching . . . preaching . . . and healing all manner of sickness . . . among the people" (Matthew 4:23).

Like a sponge I absorbed every sermon, every Sunday school lesson, every testimony, every gospel song, and every scripture. Never knowing when my mother would suddenly stop me, I anxiously attended every service I could. There was great emphasis on witnessing and winning people to Christ.

My prayers were fervent for Mother and my stepfather. Oh, how I wanted them to have this same experience! Yet, I knew God himself would have to work on this miracle! Then I decided our maid, Claudine, needed Christ. By now she had listened as I shared bits and pieces of sermons and my awesome wonder of miraculous healings and other unusual things I witnessed at church.

I began praying earnestly for her. I knew nothing about fasting. But they were discussing it at church. I read about it in the Bible, so I decided I would try it. For two days, I ate nothing. At school I sat in the bleachers and read my Bible and prayed during lunch. My friends thought I was losing my mind!

But it worked! Monday morning the phone rang and mother said something like, "If you can just come and be here with the children; don't worry about cleaning or cooking. I just can't miss work today. Can you come?" Soon after she left for work, Claudine arrived. I was rushing to get ready for school. She came into my bedroom and said, "Miss Jackie, you've been talking to me about God, and for the first time in years I went to church Sunday. My husband was drunk when I returned home and he beat me. He stabbed me in the leg with an ice pick."

Before she could finish, I took her hand and said, "Oh, Claudine, that's awful. The devil didn't want you to go to church. You are hungry for God, and the devil is using your husband to hinder you." She could hardly walk. I moved my books and asked her to sit in the little bedside chair. She began crying. I felt very strange.

"Claudine, you need Jesus. I've watched you as I shared things from church and evidently the Lord has been dealing with your heart. All you have to do is kneel. No, you can't kneel—but you can pray and ask Jesus to forgive your sins. If you promise to live for Him and believe He loves you and died on Calvary for you—right now He has His hand outstretched reaching for you. Just accept Him as your Savior. That's all there is to it."

She buried her face in her hands and wept. I knelt beside the chair, and we prayed. Soon she put her hand on top of mine and said, "You had no way of knowing, but I was once a good Christian. I used to go with my family to a holiness church. When you talked about your new church, I knew what you were talking about. I've needed to get back to God for a long time. Thank you for sharing Jesus with me. I feel so clean and good."

As I walked away to get her a tissue, I remembered several services where I had seen people "lay hands" on others and they were healed. I had no idea why they used oil. Scriptures began to come forward. These are powerful promises:

James 5:16: "Confess . . . pray . . . that you may be healed."

Matthew 8:8: "I am not worthy . . . but speak the word only, and my servant shall be healed."

Mark 16:18: "They shall lay hands on the sick, and they shall recover."

Mark 5:23: "Lay thy hands on her, that she may be healed."

Luke 13:13: "And he laid hands on her: and immediately she was made straight, and glorified God."

John 15:7: "If ye abide in me, and my words abide in you, ye shall ask what ye will, and it shall be done unto you."

John 14:13: "And whatsoever ye shall ask in my name, that will I do, that the Father may be glorified."

Mark 11:24: "What things soever ye desire, when ye pray, believe that ye receive them, and ye shall have them."

Mark 9:23: "Jesus said . . . If thou canst believe, all things are possible."

There is power in His promises. When all else fails, we can stand on the Word.

I will continue this testimony in tomorrow's devotion.

Thank you, Lord, for every promise in the Holy Scriptures. Thank You for Your faithfulness. You certainly do work in mysterious ways. Over and over You prove Your love. Help me sow the Word in my heart so You may shine light on my path.

October 6

Scripture: "This is the confidence that we have in him, that, if we ask any thing according to his will, he heareth us" (1 John 5:14).

As we prayed, I thought, *Claudine could be healed if I lay hands on her, then ask and believe. That's what they did at church, and that's what the Bible*

330

teaches. I tried to explain the scriptures I remembered; I told her if we prayed, God would heal her. I told her about the woman who touched the border of His robe and was healed immediately (Luke 8:43-48) and that when Jesus heals you, others will believe on Him. He was beaten and crucified for us. By His stripes we are healed (Isaiah 53:5).

We agreed that God is no "respecter of persons" and that what He did in Bible times He could still do. Lifting up her skirt, Claudine removed a homemade bandage of white cloth, revealing a terrible wound. I stood and laid my hands on her head and began to pray. Suddenly, it was as though a bolt of electricity shot through me. I trembled. She leaped to her feet, shouting with both arms in the air. Then she ran into the dining room praising God and speaking in tongues.

When she finally "came to herself," she raised her skirt and the thigh was as clean as the back of my hand. There was no evidence of a wound. God had performed a miracle! The house where God was not welcome had become a holy place and the Healer had visited . . . believe it or not!

I didn't even go to school that day. We read the Bible and prayed and talked about the Lord until I had to hurry and help her get things straightened up before the family came home.

It was a very long time before I shared this story. It was so private and sacred that I wondered if anyone would believe it.

As a result of her testimony, friends and relatives of Claudine would come to our house for prayer meetings during school vacation time. If there is such a thing as a guardian angel, then the one assigned to me must have been quite amused. Here I was just a young girl, newly saved, conducting Bible studies and having healing services. God honored my sincerity, our faith, and His Word. For lack of a better way to describe how I felt—it was like an "anointing."

This was 1953 and there was great racial stress in the Southeast. Not with us! We were having a revival and an outpouring of the Holy Spirit. It was wonderful! They were being saved and healed—until the next-door neighbor phoned Mother to report that black people were coming to our home and we were doing that "speaking in tongues." Both were considered unacceptable to her and my mother. The prayer meetings ceased.

The ridicule I endured at school, the cursings at home, and the struggle to stay in church seemed worth it all. I had not only led Claudine to Christ but also several of her friends. They were precious to me and I loved them. Often my mind races back to those scenes of my kneeling at the blue couch and praying with them.

None of this was because of me, but all because of the power of His promises. There is authority in His Word. In simple faith I believed that *if* I obeyed His Word, *if* I served Him faithfully, *if* I believed He was sovereign God, *if* I asked anything in His name and according to His will, it would be done. Some things arrive in their own mysterious hour, on their own terms, to be seized forever.

Do you know someone who needs Christ? Do you need healing? Do you believe God answers prayer? Do you believe His Word? If not— why not?

Today, Lord, I did something I thought I would never do. I shared a miraculous story You wrote in my life long ago. Somewhere, someone needed to read this. I don't know who she is—but You do. Speak to her heart. Help her to believe Your Word and release her faith.

October 7

Scripture: "Jesus Christ the same yesterday, and to day, and for ever" (Hebrews 13:8).

When the surgeon in North Dakota operated on me only a few months after we were married, he said it was unlikely that I would ever conceive a child. That was my second surgery, and there was almost no ovarian tissue left. Almost four years later our little Donna was born. She was a big, healthy baby. She was our miracle!

I had some serious complications that kept me in the hospital for 31 days. For months I had to sleep with the bed elevated at the foot. I had to wear those ugly, thick surgical stockings, and I was on anticoagulants for a long time. But she was worth it! I had prayed and prayed for a child. My physician in Indianapolis didn't even want to confirm a baby until he heard the heartbeat. Then almost 20 months later, I was back in the same hospital, scheduled for another C-section. The nurses remembered me. After all, how many mothers and new babies stay a month with them?

When I regained consciousness in the recovery room, I sensed something was wrong. Where was a nurse? Soon the pediatrician came to me, along with a visiting famous heart surgeon from Houston. They both examined our baby and announced that she had a large hole in her heart. He drew on a linen towel and described the problem.

Remember, this was 1964. Thank God for advances in today's technology! He told me the only reason he was telling me was he knew we would want to pray. In most cases, he said the parents would not be told. The baby likely would not survive. As he walked away, I turned my head to the pillow and wept, "God, this can't be! They said I could never have one baby and now I have a second one. If she was not meant to be, why did You let me conceive and give birth? I haven't even seen her, and they tell me she may die soon. Please don't let that happen. Please let me hold her. O God, wherever she is, please be there. Please heal her. Don't let her suffer."

I began to cry uncontrollably. The head nurse came to me. She had teased me a few hours earlier and said she would have a nice, comfortable spot for me when they brought me back from surgery. This was not a comfortable spot. It was the greatest pain I had ever known. She took my hand and said something like this: "I know they gave you a bad report. I remember you and your husband from the last time you were here. You're praying folks. You just pray, and God's gonna take care of this."

I felt almost ashamed. This loving black nurse reminded me of one of the ladies who used to come to my home for prayer meetings. My faith was on display. I looked up at the ceiling and prayed again. There was a hollow hurt deep inside.

In that cold, sterile room I was reminded of the morning when all alone, I took my friend Claudine to the throne room and prayed for her healing. I reminded God that if He could heal Claudine, He could heal my baby. I had no doubts. I knew He could heal because I had witnessed it personally.

My parents said people were paid to fake healings in the Oral Roberts Crusade I had attended and that those healed at church also were just pretending. I knew better! I had witnessed God's healing power firsthand. My mother-heart ached. I knew God could look down His telescope of time; and if she would not be healthy or if her future would not be a good one, then I needed Him to take control now. I accepted the fact that His will was the most important thing. If she died, there had to be a reason. Then I experienced a strange feeling and was able to pull together these words: "It's awful, Father, but Your will be done." Immediately I had peace. I knew she would be OK.

About that time my father-in-law showed up at my side. Now, how did Paul H. Walker get past those nurses? I shared with him that 11 years ago I had prayed and God healed a lady instantly. I had never shared that story with anyone except my pastor because I wondered why God did not heal *every* time I prayed for someone. The part of my pastor's explanation that stayed in my mind is that perhaps God allowed that miracle to reveal His power, to assure me His Word was true, and to teach me that prayer, coupled with faith, could bring God into our presence to work mighty miracles. How true! Dad Walker took my hand and said, "Let's pray." He too was confident things would be OK. We agreed together.

In a few hours, I went to my room. Three days later I saw my baby

Denise for the first time. With any exertion she would turn blue, but day by day she made miraculous improvement.

She was too young and it was too soon after her birth, but Don accepted a church and we moved to South Carolina. Two weeks later, she was examined, and the doctor found nothing wrong. She was healed! There's more I will share later. But this is just a confirmation that God does hear and answer prayer . . . *if* it's His will.

Lord, it's really hard to understand everything that happens in life. We know that Your delays are not always denials. With sickness, You are an opportunity for healing. With sin, You are an opportunity for forgiveness. With sorrow, You are an opportunity for compassion. Thank You for answered prayers. Give us patience while You work out the details of our unanswered ones.

October 8

Scripture: "From a child thou hast known the holy scriptures" (2 Timothy 3:15). "For the promise is unto you, and to your children" (Acts 2:39).

It was August 1964. We had spent four happy years in Indiana. Because our baby Denise was due, I had to miss the General Assembly. What a shock to learn that they voted in a new ruling that state youth directors could only serve four years in one state. We had just finished our fourth year. Now what?

Don accepted a pastorate in South Carolina. Donna was 20 months old, Denise was less than a month old, but we packed and moved. What an experience!

When Denise was three months old, she suddenly developed pneumonia. Don was away at a ministers meeting. In the middle of the night, the physician told me to get her to the hospital immediately. A lady from the church kept Donna. I drove from Clemson to Anderson at breakneck speed, pulled into the emergency parking area, and left the car running while I rushed inside with Denise. Long after she was already being treated, they realized she had not been admitted. They were just following orders the doctor left for them upon her arrival. This was another one of those terrible times. But guess what! God healed her again!

A few years later after we had moved to Michigan, Denise developed what we thought was a little cyst on her neck. The doctor treated her for weeks. It grew and grew. Finally, he scheduled surgery. It was a very delicate procedure. We prayed; but, for whatever reason, she was not healed. She went through painful surgery. The recovery was long and slow. We fought infection. During this period of time a dear friend of ours, Bob Sustar, had surgery on his neck to remove a cancerous tumor. Denise, now 10, was becoming self-conscious of the bandage on her neck and did not know what it would look like when it healed. Bob, visiting in Detroit, took Denise aside and opened the collar of his shirt to reveal the awful, long scar he had from his own surgery. Whatever he said ministered to her greatly. She came away feeling very thankful and never complained again about her incision.

Weeks went by, and it did not heal properly. We read the Word and again trusted in the power of His promises. After consulting another physician, surgery was scheduled. This time the proper correction was made. Thank God for skilled surgeons and because there was no cancer. "The word of the Lord is right and true; he is faithful in all he does" (Psalm 33:4, *NIV*).

Denise is single and actively involved in the Mount Paran Church of God in Atlanta. She genuinely loves the Lord. Ironically, some of the same people who greatly influenced me as a teen are now mentoring her. How good God is! His promises are true. God spared her life more than once. His master design for her life is still uniquely unfolding.

Donna is married and has given us two wonderful grandsons. She and Brad and the boys live in Cleveland, Tennessee. Those who know us best say she has my disposition. I wonder. It's true, she is a neat-freak, compulsive, a type A personality, a choleric type, or whatever label best describes me. In those areas she is like me. However, the part that really "makes her tick" comes from different roots. Fortunately, she did not come from my same kind of box. She had the warmth and security of parents who loved her deeply; provided well for her; prayed for her; kept her in church; provided a good education; and exposed her to travel, the arts, and some of the finer things in life. And she knows that no matter what, we will always be in her corner. And we have a "911 number" that rings on our heart—and we come running! That's not the way it was for me. Her foundation is quite different from her mother's. She and Denise both have developed from their own life-walk the building blocks of faith and resilience. They are overcomers. I am proud of them.

But neither of my children can fully know where I came from. Nor can yours. They cannot know all the experiences and influences that brought you to where you are. However, when they begin to raise and nurture their own children, the principles and character they have developed are revealed in their own offspring. It's an amazing drama!

All those bedtime prayers, Bible stories, "little girl" talks, corrections and admonishments, and all the other "stuff" that goes into imprinting are the ingredients needed to train up our children in the way they should go; and when they are old, they will not depart from it (Proverbs 22:6). I am blessed!

God, only You see from the beginning to the end of our lives. As we deal with the in-between, help us follow Your instructions. Anchor us to the power of Your promises. Let our lifestyle reflect the image of Your Son and our Savior, Jesus Christ, today.

October 9

Scripture: "Therefore, as we have opportunity, let us do good to all people, especially to those who belong to the family of believers" (Galatians 6:10, *NIV*).

Some people come into our lives and quietly go. Others stay for a while and leave footprints on our hearts, and we are never the same.

Oh, the powerful influence people can have on our lives! Some are *positive*, some *negative*.

My first pastor made quite an impact on my life. His sermons and wise counsel ministered to me. He invested in my life, and I thought he was godlike. The two years in Minot when Don and I were first married, I greatly missed my home church. I had no knowledge of any wrongdoing there until we flew to Atlanta to go to the General Assembly in Memphis. When the Watsons met us, I could see anguish and pain on their faces. They told me that the next morning the state overseer, W.E. Johnson, would bring to the congregation the news of our pastor's dismissal. I was so shocked. It was shameful, the details unbelievable.

The scene at church was dreadful. Grown men and women bowed their heads and wept openly. I was glad I had been away, because the time span had enabled me to focus on other individuals also—not just my early church leaders. This man had taught me how to walk with God. How did he lose his way? We have been personally acquainted with other ministers who have "fallen from grace." Their fall affected many lives. Does that make me lose faith in the church or its leaders? No, a thousand times no! The Enemy is out to destroy every one of us. We have to be on guard at all times lest he sneak in when we least expect it. Remember, Christ is the One we are following.

Each time I assist Don in an ordination service, I am reminded of that scene back in Atlanta. I never teach a Ministerial Internship class that I do not examine my own life. Do I merit projecting myself as an example for young ministers and their wives? We can learn from both *successes* and *failures*.

Lee and Lois Watson embraced me with love and became my legal guardians. They became like parents to me; their children—Billy, Norma, and Gordy—like true brothers and sisters. "And every one that hath forsaken houses, or brethren, or sisters, or father, or mother . . . for my name's sake, shall receive an hundredfold, and shall inherit everlasting life" (Matthew 19:29).

God cares for people—through people. Mama Lois and Papa Lee continue to impact my life and the lives of my children. I cannot count the times I have called from distant places and asked them to pray. They are a godly couple and have often prayed down miracles! Their compassion and concern for others, their generosity, their high energy, their love for the church, their respect for leaders, their value of family ties, their work ethics, and their appreciation for the finer things of life are all significant qualities that have influenced me. When *Life* magazine did an article on Lee Watson, it only touched the surface of the story of his benevolence and citizenry.

Through the church many *mothers in the Lord* greatly influenced me, and a host of Christian women loved me and became beautiful role models—like Lula Watson, Gertrude Martin, Sister Lowndes, Grace Caldwell, Sue Duvall, Margie Abernathy, Grace Mullinax, Ruth Blackwell, Marjean Birt, and Joyleen Pealock.

Oh, there were dozens of families in those early years who touched my life. Two people who took a special interest in me were Clyde and Maudeen Cole. Had it not been for them, I would have never been able to go to church when I was first saved. Bonnie Maddox was the nurse for our family physician. When I started attending their church, she and her husband, Lynwood, greatly influenced me. In fact, I worked in his office just before moving to Minot. They are giants in the Lord. Lynwood and Lee Watson were actively involved in the early Full Gospel Businessmen's Fellowship. I marveled at how their witness won many to Christ. Their burden for the lost and their fishers-of-men attitude was a tremendous model.

Also, Chloe and Arvel Burell—no matter where we lived, they stayed in touch and helped us often. I sort of adopted them. They are beautiful people. Our Denise has found them to be good shoulders to lean on also.

How will *we* be remembered? It's quite frightening, isn't it? I guess we just have to do our best and let Him do the rest. You may be the only Bible some people will ever read. Your life is on display.

Today I want to give you a B.A. degree. Now, that doesn't mean bachelor of arts. It means *Be an angel.*

Make me a blessing, Lord. If I pass through this life and do not touch somebody's life with a positive imprint, my living shall be in vain. Others may fail me, but Your Word tells me You are faithful to the end. During those times when I am sitting at Your feet, reveal to me my shortcomings and help me grow more like You.

October 10

Scripture: "I thank my God every time I remember you" (Philippians 1:3, *NIV*).

On October 10 in Lansing, Michigan, a twin boy, named Donald Murray Walker, was born to Margaret and Paul H. Walker. He grew up in Church of God parsonages in Michigan, Florida, Maryland, West Virginia, Pennsylvania, Ohio, and Tennessee.

A few months after Don's birth, on January 29, Jacquelyn Touchstone was born to Mildred and Ben Harold Touchstone. She spent her entire life in Atlanta, Georgia.

What did God have in mind?

Don's life was spent in a loving, spiritual home of stalwart faith. His parents were pioneers in the Church of God. He has a twin brother, Dean, and one older brother, Paul LaVerne. His father was a state overseer all of his childhood and then later the director of World Missions. I accuse him of having a very sheltered life, obscure from the real world. As he was growing up, he had little responsibility at home and his greatest interest was sports!

He has a great sense of humor, a good disposition, and is even-tempered (most of the time). He inherited his father's deep voice—sometimes sounding tougher than he really is! He loves people. Idleness does not appeal to him.

During the summer of 1956 I spent several days in Cleveland, Tennessee, visiting Florence (Tidwell) Clawson. Florence was baby-sitting her sister Euverla's children while she and her husband, Ray H. Hughes, were visiting camp meetings. Don and I had our first date while I was there. That was the beginning of a new life-walk for me.

Florence and Don convinced me I should enroll in Lee College. Florence and I were roommates in the dorm. Frankly, I didn't like living in Cleveland, but I made lots of wonderful friends. Don was on the basketball team and I was a cheerleader. It was a storybook romance!

On June 7, 1958, we were married. What a union—two people with entirely different backgrounds. We soon learned that marriages are not necessarily made in heaven. They come in kits, and you have to put them together. The first few months were hectic. We planned to live in Atlanta. In August, Don's parents received a shocking appointment—to North Dakota. We felt sorry for them, so we later followed them there. Don went to college and worked part-time and I had an excellent job with the Soo Line Railroad.

While attending Minot State College, Don made a full surrender to obey the will of God for his life. On our knees at our bedside, he wept and agreed to accept his call to the ministry. That was the beginning of a new venture.

In 1953 when I promised the Lord I would be what He wanted me to be, do what He wanted me to do, go wherever He sent me, don't you suppose even then He had this in His *master plan*?

We have served the Church of God in many varied ministry roles and locations. It has been a rewarding and exciting 38 years!

What about the differences in our backgrounds? God knew best. Many times when Don would be dealing with certain issues or counseling someone with a particular problem, he and I would differ strongly on our interpretations and suggested solutions. I would give him opinions from *my* perspective that helped him see things differently than what he had filtered from his own background, emotions, and training. This also works in reverse.

Even though we have different backgrounds, I believe my heavenly Father allowed our paths to converge. Don is the greatest person in my life. When we put our lives in the hands of God and we make our daily walk one of trust—He leads us. He directs our paths. He develops our lives.

Who is the most important person in *your* life? Is it your spouse? Is it your children? Tell them how important they are. Give them a hug!

"Happy Birthday, Don! I love you."

Not all romances end with "happily ever after." I don't know where your life fits. If you feel you have had your share of sad experiences and disappointments, don't let yesterday's heartaches blur the brightness of today. Turn it over to God. He understands, He cares, and He can fix it!

*Dear Lord, thank You for bringing certain people into our lives. Some are challenges and we need Your help with them. Others are easy to love. Teach us how to be kind to both. Don't let us walk through life and not be **remembered** affectionately by someone.*

October 11

Scripture: "If ye suffer for righteousness' sake, happy are ye. . . . For it is better, if the will of God be so, that ye suffer for well doing than for evil doing" (1 Peter 3:14, 17).

I was sent from the table because I encouraged a little one (still in a high chair) to pray the blessing. I was told that religion had to go or *I* had to go. Walking away from that table, I knew the crucial hour that had been developing had come.

Locking the bathroom door behind me, I could still hear loud quarreling from the other room, but I knelt beside the tub. It was cold— my tears were hot. I telephoned my mother's father to come and get me.

Granddaddy was a building contractor. Many monuments of his work still stand in and around Atlanta. In a subdivision he was developing near his home, I found a closet in an almost-finished house that became my "prayer closet." It was sacred to me. Far in the corner on the shelf in that closet I unintentionally left a gospel tract.

After I moved away, an older couple bought the house. The man, who had once been a Christian, became terminally ill. When he found the tract, he believed an angel had put it there. At his funeral the story was told of how he came back to God. Had God planned for me to be in that closet?

During the time I was with my grandparents, they drove quite a distance to take me to church on Sunday mornings. They didn't understand the Pentecostal faith, but they felt *any* religion was better than none. Most Sunday afternoons I was taken in by a God-sent family, Lois and Lee Watson. My Sunday school teacher, Margie Abernathy, and friends like Grace, Joyleen, Marjean, and others saw that I was in church. I shall never forget them and others who took my hand and held on.

At school my friends also rejected me. I withdrew from the cheerleading squad because it conflicted with Friday night youth services. I stopped almost everything—wearing make-up, going to movies, going to dances—trying to adopt what the church taught. They even put jokes about me in the school paper. Eventually, I led several of my friends to Christ.

The Watsons asked me to come live with them. That was a major decision and a big turning point! After I had finally won the respect of my peers and had even started a Bible club, I had to transfer from West Fulton High to O'Keefe High. I had to start all over *winning friends* and *influencing people*. I didn't know anyone at the new school except the LeFevres who went to my church. The Watsons had a married daughter, Norma, who was a little older than me. She and the LeFevre teens had a gospel trio. Norma and I adopted each other as sisters and the bond still holds today.

Oh, the power of the influence of people! God put into my life many mentors and godly role-models. Someday the book will reveal their good works and their incredible impact on me. They left "thumbprints" on my life forever!

Dear Savior, we are comforted to know that You know our breaking point. The bruising, crushing, and melting process You use to design and shape us is not meant for ruin. Thank You for sending people to walk alongside us with words of encouragement.

October 12

Scripture: "The eternal God is your refuge, and underneath are the everlasting arms. He will drive out your enemy before you, saying, 'Destroy him!'" (Deuteronomy 33:27, *NIV*).

I contacted my father when I moved to my grandparents.' He was helping me financially, but I had not seen him. Our visits over the years had been minimal, but I cherished each one. He was such a kind gentleman. He took me to fine restaurants, and sometimes we would visit his father. His mother died when I was about 12. I was with her when she died at Grady Hospital. Again I questioned: "God, why did You take her? I loved her. I needed her so!"

When I made the decision to move to the Watsons,' I wrote my father to see if he could help me. He agreed. Lois arranged a meeting so that we could establish a family relationship. Chapters could be written describing the intense emotions experienced at that meeting. I dreamed of it, yet I dreaded it. However, everything worked out fine. Dad liked the Watsons; they *really* liked him. That was the beginning of regular visits when his business travels brought him to Atlanta. God was restoring what had been lost.

The last two years of high school were filled with activities (I had leading roles in several school plays, was crowned Homecoming Sweetheart, and so forth). It would have been nice for me to have had a parent there.

The very first time I remember my mother and father being under the same roof was on my wedding day. What an experience! My mother was to have a place of honor. She had no companion. My father was giving me away. I couldn't help but think, *He never had me, how can he give me away?*

My stepmother did not come. I had the Watsons, who had parented me in my critical teen years. It was as though I needed to honor two mothers. How would I arrange a receiving line at the reception? What was the proper protocol? It was emotional, but we finally worked out the details.

I shall never forget the sweet talk my father gave me just before they straightened the train to my dress and we walked down the aisle. Over the years Dad and I became very close. He had so many wonderful attributes—very well groomed, friendly, a great sense of humor, high morals, very disciplined, and an avid "golfer" (he was part of the Country Club set). But no matter how *good* he was, I reminded him often, he still needed Christ.

I prayed for years that he would have a salvation experience. We were living in Ohio when he called to say he had just watched a Billy Graham message on TV and had given his heart to the Lord. My heart leaped within me, and my mind flashed back to a tent meeting in Atlanta when I was 12 years old.

If you have been praying for someone to come to Christ—keep believing. It may not come as soon as you want it, but He will be right on time!

Thank You, Father, for the times I just leaned on Your everlasting arms and You held me. Please let someone who needs that kind of support turn to You now and receive Your peace. Remind them of the power of Your promises.

October 13

Scripture: "Then you will call, and the LORD will answer; you will cry for help, and he will say: Here am I" (Isaiah 58:9, *NIV*).

It was October when I was notified. Daddy had been fighting hepatitis for several weeks and was very ill. He was in the hospital and would call me soon. I didn't like how I felt. Don and I began praying. We called often to remind him we were praying for his healing. (I also kept reminding God that He had healed before when I prayed—please do it now!)

He got better and resumed his travels. Then on Thanksgiving Day we received a call from my stepmother (who rarely called) to tell me he was in a coma and his doctor insisted I be called.

I caught the first plane. Don prepared the children to drive down the next day. It was an awful trip! They left just as a winter blizzard was moving in; it followed just *behind* them. My storm was *in front* of me. I flew into the nearest airport and rented a car for the drive to Thomasville, Georgia. It was one of the longest days of my life. I clenched the steering wheel and prayed aloud, "Oh God, please let me get there! Please let Don and the girls get there." I prayed and cried almost the entire drive.

For several miles the highway stretched straight ahead as though it just ran off into eternity. For a fleeting moment I wanted God to just explain to me *why* I have to keep dealing with such emotional pain. Why couldn't my life just be smooth and straight, without so many curves and bumps? I wanted to remind Him of my sacrifices to serve Him. I was just before having a perfect pity party, with no one invited but pitiful, proud me! Then . . . my emotions flipped and I began to think of how good God had been to me when I didn't even deserve it. I began counting my rich blessings. I began to *praise* Him. It's amazing what happens when we praise!

Have you lost someone very special? Have you walked alone? Have you ever felt God abandoned you? When your circumstances cry, "Surrender!" don't give up. As Robert Schuller says, "Tough times don't last—tough people do!"

Father, it's difficult sharing some of my life events with strangers. I don't want to be misunderstood. Surely You meant good to come out of some of the bad places. Encourage those who read these devotions to sit at Your feet and believe Your promises. We believe nothing will come upon us that will be so great we cannot bear it—because You will help us carry it.

October 14

Scripture: "He will wipe every tear from their eyes. There will be no more death or mourning or crying or pain" (Revelation 21:4, *NIV*).

It was evening when I rushed to the hospital desk to inquire of Daddy's room. The nurse told me only *immediate* family members could visit. When I told her I was his daughter, she dropped her pen! Exiting the elevator, I saw my stepmother and several others down the long hall. As I neared them, I felt there was a volcano about to erupt in my chest. I felt like an alien. I was the unknown, unacknowledged, and rejected, now making an appearance into their world. His physician candidly told me my father was not going to make it. This was our final moment.

I requested we be left alone for a while. As the nurse slipped into a darkened corner, I went to my father's bedside and took his hand. He had not responded for hours. He was only 54 and he was dying. How could I give him up? I began to tell him how much I loved him, how we had missed out on so much together but how happy we had been these past few years. I told him how wonderful it was that he had accepted the Lord. Then I told him I wanted to pray.

He began to struggle and move his head, trying to communicate. I prayed and committed him to God. The first time he left me, I was too young to even remember. Now he was leaving again. It was my time to say good-bye. I bent to kiss his forehead, and he struggled again. The nurse stepped forward, and I could read in her eyes it would be only a few minutes. They rushed him to intensive care. I wished Don was there. Taking a deep breath, I walked out to face the other scene in the hall. My energies were spent. How could I deal with all this? I tried to speak some comforting words to my stepmother. She and her friends left to return home.

After checking into a nearby motel, I called Don. He listened to just tears and talk for a long time. I hardly slept. I relived my whole life.

The next morning was just as traumatic. I drove to the house I had never visited but had always wondered about. I did *not* want to go inside, but I had no choice. Thank God, Don and the children arrived soon. Arrangements were made for us to stay with neighbors.

Dad and my brother-in-law Paul had become friends. There had been no arrangements made for a minister. We called Paul and he came. What would we have done without him? He always knows just what to say, and he *ministered* to all of us.

Strange to me was their custom of having the body at the funeral home where people paid their respects, signed the book, then drove to the home to visit the family. I found this uncomfortable. I was there for *him*. I excused myself and drove to the funeral home to just *sit* with him those last few hours.

During this time his attorney and golfing partner came by. What a comfort he was. His visit must have been ordered of God. He revealed he was perhaps the only one there who had known about me. He told me what a good person Daddy had been and how he had regretted that our lives had been separated. He shared the many times Dad had spoken of me, my Christian walk, and my marriage to a young minister. Dad had told him he was a Christian as a direct result of the witness of my life and the many prayers I had prayed for him.

I believed God for his salvation for years. It happened! Don't stop praying for your loved ones.

Thank You for the years my father and I had to get to know each other. Thank You, Lord, for putting broken pieces together. Most of all, thank You for making it possible for him to taste of Your love and salvation. Thank You for Your faithfulness.

October 15

Scripture: "Let us . . . walk by the Spirit . . . let us go forward walking in line, our conduct controlled by the Spirit" (Galatians 5:25, *Amp.*).

No matter if it's a messy Monday, a weird Wednesday, or a fragile Friday, we can walk in the spirit of a sacred Sunday.

Our personal walk with the Lord is private—or is it? Our daily lifestyle is a book, read of all who know us. Those who are closest to us really know if we *walk* what we *talk*.

Some of us are like the duck who looks calm and serene above the water (where people see), but we are paddling like crazy below just to stay afloat! This Christian journey is very straight and very narrow. There is no room for phonies!

Most people we pass on this walk Monday through Sunday, week after week, are basically good—as good as we are—not perfect, but neither are we. If we mark every person off our list who is imperfect, we will have no one left!

Christ must be our example. There is nothing phony about Him. And we are to reflect like mirrors the image of our Lord Jesus Christ. What a challenge!

God is watching us. We are open to double scrutiny—from God and from people. We are closely observed—the way we look, the way we act, the way we react, the way we talk, and the way we handle life. God is watching you—the real you, the unvarnished, deep-down you.

Obviously, we do not see ourselves as God sees us, neither do we see ourselves as others see us.

It's only when we look . . .

> INWARD with honesty, purpose, and commitment that we can look . . .
>
> UPWARD with our worship and . . .
>
> OUTWARD with warm love for others.

Perhaps finances have you depressed. Perhaps a wayward child has your heart troubled beyond measure. Perhaps you are dealing with an inner struggle with your own husband-wife relationship. Perhaps you are stressed because you are not carrying your load maturely and with faith.

It's time to give yourself a good dose of determination and wash it down with a half-pint of persistence. Persevere! Don't allow the Enemy to camp on your mind and spirit. It's his business to discourage and frighten you. Resist him and he will flee!

God wants us to walk our walk with joy and happiness. He wants us to skip and sing. When things seem to "go sour," the Holy Spirit is like honey and sweetens things up. Too often we don't allow Him to work things out because we are in the way—doing our own thing!

What an assurance we find in the Word! Proverbs 3:21-23 tells us that wisdom and discretion will "keep you safe from defeat and disaster and from stumbling off the trail" (*TLB*). And Isaiah 30:21 says, "And if you leave God's paths and go astray, you will hear a Voice behind you say, 'No, this is the way; walk here'" (*TLB*).

We quote the Word, but do we *walk* the Word? Do we apply it to our daily journey on this path called life? Or do we simply go through life with lip service and just talk a good game? If we never apply the faith food and the principles set forth in the Scriptures, we will most definitely be knocked down by the deadly *d*'s of depression, disappointment, and doubt.

If we ever hope to influence others with a positive faith, we had best learn how to develop one of our own and use it.

Thank You, Jesus, for the pattern you have provided for my daily life-walk. I know I am not perfect, and there are times my circumstances almost overwhelm me. Hold me steady, Lord. Because You have overcome, I too can overcome.

October 16

Scripture: "Let not your heart be troubled" (John 14:1).

This summer, Don was preaching the South Georgia camp meeting, and we drove back to my dad's home. My second visit. After his death, I had returned home with absolutely nothing significant that had been his personally. We left without even a recent photograph. His wife said she could not part with anything. I needed to visit his grave site.

We picked up my stepmother, and she directed us there. On the way I observed how lonely she was. She never remarried. We still make contact during the Christmas holidays. From their large pecan orchard, she continues Dad's practice of sending pecans each year.

She enjoys hearing about the family, and we send her photographs. She's a good person and extremely devoted to her extended family. She also stays in touch with the family of Daddy's brother. Too bad we never developed a closeness. What a waste.

As we walked to his grave, I noticed the veteran's marker. As a young man, he had served his country honorably in the U.S. Navy. I was proud of him. For a fleeting moment, I remembered as a child I had seen a photograph of him in full uniform. Finally, she and Don walked back to the car. I knelt there for a few minutes telling him intimate, private things: "I miss you, Daddy, I've missed you most of my life. We got cheated."

The dry earth soaked up my tears. I looked just as a pinecone fell at my feet. I picked it up as a memento. As I turned to walk away I said, "Next time, I will see you in heaven."

This would be my last visit. I now had closure. "This is the promise that he hath promised us, even eternal life" (1 John 2:25). Today the pinecone is in my curio cabinet. It rests on a snow-white column, lifting it to a place of worth. When I see it, I am reminded of him.

We cannot change our yesterdays. It's important that we live in such a way that we touch the lives of those dear to our hearts with love and faith and trust. Circumstances and unplanned events can alter our life plans quite unexpectedly. No matter what we may accumulate in tangible goods, they really mean very little after we are gone. The things that are of greatest value are those we deposit in the hearts of others and the memories we have made.

Father God, thank You for helping me put closure to this dark chapter in my life. Let anyone who tastes of regrets and grief sit at Your feet and know that You have a way of pouring in the warm oil of your Holy Spirit that soothes and heals.

October 17

Scripture: "Remember . . . consider the outcome of their way of life" (Hebrews 13:7, *NIV*).

It has been said, "Say not that a person lived a good or bad life until you examine how they die."

On May 1, 1992, I helplessly watched as my mother was lowered into the earth. The layers of lovely, fragrant flowers failed to brighten the moment or alleviate the pain. The flowers were pretty, but death is not pretty, even with flowers.

She was all that was left. Grandparents were all gone; Daddy was gone. I wanted her to be well and live. My children loved her. They never knew the bad times. She adored them and was so proud of Don. She kept clippings of anything where he was in print. (Better than we do!)

For more than 30 years I prayed that God would bring her to a time of repentance and salvation. Almost eight years before she died, she totally lost her health. It was then she evaluated her life and had a genuine encounter with Christ. I honestly believe He mercifully extended her life those eight years to allow her time to build some bridges and make restitution. And she did.

Ironically, over the years she developed a love for our church. She was never able to attend the Mount Paran Church of God, but she was influenced by members; the pastoral staff; and Pastor Paul Walker's radio, TV, and tape ministry. God used wonderful people to impact her life.

At her funeral the room was filled with flowers sent by Church of

God friends, a Church of God minister (her son-in-law) laid her to rest, and her Church of God granddaughter sang. In 1953 I would never have thought this was possible. Isn't that like God?

Over those last few months I went back and forth from Indiana to Atlanta many times to do what I could for her. The caregiving responsibilities fell heavily on Nancy and Mike, my half-sister and half-brother. When Nancy called and said, "Jackie, come," I rushed back thinking, *This is it.*

Again my mind was on rewind. I recalled damaged emotions, bad memories, violent behavior at home, and all the times I needed her and she was not there. I remembered when I was sent away just because I had accepted Christ. I remembered how she later forfeited her parenting of Mike and Nancy too. I recalled lots of unpleasant things as I flew to Atlanta. I was digging up buried wounds of yesterday. It was an emotionally draining flight.

The next three days we didn't leave her. She was in a life-and-death struggle. Over those many hours we sang to her, and we prayed for her. They kept telling us that even though she was not responding, she could likely hear us. Very late on her last evening, I felt like singing a little song most mothers teach their young children. We sang, "Jesus loves me! this I know, for the Bible tells me so."

Then I realized I had never heard my mother pray. I had prayed for her many times over the phone and with her personally, but I had never heard her pray. On one side of the bed stood a young man and a young woman by her second marriage. She had failed them also. In the soberness of that hour, the three of us stood there and I was moved to pray a simple little prayer:

> Now I lay me down to sleep;
> I pray thee, Lord, my soul to keep.
> If I should die before I wake,
> I pray thee, Lord, my soul to take.

When we finished, there was a very feeble, whispered *Amen.* She had heard! She was lying down to sleep. He would her soul keep! I praise Him, for He is faithful.

Mother had shared with me and with visiting ministers that she had accepted Christ as her Savior several years earlier. She would quickly add that it was because she had watched my life closely and had to believe that what happened to me at an early age was real.

I share this only as a reassurance to us all that if we are faithful, God will answer prayer. His Holy Spirit did a marvelous work in my mother's life. It is written in 2 Corinthians 1:4 that God comforts us in all our troubles so that we can comfort others with what we have received from Him.

Yes, it was real for me, and it will be for you too!

Here I am, God, asking that someone who reads this story will be reminded that whoever calls on You in repentance will be saved. You often work in ways we do not understand. Help us to trust You and remain obedient—to the end.

October 18

Scripture: "The Lord is faithful to all his promises" (Psalm 145:13, *NIV*).

My mother's time had come. We knew it. We went for the nurse. While just the three of us were with her, it was as though a distinct and unfamiliar *presence* entered the room. It was incredibly awesome! As my eyes searched the room, it seemed to take on a glow. At the same time I sensed this unusual awareness, Nancy turned to me and said, "Do you feel something?" We all did! I believe angels came and lifted her spirit out of that frame we knew as Mother. Her soul was ushered into God's heaven and into His presence. We felt it happen! We watched it happen. It was real!

I share a story of death again because what I remember of Mother had an enormous impact on my life. Some of what we remember is good; some is bad. But it is from all of our experiences we learn, and grow—if down the road we are able to sort through those memories and deal with them.

As I thought of sad things, I refused to drown in them. Years ago I had forgiven Mother. You can forgive too. You can live out the kind of Christian witness Christ asks of us. Forgiveness is scriptural. It was necessary for me to forgive in order to live a meaningful and victorious life.

If you have unresolved feelings and carry with you debilitating resentments and anger, you are only hurting yourself. They will pain you and drain you. It will be healthy for you to forgive those who have wounded you. Then you can begin storing some happy memories.

Life is very short! It's like a snowflake—it will disappear before your eyes if you hold it and don't know what to do with it. If you have never accepted Jesus Christ as your Savior, you are wasting your life. When you come to the end, all you will have is *you*. And nothing will really matter then except whether or not you have been born again. But if you put your life in God's hands, He will preserve it for an eternity with Him.

Mother made a mess of her life, but God came along and fixed the mess. She made a lot of mistakes for which she was sorry. But she also had many wonderful qualities. We were not ready for her to be taken from us, but we do not question God's wisdom.

There is peace in knowing that she is with God and that her life was not in vain. We have some happy and fun memories of the last years of her life.

God was faithful to us in *all* His promises, just as His Word declares. You can stand on it!

Thank You, Father, for Your faithfulness. You promised me 30 years earlier while I was in prayer for her that there would be a day she would choose You. It was another one of Your miracles! Help me to never forget Your promises and Your power. Perhaps someone reading this today needs You as much as she did. Please help them.

October 19

Scripture: "Bear with each other and forgive whatever grievances you may have against one another. Forgive as the Lord forgave you" (Colossians 3:13, *NIV*).

I rushed back to Indianapolis to speak at a Mother-Daughter Luncheon four days after we buried my mother. It was not without emotion. I spoke on "Memory-Making Mamas," and shared some of the thoughts written for today.

Mother had many good qualities. During my childhood she was a very proud and proper lady, attractive and brilliant. She was career-oriented and held responsible, enviable positions of employment. The eldest of five daughters, she was only 15 when her mother died. In many ways she had to become the mother figure to her younger sisters. Who knows, maybe later in life she just could not accept all that was expected of a mother to her own offspring. Nevertheless, she had many attributes I admired. She never met a stranger. She loved to do good deeds for her friends and neighbors. She was cheerful and had an uncanny way of putting negative things behind her and dwelling only on good things—real or unreal! She was a survivor!

As the song implies, memories may be beautiful; yet what's too painful to remember, we simply choose to forget.

The most beautiful memory I have ever been able to picture is that of a close and loving mother-daughter relationship. I love my daughters dearly. They bring me great joy. We have come from diapers to dolls, to daring young men, to grandchildren. Every family experiences some times of frustration, some fears, some disappointments, some sorrows. These are growing experiences for both mothers and daughters. They bring forth the fragrance of maturity. (You are making memories!)

Every daughter deserves a mother she can respect and emulate. The workshop of character is everyday life. Today, when almost anything goes, we desperately need mothers who still believe in modesty and manners and old-fashioned virtues and who aren't ashamed to say so! Today, more than ever, we need mothers of love who will spend time and teach their daughters the value of being feminine and gentle, yet morally strong and in control.

Don't dare give up on that son or daughter who may be "out of sorts" right now. Give each one your total support and love. (You are making memories!) How will your children remember you? What qualities about you will they remember most? The family photo album will always remind them of how you looked, but they will remember who you were—what you were like. Unfortunately, when we became mothers, our child did not come with a learner's manual. We all make mistakes.

There is a past which is gone forever, but there is a future which is still our own.

Memories we are making are ultimately our own responsibility. We shape our lives and the lives of our children. The process never ends. We shall not despair, for we remember that our Helper is omnipotent!

We cannot know what may happen to us in this strange adventure called life. But we can decide what happens *in* us—how we react, how we handle things—and that's what counts in the end. We have to take the raw stuff and make it into something of worth and beauty. That's the real test of living. Life is an adventure of faith if we are to be victors and not victims.

Mother may have failed me in many ways, but I choose to put those memories behind me. Rather, I rejoice in her merciful pardon and salvation. It was a long time coming, but God was faithful to His promise. "Death has been swallowed up in victory. Where, O death, is your victory? Where, O death, is your sting?" (1 Corinthians 15:54, 55, *NIV*).

My Father, let the influence of those who touch my life be held as a precious memory. Remind me often that I too am casting a shadow on someone not far from me. Help me to live a holy life, above reproach, and let the beauty of Jesus be seen in me. Make my life a blessing to someone today. Help me leave memories worth recalling.

October 20

Scripture: "But we also rejoice in our sufferings, because we know that suffering produces perseverance; perseverance, character; and character, hope" (Romans 5:3, 4, *NIV*).

Valued for its iridescence, the opal is October's gemstone. Its sparkling color comes from the unique structure of layered silica. Light passes through the layers and catches on tiny cracks as it bends, refracts, and creates flashes of color.

Year after year, event after event, we too are *layered* with a myriad of experiences. When God's light shines on us, we have iridescent color unique to our own life-walk. Some things happen in our lives we don't deserve, and at the time, we think we shall never survive. He takes the unfortunate layers of events and blends them with good things to ultimately make us a gemstone of brilliance.

Childhood was not very secure for me. It was difficult at the age of 14 to leave home or give up my faith and baptism in the Holy Spirit. My mother and stepfather could not accept my decision to be a Christian and attend the Church of God. It was a bad time for them in their own marriage and I became a whipping post. But God made something good of what appeared to be so bad. I had to learn to forgive and forget the pain.

Where is God when we hurt so deeply? I'll tell you. He is standing "somewhere in the shadows." Look for Him—you will find Him. He will mend the brokenhearted. He is faithful to do the impossible!

Do not continue to dwell on tearful, tough memories. Make a decision to turn around. Stop looking back and begin to look forward. You cannot put toothpaste back in the tube. Yesterday is like spilled water on the sand; it cannot be recovered. However, you can surely make a difference in today and tomorrow. Purpose to have a triumphal trust. You must have a tough faith and a tough commitment.

We pass people on our journey who have unfortunate cracks and unplanned bends in their lives that appear to mar them. A designing hand chisels carefully to give new shape and purpose. Tears and fears are polished away, revealing layers meant as new paths and allowing for glorious light. Miraculously, someone as colorful as an opal can emerge.

Is there one like me in your church? There are valuable gems all around us—only needing someone to notice. Have you extended a hand in love and concern? Can you embrace a young person with acceptance? You may not realize the impact your love will have on that young life until later down life's journey when you find that *you* helped place a *layer* that would be part of something precious.

Thank You, Father, for assuring us that any persecution can become a blessing because it forms layers as a backdrop for the radiance of the Christian life.

October 21

Scripture: "Whatever things you ask when you pray, believe . . ." (Mark 11:24, *NKJV*).

On a busy February afternoon in 1996, I rushed to my annual routine mammogram appointment at the hospital. Upon arriving home, I received a report of very unusual and suspicious tissue in *both* breasts and word that I should return the next morning for more tests. I spent an anxious night.

The alarm awoke me—*Welcome to a terrible Tuesday!* New mammograms were taken, then another set. I excused myself to the rest room. I don't even know if I was alone. I fell apart! Crying and praying openly, I asked God to please not let this be. I quoted some of His promises. I felt the Enemy was angry because of what I had written for publication. (I had already completed my month's assignment of devotions—I had to blame someone!)

My mind raced back to my little bedroom in Atlanta 43 years earlier, back to a hospital in Indianapolis, back to a healing in Michigan, and back to a hospital in South Carolina. He was the Great Physician then—and many other times; I knew I could also give this situation to God, my Father! I can't explain it, but suddenly I had peace. How strange it is that anytime I needed reaffirmation of God's healing power, I am driven back to those earlier experiences! It was through them that God planted me on an absolute. I do believe things happen for a reason.

When I returned, I had lost my turn. While I was waiting, another physician came by and entered a little cubicle. I overheard my name, so I walked in. They were comparing the X-rays from 1995 with the current ones. Circled in white were the areas of concern. Not too pleased I was there, they made brief observations and requested that I have a third set made, magnifying the specified areas. Unbelievably, once more they needed to magnify. This was now the *fourth* set of mammograms!

Soon, the older physician stepped in the hall. I shall never forget the scene. With raised hands, speaking to the radiologist, he said, "I don't give a (expletive). They're not there now. We just can't explain it!" I was told, "Mrs. Walker, you can leave now. Strangely, there's nothing there anymore." I briefly witnessed to the technician who had done the testing.

For a few moments that morning a very unlikely place for worship had become a "house of prayer." God's power and presence know no boundaries. He manifests His love and peace wherever we lift our hearts to Him.

God is still God of all! He turned a terrible Tuesday into a day of triumph!

Thank You, Father, for Your healing touch. Please continue to keep me in Your care. Keep me from evil. You have healed me one more time, and I just can't praise You enough. No matter what might have happened that Tuesday, I know You would have kept me in the hollow of Your hand. I praise Your holy name!

October 22

Scripture: "For it is God who works in you to will and to act according to his good purpose" (Philippians 2:13, *NIV*).

> Blessed are those whose dreams
> are shaped by their hopes,
> not by their hurts.

Look into your future—it's unfolding now. You are responsible for shaping your future. Don't bury dreams! You are never too old or too cold that you can't look up and look out to suddenly sense new energy to break free from a mundane comfort zone. Don't be a prisoner to your unfulfilled goals. Make them happen!

Most people who made significant marks on the 20th century started out as uneducated, poor, simple, unconnected people who had only a dream.

Don't say your dreams died because your family rejected you, you could not receive the education you wanted, you never met the right people, you had too little money, your marriage failed, or your children failed you. Nothing, and no one, can kill dreams unless you allow that to happen. God can help you have hope instead of hopelessness, and He can give you anticipation instead of regret. If then you fail to realize your dreams, perhaps it is that your dreams were of your own selfish desires and were not submitted to God's plan for your life.

As a young girl I daydreamed of traveling the world and of meeting important people. The Lord has blessed me to experience extensive international travel and see most every famous site I ever dreamed of. And I have met numerous well-known and significant personalities. So in many respects, lots of daydreams have been fulfilled. We live a comfortable life, and I have a wonderful husband and family—another dream fulfilled. Did all that just happen? No. Some of it we worked at *making* happen.

A few years ago I decided to enter network marketing to generate extra money to purchase a retirement home. This was totally new for me. I learned as I went. But it turned out to be profitable, fun, and fulfilling. I found myself a savvy businesswoman swimming in this new stream. I had unusual opportunities to share Christ with wonderful, new people I would otherwise have never met. I traveled all over the country and several times overseas—at somebody else's expense. Can't beat that! After a short involvement (and the house paid for), I found it was going to be difficult to juggle that business and my ever-expanding church commitments, so I bowed out in order to keep my priorities in line. I only make these references to assure you that no matter how old we are we can take on new challenges and make positive things happen. We can do more than just dream.

Give yourself a push! Break loose from the concrete of procrastination. It sets up harder every time you say, "I will put that off till later."

Uncover your buried dreams. Ask God to help you. Deep within many lives there is a forgotten scrap of a dream and a lonely melody trying hard to return it. Let it happen.

Dream. Nothing is impossible with God!

Dear Lord, surely I am not just an accident. I still believe that I am Yours and that You have plans for me. I don't want to achieve only for vainglory. I only want to be all that You want me to be. I want to effectively touch lives and glorify You in all I do. Open doors for me and help me to have courage to step through them. As I sit at Your feet this moment—whisper Your plan to me. I am still, and I am listening.

October 23

Scripture: "Remember how fleeting is my life" (Psalm 89:47, *NIV*).

Don't pretend to be what you do not intend to be!

Never before has Christianity been examined and shared on the media as today. How sad when Christians fall on their journey. The whole world looks on. The world is looking at us with mixed emotions and many preconceived opinions. We must be accountable to God, to the church, to our families, and to ourselves. Whatever we sow, we shall reap.

What has been before us and
What lies behind us
Are small matters
To what lies within us!

I purchased several hundred bulbs for our grounds. With great care I placed each bulb where it should be planted, arranging them so that the daffodils, the tulips, and the iris, our state flower, would create a nice pattern. As I walked away to another section of the lawn, looking back, I could not remember which bulb was where. I had not labeled them.

With the help of a professional, we managed to get all of them in the ground. I could hardly wait until spring to see this colorful display.

It's amazing. Inside a little bulb sleeps color and life that will burst through warm, moist soil, pushing up a stem to support a flower that in turn will support other life.

It doesn't matter that I anxiously awaited spring for the bulbs to give birth to beautiful flowers. They slept and did not fret about what was ahead. Nor did it matter that they were just dry, oddly shaped things in a box, then separated from the others and laid in a strange place to be buried in a totally different environment. Anyway, what was behind them was only temporary. They were destined to experience a transformation that would soon make them wondrous things of beauty. If these bulbs had knowledge, they would have known that within them lay hidden beauty, hidden fragrance, hidden admiration, and hidden worth. They were planted deep enough to withstand winter's blasts of cold and blankets of snow. God would name the day and time they would push through the earth and bed of mulch to sing the song of spring in full harmony, blending with those near them. Time after time they would lift their heads and draw the attention of others.

I randomly selected bulbs, but I could not tell exactly what time they would bloom. (It was only faith and my imagination that allows me to see a golden daffodil within those brown bulbs). The Master Gardener handpicked you "out from among others" and placed you in a specific place. For a season He nurtured you and prepared you for a new life—almost like an incubation period. His plan was for you to develop into a mature Christian. He prepared a time and place for you to show forth His glory in a lifestyle of loving service designed to exalt Him.

When God selected you, He knew just who you were and what uniqueness He could develop in you. He sowed you, expecting something! He wants you to bloom where you are planted.

There is no mystery to Him. Unlike my carelessness, He knows your label. He knows exactly where you fit into His master plan. The world is watching you. If you are a regal iris, don't pretend to be a daffodil. If you are a tulip, don't pretend to be an iris!

How shocking it would have been if none of the bulbs I planted had come up in the spring. What a disappointment! If only green stems and graceful leaves had come up with no colorful blossoms and rich fragrance—I think I would have cried.

I know some people like that. They never make a decision to be something meaningful, and remain ugly, dried-up, oddly shaped stumps of life. Others go through the motions but just look like a flower. They have a stem, they have a leaf, but there is never a blossom. How that must grieve the heart of God.

Early-spring flowers have short lives. Our lives too are so short and they are not meant to be unto ourselves. We must earnestly seek to please the Master Gardener. We are blessed of Him so that we may bless others.

Yes, God, You are the Master Gardener, and I pray that You will make my life one of beauty. As my world looks on, let me reflect Your glory. Help me blend with those around me in full harmony so that the unbelieving world can know we have been touched by Your hand. May they see the uniqueness You designed and glorify our Father in heaven.

October 24

Scripture: "As His divine power has given to us all things that pertain to life and godliness, through the knowledge of Him who called us by glory and virtue" (2 Peter 1:3, *NKJV*).

When my husband was pastoring in South Carolina, a military chaplain came to our door announcing the death of one of the young boys from our church. He had been killed in Vietnam. His chaplain wanted Don to accompany him to the family's home, but Don was out of town at a State Ministers Meeting. I went with the chaplain and his wife as he delivered the horrible news to the parents. It was a hot summer night. Through the screen door, we could see the mother standing at the dining table wrapping a "package from home" to mail to her son. What a heartrending sight! I shall never forget. I marveled at the ministry of this chaplain, whose full duty was to simply carry death notices. He embraced this family with respect, honor, compassion, and love. (He deserved a click of the heels and a proud salute!)

The days spent awaiting the arrival of the young boy's body seemed eternal. Finally, her son came home. He had paid the ultimate price for his country. A military escort hand-delivered his bloody, muddy boots. He was so young and looked so handsome in his crisp uniform, preserved under glass like a numbered, limited-edition collector's sculpture. The family's faith would surely be on display. Immediately they sought comfort in the Holy Spirit. They knew the Word; they knew God's voice; they were endued with a power unexplainable to the unbelievers. Their loss was great. Their coworkers, neighbors, community leaders, and others were amazed at the great faith of these parents. Their stamina and the spectacular demonstration of their faith underscored the power of promises from the Scriptures: "I am the resurrection and the life. He who believes in Me, though he may die, he shall live" (John 11:25, *NKJV*); "I can do all things through Christ who strengthens me" (Philippians 4:13, *NKJV*); "He will wipe every tear from their eyes. There will be no more death or mourning or crying or pain" (Revelation 21:4, *NIV*).

Recently I was told a story about a Sunday school teacher who asked her students to bring an object to share on Easter Sunday morning that would depict the Easter story.

- One boy brought a rock. The teacher said, "But, Ronnie, this rock has no life." He turned it over to reveal moss growing underneath—*new life!*
- One girl brought a fluffy Easter bunny. She knew only of the commercialization of Easter.
- One girl brought an Easter lily, representing the fragrance of spring.

Little Jeremy sat timidly at the back of the room, clutching his little brown paper bag and waiting his turn. Unfortunately, he was not as articulate as the others; he had some mental and physical challenges, and he was also very ill. But he was a bundle of love! After the other boys and girls were finished, he called out to the teacher, "I brought something!" He walked to the front of the class and reached into his little bag and brought out a plastic egg that could be opened. The other children began to snicker. The teacher opened the egg; there was nothing. The children broke into full laughter!

"But, Teacher, it is empty—just like the tomb! Jesus had a *new life!*"

Only a few weeks passed and little Jeremy was hospitalized and died.

On his casket were no flowers, but lovingly placed on a mound of greenery were dozens of plastic Easter eggs. *He is not here—He is risen!* (Luke 24:6).

Our days on earth are numbered. But when we lay our heads down on eternity's pillow, He will cover us with *new life!*

My Father, in heaven, how I praise You for adopting me into Your everlasting family. Thank You for Jesus. When You send for me . . . I shall not fear, for You will be with me. I don't want to do anything that would cancel my reservation for that flight home. Help me, Father, to live a life of faithfulness.

October 25

Scripture: "Call upon me . . . I will deliver you, and you will honor me" (Psalm 50:15, *NIV*). "Cast your cares on the Lord and he will sustain you" (Psalm 55:22, *NIV*).

God has no problems—only plans!

Someone recently said we ought not to think of *problems* but rather of *purpose.* Life is filled with things we cannot do anything *about* but which we are supposed to do something *with.* How do we iron out the wrinkles of life?

Let me suggest God loves to hear us shout when we're desperate, "H-E-L-P!" Just dial 911-HEAVEN. There were times I called on Him simply saying, "I think I'm going to cry, Lord! And I have no shoulder to cry on but Yours." It's as though He once spoke to me saying, "Those who never taste of bitter never know what sweet is." He also reminded me that Jesus knew about rejection, misunderstanding, and betrayal!

Edward Everett Hale said, "We should not attempt to bear more than one kind of trouble at a time. Some people seem to like to bear three kinds: All they have *had*, all they *have* now, and all they *expect* to have."

Winston Churchill once said, "Kites rise highest against the wind, not with it." So if there is a stormy wind blowing in your life today, catch the wind and soar above it! James 5:11 says, "Blessed [are] those who have persevered" (*NIV*).

In you are terrified by your circumstances, don't surrender. Don't get stuck in pain. Be faithful . . . endure. Only those that endure shall be saved! Seize the opportunity to shape and solve problems.

When I made my decision to follow Christ, I could not forecast the future. Neither can any of you. Quite candidly I have shared some of my experiences simply to assure you that God does not abandon us. He is always there. There were times when fears, uncertainties, and insecurities made my knees knock. That's a good time to kneel on them! He showed me sin is an opportunity for forgiveness; sickness, an opportunity for healing; sorrow, an opportunity for compassion.

We must take one day at a time. Today is tomorrow's yesterday, so how do you want to remember it? It's sort of like memory-in-the-making—a deposit in the bank of time.

I certainly have not been perfect. But I assure you, God has been faithful to me. In fact, my favorite gospel song is "Great Is Thy Faithfulness," especially when sung by Debbie Wesson Sheeks. I told her once she must sing that at my funeral. She, too, has experienced His great faithfulness. Believe this: "The Lord is faithful, and he will strengthen and protect you" (2 Thessalonians 3:3, *NIV*).

God is not looking at your circumstances as overwhelming. If you are lonely, if you are ill, if you are financially overloaded, if you are disappointed beyond measure, if you are wounded—scream to the Father for help.

HELP, God! I don't even have to tell You of my circumstances because You know them even better than I. You have told me to rejoice and be glad for what is happening. I am having a struggle doing that. Reassure me that You have not forgotten me, that You are still in charge of my life. Thank You for the many times You have smoothed out the rough places. Help me be patient as You direct my path today. I love You, Lord, and no matter what comes my way, I am determined to live for You.

October 26

Scripture: "Run in such a way as to get the prize" (1 Corinthians 9:24, *NIV*).

Win-or-lose, cheerleaders have to wear a smile. Their purpose is to generate enthusiasm and encouragement and to display strong support for the team.

I loved the football season, but I hated having to cheer in the rain and the cold. Isn't that so like life? We like the warm and sunny days much better.

We function fine and can even handle minor losses when things are going well. When things are sunny, we can roll with the punches. But when things get dark and murky, then even a very little thing can disappoint us and cause us to give up and quit giving our best. It is a real challenge to sustain enthusiasm during the rough times—to put on a happy face and wear a smile!

Jesus is our cheerleader! He gives us three cheers:
1. "Be of good cheer: it is I; be not afraid" (Mark 6:50).
2. "Be of good cheer; I have overcome the world" (John 16:33).
3. "Be of good cheer; thy sins be forgiven thee" (Matthew 9:2).

Even when it appears we are losing, He does not abandon us but continues to cheer us on. Have we not also read there is a host of heavenly witnesses watching our performance and cheering us on (Hebrews 12:1)?

The instant replays of TV do not happen in real life. For many of life's situations, there is no second chance. We can't raise our children again. We get only one chance to make a good impression. Words we wish we had not spoken can never be retrieved. Scars can't be completely removed, and the tearstains left on the fabric of our emotions are usually permanent. What has happened cannot be changed; but it is possible that we can still influence certain aspects of what is still to be.

Most sporting events give trophies and awards to winners. Often the Most Valuable Player is singled out from the rest.

We are promised an award for a good performance also. If we train properly, stay alert, know the strengths and weaknesses of our opponent, play fairly, don't surrender to temporary setbacks, and have a driving desire to reach our goal—we are rewarded. We may get bumped around, but we can bounce back! We can be our own cheerleader. Don't listen to any voices that would discourage you on your journey. Just strive for the victory!

In life's game there are risks. But the love of God surrounds us. God offers His game plan, the Bible. In it He shows us where to walk, warns us of dangerous places, instructs us when we're off course, and comforts us when we don't make it. He also encourages us to maintain a cheerful heart. So what if you goof? So what if you are not the MVP? I'm told it takes more skill than one can tell to play the second fiddle well!

John Bowell said, "Blessed is she who has learned to laugh at herself, for she shall never cease to be entertained." Abraham Lincoln once said, "Most folks are about as happy as they make up their minds to be." So if you fumble the ball once in a while, just laugh about it. Don't get violent and behave as a child. Learn from your mistakes. Swallow your pride. (I've found it's not fattening!) Remember, no one can make you feel inferior without your consent.

I hear You, Lord; I hear You as You remind me to be of good cheer. You have overcome, so I can also! Reveal to me the game plan and I will do my best. Thank You for allowing me to be on this team. It won't be a loss. It won't be a tie. We will win!

October 27

Scripture: "A cheerful look brings joy to the heart" (Proverbs 15:30, *NIV*). "She is clothed with strength and dignity; she can laugh . . ." (Proverbs 31:25, *NIV*).

A smile can greatly increase your "face value!"

In the squeaky places of everyday life, laughter is a marvelous oil; just one drop can reduce friction and release tension. "A cheerful heart is good medicine, but a crushed spirit dries up the bones" (Proverbs 17:22, *NIV*).

If we are to have a radiant life, we must enjoy laughter. Are you an anxiety addict? Are you a wretched worrier? Scripture admonishes us to "fret not" (Psalm 37:1, 7, 8; Proverbs 24:19). That's really tough for women. We spend a lot of time fretting. When we move past worrying about our own lives, we begin to worry about our children, and then we start on the next generation, worrying about the grandchildren. Attitudes are outer expressions of inner thoughts. It's time we adjust our attitude. It's important for us to have a healthy inner spirit so that we can have "mouths . . . filled with laughter, [and] tongues with songs of joy" (Psalm 126:2, *NIV*).

"Good humor is a tonic for mind and body. It is not a sin. It's an escape hatch—like a safety valve. Humor is the best antidote for anxiety and depression. It is a business asset. It attracts and keeps friends. It lightens human burdens. It is the direct route to serenity and contentment" (Grenville Kleiser).

Joy is a missing ingredient in many Christian women's lives. Scripture tells us, "The joy of the Lord is your strength" (Nehemiah 8:10). Joy comes from inside. It doesn't depend on circumstances. When His joy invades our lives, it spills over into everything we do and onto everyone we touch. Where is your sense of humor? Have you begun to shrivel into a bitter, impatient critical Christian? A joyful heart is what you need! God wants us to have life and to have it more abundantly.

Shake loose those things that have bound your spirit and robbed you of laughter. Say no to negativism and yes to laughter. God must surely have a sense of humor. I think maybe God smiled when Erma Bombeck prayed, "Lord, if You can't make me thin, then make my friends look fat."

A smile is understood in every language. A warm smile sends a message of warmth and of approval. A smile happens in a flash, but the memory of it can last a lifetime.

Hearty laughter is contagious. It's also healthy!

No matter what is happening around us, we can refuse to be discouraged and trodden beneath the feet of our negative experiences. Living life to its fullest means making life a memorable experience. Surely we do not want to be remembered as sour, whiny, depressed, pitiful, and wimpy women. Let's be sure, however, that our joy is genuine. Be careful not to wear a mask of happiness and joy to impress others but upon entering your home you remove the mask and reveal a totally different personality. Your family deserves better, and so do you!

It's true I can't know what you are facing, but I know One who does. He stands at the portals of glory just waiting for you to allow Him to clean out the cobwebs in the corner of your mind. When He is finished with a little housekeeping in your inner soul, He will then put a nice curve on your face. That's what a smile is—a curve that straightens out a lot of things!

O God, where has my joy gone? When did I lose it? I don't want to be without laughter in my life. Show me today where I must give attention. Restore my joy; let me share laughter and happiness with those nearest me. I pledge today to begin smiling more—for the sheer joy of knowing You!

October 28

Scripture: "Let us not be weary in well doing" (Galatians 6:9).

The power of the performance of our lives should reveal obedience, conformity, and submission.

One woman said, "I feel like a plumbing fixture. No one notices me until something goes wrong!"

That might appear to be the case. But it is not true. According to the Bible, our lives are like books: they are read constantly, often by those we least expect are interested.

Someone said life is a song. If that is true, we need to learn to sing on pitch!

The story is told of a great choir scheduled to present a musical in a distant city. The weather forecast warned of a great storm; travel was discouraged. The choir members wanted to cancel the engagement, because they suspected attendance would be low. However, the conductor admonished them to do their best to keep their commitment so those who did come would not be cheated out of the performance.

After their grand performance to only a small audience, the conductor brought to them a note and read with much excitement: "Thank you for a wonderful performance. You blessed me." It was signed "Your King."

How about us? Even in an arena that seems small and insignificant compared to others we know, are we performing at our best? The King is watching!

There is a grand lady first conceived as a gesture of international friendship and now has become a global symbol of freedom. She wears a flowing robe and a spiked crown. At her feet are depicted broken chains of tyranny. Her performance is only to stand tall, at her full height of 306 feet, on a tiny island in New York Harbor. She was first dedicated by President Grover Cleveland on October 28, 1886. She bears a message memorized by schoolchildren and millions of immigrants:

> "Give me your tired, your poor,
> Your huddled masses yearning to breathe free,
> The wretched refuse of your teeming shore.
> Send these, the homeless, tempest-tost to me,
> I lift my lamp beside the golden door!"

She holds a torch aloft in her right hand and carries in her left one a book inscribed July 4, 1776. Our Statue of Liberty! What a highly visible and grand performance for 110 years. I was there a few weeks ago to see her once again.

Christian women bear a lamp leading those in darkness to the marvelous Light. We hold in our right hand a book describing liberty purchased over 2,000 years ago by a man whose life was a performance never to be forgotten. He left the flowing robes of Glory to take on the seamless robe of common man. He removed His crown when He came to walk among humanity. He laid down His life to purchase our freedom. But He broke the chains of death to rise again!

He is the lamp. He beckons the tired, the poor, the huddled masses, the homeless, and the tempest-tossed. For more than 2,000 years He has stood highly visible to set men and women, boys and girls free from the bondage of sin.

We must never drop the torch nor fail in our mission to carry the message of His love and His sacrifice for the atonement for sin—to set men and women, boys and girls, free from the bondage of sin.

Our performance is important. He is counting on us!

Dear Lord, I feel very insignificant when I look around at many others who are far more talented than I. My torch may be only a candle, but nothing is lost of its light when we light another candle. Help me, even if it's a little thing, to do something for those who need my help, something for which I receive nothing more than the privilege of doing it . . . performing for You.

October 29

Scripture: "I thank my God upon every remembrance of you" (Philippians 1:3).

It has been my spectacular opportunity to watch grand performances by some very special women. The power of the performance of their lives left inspirational imprints on me and hundreds of other women who have been privileged to know them personally. At the risk of omitting others whom I admire, I am naming a few that surface to my heart today.

- *Mary Graves*—one-of-a-kind who was "light-years" ahead of her time. She was articulate, well-educated, driven with ambitious goals, and successful in challenging ventures for lady ministers. She inspired thousands. She was a true motivator, and a knowledgeable woman of the Word. She looked down the tunnel of time to see the day when Christian women would be used in significant ways in ministry.
- *Evelyn Knight*—a kind and graceful lady with the gracious gift of hospitality. A devoted mother, whose family rises up to call her blessed. Drawing from years of varied roles in ministry, her coaching of others in similar ministries has been of great value.
- *Edna Conn*—a stalwart example of faithfulness and trust in God no matter the circumstances. A wise woman, standing tall yet walking humbly. A mother who gave birth to 12 children of her own and a mentor for hundreds who have had the blessing of knowing her.

- *Marge McClain*—a speaker, teacher, server, soulwinner, survivor of attacks by the Enemy, and a busy woman. She was mentored by my dear Lula Watson, my special prayer warrior. Marge has many of Lula's outstanding qualities.
- *Annette Watson*—an overcomer, anointed minister, and a mix of humor and holiness. She is an uncommonly powerful Christian woman. She is a loyal confidante, and her joy is truly contagious.
- *Willie Mae Willis*—one who from her childhood led a colorful life caught up in service to God. I personally treasure the many deposits of love and support she invested in my own life and that of my family.
- *Gladys Lemons*—one whose roots in our denomination go very deep. Our very first appointment in ministry was with her and her husband, David. They both modeled the same unwavering pledge to the church and willingness to make whatever sacrifice necessary to ensure its well-being—the same traits I have observed in my husband's family. Her poise and graceful femininity have always been admired. She is a lovely Christian woman.
- *Carmelita Walker*—just like a real sister, she is more than just a friend. Once in a while God designs a rare thing of beauty that cannot be duplicated. Such is Carma. She is well-educated, well-traveled, articulate, contemporary, stable, and influential worldwide. I dearly love and admire her. She has never known anything but life in a parsonage. She carries the torch of ministry with dignity and graciously wields valuable influence on thousands of lives. A loving wife, a model mother, a student of the Word, a woman of prayer, and the family *ear* for all kinds of problems—she is a unique blend of outstanding qualities.

These are but a few of the women who have influenced and continue to influence me as a minister's wife. I have given a brief view of how I perceive them. The performance of their lives made permanent marks on me.

A tombstone with a significant message could read, *She went about doing good.* We would certainly hope no one would suggest one of these as an appropriate summary of our lives: *Here lies a perfect procrastinator* or *Here lies a pitiful performer* or *Here lies the beautiful shell of an ugly person* or *Here lies an angel who carried a pitchfork.* We shall be remembered by the power of our personal performance. How are you doing?

Thank You, Lord, for those who have had great positive influence on my life. I am sure You placed them on my path. Teach me by their example. Help me to also leave loving memories of godly and admirable qualities. That will not happen unless You are involved in my life.

October 30

Scripture: "When he [Abraham] was called to go out into a place . . . he went out, not knowing whither he went" (Hebrews 11:8).

Even when you don't know where you're going—remember, God knows! Recently my husband and I visited the Holy Land and then traveled to Greece and followed some of the steps of the apostle Paul. Today I was reading something that spoke to me and made me consider that Jesus really had no "big connections." VIPs did not seek Him out. He never visited exciting, glamorous sites that were important in His day. From our hotel in Athens we could see the Parthenon on the Acropolis. Jesus never saw that. When we were in Rome, it never occurred to me that Jesus was never there. When we walked the ancient streets of spectacular Ephesus, I did not consider that Jesus never visited there. He lived and died without having traveled extensively. He came to this world on a mission. He lived among people who were oppressed, lonely, sick, depressed, fearful, and troubled. Some were cynical and embittered people.

It just proves great people don't always do the things we associate with greatness. Some of the most effective people for the cause of Christ have been simple, humble folks who were faithful to His calling. Jesus proved God exists, that life continues after death, that heaven is a real place. He did that by dying and rising again. What a trip!

I have not always known where I was walking. Jesus knew full well what His journey was all about and where He was headed. He also knows the same about our lives. What a comfort that is!

When you don't know where you're going—walk with God! Charles Stanley recently gave this illustration: You know, we can be walking with God and yet not be *with* God. For example, have you ever gone shopping with a 3-year-old? They can be walking with you, but their interests are any place but with you. If you don't watch closely, as quick as lightning they can be out of your sight. That's how some people walk with God—afar off. They say they are walking with Him, but they are easily distracted.

Jesus speaks to us today and beckons us to walk with Him. To have a persistent faith and a powerful performance in our Christian life, we must take bold and courageous steps of faith, undergirded by the power of His promises.

Do you like *cans* or *cannots*? You *can* be born again. Character *can* be changed. You *can* become a different person. Your life *can* be a thing of beauty. There *can* be solutions to your problems. There *can* be light behind your shadows.

Life is a boundless privilege. Jesus is the author and finisher of our faith!

Yes, Lord, we want to walk with You. We may not always know our path, but we follow You. We know You know where You are leading.

October 31

Scripture: "[I] will be a Father unto you, and ye shall be my . . . daughters, saith the Lord Almighty" (2 Corinthians 6:18).

As I began to pray about what I should draw from my own memory bank for this month's devotions, I felt compelled to share much of my own life-walk. I have struggled with some of the personal glimpses into my past as I have remembered and, for the first time, put into print many life experiences.

What I have submitted for print is from a spirit of reflection; I trust it has been a source of inspiration or encouragement to someone who needed it. God has been faithful to me; I am nothing without Him. He has brought me every step of the way. Much of the time He *carried* me. I believe God uses even the bad things that happen in our lives to make us stronger people. If something from my yesterdays has caused you personally to reflect on your past and gain insight you did not have prior to reading these pages, if something I have shared from my own experiences has given you inspiration, then I will feel rewarded for my contribution to this book. I believe the things that happen in our lives have a purpose.

Tomorrow we begin November's emphasis on "Giving Thanks." Today, I pause to give thanks for my past. Not all of it would I have chosen; nevertheless, even the tiny pieces have all been touched by the great Artist, and my mosaic—though not quite finished—is already full of color. Some of the pieces have been experiences God gathered from various places in the United States as well as from several foreign countries.

There are yet some blank spots. I just wonder what He has in store for me these remaining years. I step into tomorrow with courage and great anticipation. I know that I shall always experience the power of His promises and He will continue to allow the power of people to influence me. There's no turning back! My prayer is that He will never let the power of persistence dim in my life and that the power of my performance will ultimately win His favor with a "Well done, My good and faithful daughter."

When the final piece is placed into the mosaic called *Jackie's Life*, it will not be displayed in a museum nor listed in a directory of fine art.

But it will be valuable because my Father designed it. He was near me when every piece was chiseled out of my life experiences. He employed the hands of my guardian angels to carefully ensure its development. It will be protected for all time. He made a covenant with me long ago that He will never leave me nor forsake me (Hebrews 13:5). He said that if I would observe all things He commanded me, He would be with me always, "even unto the end of the world" (Matthew 28:20). He made those promises that my joy might be full (1 John 1:4). He said, "[I] will be a Father unto you" (2 Corinthians 6:18). He told me to "be joyful in hope, patient in affliction, faithful in prayer" (Romans 12:12, *NIV*). I believed the scripture "He is the Rock, his works are perfect, and all his ways are just. A faithful God who does no wrong, upright and just is he" (Deuteronomy 32:4, *NIV*).

I stood on His promises. I made a commitment to God and meant it! Some of the colors of this mosaic I did not like and did not understand their placement, but He knew all along what was best. I will have to wait until the final piece is put in place to see the final work. Of course, that will be at the end of this earthly life and the beginning of my life with my Father in heaven.

My trust in God allows me to embrace the yesterdays, live in harmony with today, and enthusiastically look toward the adventure of my tomorrows. "Thanks be to God! He gives us the victory through our Lord Jesus Christ" (1 Corinthians 15:57, *NIV*).

"Let the words of my mouth, and the meditation of my heart, be acceptable in thy sight, O Lord, my strength, and my redeemer" (Psalm 19:14).

NOTES

NOTES

November

Giving Thanks
Kathy Sanders

Kathy Sanders was born in Dodge City, Kansas, but she was raised on a ranch in Texas. As a small child she accepted God's call to a teaching ministry. This call was put into practice as she and her husband, the Reverend Ray H. Sanders, planted over 50 churches through metro evangelism. It was during the planting of one of these churches that Kids Klubs first began. Subsequently, she wrote the *Kids Klub Manual*. At another church Kathy started a girls club, which was the forerunner of the national Girls Clubs program.

Kathy is the author of *So You're a Girls Club Counselor* and *How to Make Your YLA Click*. She served as Girls Club coordinator for three years, state Ladies Ministries president for 16 years, and member of the International Ladies Ministries Board of Directors for seven years, chairwoman four years. Recently Kathy created a Bible study program she calls *Apple Seed*.

Kathy and Ray have three daughters. Delta is married to the Reverend Mark Schrade. They have one son, Gabriel. Their daughter Ginger is married to the Reverend Jeremy Robinson. Tonya, the youngest daughter, is currently involved in commercial pilot training. All the Sanders are graduates of Lee College.

November 1

Scripture: "While the earth remaineth, seedtime and harvest, and cold and heat, and summer and winter, and day and night shall not cease" (Genesis 8:22).

November! You are my favorite month of the year. There are so many things about you that cause my heart to rejoice. Your *sights*, your *sounds*, your *smells*, your *invitation* to pause, to think and give thanks.

November 1—today is the day we complete our fall decorating. With great pride my husband, Ray, takes the clusters of Indian corn from his personal garden and hangs them over the light post, garage lights, and doorways. He binds the corn shucks together, adding a bail of hay, his homegrown pumpkins and squash, and, of course, a bushel basket of colorful leaves to his display at the end of our driveway.

In October, I bring out the fall pictures with the red barns, golden grain, and corn shucks. The ceramic pheasant pitcher is placed on the mantel in the center of the crisp red and yellow leaves, surrounded by ceramic miniature golden pumpkins, yellow squash, and white corn. Straw scarecrows dressed in patchwork garments enhance the den's bookcases, along with smiling jack-o'-lanterns.

But today, November, is your day. I will fill the horn of plenty and place it on the kitchen table. I will turn the jack-o'-lanterns around to become a crop of golden pumpkins. And my favorite, I will place pilgrims, which have become the symbol of giving thanks, throughout the house as a reminder of what the month of November is all about—a time to give thanks to our Creator for His bountiful harvest of blessings. Oh, what *sights* you bring!

And *sounds*! Listen to the rustling of the fallen leaves. Some days the leaves gently float from tree to ground, while other days your November winds gustily pick them up and toss them to and fro. There's the sound of the honking of a flock of wild geese flying by in perfect formation on their journey south. The sound of crackling logs of the first fire in the fireplace invites me to come and sit at His feet.

Then there is your *smell*. I have replaced the raspberry-and-strawberry-scented candles of spring and summer with the baked-apple and pumpkin-cinnamon ones. This aroma will remain in my house until my taste buds are overtaken with the smell of turkey, sage dressing, and pumpkin pie steaming from the oven.

And then there is your *invitation* to pause. The harvest is in. We have plucked the corn, shelled the peas, canned the green beans, and frozen all the okra. Tomato salsa has been made, and all the garden and yard tools cleaned and put away until spring. The hustle and bustle of the Christmas holidays knock, but I bolt the door and refuse to let them in.

I want to savor November's quiet moments—moments of reflection and meditation that only this month can give.

Creator of all seasons, I especially thank You for fall, a time when You and I are drawn together into a world all our own.

November 2

Scripture: "Whatsoever things are true . . . honest . . . just . . . pure . . . lovely . . . of good report; if there be any virtue, and if there be any praise, think on theses things" (Philippians 4:8).

November is the month that draws our focus away from ourselves to center on giving thanks to God. And how can I abound in giving thanks? By T-H-I-N-K-I-N-G. In the old Anglo-Saxon language the word *thankfulness* means "thinkfulness." The more you think, the more thankful you will be.

Thirty days hath November. This gives me thirty days to think so I can thank. Each day this month let me think of a different aspect of giving thanks.

The word *thanks*, in one form or another, is found more than 140 times in the Bible. In reading the Psalms one readily recognizes that David passionately expressed thanks and used the term more times than any other Bible character.

However, in reading the New Testament, one will certainly note that Paul easily qualifies for second place. In each of his letters, he touched on thankfulness, usually within the first chapter—in 10 of them, within the initial verses. In studying his letters, one finds that he admonished the Christian not merely to give thanks sometimes but at all times and for all things. This was not something he taught mechanically but from his own personal experiences. The spirit of praise and thanksgiving were as natural to him as breathing.

Thankfulness is an integral part of the Christian faith, although oftentimes it is hard to give thanks when we are hungry, when we are hurting, or when we are bereaved. However, it has been my observation that Christians who live with an attitude of thankfulness when things are going well, do not lose their appreciation for the goodness of God during times of adversity.

My sister-in-law was just such a person. Ravaged with pain because of cancer, she was an inspiration to all who visited her. Those who went to see her with the purpose of encouraging her left her bedside with their own faith built up. She was always thinking on the good things in life.

I realize for some it is hard to have a joyful attitude as they face the holidays alone. Others who have been victimized by flood, sickness, financial reverses, fire, or drought might sincerely ask, "How can I be thankful for all that has come to me this past year?"

I would say, "Think of the Christ who knows all things and really cares for you. Bring your mind into agreement by thinking of the positive and thanking Him for the good things He has bestowed upon you."

When I pause to think of You and all the positive things involved in Your character, I must stop and give an offering of thanks.

November 3

Scripture: "How precious also are thy thoughts unto me, O God! how great is the sum of them" (Psalm 139:17).

Where do I start when it comes to thinking of thanking God? Do I begin with the spectacular or the ordinary? Sitting at His feet, I was pondering the many facets of my life. Where did it all begin?

One of my favorite scriptures states that before the foundations of this earth were ever formed, He thought of me.

If I literally believe that, then . . .

- before there was ever the canopy of a blue sky,
  He thought of me.
- before there was ever the brilliance of a red sun,
  He thought of me.
- before there was ever the romance of a harvest moon,
  He thought of me.
- before there was ever a towering green sycamore tree,
  He thought of me.
- before there was ever a white snow-capped mountain,
  He thought of me.
- before there was ever a drop of dew on a blade of grass,
  He thought of me.
- before there was ever the shrill of the whippoorwill,
  He thought of me.
- before there was ever the flapping tail of a mammoth whale,
  He thought of me.
- before there was ever the sweet fragrance of a red rose,
  He thought of me.
- before there was ever the sand dunes of a parched desert,
  He thought of me.
- before there was ever the hurricane winds of a raging sea,
  He thought of me.

- before there was ever the sound of a sweet baby's coo,
  He thought of me.
- and before there was ever the blackness of sin,
  He thought of me.

And if He thought of me, what did He think?

He thought of a little freckled-face girl whose heart was tender toward Him, and He said, "I love you!"

She said, "Me loves you, too."

Not only did He think of me, but He thought of you—before there was ever a sky, a sun, or moon. And He said, "I love you!" Take time today to think of Him, and thank Him. And be sure to say, "I love You!"

Everlasting Father, thank You for thinking of me. And because You thought of me, I am thinking of You, and I thank You!

November 4

Scripture: "In every thing give thanks: for this is the will of God in Christ Jesus concerning you" (1 Thessalonians 5:18).

You've got to be kidding! Thankful *in everything* that happens to me? Some things, yes. But *in all* things?

You can't be talking about the Friday I was running late for work and had both a mailout deadline for the *Apple Seed* (a daily prayer exercise and devotional I mail out each month) and a speaking engagement that night, which required a two-hour drive.

Standing at the kitchen sink that morning before work, I felt water at my feet. "Ray! Help!" I frantically called. My husband soon discovered a loose pipe from the garbage disposal. We had to take everything from under the sink, mop up all the water and debris, pitch the sopping wet throw rug in the washer, and mop the floor. I still had my deadline and my speaking engagement, and I was to be thankful?

Of course I was late for work, but I could still make it. I would just get in there and get it done. Wrong! My husband had an unexpected visit with a couple who needed counseling. He wanted me to attend the session. "Lord, do you understand what's going on here? I don't have time for this."

You have heard of Murphy's Law? When it comes to computers, it's Kathy's Law. Having skipped lunch, stomach growling, nerves getting a little tense, I glanced at the clock while I was making my last-minute changes on the *Apple Seed* and somehow hit the wrong key on the computer. (If you know about retrieving a totally lost file, you know more than I do.) But—with help—I was able to find the lost file, and it was ready for printing. For that, I was thankful.

Need I go on? The printer jammed as the clock ticked on. The labels got stuck in the printout machine, and the paper folder was on the blink.

Uh-huh, was I being thankful *in* this? To be honest, this scripture was as far from my mind as China is from Lexington.

When I discovered I had printed the front page of the *Apple Seed* on the wrong side to run through the postage meter, my "tear dam" broke. I would have to rerun all the labels and put the *Apple Seed* in oversized envelopes, which of course would cost more postage. Thankful *in* everything?

In thinking on this scripture, it is hard for me to imagine Paul smiling during all the perils he went through, recorded in 2 Corinthians 11. As he was hit in the head with a stone outside of Lystra, I can't see him saying, "Thank you for that stone. Would you please throw another one?" As the whip slammed across his back, do you think he said, "I'm so thankful I am having this experience." There were other times. When he and Peter exchanged angry words about their ministry to the Gentiles and when he was tossed to and fro in a ship, Paul's lips could not utter thanks.

No, his mind was on what was happening to him at that moment. It was when he was writing his letters and reflecting back upon his experiences that he wrote of thankfulness.

It was when I got in my car, driving to my appointment, that I took a deep breath and said, "Thank You, Lord, for the opportunity I have in sending out the *Apple Seed*. Thank You for fellow secretaries who saw my dilemma and put aside their own work to help me meet my deadline. And thank You, Lord, that not every day is like today. There are some days when everything goes right. Let me stop and be thankful *in* those days.

Lord, I pause now and think back to all the days that were good days, and I thank You!

November 5

Scripture: "We give thee thanks, O Lord God Almighty" (Revelation 11:17).

When I first met Rose she was just learning to walk and talk. She was all girl, dressed up with some type of decorative ribbon in her silky blond hair, usually matching her lacy socks. Her natural ruby lips and fair complexion gave her the look of a porcelain china doll. Rolling her big blue eyes was a sure temptation to steal a kiss from her baby-soft neck. For everyone but me, that is. For some reason, Rose didn't like me. She didn't want me to hold her hand or whisper in her ear. She didn't want me to touch her ruffly dress. Having three girls of my own, I had always been partial to little girls and was always able to make friends with them very easily. But not Rose!

Her mother and I became very good friends. She came often to my office, bringing Rose with her. I always gave her a piece of candy from the candy basket on my desk, but that couldn't bribe her to give me a kiss.

On one particular visit, I gave Rose a piece of candy. Her mother nudged her, "What do you say?" Rose just looked at me. Her eyes stared straight into mine. Nothing came from her lips.

"Now, Rose, what do you say?"

"M-m-m," she grunted, glancing the opposite direction.

"Come on, Rose. You know what to say," her mother persisted.

Still nothing.

Getting a little embarrassed, her mother firmly stated, "If you don't say it, I'm going to make you give back the candy."

Reluctantly, Rose ducked her head, forcing out a "Fank oou," but there was no real gratitude. The one and only reason Rose said thank you was to keep her candy.

How often does God give us a blessing, desiring that we respond with love and gratitude to Him, only to see us take the blessing and hurry on our way. Or like Rose, we really do like the gifts He bestows upon us; but remembering what He has given us before, we become accustomed to them and just expect them.

Failure to express gratitude is a weakness we all share. It is much easier to say "Give me" than to say "Thank You." May I never take for granted the little things that come from the heart of God.

Heavenly Father, thank You for a beautiful little girl who now has become a very special, loving friend and for each generous hug she freely gives me.

November 6

Scripture: "Then was our mouth filled with laughter, and our tongue with singing . . . [for] the Lord hath done great things for them" (Psalm 126:2).

"It's for you," Ray said, shrugging his shoulders, as he handed me the phone.

I glanced at the digital clock. The red light illuminated the numbers 6:07. Who would be calling me this time of the morning? "Good morning," I said.

"Hello, Kathy. This is Edna. I don't know if you remember me. I was introduced to you as we sat at the same table at the conference in Gatlinburg."

"Oh, yes. I remember you. How could I forget your pleasant voice," I replied. She was a very tall, striking businesswoman who carried herself with poise and grace. I remembered that in the three short days of the conference, we had established a bond between us by being together, chatting, and laughing about the least little thing.

"I know it is early," she continued, "but I was wondering if you could do something for me?" I could tell there was an earnestness in her voice.

"Sure. Anything," I replied.

"Would you laugh for me?" she asked.

I was silent . . . maybe I didn't understand exactly what she said.

She knew I didn't know how to respond to her request, especially at that time of the morning. So she repeated herself.

"Would you laugh for me, or maybe chuckle, or just smile out loud?"

"Laugh? You mean laugh, laugh?" I questioned.

"Yes. I mean just laugh," she said.

I have had my share of requests, but never this one. My voice cracked as I continued to ask how I was going to do this. As Edna tried to explain, she began to chuckle, thinking of her request. In a matter of seconds we both, simultaneously, burst into laughter.

After Edna and I calmed down enough to carry on a conversation, she shared with me the terrible trauma going on in her life. She had cried for the past few days and most of the night. In the middle of the night she thought, "I am not going to cry any more. But how can I stop?" Then she thought of the good times we had in Gatlinburg. The times we laughed together and prayed together.

"So, I just decided to call you, but I knew I had better wait until morning. I've been waiting, but I got so excited just thinking about it and couldn't wait any longer. And here we are," she said.

We had a wonderful visit and ended it with a special prayer time. Oh, her problems were still there. I certainly didn't have the power to remove them, but I was very thankful I could share laughter with a dear friend.

Lord, I do thank You for the gift of laughter. Help me to be sensitive to someone today who may just need a chuckle.

November 7

Scripture: "Now unto him that is able to do exceeding abundantly above all that we ask or think, according to the power that worketh in us" (Ephesians 3:20).

My favorite story Mom and Dad used to tell was about God's provision for His children. After my Dad was healed of a major heart attack, it took some time for him to get back strength enough to get a job. My mother sold greeting cards to put food on the table. One day she said to my dad, "I have nothing in the house but flour, and all I have is 25 cents. I know the old pickup doesn't have much gas, but if you will go to the store and buy some milk, I will make milk gravy and biscuits for the kids and us to eat."

Dad, a babe in Christ, didn't know how to pray a fancy prayer; but after pulling up in front of the store, he simply bowed his head and said, "Lord, I need a miracle for my family today. I need You to supply our needs. Amen."

When Dad came home with a little sack of cookies, Mom threw a fit. "*Why* would you take our last bit of money and buy cookies?" (Dad would then pretend to pull up the tail of an apron over his face, portraying Mom coming to tears.)

I can still see Dad's eyes dancing as he continued the rest of the story. "I realized I had better tell your mom what happened before I was thrown out of the house," he chuckled, giving my two brothers and me a wink.

"As I got out of the old pickup and started into the store, I heard someone call, 'Pete! Pete Huckelbridge.' I stopped and turned around to see who was calling me. I immediately recognized the posture of the man headed my way. It was that of Charlie Boyd. Why, he was the richest rancher in them parts of the country. They said he had more oil wells on his property than Fort Knox had gold bars." I was too young to know about Fort Knox, but I knew by the tone of Dad's voice it was a whole lot more than I could count.

"Go on, Dad; tell us the rest," we begged.

"Well, I don't rightly know how such a rich man knew my name, except the good Lord told him. You do know He knows your name and where you live?" Then, with a pause, he looked at Mom and finished . . . "And how much flour you have in the barrel."

Mom would shake her head and roll her eyes. "Go on, Pete!"

"Charlie put his hand on my shoulder. 'Pete,' he said, 'I heard you have been sick for some time, but you're doing much better now. I have a proposition for you. Tomorrow my family and I are going on a month's vacation, and I need someone to drive out to the ranch to do some chores for me. I understand that you're a pretty good ranch hand.'"

We always laughed at this point as Dad tried to put on airs and say, "Yes Sir, the best!"

Mr. Boyd began his proposition with, "I have a milk cow that needs to be milked, and you can have all the milk."

"Thank You, Jesus!" Dad was about to get happy.

"And eggs? I need you to gather the eggs out of the hen house as well as the barn. Take 'em all home with you."

"Oh, sweet Jesus!" Dad was on his feet.

Mr. Boyd continued, "And do you have a freezer? It's going to be butchering time when we get back, and my wife would like to have our freezer emptied. There's chicken, ham, bacon, pork chops, roast, and even ice cream. Take it all."

By this time, Dad was doing a little "holy jig," Mom was wiping her eyes with her apron tail, and my brothers and I were crying too. "But there's still one more part."

"Can I tell it, Dad?" one of us kids would plead.

One of us would stand up, pretending to be rich Charlie, and say, "By the way, Pete, I have a new pickup you can drive, and here's the key to the ranch gas tank. See you at the ranch in an hour."

Oh, yes, God can supply all our needs and do exceeding abundantly above all that we ask, providing some cookies along the way.

Sweet Jesus, thank You that as a child I was taught what faith really was. Not by words but by the actions of parents who simply knew what it was to trust in You.

November 8

Scripture: "I will praise You with my whole heart" (Psalm 138:1, *NKJV*).

"Let's all raise our hands and give thanks to God for His many blessings," I heard the worship leader instruct. As automatically as breathing, I raised my hand, and my mouth started saying words of thanks; however, my mind was on a ladies retreat I was having the following week. After several minutes, the leader abruptly interrupted the praise and my thoughts, "All those who were saying words, but whose mind was somewhere else, I want you to go to the back of the sanctuary. All those whose mind, soul, and spirit were actually communing with God, I want you to come to the front of the sanctuary."

Immediately some worshipers started out of the pews toward the front, and then there were those of us who hesitated. I glanced around to see if I were the only one trapped. I knew if I went to the front, the Lord could strike me dead for lying, but if I went to the back, everyone would know I was not really praising God.

Thankfully, the leader stopped his order before very many made their move. Explaining the object of his point, he asked, "How many were really offering a sacrifice of praise and thanksgiving from your heart? How many were just giving lip service?"

The object lesson itself lasted less than 30 seconds, but the reality of its meaning will last my lifetime.

Under the law of the Old Testament, God instructed Moses to institute many kinds of offerings. There were burnt offerings, meat offerings, peace offerings, sin offerings, and many others in the Hebrew ritual. There were three sorts of peace offerings: thank offerings, votive offerings, and voluntary offerings.

The thank offering stimulated an element of joy in its presentation for sacrifice. Although it was spontaneous and not compulsory, certain statutes regulated it. Violation of these guidelines resulted in the sacrifice not being accepted (Leviticus 7:18). In fact, the offering became an abomination unto the Lord.

Are the requirements for bringing our thankoffering to God any less reverent than they were then? We must be careful as we come before God with our praises and thanksgiving, careful that we do not offend God with our flippant words and memorized phrases and thereby cause our giving of thanks to become a stench in the nostrils of God.

May the fruit of my lips be acceptable to You as I bring my sacrifice of thanks, O Lord God.

November 9

Scripture: "If thou, Lord, shouldest mark iniquities, O Lord, who shall stand? But there is forgiveness with thee" (Psalm 130:3, 4).

My husband and I were traveling on Interstate 75 out of Knoxville. Clipping along at 65, well maybe 70, miles per hour, I was the driver behind the wheel of our van when I saw the two orange signs on either side of the road: CONSTRUCTION AHEAD. The next sign stated, CONSTRUCTION NEXT 17 MILES. Having traveled this road before, I knew it would take us into the mountains.

Observing the speed of all the trucks, cars, vans, trailers and buses, one would not have known there had been blinking lights signaling, REDUCE SPEED TO 45, until you saw the next sign, BOTH SHOULDERS CLOSED 500 FEET. Immediately large cement road barriers began to narrow the road until they were sitting right on the white lines at the edge of each lane.

I pulled into the right lane behind a piggyback semi truck, while cars failing to reduce their speed continued to pass us. I clenched the steering wheel as each one passed. I like neither the penned-in feeling nor the black marks going up the sides of the barriers, a haunting reminder that someone had lost control.

"Go around him," Ray suggested.

"I can't. There's not enough room," I replied.

"Sure you can," he said. "There is the exact amount of room as there was before the barriers."

"Well, it doesn't seem like it."

"Go ahead!" Ray persisted.

I gripped the stirring wheel as I turned my blinker on and pulled out into the passing lane. *There can't be over an inch on either side*, I thought as I started around the big truck. By now we had reached the top of a hill and were on our way down. We all know what 18-wheelers do when they start down a hill. They put the pedal to the metal. *Oh, great!* I thought.

I glanced in my rearview mirror. "Oh, no! Where did he come from?" Out of nowhere came another semi truck, bellowing down the hill right behind me, blinking his lights. My knuckles were white, my jaws were locked, my neck muscles were strained, and my eyes were fixed. I realized there was no room for the slightest mistake. At that moment, a mistake of six inches could have brought us death.

Well, it is obvious that I made it around the first truck and got out of the way of the second one, but not without some very tense moments. What a relief it was to get back on the highway with extra room on the shoulders.

I am so thankful that the Lord allows us some breathing room on this narrow road of life. I have made many mistakes on my spiritual journey, and no doubt I will make many more. But although some brought very tense moments, thanks be to God, none of them brought spiritual death.

Sweet Jesus, giver of life, thank You for giving us room for mistakes and forgiving us of our shortcomings.

November 10

Scripture: "What shall I render unto the Lord for all his benefits toward me?" (Psalm 116:12).

Throughout David's writings one can sense his gratitude toward his Creator by the words, phrases, and sentences he uses in giving Him thanks. Whether he was sitting at His feet by the cool water, running for his life from an enraged king, or just ruling the kingdom, David knew from whence came his help. In this Psalm he numerates some of these benefits.

For physical benefits he wrote, "Blessed be the Lord, who daily loadeth us with benefits" (Psalm 68:19).

Although we in America seem to live in a land of materialism, we can count our daily benefits by taking inventory of the material goods which He has entrusted us with. For our homes, our jobs, our transportation, our food, and our clothes—for all of these things we are grateful.

In times of walking through the valley, he wrote, "I was brought low, and he helped me" (Psalm 116:6). Life does not always consist of walking on the mountaintop. There are times when the everyday stresses of life engulf us and pull us low. It is in those times we are thankful we have His assurance that He will help us.

In a far more earnest realm of gratitude, David wrote, "Thou hast delivered my soul from death" (v. 8). Perhaps David was thinking of more than the many times God had delivered him from the threats of King Saul. There were other times when in the midst of heartaches, hurts, or despair he felt his soul would surely break. But the gentle Shepherd delivered him. That same Shepherd is still delivering His sheep today.

"Thou hast delivered . . . mine eyes from tears" (v. 8). How many times in the midst of our sorrow has the Comforter come to us, wrapped His arms around us, and gently pulled us close to Him! David said, "Not only is He a deliverer of my tears, He is a keeper of my tears. God knows, He understands, He cares."

"Thou hast delivered . . . my feet from falling" (v. 8), he continued. At one point in David's life, he got his eyes off God and on man. He saw the prosperity of the wicked and the suffering of God's people. He saw the corruption of the wicked who seemed to be blessed regardless. He even questioned if living for God was worth it (see Psalm 73). Then he went into the house of God; and there, in the presence of God, he understood that their feet were in slippery places and their end was destruction. It was there God became the lifter of his head. When we get our eyes on people, surely our feet will slip, but how thankful we are that He holds us up by His outstretched hand.

For freedom he wrote, "Thou hast loosed my bonds" (v. 16). When we acknowledge our gratitude for the freedom God has given us from the power of sin and for the way He has loosed us from the bonds of guilt and condemnation it carries, our heart rejoices.

For his relationship with the God of Israel he wrote, "I am thy servant" (v. 16). As God's servants, we have the privilege of enjoying His divine fellowship, companionship, protective care, daily provisions, and grace to help in time of need. What a privilege to be called "servants of God."

Lord, I do thank You for all Your benefits toward me.

November 11

Scripture: "He hath made every thing beautiful in his time" (Ecclesiastes 3:11).

As I went outside to go to work, I could feel the crispness of the gusty wind. It was as if the first winter frost was rattling the front gate, wanting to get in. "But the trees are still so brilliantly bright, and my flowers are still blooming. I'm not ready for you, Winter. Please go away and let Autumn stay," I wanted to shout.

My office window was a perfect frame for the beautiful trees with their leaves of many colors. I tried naming all the colors. There were brick red, crimson red, and fire engine red, along with the yellow hues of goldenrod, canary, and mustard. There were many tones of browns and different rich oranges and a variety of shades of mauve. What beauty to behold, but I knew time was getting short. Fall would soon be gone. It would not be long until all I would see would be barren limbs and twigs.

As I sat at my desk, I could see one tree that stood out from the rest. It wasn't as big as some of the others, but its flamboyant red leaves drew me to the window for a closer view of its beauty. *Oh, how God must be pleased with the beauty of this tree!* I thought. *Let me take a moment to savor the beauty of this day.*

I noticed the wind had picked up. I saw leaves whirling and tumbling and nodding and drifting to the puffs of the whistling wind— an unpredictable wind. By noon the relentless wind had snapped over half the leaves from their life support.

How sad I felt as I glanced out the window to see the trees being stripped of their beauty. By late that afternoon most of the leaves had been torn loose and had rustled to the earth, where they would wait until they were either raked into a pile to become a fiery inferno or sucked into a machine chopping them into mulch. How barren it had become in just one day.

Wait—it was barren, all except for one leaf that was still hanging on for dear life. One red, heart-shaped leaf from what had been a brilliant red tree. The autumn wind had failed to shake it free.

This little leaf became a focal point for me. Throughout the winter months I would periodically look for the leaf. Each time it was there. On frigid mornings when every blade of grass was covered with translucent glasslike frost, the little leaf would glisten in the sunlight as if it were a crystal ornament on a Christmas tree. When the falling snows came, the little red leaf became part of a beautiful winter wonderland.

And then it happened. When or how, I don't know. But one day I glanced out the window and the little leaf was surrounded by the most beautiful tender buds. In fact, the whole tree, once dressed in her flaming red gown, was now clothed in a pinafore of mint green.

I refocused my eyes on the little leaf which seemed to be looking right at me. "I've got to be going now," it seemed to say. "But first, thanks! Most people would have thought I was nothing but an old shriveled up leaf. But you took the time to see the beauty in me during these long winter months, giving me dignity while new life was being formed. I must go now and start mixing my paints of red. See you next fall!"

Creator of all beauty, thank you for the variety of color You have given to this world to make it such a beautiful place to live in.

November 12

Scripture: "I thank my God upon every remembrance of you" (Philippians 1:3).

I think I'll take these down and put them in a garage sale, I said to myself, as I started dusting my four racks of silver-plated collectors spoons. *No one sees 'em here in the washroom. They are just junk collecting dust,* I continued.

I had read that spoon collecting first became popular as a hobby in the 1890s. During that time the first patent was issued for a Niagara Falls commemorative spoon. This began a long line of spoon collecting, each spoon depicting a favorite travel destination.

I wonder if everyone else's collectable spoons collect as much dust as my collectibles collect. I had joined back into my conversation with myself. *Now really, what good are they doing out here?* I reached up to start removing the spoons, taking down the first one, which was from Alaska. *Wanda took me to downtown Anchorage, and this and a cup of coffee were all we bought. We had such a wonderful talk.* After dusting it, I put it back, reaching for another one. *This one is from Montana when we were with the Spiveys and the bear came up on their porch. How scared the girls were.* I put it back. *Here is the one from our first trip to Disneyland; we went with Phyllis and Danny.* I put it back. *And this one is from Hawaii where Jimmi had such a wonderful retreat. I can't get rid of it.* I placed it back with the others.

I started laughing as I took down the one from Mexico City. *How could I get rid of this one? That's where Shelby, Dot, and I got lost. We couldn't speak any Spanish and couldn't find anyone who spoke English to give us directions. We got so tickled and needed a restroom so bad. Of course we didn't know how to ask for one.* I put it back on the rack.

One by one I took the spoons down, holding each for the duration of my thought about that particular time, place, and moment. *Were there any I could get rid of? Korea with the Hans? Of course not! Philippines with Estelita and Ramy? Never! New York with Vera and J.D? Nope! How about the one from Virginia when we were with our dear friends Aubrey and Marian? No!*

Again I started laughing out loud as I dusted the spoon from the Bahamas. *Jackie and I were 'International Winners,' you know! We marched right out onto the beach to have our devotions; she in her midcalf skirt and I in my culottes, with Bible underarm. Did we ever get the stares!*

Did I say these were junk and I was going to put them in a garage sale? I don't believe so! What price could I ever put on the memory that each spoon represents? Or who could pay me enough money to replace the special times spent with special friends? Not possible! They are not junk. They are time capsules holding the wealth of friendship.

Lord, I do thank You for every remembrance of the friends you have given to me.

November 13

Scripture: "Thou shalt make them drink of the river of thy pleasures. For with thee is the fountain of life" (Psalm 36:8, 9).

Minnesota, the land of 10,000 lakes. If there isn't a lake there now, just wait, for during the winter certain parks are designated to have the fire hydrants turned on to make small ponds for ice skating or little-league hockey.

There is one lake, Lake Itasca, that is really not known except to the people who live around it. Yet that which it supplies is known around the world.

While living in Minnesota, we went to visit Lake Itasca. As we walked around the lake, Delta ran to a trickling stream which was coming from the lake. "Look, I can put one foot on one side and the other foot on the other side," she shouted. "That's nothing. Look at me," hollered Ginger. "I can jump across it." And she did. Tonya just sat down in the middle of the water and began splashing. It certainly wasn't hard for the 7- 5- and 3-year-old girls to stretch themselves across this little stream.

Yet the little stream of water that is only a few inches wide and a few inches deep soon begins winding its way southward, coming together with another little stream and another and then another and another. The melting snows and gentle spring rains also feed the streams until in just a few miles it is no longer a stream but a flowing river. Just a few more miles after that its borders expand and its bottom digs deeper as it picks up speed, rushing toward the Gulf of Mexico. By the time it reaches its destination 2,487 miles away, it is over 3,000 feet wide, more than 100 feet deep, and is known as the Mighty Mississippi.

From its small beginning—where the girls enjoyed jumping, wading, and splashing—to the power-driven forces of its moving mighty barges, the river expands to such enormity that we can hardly imagine that the small stream at its headwaters could be a part of the same body of water. People, animals, plant life, agriculture, electric companies, industries, and thousands of other entities participate in what the powerful river has to offer.

David says those who put their trust in God will drink of the river of God's pleasures. God's pleasures are certainly not the amusement, thrills, and happiness of the world's standard. They are, rather, His delights . . . His promises . . . His gifts.

We begin our trust as little streams, not knowing the impact and power that trust will bring. The farther He leads us along, the more we trust and the deeper we walk in faith. God adds more experiences in our lives that bring more of His pleasures. He delights in blessing us with all spiritual blessings in heavenly places in Christ. He has predestinated us to be His adopted children, accepted in the Beloved. With this He gives us strength, boldness, and His power.

Lord, whenever I see a river, may I remember to thank You for the pleasures You give to all who will trust in You.

November 14

Scripture: "Ye should shew forth the praises of him who hath called you out of darkness into his marvellous light" (1 Peter 2:9).

While living in Kentucky we had the privilege of knowing a man who owned a coal mine. One day he took his pastor and wife and Ray and me seven miles back into his mine.

As we were putting on all the miner's garb—the jumpsuit, hard hat with a spotlight on the front, (our only light in the mine), and other paraphernalia, I looked at the dark hole with rail tracks leading under the humongous mountain. The rail cars were about 36 inches wide and 4 feet long, and the bed of the car was about 6 inches off the ground. And I was about to get on one and go into that dark hole?

Mike, the owner, got on one car, Ed and Angie on one, and Ray and I were on another. Angie and I had to sit on the bottom of the car between our husband's legs. Mike told us that once we were in the mine there would be times we would all have to lie on our backs because some passageways were only 27 inches high.

What interesting stories Mike told as we went from one chamber to another. He shared the history of the early miners, the risks they took and how before the rail cars men and beasts carried the coal out. Many mules taken back into the far mines never again saw light. In fact mules were bred in the mines, and many were born and died without ever seeing a shaft of light.

Mike was right. Many times we lay on our backs as we passed through passageways, and even some chambers, with the ceiling only two or three inches from the tip of our noses. Just a slight blow and black coal would fall on our faces.

At one point Mike asked us to turn off our lights. What words in the dictionary could describe the darkness? You could feel it! Sense it! Hear it! And somehow, even see the blackness of the moment.

After spending several hours in the unfamiliar, dark, damp world uniquely its own, we headed out of the mine. What a beautiful sight it was as we took a turn into a chamber that had sun rays beaming on the passageway leading us out of the dark hole. What a marvelous feeling to be standing in the warmth of the bright sun once again.

Could Peter have known the black darkness of the mines when he wrote to the early Christians admonishing them to give praises and thanks to God for bringing them out of their spiritual darkness into the light of God's Son?

There are millions in this world who have never even heard the name of Jesus—who live in a darkness as black as a coal mine without even a ray of hope. Yet how many times have I heard His wonderful name? Hundreds? More! Thousands? More! Tens of thousands? Probably more! Blessed is the name that gives hope.

Jesus, Light of the World, thank You that in Your divine wisdom You called me from the darkness of sin to give me the light of Your salvation.

November 15

Scripture: "For he performeth the thing that is appointed for me: and many such things are with him" (Job 23:14).

I was cruising along at 65 miles per hour on my way to speak at the South Carolina state ladies retreat. Suddenly my car gave a jerk. The gas gage was half full, so I knew I wasn't out of gas. Jerking again, it completely died in the middle of the freeway. I was able to coast through three lanes of heavy traffic to get to the shoulder before it came to a complete stop. I had no idea what caused the problem. All I knew was I was excited, for I was going to receive a miracle.

I had just been challenged that morning at a World Evangelism Conference by the miracles God was performing among the missionaries. "You have to *need* a miracle, then ask for a miracle, *believe* for the miracle, and *acknowledge* the miracle to *receive* a miracle" was their testimony. This was going to be my miracle! That night I was going to be able to share my miracle with the ladies of South Carolina, of how my car died, I prayed for it, and God healed it.

After praying for the car, I tried to start it. Nothing. I sat there several minutes praying. Again nothing. Now, wait! I needed a miracle. I had asked for one. My faith was certainly strong. I had even told the Lord how I was going to give Him glory.

Finally, I got out of the car and raised the hood. A truck driver saw a damsel in distress and brought his 18-wheeler to a screeching halt. "Looks like you need some help." Now how was I going to tell him, "No, not really. I'm just waiting for God to heal my car. You see, I'm expecting a miracle"?

To spare you all the major and minor details, the truck driver, Robert, and I spent over four hours that afternoon on the side of the road, jumping and rejumping my car to get it to a garage. There I was told I had to buy an alternator.

"Lord, why didn't You give me a miracle that I could share. I really needed one. Now it is too late for me to speak tonight. This is so embarrassing. I was really expecting a miracle."

"How do you know that I didn't perform a miracle," the Lord impressed upon me. "What about Robert? Did he not tell you he was a backslider raised in a Pentecostal home? Did you not share with him how you felt I sent him along to help you? Do you think it strange that out of all the truckers on the road the one who stopped to help you had just had a flat tire in your hometown of Sweetwater, Texas, the day before, creating another cord of bonding?

"Even if you don't perceive that I performed a miracle for you, I performed one for Robert's parents. They too asked for a miracle. They asked Me to send a laborer in Robert's path to point him back to the Lord. And I appointed you to be that laborer. I don't perform coincidences; I do perform miracles."

Robert didn't pray the sinners prayer with me that day, but I do know the Holy Spirit used me by bringing to his remembrance those things he was taught as a child. And the Scripture says when he is old he will not depart from that training.

Lord, thank You for the appointed miracles You perform along life's way, miracles that I might often consider only coincidences.

November 16

Scripture: "Do not say, 'Why were the old days better than these?' For it is not wise to ask such questions" (Ecclesiastes 7:10, *NIV*).

"Dad, tell us again about Aunt Kathleen chasing rabbits on her horse. How you and Uncle Jack laughed, knowing she was going to get a spanking as you saw Grandad looking from the top of the hill, and how . . . ."

"I don't think we need to hear that story again," I quickly interrupted my niece. But as usual, both Kent and Jack could hardly wait to give their version of the incident.

It was that time of year when I had gone back home to see my family: my mother, stepdad, two brothers, sisters-in-law, and all my nieces and their husbands or boyfriends. I was the only one in my family who had moved away, so going back to West Texas for a visit was a big deal for us all.

One evening had to be at my brother's house for barbecue, snapshots, and storytelling—childhood stories of my two brothers and me. Every year the same stories were requested—me chasing the rabbits, Jack burning down the horse barn, and Kent being bit by the rattlesnakes. Of course every year the stories got bigger as the "Let me tell you about the time" mood continued for the whole evening. We laughed, and sometimes become somber, at stories we shared.

"You all had so much fun when you were little. I wish I had lived back in the good ole days," Marsha, my niece, remarked.

Good ole days, I thought. *That's what I used to say as a child when we went to visit my aunts and uncles. We would sit on the floor for hours listening to stories such as Aunt Anna's about cousin J.R. getting a burr caught in his throat, and Grandma taking him to get a hair cut before taking him to the doctor.*

It is tempting to think that everything was good in the past and that things are now mundane, going from bad to worse. The writer of Ecclesiastes reminds us that glorifying the good ole days is not wise. As others have noted, "The best thing about the good ole days may be that they are in the past."

We may relish fond memories, learn from experiences, and enjoy reminiscing with our family and peers. But living in the past robs us of living in the present. Yet it is this blending of the past in harmony with the present that has shaped us for the future.

Lord of all ages, thank You for memories of the past, experiences of the present, and hope for the future.

November 17

Scripture: "It is of the Lord's mercies that we are not consumed, because his compassions fail not. They are new every morning: great is thy faithfulness" (Lamentations 3:22, 23).

Twenty-six times in Psalm 136 are the beautiful words, "For his mercy endureth for ever." Eleven other times in the Bible are the same words regarding the nature of God: "For his mercy endureth for ever." "Endureth for ever" means nothing can stop His mercy. It comes from a Hebrew word meaning "to conquer." So His mercy conquers forever.

David wrote, "Surely goodness and mercy shall follow me all the days of my life: and I will dwell in the house of the Lord for ever" (Psalm 23:6). Did David know what the mercies of the Lord were? Not only did he cry for mercy for the known sins of his character, but in Psalm 19 he asked for mercy to be cleansed from even his secret faults (v. 12): those sins of which he was not aware, those unholy motives, those tainted purposes, the things he should not have done as well as the things he should but did not do. He was able to shout, "Thanks be to God! His mercy endureth for ever!"

Saul tasted God's mercy on the road to Damascus. God told Ananias concerning Saul, "He is a chosen vessel unto me" (Acts 9:15). Yes, His mercy does endure forever!"

The apostle Paul continued to cry for this mercy when he too was struggling with his carnal flesh. He found himself doing the things he didn't want to do and the things he wanted to do, he didn't do. "O wretched man that I am! who shall deliver me from the body of this death? I thank God through Jesus Christ our Lord" (Romans 7:24, 25). "His mercy endureth for ever."

It is not only in our fleshly sins that God's mercy endures forever but also in our hardships.

During my mother's illness and death, I knew God's mercies were new every morning. She did not know that she was a diabetic until the day my stepdad took her to the hospital because dark red lines were going up her leg. She had been home-doctoring a corn on the bottom of her foot, not realizing it had made an inner sore. Gangrene had set in. As we stood around her bed, the doctor said he would have to amputate her leg. We felt His mercy that endures forever.

I think one of the hardest things I've ever had to do was to put my mother in a nursing home. Mother and PaPa's home was the typical grandparents' home: pictures of children, grandchildren, and great-grandchildren were in every room. Throughout the house was scattered a variety of whatnots, gifts they had received over the years from each of us. Their hobby was working in the yard. It was an oasis of lush green grass and assorted beautiful flowers in the middle of this west Texas town.

How could I hold back the tears at the nursing home as I tried to arrange a few of her personal belongings on the one nightstand and one small shelf over her bed. She had to share a four-drawer chest with her roommate who had Alzheimer's. Her tiny closet could barely hold the few clothes she took. In all of this I found His mercy endures forever.

After several months in the nursing home, Mother discovered the seam of her hose had rubbed a little blister on her second toe. Because of her sugar level, the doctors could not get it to heal, and her second leg had to be amputated also. But His mercies were our strength every morning.

I often wondered what my reaction would be if and when I received a phone call that Mother had slipped into a coma and to please hurry home. But God's mercy is so good. I went to Texas for a week's visit. What a wonderful time Mother and I had! She never lost her positive attitude, and we talked about everything we had ever done or hoped to do. The night before the day I was to leave, Mother was talking and laughing when she sneezed three times, had a massive heart attack, and died. I am so thankful to God that the dreaded trip was one I did not have to make. I was already there, and the memory of precious times together was fresh in my heart. His mercy endureth for ever!

If you are not in right relationship with Christ, His mercy endureth forever!

If you are struggling within yourself, His mercy endureth forever!

Do you have heartaches? His mercy endureth forever!

Is your body filled with disease? His mercy endureth forever!

Lord, today I am so thankful that Your mercy endureth forever!

November 18

Scripture: "I thank my God through Jesus Christ for you all . . . that I might have some fruit among you" (Romans 1:8, 13).

"Kathy, our church wants to have an appreciation day for you and Pastor. Can we set up a date?" asked Lynda, the clerk of our church.

"You'll have to talk to my husband and let him check the church calendar," was my reply.

The date was set for the first Pastor's Appreciation Day of our newly organized church. Almost all of the members were new converts who did not have a church background, so this was all new to them. Lynda had received a letter from the state office suggesting each church set aside a day to show the pastor and his family their appreciation. Our little church wanted to do its part.

For several services I saw ladies going around whispering to one another, glancing my way. I knew they were planning a big day, but I didn't know what.

I remembered the pastor appreciation days my mother helped plan. A week of someone doing good deeds for the pastor's family. The meals that were brought in. The surprise gifts each family member received. The nights different ones kept the pastor's children so he and his wife could have quiet nights alone. *Wouldn't it be nice if someone would keep our three children, just for one night,* I daydreamed.

A week before the big day, Lynda called. "I know your family likes Mexican food, so we are going to have a Mexican dinner for you. Does that sound good?" "Great," I answered.

A few days before the big day, Lynda called: "Your house is bigger than mine, and you have a fenced-in yard for the kids, so could we have the dinner at your house?" "Sure, why not," I responded. I was thinking they must be going to do something for our house.

The day before the big day, Lynda called. "Kathy, we were talking, and we all agreed that you can cook Mexican food better than all of us. If I bring the food over, could you cook it?"

That's it, new pans! Lynda knows I need some new pots and pans, "Why sure, I'd love to," was my reaction.

The day of the big day, Lynda called. "Kathy, I don't have the car today. Can Pastor go to the grocery store to get the food? I'm really sorry."

Now wait. Something is definitely wrong with this picture, I thought.

Ray went to the store and bought the supplies. I spent all morning preparing the food for tacos, enchiladas, and cheese sauce. Ray and I served 40 people their pastor's appreciation dinner. Ray and I cleaned up all the dishes. And all the people had a wonderful time.

There were no pots and pans. There were no surprise good deeds. There were no special gifts. There was no baby sitting. No nights alone.

But what we did receive was an imaginary basketful of "We love you, Pastor."

"Thank you, Pastor, for starting this church."

"If you didn't care, Pastor, I would still be a sinner."

"Because of your concern our marriage is back together!"

"My children are all saved because of your ministry."

An imaginary basket filled with the fruit of our labor. Oh, the pots and pans would be worn out by now, and the good deeds forgotten. And now with our children all grown, Ray and I have all our nights alone. But the fruit that was in that imaginary basket that day still remains today and will remain throughout eternity.

Lord, thank You for the opportunity to serve such sincere people who at that time did all they knew to do to let their pastor and family know they loved us.

November 19

Scripture: "The Lord is my rock, and my fortress, and my deliverer; my God, my strength, in whom I will trust" (Psalm 18:2).

It was the first time Tonya, our youngest daughter, had been home after receiving her single-engine pilot's license. How very proud we were as she showed us her memorabilia of things she had accumulated—the torn T-shirt of passing the first-stage check, her log book; the write-up in the paper of "Flight Attendant Turns to Pilot," a cross-country map of her flights, and the earphones to talk to the tower.

"Well, let's go out and rent a plane, and you can take us for a ride," her dad said as he got up from his chair.

Ray and I had discussed this matter before Tonya came home. "I don't know if I'm ready to get in a plane with her," I had commented.

"You will have to go up with her. We have to show her we have confidence in her. Just be prepared," he said.

Easier said than done, I thought.

We all three went into the office to rent a single-engine plane. "The only one I have available right now is a two-passenger," the clerk stated. "Who's going to go up first with her? Her mom or her dad?"

"Her dad," I quickly interjected.

I stood outside the fence as I watched the two of them taxi down the runway. Then it was up, up, and away.

It's interesting how in moments like this your mind can have instant recall of thoughts and memories that seem to have been packed away in the attic with all the toys, coloring books, report cards, and other keepsakes. Where was my little girl with the long blond ringlets? The little girl who was always turning somersaults and doing gymnastic routines? The little girl who looked so beautiful in her green prom dress? The little girl who said, "Mom, please don't cry," as we drove off, leaving her for her first year at Lee College? Where was that little girl? She was up flying a plane!

My thoughts were interrupted 30 minutes later as I saw the little plane coming in for a landing. Perfect!

Now it was my turn. I slowly climbed into the plane. Ray shut the door and turned the handle to lock it. "Click." I was in. I buckled the seat belt, pulling on it a couple of times to make sure it fastened. Tonya handed me a set of head phones. I put them on, adjusting the size. I could feel my heart rate speeding up. Then Tonya looked at me. "Are you scared," she asked?

"Oh, ah, just a little bit," I managed to utter.

"Mom, trust me. Everything is OK. I have everything under control. Leave the flying to me," she said with confidence.

Asking for runway clearance, my baby and I took off into the blue horizon. My life was totally in her hands, and, at that moment, my fear was expelled. I had confidence she was in control.

How many times does the Lord allow us to be in situations in which we have to have confidence that He is in complete control. Are we sometimes nervous? Oh, yes! Do we sometimes wonder if He really knows what is going on? Sometimes, yes! But when we realize all that He is to us and that He loves us more than we love ourselves, we can trust Him to take care of us.

O, God, my strength in times when I would be afraid, let me completely put my trust in You. Thank You in advance for expelling all my fears.

November 20

Scripture: "And the prayer of faith shall save the sick, and the Lord shall raise him up" (James 5:15).

Not everyone hears God speak in an audible voice. Most of us must take by faith the promises God has given to us through His Word. However, my husband is one of the few who has heard God's voice.

When Ray was 9 years old, he had rheumatic fever. This left him extremely weak and bedridden, unable to even put his feet to the floor for over nine weeks. The doctors told his parents there was no hope for him. In fact, they suggested his parents go ahead and make some preliminary funeral arrangements and choose a burying place for him.

During the Sunday morning service, the pastor had such a burden for Ray he asked all those of the church who believed God would heal Ray to join him in prayer around the altar. The Spirit moved greatly upon those who responded. At the close of the prayer, it was suggested that all those who believed go immediately to the Sanders' house to pray for him.

The house filled with prayer warriors believing Ray was going to be raised from his bed of affliction. They prayed all during lunch. Nothing seemed to happen. They prayed for another hour. Ray still was too weak to even sit up. They continued to pray. Still no healing. By mid-afternoon, one by one the families began to leave, though Ray's body was still in intense pain.

After everyone was gone, Ray's dad went to the chicken yard to gather the eggs, while his mother went to the kitchen to cook supper. His four brothers and sister left his room, leaving Ray alone. As Ray lay completely exhausted from all the afternoon's activity, the Lord came into his room and spoke to him as clearly as if it had been his dad speaking to him. "Ray, get up and go to church tonight. I have healed you for a testimony."

Immediately Ray leaped out of the bed, calling for his mom and dad as he ran down the hall. His mother came running from the kitchen, and his dad, hearing Ray's voice, came running from the henhouse, eggs strewn everywhere. Being a family of faith, they knew God had just performed a miracle of healing. They embraced Ray and gave God the glory.

Needless to say, after Ray walked up 21 steps into the sanctuary of the Langly Church of God that night the service was filled with praise and thanksgiving. That was over 50 years ago, and Ray is still healed.

Thank You, Lord, for Your healing power that healed a little boy who grew up to be my husband.

November 21

Scripture: "Thou shalt have no other gods before me" (Exodus 20:3).

What a joy it was to have as our houseguest for six weeks Brother Joseph from India. While Ray was a World Missions representative, we often had people from around the world stay in our home for different lengths of time. Brother Joseph came to America prior to the Church of God General Assembly and was traveling with my husband and preaching in mission rallies.

Fascinated with my cooking and kitchen gadgets, Brother Joseph shared how they had only one electric outlet in their home, and it held one naked lightbulb hanging down from the ceiling in their main room. Consequently, there was no refrigeration, so his wife had to go to the market every day to buy food. She prepared and cooked it outside the house on some type of open-fire stove.

Brother Joseph became hooked on the Discovery Channel that came from our "corner box," the TV. He would sit with great intensity watching the films of underwater life or the behavioral patterns of the wild animals of Africa. He was spellbound by the habitation of snakes or birds or insects that drew him back to the corner box each day.

After several weeks of continuously watching these educational yet fascinating programs, one day he got up from the couch with a distraught look on his face. "Brother Joseph, are you OK?" I questioned.

"Oh, no, Sister Kathy," he said. "Everything is not OK. Many years ago I promised the Lord I would meet with Him every day at this time," pulling up his sleeve and pointing to his watch. "But since I have been in America, I have not kept my promise to the Almighty God. My promise has been to the corner box. The Lord, He is waiting for me," he said as he went to his room.

I stood there, feeling as if a saint had just walked through my kitchen.

Brother Joseph also became fascinated with and enjoyed other things about our home. Our van was one. He didn't own a car. In fact, he had never driven one. He did all his traveling by foot, on his bicycle, or by public transportation.

Since it was August, our air conditioner was also a hit. And a dish washer? His wife wouldn't believe it. Canned biscuits, instant grits, microwave oven, and the electric knife were always conversational topics.

When Brother Joseph was preparing to leave to go back to India, I asked him if after seeing all the conveniences of America, he would like to bring his family here. I will never forget his words, "No, No, No. In America, you have too many gods between you and the real God. I would never want my family to be so tempted."

Lord, I thank You for all the conveniences America has to offer, but never let me put anything between You and me that might hinder my sitting at Your feet.

November 22

Scripture: "By him therefore let us offer the sacrifice of praise to God continually, that is, the fruit of our lips giving thanks to his name" (Hebrews 13:15).

The ancient people sometimes argued that a thank offering was more acceptable to God than a sin offering. When a man offered a sin offering he was trying to get something for himself, while a thank offering was an unconditional offering of a grateful heart. The sacrifice of gratitude is one that anyone may and should bring.

Curtis Hutson said, "Thankfulness, or its opposite, is the thermometer by which our spiritual temperature is gauged, the oil of gladness that lubricates life's activities."

When I think of the sacrifice of a thank offering, I am reminded of the following story.

A farmer went to his pastor and said, "Our son was killed in the war, and we would like to give $200 to be used for a memorial."

Standing close by was another man along with his wife and his strong, healthy son who had served in the same war but had come back without a scratch. He said to his wife, "Honey, write out a check for $500."

She asked, "Why?"

He said, "To be used as a memorial for our son."

"But our son wasn't killed in the war. He's here this morning, strong and healthy," she affirmed.

"That's just the point. If they can give $200 to the church when their boy was killed, we can give $500 because our boy went through the war and God allowed him to return to us."

Gratitude is an attitude achieved in the school of faith. It declares that God is so good and so great that He begins every day with material blessings by letting us meet new faces, allowing us new opportunities for service, revealing new truths, and opening to us new doors for spiritual growth. Multitudes of blessings fall unnoticed into our lives each day. When we make a conscious effort to appreciate our blessings fully, we will offer the sacrifice of thanksgiving for all things.

Matthew Henry, the famous Bible expositor, was once accosted by thieves and robbed of his pocketbook. He wrote these lines in his diary: "Let me be thankful, first, because I was never robbed before; second, because, although they took my purse, they did not take my life; third, because, although they took my all, it was not much; and fourth, because it was I who was robbed, not I who robbed."

Gratitude is one of the greatest Christian graces; ingratitude is one of the most vicious sins. Gratitude should ascend like incense to the throne of God, filling the throne room with a misty cloud of thanksgiving.

Lord, may the thoughts of my heart be thoughts of gratitude that cause my lips to speak words of thanksgiving.

November 23

Scripture: ". . . while you are enriched in everything for all liberality, which causes thanksgiving through us to God" (2 Corinthians 9:11, *NKJV*).

My mother had this in her scrapbook of poems.

A Good Thanksgiving
Said old Gentleman Gay, "On a Thanksgiving Day,
If you want a good time, then give something away."
So he sent a fat turkey to Shoemaker Price,
And the shoemaker said, "What a big bird! How nice!
And, since such a good dinner's before me, I ought
To give poor Widow Lee the small chicken I bought."

"This fine chicken, oh, see!" said the pleased Widow Lee,
"And the kindness that sent it, how precious to me!
I would like to make someone as happy as I,
I'll give Washerwoman Liddy my big pumpkin pie."
"And, oh, sure!" Liddy said, "'tis the queen of all pies!
Just to look at its yellow face gladdens my eyes!
Now it's my turn, I think; and a sweet ginger cake
For the motherless Finigan children I'll bake."

"A sweet cake all our own is too good to be true!"
Said the Finigan children, Rose, Denny, and Hugh;
"It smells sweet of spice, and we'll carry a slice
To poor little lame Jake, who has nothing that's nice."
"Oh, I thank you and thank you!" said little lame Jake;

"Oh, what a bootiful, bootiful, bootiful cake!
And, oh, such a big slice! I will save all the crumbs
And will give 'em to each little sparrow that comes!"

And the sparrows, they twittered, as if they would say,
Like old Gentleman Gay, "On a Thanksgiving Day,
If you want a good time, then give something away!"

—Annie Douglas Green Robinson

Lord, I thank You for the many personal gifts that have been given to me by special friends. May they in return be blessed by You.

November 24

Scripture: "And these stones shall be for a memorial unto the children of Israel for ever" (Joshua 4:7).

Family traditions. I don't remember how or when or why some of the Sanders' traditions got started. I suppose when Ray and I were married we each brought our own ideas into each holiday festivity. Then with the addition of each of our three children, some traditions developed "just because." Sons-in-law and grandchildren also added new traditions to the old.

Of all the holidays, Thanksgiving is Ray's favorite. He says that most holidays honor a person or observe an event, but Thanksgiving Day is unique because its purpose is to express gratitude. And now that the girls are married and spend every other Thanksgiving with their in-laws, the years they all come home are very special.

I suppose of all our traditions, Thanksgiving is the most meaningful. Unlike most, we have never started cooking dinner until the morning of Thanksgiving. (That is except for the batch of million dollar fudge I cook the day before to have it hidden before Delta arrives. When she was little, I would cook and hide it after she had gone to bed. We all timed her to see how long it would take her nose to sniff it out.) A menu list is posted on the frig with each of our names beside the main dish we are to prepare. I always make the turkey and dressing, Delta the corn souffle, Ginger the sweet potato casserole and Tonya the lime jello salad. From there we all pitch in for the other incidentals. What fun we have with all four of us girls in the kitchen. However, since the first year our son-in-law, Jeremy, hand mashed the potatoes to a creamy, fluffy, white dish, no one would dare take away his contribution.

After dinner Ray will put on an apron and wash the dishes, and Tonya will dry them as the rest of us clear off the table and put the food away. Our son-in-law Mark will pull the vacuum out and vacuum the floors so we can play games the rest of the evening and into the night.

Without a doubt, our most important and treasured tradition of the year occurs after all have been seated and are ready for our Thanksgiving dinner. Following a custom of the Pilgrims, before dinner Ray will place five kernels of corn upon each empty plate to represent each individual's five most prominent personal blessings of the year. After he has read a thanksgiving psalm, we go around the table, one by one, expressing gratitude for personal blessings. Even though all of us are in public life, which causes us to express our feelings more openly, this is not a time of just expressing gratitude, but of definite thought-provoking expression from the soul. During this time of laughter and tears, our family once again bonds through reflections on our joys and sorrows, victories and failures, hopes and dreams.

Dear heavenly Father, I pause to thank You for my family today—for the joys each one personally brings to my life.

November 25

Scripture: "Every day will I bless thee; and I will praise thy name for ever and ever" (Psalm 145:2).

As a young mother of three small girls, I struggled trying to juggle all the activities in my life. I was a wife, when I had the time; a mother, wearing all the hats that involves; a teacher's aid at the school; the pastor's wife of two infant churches; Sunday school teacher and children's church teacher in both churches, one in the morning and one on Sunday afternoon; plus the state Ladies Ministries president and the person who did anything else that needed to be done. Was I ever WORKING for God!

I was miserable, totally exhausted, and, can I say it, spiritually dead and resentful.

One day in the midst of my despair, a blessed elderly lady of our church called to ask me to her house for prayer. Why did she need me to come to her house? Why couldn't I pray over the phone? She of all people knew how busy I was, for I delighted in telling people how thin I was stretched, especially Sister Blair.

Arriving at her home, I smelled the sweet aroma of baked goods. "I've made some fresh apple dumplings and brewed some hot tea. Let's have a little chat," she invited.

Chat! A chat? You called me here to have a ladies' chitchat? I thought.

We spent just a few minutes on small talk; then she began. In her abundance of spiritual wisdom, she told me how much she appreciated my spiritual zeal and the many things I was doing for the church, my family, and other people. I'm sure I must have lifted my wings a little higher, until she told me the real reason she had asked me over.

"Sister Sanders, how much time do you spend alone with my blessed Jesus?" she tenderly asked. Although I knew exactly what she meant, I tried to detour the question by pinpointing the time I took in preparing programs, lessons, and activities. When she reached across the table to hold my hand, her eyes looking deep into mine, I broke. Putting her arms around me, she moved us to her couch where I poured out my soul.

Of the many things Margaret Blair shared with me that day about the necessity of letting works go and getting into Jesus, this one has made the greatest impact on my life.

She showed me, beginning in Psalms, how to underline every praise and thanksgiving with a blue-leaded pencil. You must begin every day by reading a praise unto God. There are some mornings you may be down and do not feel like praising. Just turn to Psalms and start reading everything underlined in blue. It will not be long until your heart will be lifted up.

Turning to Psalm 55, she said, "If you don't read the blue you might start your day with this: 'My heart is sore pained within me: and the terrors of death are fallen upon me . . . . Horror hath overwhelmed me' (vv. 4, 5). And you certainly don't want that!"

Many years have gone since that day in Minnesota, but Margaret's instructions of sitting at His feet are still as wise and real as they were then.

Lord, thank You for people in my life who live close enough to You and that care enough for me to show me my shortcomings in tender love.

November 26

Scripture: "Bless the Lord, O my soul, and forget not all his benefits" (Psalm 103:2).

Thanksgiving to the Christian should not consist of one day that is set aside to observe the benefits God gives His people; giving thanks should be our way of life. So many of us are prone to count our crosses and not our blessings, to enumerate our difficulties and not our gifts, to think upon our trials rather than our triumphs.

David certainly did not pen the phrase, "Count your blessings, name them one by one," but he did do just that on a number of occasions. Psalm 103 is just such a list. The wonderful news is that this can be our list too. Meditate on these benefits God gives His people:

1. Forgiveness of all sin (v. 3)
2. Healing of all diseases (v. 3)

3. Redemption from all destruction (v. 4)
4. Crowning with lovingkindness (v. 4)
5. Crowning with tender mercies (v. 4)
6. Satisfaction with good things (v. 5)
7. Renewal of youth like eagle's (v. 5)
8. Justice—deliverance from all oppression (v. 6)
9. Knowledge of God's ways (v. 7)
10. Knowledge of God's acts (v. 7)
11. Mercy and grace (v. 8)
12. Patience of God and slowness to anger (v. 8)
13. Plenty of mercy (v. 8)
14. Temporary, not continual, reproof (v. 9)
15. God's anger which soon passes (v. 9)
16. Merciful dealings with our sins (v. 10)
17. Withholding of the punishment we deserve for our sins (v. 10)
18. Infinite mercy toward those who fear Him (v. 11)
19. Removal of sins far away (v. 12)
20. Fatherly pity to His children (v. 13)
21. His knowledge of our frame and His love regardless of this (v. 14; see also Romans 5:8)
22. His memory of our frailty (v. 14)
23. Man's brevity of life, no longer living under the curse (v. 15, 16)
24. Eternal mercy (v. 17)
25. Mercy upon them that fear Him (v. 17)
26. Eternal righteousness (v. 17)
27. Righteousness to covenant keepers (v. 18)
28. Righteousness to the obedient (v. 18)
29. A dependable throne of grace (v. 19)
30. Membership in God's Kingdom (v. 19)

During this season let's take time to step aside from the maze of things round about us and make our own list of at least 30 blessings.

Lord, these are only a fraction of the benefits You give to me. If I could count them, they would be more than the stars in the sky or the sand in the seas. Thank you for Your unmeasurable benefits.

November 27

Scripture: "Let us come before his presence with thanksgiving" (Psalm 95:2).

Here is another poem from my mother's scrapbook.

Thanksgiving

T —thanksgiving is the attitude of praise we give to Him.

H —happiness is what He gives, and it's precious as a gem.

A —absolute adoration, is just another form of praise, one that can be freely given, and used throughout our days.

N —necessary is the love we give to God and others, for joining together with Christ our Lord, has made us sisters and brothers.

K —kindness is something to be used, and not put on a shelf, for its soothing touch should be shared and not kept to oneself.

S —salvation brought great love and peace because of God's concern, and striving to help others receive Christ should be the Christian's yearn.

G —giving is what God did in Love when He gave us His only Son, so giving our love, our substance, and time, should be easy for everyone.

I —invitation has been made, the meal has been prepared through God's Word and sacrificed Son, the truth has been declared.

V —victory for the heavenly race has already been won by our Lord, Jesus Christ, God's only begotten Son.

I —inheritance of heavenly things, awaits God's children today, but in order to receive, we must obey God's Word and pray.

N —nothing should ever be allowed to separate you from His love; constant praise will keep you in touch with our Father up above.

G —gladness fills the hearts of those, who know at the end of their days that they shall be in Glory with Him.

—Natalie J. Thomas

Let all that has breath, give praise!

Father, as I come into Your presence, my mouth is filled with thanksgiving for all You mean to me this day.

November 28

Scripture: "For they heard them speak with tongues, and magnify God" (Acts 10:46).

Sitting at His feet causes different moods, thoughts, expressions, and reactions. There are times I just want to sit in His presence and think— think of His personal blessings to me, think of His creation, think of His promises, or think of His protection of His people throughout history.

Other times I find myself going to the piano, playing and singing softly, "Peace, peace, wonderful peace," or "Standing somewhere in the shadows you'll find Jesus." What communion I have with Him as the tears freely run down my face. But then there are times I would like to be on the housetop, singing at the top of my voice the crescendo, "You ask me how I know He lives, He lives within my heart."

I remember one time while sitting at His feet I became so full of His Spirit I started walking around the house with my hands lifted as high as I could get them. I had so much praise within me that wanted to get out, but I just couldn't find the release of expression I wanted. I suppose my subconscience mind took me back to my cheerleading days, and as I was speaking in a heavenly language, I started doing "victory cartwheels" in the middle of my living room floor. I couldn't help but laugh at myself, but what a wonderful time I had in expressing my love to my Lord!

We take the scripture ". . . for we know not what we should pray . . . but the Spirit itself maketh intercession for us" (Romans 8:26) to mean that when we are frustrated, at a point of decision, disheartened, or in suffering, the Spirit will go before the Father and make intercession for us. Although the Spirit does do that for us, what happens when we are so full of gratitude to the Father that we cannot find the words to express the inexpressible? How can we respond to such appreciative feelings too deep for words?

Speaking in the Holy Ghost with the evidence of speaking in tongues is our outward response to our inward ecstasy. It is a loving response to the wonder and glory of God, who gives not only His Son, His life, and His love but even the gift of words with which to thank Him. When we comprehend that the gift of tongues is really the gift of praise which gives us a greater capacity to worship God, we begin to see why all should speak with tongues. A newer, deeper, and more joyous ability to praise God will strengthen anyone's life. Tongues give expression to praise and thanksgiving.

We don't have too much difficulty putting our obvious needs into words. But heartfelt, overflowing praise to God does not come easily to us before we are baptized in the Holy Spirit. That's what speaking in tongues is all about. It is supremely the gift of praise! When a child of God opens her life to the presence and love of her Father, she will experience a great desire to praise Him, and the Spirit will be able to express what she cannot.

Thank you, God, that when I cannot find words to express my gratitude to You, Your Spirit will make intercession for me to You.

November 29

Scripture: "Continue earnestly in prayer, being vigilant in it with thanksgiving" (Colossians 4:2, *NKJV*).

The Pilgrim fathers who landed at Plymouth rock over 300 years ago knew nothing of the bountiful prosperity which America enjoys today. How touching is the picture of William Brewster, rising from a scanty Plymouth dinner, consisting of a plate of clams and a glass of cold water, to thank God "for the abundance of the sea and the treasures hid in the sand." This is quite a different picture from America's Thanksgiving today with the traditional turkey-and-all-the-trimmings dinner, the gaiety of visiting with family and friends, the football classics, and the time of relaxation and enjoyment. Where is the pause for the time of giving thanks?

In 1623, Governor William Bradford issued the following proclamation to the people of Plymouth Colony:

To All Ye Pilgrims:

> Inasmuch as the great Father has given us this year an abundant harvest of Indian corn, wheat, beans, squashes, and garden vegetables, and has made the forest to abound with game and the sea with fish and clams, and inasmuch as He has protected us from the ravages of the savages, has spared us from pestilence and disease, has granted us freedom to worship God according to the dictates of our own conscience; now, I, your magistrate, do proclaim that all ye Pilgrims, with your wives and little ones, do gather at ye meeting house, on ye hill, between the hours of 9 and 12 in the day time, on Thursday, November ye 29th of the year of our Lord one thousand six hundred and twenty-three, and the third year since ye Pilgrims landed on ye Pilgrim Rock, there to listen to ye pastor, and render thanksgiving to ye Almighty God for all His blessings.

—William Bradford

Ye Governor of ye Colony

America today has a spirit of dissatisfaction that is reflected at every level of our society. Everybody is grasping for more of this world's material things. But when they have attained their goals, they find nothing but emptiness.

It was not for materialism that the pilgrims founded America but for the privilege and freedom to worship the Almighty God according to the dictates of their consciences. For the fathers of our country, the Bible was a book of spiritual authority, which was born in the Christian faith, nourished by Christian faith, and preserved by Christian faith. America is what she is today by the grace of God. But America is not immune to

God's judgment if we depart from faith in God. America's strength today lies not in our military power but in our moral and spiritual power. We can have enduring peace only as we continue to value our spiritual resources and trust in the Almighty God.

Solemn warning is given in Romans 1:21 where we are told that the people of old fell from His favor through ingratitude, even though they had known him. Therefore, God's wrath was turned toward them, and He allowed them to commit every vile sin imaginable.

One of the sins charged against the false profession of the last days is that of unthankfulness. "For men shall be . . . covetous . . . blasphemers . . . unthankful, unholy . . . fierce, despisers of those that are good, traitors . . ." (2 Timothy 3:2-4). Unthankfulness is listed with covetousness and blasphemy! Truly, today's America has all the signs of living in the last days.

Lord, I thank You for those who were willing to pay the price for a nation free to serve You. May I be thankful for America as I continue to pray for her.

November 30

Scripture: "Thanks be unto God for his unspeakable gift" (2 Corinthians 9:15).

No giving of thanks could be possible without the greatest blessing of all—God's. And yet it cannot be expressed with words. Even Paul, who was quite a master of words, found himself without words to describe this blessing. He could only describe it as an "unspeakable gift." And what was so wonderful that it wouldn't go into words? The gift God sent which was His only Son, Jesus Christ, to die for me that I might have eternal life.

In all God's infinite plans, in all God's minute workings, in all God's indescribable creation, nothing else in the universe is as important as the forgiving, saving, and restoring of man to the fellowship of God.

I am always a little embarassed when asked if I remember the time and place I was saved. Born into a Christian home, I have always had a tender heart toward God.

As a little freckled-face girl, raised on a west Texas ranch, I would often climb to the top of the windmill where I would sit and ponder about God for hours. I would look as far as I could into the horizon, wondering what God had beyond and how I fit into His plan. In my simple childlike faith, I knew Christ died for me because He loved me. I had discovered the reason for His gift: He loved me! It was just that simple. I didn't try to discover why God loved me. I certainly knew it was not because of my goodness, for many a climb was immediately after a spanking. It was . . . He just did. Sometimes I would stand on the ledge singing to the whole world, "Jesus loves me! this I know, For the Bible tells me so."

Sometimes I wish I could go back to my windmill ledge and retrieve that same childlike faith. Somewhere through the years of adulthood, I have often been pressed to find answers—answers to questions that are not even asked. I cannot begin to explain God's love for me. How can I select the words to describe a gift so vast that it explodes man's finite mind to comprehend? Yet this gift is so small that it abides in the tiniest recesses of my heart. I cannot fathom why He chose to give His Son to forgive someone like me. He just did!

How God longs to forgive sinners! The forgiveness and salvation of sinners is first in His plan.

When Charles Wesley experienced the joy of divine forgiveness, he told a Moravian friend of his new sense of pardon and added, "I suppose I had better keep silent about it."

"Oh, no, my brother," came the reply. "If you had a thousand tongues you should go and use them all for Jesus." Charles Wesley went home and wrote the hymn:

> O for a thousand tongues to sing,
> My great Redeemer's praise;
> The glories of my God and King,
> The triumphs of His Grace!

We have come to the end of a month of thinking so that we can thank God for His many blessings. Let the most profound gratitude go out from grateful hearts to a forgiving God whose mercy is everlasting. When we realize that we have been redeemed, not with gold but with the blood of Christ, we can say each morning, "Thanks be unto God for his unspeakable gift."

Dear Father, Creator, Protector, loving Savior, and Holy Spirit, today my heart is filled with thanksgiving for all Your blessings to me.

NOTES

NOTES

December

Unwrapping Your Gifts

Saundra Jennings Rose

Saundra Jennings Rose has served as state president for Ladies Ministries for 12 years. She served in North Dakota/South Dakota and Kentucky and is presently state Ladies Ministries president in North Georgia. She and her husband, the Reverend Delbert D. Rose, also pastored for 18 years. She has a bachelor of arts degree from Northwest Bible College.

For the last three years, Saundra has conducted seminars on "Discovering Your Spiritual Gifts" on both state and national levels. She has been a speaker for Women's Aglow, camp meeting Ladies Day, and state retreats.

Saundra and her husband have two children: Tanya Dashe and Christopher Todd.

December 1

Scripture: "As each one has received a special gift, employ it in serving one another, as good stewards of the manifold grace of God" (1 Peter 4:10, *NASB*).

Unwrapping your gifts! What an exciting and appropriate theme for the month of December. This is the time of the year when our minds are overflowing with thoughts of giving and exchanging gifts in celebration of the birth of the Christ child, Jesus.

During the Christmas season four years ago, I received a gift from a friend. I didn't unwrap the gift for quite some time. It was wrapped in gorgeous gold and burgundy paper, tied with a beautiful gold bow. Since the package was so attractive under my Victorian Christmas tree, I decided not to open it.

I know you are thinking, *How could you leave a gift without opening it?* I thought I knew what was in the package because Debbie had told me earlier she had purchased several of the same items for gifts.

A couple of months later I was preparing to teach a class on spiritual gifts at a conference at Ridgecrest. Remembering the unopened Christmas gift, I retrieved the gift for my visual illustration.

"Too many believers look like beautifully wrapped gifts under a Christmas tree," I began. "Can't you just see some Christians who come Sunday after Sunday and sit on the pews like packages all wrapped up in gorgeous paper and tied with big ribbons? In reality, they should look like the day after Christmas with all their gifts unwrapped, being discovered and used. In 1 Peter 4:10, we read that each person has received a special gift or gifts. The gifts are to be used to serve one another for the good of the whole body. No one has been left out."

At that point I proceeded to unwrap my Christmas gift. It was a beautiful, etched crystal cup I could have been using for my freshly brewed cup of gourmet coffee or raspberry tea. Instead I had been delighting so much in the wrappings that I neglected to enjoy the gift! How often do we do this with spiritual gifts?

When you unwrap the gift(s) God gives you and begin utilizing each gift for the kingdom of God, you are in essence giving back to God a gift, as well as serving and ministering to the body of Christ.

As you read the devotions for the next few days, ask the Holy Spirit to speak to you about how He wants to work in your life. While quietly sitting at His feet, unwrap and discover the gifts He so graciously gives.

Holy Spirit, teach me how to take that first step toward discovering, developing, and using my gifts. Create a desire within me to be obedient to Your Word by finding my place of service in the body of Christ.

December 2

Scripture: "All these [gifts] are the work of one and the same Spirit, and he gives them to each one, just as he determines" (1 Corinthians 12:11).*

As we continue unwrapping our gifts, let's define spiritual gifts as God's provision for the Holy Spirit to minister through a believer to serve Him and His church more effectively. They are energizers and divine motivators. When we operate within our gifts, we experience a want-to rather than a have-to attitude.

Our scripture today emphasizes that it is the work of the Holy Spirit to administer the various gifts to the body just as He wills. Often I use an object lesson to illustrate this verse. At the beginning of class, small gifts are given out wrapped in different types of paper—comic strip, Handi-Wrap, brown paper bag, foil, fancy gift wrapping. In each gift are different amounts of candy.

I start the class by asking, "Did all of you receive a gift when you came in the classroom today? You had no choice in the gift you were given. It was simply handed to you. Neither did you have a choice in the number and variety of candies inside." Then I explain: "The various types of wrapping paper represent our uniqueness. We are wrapped in different personalities. Some of you have a wonderful sense of humor (comic strip); others are open and transparent (Handi-Wrap); some are rather quiet and reserved on the outside, but on the inside are beautiful people (brown paper). Another personality represents the bright, shining intellectuals (foil paper), and then, there are the gorgeous and beautiful types (fancy wrapping paper) we all want to be.

The spiritual gifts in your life will be manifested according to your own unique personality. The number of candy pieces in your gift is representative of the Holy Spirit's giving to each person the number of gifts that He determines. To some He may entrust only one gift which may be used in a highly developed ministry that will provide a vital contribution to the life and growth of the church. Another person may have a mixture of gifts providing a more varied ministry to the body. Always remember, whether he has one or many gifts, each believer is *equally* important and necessary for unity in the body of Christ.

Maybe you can identify with this feeling. Early in my Christian experience I allowed fear to hinder me from becoming involved in certain areas of ministry and from functioning according to my gifts. Because I compared myself with others, inferiority and intimidation

*The Scripture references used for this month's devotions are from the *New International Version* unless otherwise indicated.

413

overcame me. I almost became immobilized! But, praise God, you and I do not operate in our own strength. When we exercise our gifts, the Holy Spirit empowers us. He flows through us, enabling us to do what He has called and equipped us to do!

In the next few sessions we will review several of the body ministry gifts. See if you recognize any characteristics in these gifts that may assist you in unwrapping and identifying your gifts.

Father God, forgive me for comparing myself with others. Thank You that I can effectively operate in the gifts You have given me through the power of the Holy Spirit.

December 3

Scripture: "We have different gifts, according to the grace given us. If a man's gift is . . . teaching, let him teach; if it is encouraging, let him encourage" (Romans 12:6-8).

Those who have the gift of teaching have the ability to communicate the Word of God, making the truth relevant so that others will learn and grow. Those who have the gift of exhortation (encouragement), according to Leslie Flynn, have the ability to strengthen the weak, reassure the wavering, steady the faltering, console the troubled and encourage the halting.

Maria Pream from Austria spoke at the ladies meeting at the 17th World Pentecostal Conference in Jerusalem in September 1995. She is an excellent example of a woman who ministered mightily in both of these gifts. She not only presented the truth so others could learn, but she also spoke a message that was uplifting and reassuring. She began by praying, "Father, You love each lady here today as one of your darlings. Open our ears to Your Word and help us to realize You are 'crazy' over us, Your daughters."

Her prayer, taken from Song of Solomon 4:7, immediately ministered encouragement to my heart. The Holy Spirit captured my attention. I wanted to hear what the Father had to say.

"The Lord rejoices over each of us today," Maria said. "We are precious to Him . . . we are His darlings! Too often we look at that one thing in our life that is missing. I did. We say, 'If I had more education . . . if I were slim . . . if I were married . . . if I were single . . . if I were tall . . . and so forth.' Instead of *being*, we start *doing*; and our whole identity is based on what we do. We have a work relationship instead of a love relationship with the Father. If you feel like a big zero and work hard to keep it filled, God may put a knife in your zero. He did mine. And when I said, 'Lord, I give up,' He replied, 'Finally, you got the message

414

and now we can work together.' God revealed to me once again that salvation was a free gift, and my sins alone were enough to crucify Jesus. I was not to live *for* Him, but let Him live *in* me. If you allow the Holy Spirit, who is number one, to come in front of the zero, you become a 10."

She concluded by saying, "The Lord wants to lavish His love on you today, His darling daughters. Open your hearts and allow Him to pour buckets of love on you."

I left with the assurance that I was indeed loved. There was a deep desire in my heart to have a more intense love affair with Jesus Christ. Through the gifts of teaching and exhortation, I was blessed.

Can you think of a time when God used you in one of these gifts to minister to another? Have you been affirmed by someone anointed by the Holy Spirit who unwrapped these gifts and touched your life? Thank them, and give thanks to your heavenly Father.

Holy Spirit, thank You for placing people in our lives who comfort, encourage, and teach us Your truths. Help us to be used in strengthening others.

December 4

Scripture: "Through love serve one another" (Galatians 5:13, *NASB*).

In our devotion for today, we begin by unwrapping the gift of serving, or helps. The person with this gift has the ability to minister to the body of Christ by meeting the needs of others through practical service. The following incident is an example of this gift in action.

Excitement permeated the air! Seniors, families, friends congregated! Cameras flashed! The orchestra sounded the downbeat! It was graduation day at Lee College! My daughter Tanya proudly accepted her diploma. This was her commencement—her opportunity to step into the real world and embark on a new career. During the commotion of greeting friends and moving through the crowd, I felt a tap on my shoulder. What a delight to see an old friend. After embracing we began reminiscing about the "good ole days." Judy had accepted Christ during our first pastorate in Illinois almost 30 years ago. After a few minutes of chatting, she changed to a serious note. "Do you know what I remember most about you as a pastor's wife?" she asked. As I thought back over that period of almost 10 years, I recalled the various areas of ministry—teaching Sunday school, serving as Ladies Ministries president, leading a Tuesday morning prayer group, playing the organ, conducting Vacation Bible School. As a young and enthusiastic pastor's wife, I thought I should be involved in all these ministry opportunities, plus any others I couldn't get someone else to do. Before I could answer my friend, she said, "I remember a very discouraging time when I fell and broke my leg. I had three small children and was expecting my fourth. I didn't know how I was going to manage my house and family. You and two other ladies from the church washed my clothes, cleaned my house, mopped my kitchen floor, bathed the children, prepared meals for the family, and ministered to my needs. I will never forget what you did."

I wondered . . . how often have I minimized the value and importance of the "basin and towel" ministry? What a tremendous blessing it is when given in love with the spirit of a servant's heart! You see, she didn't need someone to teach a Sunday school lesson, play the organ, sing a song, or even conduct a prayer meeting (those up-front gifts many envy). Instead, she simply needed love in action operating through the gift of serving.

Gloria Gaither once said, "It is neither less nor more spiritual to clean the bathrooms in the church than to preach behind the pulpit, because there are no status jobs in the kingdom of God."

Lord Jesus, thank You for setting the example of servant leadership during Your ministry here on earth. Help me to always be sensitive to the needs of others and have a willing heart to serve.

December 5

Scripture: "Offer hospitality to one another without grumbling" (1 Peter 4:9).

In the following illustration you will see the gift of hospitality opened and in full use.

We had just moved to the Atlanta area. My husband had just been appointed to serve the churches as overseer in North Georgia. Arriving at the state office one morning I found a handwritten note, scribbled in pencil, on my desk. It read: "Dear One, This is that sweet, wonderful Reba. Sorry I missed the banquet Monday night. So you will recognize me, I am beautiful and weigh 110 pounds. Welcome to Georgia. Reba."

Well, I didn't know Reba, but I recognized her great sense of humor, and I already liked her. I asked the office staff, "Who is this person?" They quickly informed me, "You will find out soon enough. And, by the way, she does weigh more than 110 pounds!"

More than five years have passed since my first encounter with Reba. Among her many talents and gifts, one is outstanding. She fits to a tee Webster's definition of *hospitality*: "welcoming guests with warmth and generosity, fond of entertaining, and well-disposed toward strangers."

Yes, she could be called Miss Hospitality without doing any injustice to the title. Her door is always open to family and friends, as well as strangers. When I drop by, she says with a big smile, "Babe, wouldn't you like something to eat or drink? I've just made a big pot of vegetable soup and cornbread." Before I have time to answer, she sets the table, fills a plate, pulls out a chair, and what was intended to be a short visit turns into a full hour of food, fun, and fellowship (and extra pounds).

Often she calls her friends and neighbors to say, "Doll, why don't you come over tonight for chicken pan pie." Or "I just made a fresh peach cobbler. Come by and pick it up." I suppose you have guessed by now, Reba affectionately calls everyone "Babe" or "Doll."

Since her front door is never locked, a minister friend went by recently. Finding no one home, he made himself a sandwich and enjoyed a time of rest. He left a note that said, "I was hungry and knew you wouldn't mind if I had something to eat. Thanks for the food. Jim."

For years Reba has cooked for hundreds at the state ladies retreats, decorated and catered weddings, and prepared meals for the seniors at her church. Karen Maines says in her book *Open Heart, Open Home*, "Entertaining puts the emphasis on things rather than people. Scriptural hospitality seeks to minister and does not seek to impress, but to serve."

Reba's generous spirit indeed fulfills the scriptural mandate to offer hospitality without grumbling—seeking to serve, not impress! I know. My family along with many others are recipients of her kindness. Maybe this is the gift God would have you unwrap today.

Holy Spirit, my prayer today is that I might learn to cheerfully open the gift of hospitality and minister to others during the holidays and coming year.

December 6

Scripture: "We have different gifts, according to the grace given us . . . If it is contributing to the needs of others, let him give generously" (Romans 12:6, 8).

Today, the spiritual gift we will unwrap is the gift of giving. Let's begin!

How would you define the Christmas spirit? Would it be the sounds of familiar carols echoing through the busy shopping malls, family gatherings, a tree covered with white twinkling lights surrounded by a sea of beautifully wrapped Christmas packages, or maybe the cheery greeting cards that keep us in touch with family and friends? Although all of these play an important role in creating the festive air of the season, they only represent an atmosphere for the real significance of Christmas—the birth of Christ.

The real spirit of Christmas can be found by unwrapping the gift of giving. Jesus himself demonstrated this by His life as well as His words . . . "Inasmuch as ye have done it unto one of the least of these . . . ye have done it unto me" (Matthew 25:40, KJV). Those who give liberally and joyfully to provide material resources to the body of Christ have the gift of giving operating in their lives. They give without expecting to receive anything in return. All believers should do this, but there are those for whom this is a special gift, their ministry.

Today I was reminded of a couple who attended our church in Anderson, South Carolina, and often demonstrated the gift of giving. Their kind generosity during one particular holiday season stands out vividly in my mind. One Sunday they asked me, "Would you do us a favor? We feel impressed to give a Christmas gift of money to a single mother in the church who needs financial assistance. We didn't want to send cash through the mail, so would you please take this envelope to her? We would rather she not know where the gift came from. Just say it is from someone who cares." This is characteristic of a person operating in the gift of giving. They prefer for their giving to remain anonymous, and they are sensitive to the needs of people.

That Sunday night after church I had the privilege of handing her the envelope. She was overwhelmed when she opened it. Tears filled her eyes. "How can I accept such a generous gift?" she asked. "They are giving it in Jesus' name because they care," I replied.

It was very difficult for her to imagine that someone would be so sympathetic to her needs, would give her a gift of this nature, and would want to remain anonymous. Again, I was reminded of Matthew 25:40. This is the true Christmas spirit. Proverbs 19:17 says it like this: "He who has pity on the poor lends to the Lord, and He will pay back what he has given" (*NKJV*).

What a deal! You can't possibly lose. Why not unwrap the gift of giving during the holidays by placing money in envelopes to give spontaneously when you are touched by the Christmas spirit?

Lord Jesus, may the true spirit of Christmas fill my heart this year and overflow to others. My desire is to minister to You by giving to those less fortunate. Lead me.

December 7

Scripture: "We have different gifts, according to the grace given us. . . . If it is showing mercy, let him do it cheerfully" (Romans 12:6, 8).

It is time to unwrap the gift of mercy, or benevolence. One who has this gift is one who has the supernatural ability to manifest practical, compassionate, and cheerful love toward suffering people. This will be our last devotional on body ministry gifts, although by no means have we unwrapped all the spiritual gifts.

Pat and John Meeks have definitely been called and equipped with the gift of mercy. The Meeks began the Inman Park Mission at Little Five Points in the heart of downtown Atlanta, Georgia, almost six years ago. Weekly they give practical help by feeding the hungry, clothing the poor, and ministering to the destitute, sick, and hurting. Pat related this heart-warming story that happened at the beginning of their inner-city ministry.

> A few weeks after we began the new work, two young men (James and John) visited our church. James was raised in a Church of God home and had relatives praying for his restoration. John knew very little about salvation. They were well educated, had a thriving business, but both had AIDS. These men were gloriously saved that morning and delivered from their former lifestyle. They were later baptized in water and joined the church.
>
> James lived approximately two and a half years longer than expected and died with a glowing testimony of the saving grace of Jesus. On two occasions just before his passing, a bright beautiful light came into his room. He was filled with peace and joy.
>
> As John's illness worsened he lost his eyesight, but rejoiced in his salvation and looked forward with great anticipation to his home going to heaven. Some of his last words were, "Praise the Lord! You don't have to feel sorry for me. I've hidden His Word in my heart, and although I am blind, I can see better than most people with good eyesight."

Pat concluded by saying, "We were blessed by these lives that were so drastically changed. Although we rejoiced in their victorious home goings, we miss them greatly. Many lives were touched and restored because of James's and John's testimonies during their illnesses. To God be the glory!"

I wonder how many churches would respond to James and John with the same compassionate spirit? How would you respond? I'm so thankful Pat and John answered the call to be Christ's hands extended to those in need in the inner city of Atlanta. Do you have a burden to comfort and console those who are hurting? Are you willing to sacrifice, if necessary, in order to help those in need?

If you see these characteristics in your life, it might indicate God has equipped you with the gift of mercy.

Lord Jesus, help me to be aware of those whose needs I can meet this Christmas by providing food and clothing. May I always extend compassion and mercy to the lost.

December 8

Scripture: "If I speak in the tongues of men and of angels, but have not love, I am only a resounding gong or a clanging cymbal" (1 Corinthians 13:1).

The class I taught was studying a series on unconditional love. It appeared as if the Lord had given us a living example to see how we would respond. Mary (not her real name) didn't always smell good or look neat. But Mary became an instrument God used to teach me and others the real meaning of unwrapping and giving away the gift of love.

One Saturday I received a call from a couple who attended the young married couple's class. "Would you mind if we brought a woman to Sunday school tomorrow that we met this week on the streets? She doesn't wear clothing normally seen at church, and we were just wondering if we should invite her?"

"Certainly. Ask her to come," I replied.

The next day John and Patti arrived at church with Mary who appeared to be in her 50s. She was wearing a pair of tattered brown pants, a faded shirt, a dirty green nylon jacket and an old stocking cap she kept on during the entire morning. This was the same attire she wore daily as she walked the streets of Anderson. Needless to say, she stood out in the crowd that Sunday.

Mary could hardly make eye contact with anyone. She sat with her head down during most of the Sunday school class. It was evident she desperately needed someone to show her love and acceptance. Patti and John, young enthusiastic Christians, continued to bring Mary to church. As always, she wore the old stocking cap.

One week Patti informed the class of Mary's birthday. The next Sunday we celebrated with colored balloons, ice cream, cake, cards, and gifts of money. You could sense she was touched with the outpouring of love from the class members. With tears in her eyes she thanked us repeatedly for our kindness.

A few Sundays went by and Mary was not there. Patti had been unsuccessful in locating her. Everyone was concerned. From the hospital staff we later learned her sad story. Before she was born, Mary's mother tried to abort her. The trauma caused a multiplicity of physical and emotional problems. She was deserted by her mother and other family members. She had no one. Because of the excruciating pain in her head, she underwent surgery several times, often having to have holes drilled in her skull to relieve the pressure. Now I knew why she always wore that old stocking cap.

How grateful I was that this class passed the test of love. Yes, Mary . . . eccentric and rejected by society . . . was introduced to the unconditional love of Jesus Christ. Her life would never be the same.

In today's scripture, Paul explained the absolute necessity of love and how it is the qualifying factor for exercising any of the spiritual gifts. In essence, he was saying that the most magnificent manifestation of spiritual gifts and the most heroic self-sacrifice mean nothing without love.

Perhaps there's a Mary or a John struggling in the darkness, walking the streets of your city, a person whose life could be illuminated by unwrapping the gift of love. Why not invite a lonely, forgotten, or deserted person to your home for a meal or to share in a worship service with your family during the holidays.

Father, this Christmas may I share what You have so graciously given to me that I may touch the life of at least one person who needs Your unconditional love.

December 9

Scripture: "But I, when I am lifted up from the earth, will draw all men to myself" (John 12:32).

During the Christmas season several years ago, I read an interesting article in *Virtue* magazine about a new concept in giving and receiving gifts. Instead of just another white-elephant gift exchange at a church Christmas gathering, they held a spiritual gift exchange. Everyone was instructed to come prepared to give a gift others would remember all year long. *Very interesting,* I thought.

For instance, one person made an acrostic of the word *joy* and typed it on a hole-punched card with curling ribbon on the side. It read . . .

J ump for joy—celebrate life.

O bserve the common—let it become miraculous.

Y ahoo! Let joy be unleashed. Let it saturate your life.

The group was then asked to place the card in their Bibles or somewhere in their home to remind them not to take life so seriously but to rejoice and be happy in Jesus. The person who wrote the acrostic said, "Every time one of the group saw me the following year, they would yell, 'Yahoo!'"

Another gift reflected what the person had been going through that year, perhaps giving a word of encouragement: "Do not be afraid or discouraged because of this vast army. For the battle is not yours, but God's" (2 Chronicles 20:15).

One person told the story that inspired the writing of a favorite Christmas carol. Then the group sang the carol.

Someone else read a poem:

> O God who scarfs this Christmas world with snow
> And lights star tapers so that all may see,
> Please leave beneath the tinseled pine's clear glow
> Your gifts of faith, love, hope, and charity.
>
> —Author Unknown

Another participant passed out candy—sour ball suckers, reminding the group of the bitterness of sin. Then she gave out candy kisses and talked about the sweet redemption that a babe in Bethlehem brought to this world. Sin has no sting for us who are redeemed through the Cross.

One person gave everyone a penny and talked about the costly gifts of the wise men—gold, frankincense, and myrrh—and their significance. She then asked them to give their penny away to someone else and tell that person what type of gift they had been to them. "Neat idea. I am going to use this one next year," I said aloud.

Then another idea flooded my mind. Why not give the gift of prayer? Pass out a signed Christmas card to the group as a reminder for them to save their cards and pray over a different family each day in the coming year. This would be a gift that would last all year long, and keep family and friends close in thought as well.

Maybe you can also think of a spiritual gift exchange you could unwrap in a similar setting this season to exalt the name of Jesus Christ. Why not try it at family gatherings, perhaps on Christmas Eve. It's not costly, but the effects may be remembered long after the season has passed.

Jesus, may I reflect and lift up Your name in my giving this Christmas so that others will be drawn to Your kingdom and experience Your joy.

December 10

Scripture: "Therefore encourage one another and build each other up" (1 Thessalonians 5:11).

Recently I received a beautiful card from a friend. She shared that she and other family members were going through a difficult time. She ended the note by writing encouraging words to me. The timing was just right. How I needed that gift. It lifted my spirit! I wondered if she realized she had discovered something that would be of tremendous strength to her. One sure way I have found to cure discouragement in my own life is to encourage someone else.

Immediately I picked up the phone and called to assure her of my concern and prayers. Within a short time a third party was on the line—the Holy Spirit—confirming to my friend that He was her counselor, strength, and guide during the difficult trial. Even though we were miles apart, we rejoiced together. Discouragement vanished, and the atmosphere was filled with praise.

Part of the problem of discouragement in my own life is that I become so introspective that I cannot see beyond my own difficulties. Comparing my problems with those less fortunate always places them in proper perspective.

Today why not unwrap the gift of encouragement and freely give it away. There are many ways to express this gift. Consider some of the following:

- Think of someone who made a difference in your life and tell them.
- Put a love note in your child's lunch box or your husband's coat pocket.
- Be gentle and patient with an angry person.
- Compliment at least two people every day during the rest of December.
- Wish someone a happy holiday with music. Dial 1-800-422-SONG and Send-A-Song will deliver your specially selected Christmas song and recorded personal greeting over the phone.
- Give kind words to the salesclerk, the mailman, the paperboy.
- When you get off a crowded elevator, wish everyone a Merry Christmas.
- Mend a quarrel—release a grudge.

Discouraged and disillusioned people will more than likely cross your path in days to come. In whatever way you can, be an encourager. Give the gift that keeps on giving long after you are gone. It may be only a pat on the back, a hand on the shoulder, a comforting word, a sincere compliment, a smile, or perhaps an expression of gratitude. These few lines say it best:

> I am only one, but I am one.
> I cannot do everything, but I can do something;
> And what I should do and can do, by the
> Grace of God I will do!
>
> —Anonymous

Heavenly Father, as I sit at Your feet today, make me sensitive to those in my world who need the gift of encouragement. May I unwrap this gift and give it as willingly as You gave Your Son Jesus to this world.

December 11

Scripture: "How much more will your Father in heaven give good gifts to those who ask him" (Matthew 7:11).

I was reading the Sunday newspaper when the following ad caught my attention:

> IMAGINE for a moment that Christmas Day has arrived. You've received lots of cards and several gifts. Then, you receive one last gift—a video cassette. You put the cassette into your VCR and meet an attractive host who shows you a wide variety of fine quality merchandise from one of your favorite shops. After a few minutes, the host prompts you to select any item you want and call a toll-free number to place your order. You are told, "It will be shipped in less than two weeks, all expenses paid." The ad continues:

> Hard to imagine? Not anymore.

> That product has arrived.

> You don't have to be a mind reader to be a

> Good gift giver.

Apparently, the new rage is gift videos, available for any gift-giving season—Christmas, birthdays, Mother's Day, graduation, weddings, and so forth. The article goes on to say, "Cost starts at only $25 and your gift can be shipped to that special someone."

As I finished reading the advertisement I thought, *This is certainly a revolutionary gift idea . . . exciting and different. And I imagine a lot of people will buy into this new concept of gift giving this year. I might even consider it for my son, Todd, because I never know what to buy him.*

Then my mind started clicking . . . I could make my own video with the things I would like for Christmas and the stores where they could be purchased, and give it to my husband. After all, he says he never knows what to get me. I laughed. Maybe I'm on to something really great this year!

As I seriously considered this, I was reminded of the scripture in Matthew 7 and the contrast that was given. Though we as parents are imperfect, our Father in heaven is infinitely perfect. So if we who are imperfect give good gifts to our children, imagine how much more our heavenly Father will give us what we need if we just ask.

After a few moments I thought, *But how sad! Most people would rather receive a video of $25 gifts than accept the free gift of God's love and salvation.*

Yes, the Father is a good gift giver; He is ever giving gifts to His children—love, joy, peace, forgiveness, eternal life—simply for the asking.

What do you need today?

Father, may I come boldly into Your throne room this morning and make my requests known to You. Thank You for the assurance that it pleases You to give to me . . . if I but ask.

December 12

Scripture: "For thou didst form my inward parts; Thou didst weave me in my mother's womb. I will give thanks to Thee, for I am fearfully and wonderfully made" (Psalms 139:13, *NASB*).

Stella Miller, or Mosis, as she was affectionately known by her family and friends, was my maternal grandmother. She was an extraordinary person. The best way to describe her is to say that she dearly loved life! She would say, "God's great, big, wonderful world is something to behold. I love the change of seasons; every shimmering blade of grass speaks of God's creation, and all the creatures reveal His mighty handiwork." She would pick up a piece of driftwood and say, "Isn't this a thing of beauty?"

But as colorful and full of variety as the plant and animal kingdoms were in her eyes, nothing was more magnificent than what God had created in His own image—human life. So her greatest love was for people, all people—red, yellow, black, and white. She gave dignity to each person she met. She passionately loved children and accepted the birth of each of her five children as a gift directly from the hand of God. In my conversations with my grandmother, she often referred to Psalm 139 and commented, "Saundra, God has a special plan for each life. Isn't it wonderful to know He was involved in our lives even before we were born? While we were yet being formed in our mother's womb, He numbered the length of our days!" She would conclude, "Yes, we are fearfully and wonderfully made."

In 1973 when abortion became legal in America, she was appalled! I have heard her prevail in prayer, grieving over the million and a half babies aborted each year, some even up through the seventh month of pregnancy. In her 80s, she penned the poem titled "Unnamed." How appropriate during this season of the year when we are celebrating the birth of a baby who changed the course of history that we remember to protect, value, and be grateful for this priceless gift, the gift of life.

Unnamed

> A cry goes up to the ears of God
> From unborn babes sleeping 'neath the sod.
>
> Never a chance for a downy bed,
> No place to lay his little head.
> A tiny little fist closed up tight,
> Not knowing what would happen to him that night.
> No one came to his defense—
> All was silent except the steel instrument.

He might have been a prophet or a man of fame,
But an aborted baby is given no name.
Yet the God of all mercy who rules on high,
Will give him a name that will never die.
He'll go down in God's Hall of Fame
With millions of others who were never claimed.

Another little martyr,
The small and the weak,
God will finish His product,
And place a kiss on his cheek.

There may be a choir of unborn babes,
Who failed to make it in the human parade,
But they made it home to the Father on high,
Who said, "So you were not welcome; neither was I."

Little mysteries so pure and sweet,
Never touched by the filth of the streets.
Lord, shelter these little ones safe in your arms.
They are kept now from all danger and harm.
Give them the love they missed down here;
May they never remember a sorrow or tear.

O God, hasten Your return from on high,
And cut short the wail of the infants' cry!
Fold them to Your heart as You weep;
With a tender lullaby, sing them to sleep.

—Stella Miller

Father, I give thanks to You for I am fearfully and wonderfully made. You have designed and created each precious gift of life with Your own hands. Help us to always defend and cherish life.

December 13

Scripture: "To everything there is a season, a time for every purpose under heaven" (Ecclesiastes 3:1, 2, *NKJV*).

Time is one of the greatest gifts God has given us. And since God is a generous God, it makes sense that He has given time in abundance to do the things He has called us to do. Yet we live the frantic lifestyle of beating the clock rather than sitting at His feet and allowing the Holy Spirit to help us prioritize and manage our time.

Sitting in the den one morning after spending a restless and sleepless night trying to juggle all the things on my "to do" list, I slumped back in the rocking chair with a feeling of hopelessness. Exhausted, depressed, and weary from the struggle of it all, I thought there was no possible way to accomplish all I had to do. Sinking deeper into the chair as if to hide from the nagging thoughts swirling around in my head, despair overwhelmed me. *I don't have the time. . . . Where does the time go? . . . Christmas will soon be here! . . . If only there were more hours in the day!*

Then my thoughts turned to Jesus, our example, who entered this world during one of the busiest rush hours in history. The little town of Bethlehem was bustling with weary travelers, pushing and shoving their way through the narrow streets, trying to find a place to rest. The inns were full. Yet it was the Father's time to send His Son into the world.

So Jesus knew about busyness. Yet in His lifetime He never appeared rushed. He was tired at times . . . sorrowful at times . . . discouraged at times . . . but He was never in a frantic hurry.

The longer I sat and meditated, the more I realized that anxiety flourishes with too much to do and too little rest and relaxation. The hustle and bustle of shopping and the long lines had polluted this reflective season with stress and self-imposed expectations.

Time is a collection of moments, and for me time was flying by, leaving so many details unattended. But Jesus didn't model a pattern of burnout. Instead He paced His life. He often took time out in the wilderness to regroup, to walk along the seashores of Galilee, to reflect and relax at a wedding.

I have been driven by things that rob me of that balanced lifestyle—promotions, plans, and programs, rather than His purposes. I needed to be reminded that there is a season for everything, and the Father makes no mistakes in His distribution of time or of what He requires of each person.

I began to eliminate some things on my "to do" list, determined to take more quiet time to just rest and listen to that "still, small voice." My spirit felt renewed, my body refreshed, and I even became eager to unwrap the gift of time and begin my day.

> Yesterday is a cancelled check.
> Tomorrow is a promissory note.
> Today is ready cash . . . spend it!

Lord, I am not asking for more time. Just give me wisdom to use the time You give me each day to fulfill Your purposes in my life.

December 14

Scripture: "I have learned the secret of being content in any and every situation" (Philippians 4:12).

As a young bride of 23, I was still making the adjustments of married life when my husband accepted a pastorate in Kincaid, Illinois. Kincaid was a small mining town of 1,500 people, most of whom were coal miners. After seeking God for His will about our future, we believed this was right.

When we arrived, we found a neat four-room parsonage with a space heater in the living room that kept that room hot—really hot—and the other rooms cold—really cold. The exception was in the summer when all the rooms stayed hot.

Needless to say, our pace of living was much slower in this rural setting. It was quite a change from the bustling city life in Washington, D.C., where my father pastored the National Church of God. Now I was hundreds of miles from home, a new bride, in a new church, in a new town, and a new pastor's wife!

The church members were also going through a time of adjustment. They were brokenhearted by unfortunate events that recently occurred in their church. Several ministers had been contacted by my father-in-law who was state overseer in Illinois, but none had felt the call to come to this particular church. Perhaps it was God's sovereign will that we be appointed "to the kingdom for such a time as this."

I learned quickly there was no time for loneliness, regrets, or looking back to yesterday. This proved to be a time of contentment and fulfillment. There were hurting people who needed to be reassured that their wounds would heal; that God had sent us to love and encourage them; and that my husband would be a tender, caring shepherd. In the midst of sacrifices we experienced incredible joy and satisfaction during the next 10 years. One of the greatest joys was seeing many young couples converted who are now leaders in the church. Five of these couples accepted the call to full-time ministry.

How thankful I am that God allowed us to minister in that "little place." Years ago I clipped the following poem and placed it in my Bible. It is a reminder to me that the gift of contentment comes from being obedient to God's will, wherever you are. Does it speak to you today?

Little Things

"Father, where shall I work today?" I asked,
And my love flowed warm and free.
He pointed me out a tiny spot,
And said, "Tend that for Me."
I answered quickly, "Oh, no, not there!
Why, no one could ever see,
No matter how well my work was done.
Not that little place for me."
The word He spoke was not stern;
He answered me tenderly:
"Ah, little one, search that heart of thine.

Art thou working for them or Me?
Nazareth was a little place,
And so was Galilee."
—Author Unknown

Good Shepherd, thank You for helping me find contentment in every situation in life that You are leading in. May I sit at Your feet today . . . listen for Your voice . . . then follow.

December 15

Scripture: "A friend loves at all times, and a brother is born for adversity" (Proverbs 17:17, *NKJV*).

Ralph Waldo Emerson once said, "Friends are presents you give yourself." And it is true. To have a friend you must unwrap that gift of friendship by being loyal, faithful, and loving in adverse circumstances as well as good times.

Since my father was in the ministry and I married a minister, I have had the privilege of living in different parts of the country and meeting many friends. I consider each one a special gift from God. However, there are those long-lasting friendships that span many years and grow stronger with each year. Recently a special friend of more than 30 years gave me a gift I will always cherish. The gift was beautiful, and the thoughtfulness and love with which it was given made it more meaningful. The framed print read:

> Sisters by Heart . . . We've shared so much laughter,
> Shared so many tears. We've a spiritual bond that
> grows stronger each year. We're not sisters by birth,
> but we knew from the start, God put us together to be
> Sisters by Heart.

Jan and I are not together every day because we live in different states; however, when we do see each other we talk for hours, discussing every significant event in our lives and in the lives of those we care about. We are comfortable sharing our inner thoughts, coming to a deeper understanding of our own lives and our relationship. In addition to the times of fun and laughter, we've walked through times of adversity and heartache. By joining our hearts in prayer we have seen God work in miraculous ways in our lives and in the lives of our family members.

It has been said that friendship is at its best not in prosperity but in times of trouble. I have found this to be true. No, we're not sisters by birth, but our times of sharing laughter and tears has created a strong bond of friendship and sisterhood that grows stronger through the years.

The Bible says to have friends you must show yourself friendly (Proverbs 18:24). Since it is the season for giving, why not rekindle the gift of friendship by writing or calling a friend you have not heard from for some time. Or maybe you could make a new friend by inviting someone to lunch during the holidays. Don't forget, friends are presents you give yourself.

Lord Jesus, help me to unwrap the gift of friendship in the days ahead and always be a friend who is loyal and true. And thank You for a friend who loves through adversity as well as in times of joy and happiness.

December 16

Scripture: "The Angel of the Lord encamps around those who fear Him—who revere and worship Him with awe; and each of them He delivers" (Psalm 34:7, *Amp.*).

Angel mania best describes the fascination and focus placed on angels in the last few years around the world. Everything is coming up angels! Neiman Marcus carries an expensive perfume called Angel, and cherubs are available in all shapes and sizes. Guardian angel shoulder pins can be purchased at most department stores and card shops.

This Christmas the stores are filled with pictures, decorative jars, pillows, and afghans adorned with angelic beings. Seraphim Classics by Roman offers a splendid collection of exquisite angels. And of course, at this time of year we associate angels with the proclamation of Jesus' birth as they praised and glorified God saying, "Glory to God in the highest, and on earth peace, good will toward men" (Luke 2:14, KJV). We might even think of angels as gifts from God. Hebrews 1:14, speaking of angels, says, "Are they not all ministering spirits sent forth to minister for those who will inherit salvation?" (*NKJV*).

My grandmother who lived 97 years certainly viewed them in that light. She had an awesome experience in her devotions one morning not long before she died. This is her story:

> This particular morning I was filled with so much joy just thinking upon the goodness of the Lord and how wonderful He had been to me and my family that I could hardly contain myself. Overflowing with thanksgiving, I went into the living room to the piano and began playing and singing praises to the heavenly Father. I wasn't surprised when I sensed that my daughter who lived across the street had entered the house and joined me in singing. However, when I turned to acknowledge her presence, there was no one there. I went to the phone and called her. "Why did you leave so abruptly after we finished singing this morning?" She replied, "Mother, I have not been at your house at all today."

My grandmother then checked the doors and found they were still locked. Immediately she realized that she had been graced with a presence from another world that morning! What love and peace filled her heart. I am not surprised because the Bible says, "The angel of the Lord encamps around those who fear him" (Psalm 34:7), and the *Amplified Bible* goes on to say, "who revere and worship Him in awe."

That is exactly what she had been doing. Since one of the duties of angels is to praise and glorify God, why would it be difficult to believe they had joined her in singing? Yes, angels are gifts from God, sent as ministering spirits to provide guidance, assistance, and reassuring evidence of a loving God who forever watches over us!

Why not end this devotion by singing a hymn or chorus of praise to Jesus? First, read Revelation 5:11-14 which foretells the angels encircling the throne, singing: "Worthy is the Lamb, who was slain, to receive power and wealth and wisdom and strength and honor and glory and praise!" (v. 12).

Lord Jesus, thank You for the gift of angels who minister to those who are heirs of salvation. I offer praise and worship to You today for Your loving-kindness.

December 17

Scripture: "'For I know the plans I have for you,' declares the Lord, 'plans to prosper you and not to harm you, plans to give you hope and a future'" (Jeremiah 29:11).

It was October 1980. My husband and I, along with our two children, were living in the beautiful bluegrass country of Lexington, Kentucky. I was not aware that the next few months would hold threatening storms, but God's Word would be the gift of hope to give us strength in weathering these adverse and despairing winds.

My only sister, Miriam, who lives in Detroit, Michigan, called to say, "The doctor is going to remove a lump even though he believes it is benign. I think everything will be OK. But would you just pray?

On November 3, the terrible news came. Cancer! What a devastating word. The specialist revealed a bleak situation. The cancer was rare, but the kind that grows and spreads quickly. Her doctors gave us little hope that the spread of the cancer could be arrested.

Immediately I called ministers and wives throughout the state of Kentucky to intercede for her. Bill Stuthridge, a pastor in Kentucky, called the state parsonage the following Sunday morning. "I have a word from the Lord for your sister, Miriam," he said. "Please have her read Jeremiah 29:11. This is a promise for her."

When I called to give her the message, she was overwhelmed. "God gave me the same scripture in my devotions this morning. I opened my Bible and He spoke clearly to me first from Isaiah 21:12, "Turn again to God, so that I can give you better news. Seek for him, then come and ask again!" (*TLB*).

"Excitement filled my heart," she said. "I knew He was saying I could now hear a good report from the doctor. As I continued to read, I turned over randomly to Jeremiah 29:11, and hope filled my heart with the assurance that He would give me life," she declared. "And now He has confirmed His Word again!"

We cried and rejoiced together. That same day while Miriam was traveling to Harper Hospital to be admitted for exploratory surgery, she opened a book to read. She was amazed to discover it contained a story of a lady who had cancer. And guess what scripture was given for her comfort?—Jeremiah 29:11.

God wanted to speak through the storm loud and clear to make sure the message was received. Five days later, the results of the exploratory surgery came. Everything looked normal! To God be the glory!

That was 15 years ago. The gift of hope in this seemingly impossible situation was the best present our family could have ever received. Today, the doctors review Miriam's medical records and marvel that she is still alive.

If circumstances in your life bring turbulent winds of adversity, remember God has promised "plans to prosper you and not to harm you, plans to give you hope and a future."

Father, thank You because we do not have to fear the storms in our life. You walk with us through those times and give us hope for the days ahead.

December 18

Scripture: "God turned into good what you meant for evil" (Genesis 50:20, *TLB*).

While shopping at Perimeter Mall in Atlanta a couple of years ago, I became frustrated with the crowded parking lots, the bustling crowds pushing and shoving for sale items, the tinsel and bright lights being strung as early as September to beckon the consumer to buy more. Everything seemed hollow. I could see no visible sign of the Christ of Christmas. *This season becomes more commercialized every year,* I thought. *As far as the world is concerned, it's just another holiday to make money.*

Leaving the noisy mall and my intended gifts unpurchased, I felt disquieted in my spirit. As I pondered the situation, the Holy Spirit quietly and gently reminded me of the words Joseph spoke to his brothers who sold him into slavery: "God turned into good what you meant for evil" (Genesis 50:20, *TLB*). I believe He was saying to me, "You too can see Jesus in the things that seem unrelated to Him if you allow the Holy Spirit to enlighten your understanding."

I was excited a few days later when I found an article listing various items that could be used to teach spiritual truths to children at Christmas. The holidays could be turned into holy days in the midst of all the commercialism by simply unwrapping these nuggets—gifts from God's Word for this season. Perhaps you and your family can also benefit from the following examples:

The candy cane. Its shape reminds us of a shepherd's crook, and the words of Jesus: "I am the good shepherd, and know my sheep, and am known of mine" (John 10:14, KJV). The red stripes help us remember the blood of His sacrifice: "With his stripes we are healed" (Isaiah 53:5, KJV). The white of the candy cane symbolizes the purity of Jesus and is a reminder that He cleanses us: "Wash me, and I shall be whiter than snow" (Psalm 51:7, KJV). When turned upside down, the candy cane becomes the letter *J* . . . for Jesus!

Christmas lights. Jesus said, "I am the light of the world. Whoever follows me will never walk in darkness, but will have the light of life" (John 8:12).

Holly. The thorns and bright berries are vivid reminders of the crown of thorns Jesus wore, and the drops of His blood. Also, we can focus on the promise given in 1 Peter 5:4, "When the chief Shepherd shall appear, ye shall receive a crown of glory that fadeth not away" (KJV).

The Christmas wreath of evergreens. This represents eternal life that is ours in Christ Jesus. In ancient times after a race was won the wearing of a wreath symbolized a glorious victory! What could be more glorious than Jesus' birth and His defeat over sin, death, and the grave? "Be faithful until death, and I will give you the crown of life" (Revelation 2:10, *NKJV*).

After reading these verses that apply to the various ornaments used at Christmas, my heart overflowed with gratitude. I wondered how many other Christmas decorations were also associated with scriptures that could give new meaning to this festive season celebrating the birth of the Lord Jesus Christ. This subject will continue in tomorrow's devotion.

God, thank You for speaking to my spirit through the gift of Your Word and giving me a new perspective on the celebration of Christmas.

December 19

Scripture: "All things were created by him and for him" (Colossians 1:16).

Paul said of Christ: "All things were created by Him and for Him." Therefore, I can accept the traditional Christmas decorations as symbols of gifts from God: all things beautiful reflect His creation. Unwrapping these symbolic gifts became delightful because they reminded me once again to worship and celebrate the birth of Jesus Christ, our Lord and soon-coming King! Let them minister to you as well.

Christmas bells. Bells remind us of our High Priest, Jesus Christ. "But Christ came as High Priest, of the good things to come. . . . He entered the Most Holy Place once for all, having obtained eternal redemption" (Hebrews 9:11-12, *NKJV*). Also, Exodus 28:33-35 gives the details of the priestly robe and the significance of the gold bells which were attached to the hem of the skirt.

Christmas trees. Hosea 14:8 uses examples of nature to show God's faithfulness. "I am living and strong! I look after you and care for you. I am like an evergreen tree, yielding my fruit to you throughout the year. My mercies never fail" (*TLB*).

Christmas star. Perhaps the purest object in our Christmas symbolism comes directly from the Christmas story. "Where is He who has been born King of the Jews? For we have seen His star in the East and have come to worship Him" (Matthew 2:2, *NKJV*). A star also causes us to think beyond this star of Bethlehem to the words of Revelation 22:16, "I, Jesus . . . am the Root and the Offspring of David, and the bright morning star."

Christmas gifts. Let our giving be a reminder of God's unselfish gift to mankind. "For God so loved the world, that he gave his only begotten Son, that whosoever believeth in him should not perish, but have everlasting life" (John 3:16, KJV). Wrap each gift this year with a prayer that the receiver will be led into a deeper relationship with Christ. For indeed God's presence with us is His greatest present to us.

When I returned to the mall to purchase my last Christmas gifts, my attitude was different. I saw the twinkling lights on the trees, the bright evergreen wreaths with their shining red berries, all the gorgeous gift boxes, and I smiled. *I've always loved Christmas, and now it has a deeper meaning,* I thought. The decorations were beautiful! "The whole world is really unwrapping His gifts and celebrating His birth without even realizing it," I laughed quietly.

Idea: Give out candy canes to visitors who come to your house this year. Type the scriptures that explain their significance on a card and attach them with a ribbon. Kids will love it. Adults will too!

Jesus, thank You for reminding me that all things were created by You and for Your pleasure. Help me to share these wonderful gifts from Your Word with others this year.

December 20

Scripture: "Unless you change and become like little children, you will never enter the kingdom of heaven" (Matthew 18:3).

Every time a clock ticks a baby is born! There have been billions of births during the course of history, but never one like the birth of Jesus Christ. Sometimes as adults we become so familiar with the Christmas story that we lose the wonder and excitement of it all! Is this not what our Lord meant when He said, "Unless you change and become like little children, you will never enter the kingdom of heaven"?

This summer while vacationing in Florida with the family, my nephew Zachary, who is 2 years old, reminded me of the thrill and wonderment of a child. Whenever we stopped at blinking railroad lights, he squealed with excitement, anticipating the choo-choo train's arrival. The arrival of the train with its loud whistle, brought still louder cries of delight. Even dreary clouds and rain did not dampen Zachary's day. He found joy and satisfaction in the simple things.

As I approach this beautiful season of the year, I want to take a fresh look at the mystery of the incarnation of Jesus Christ, the Creator of the universe who was willing to come to earth as a tiny baby. I want to experience a childlike faith that will enable me to go beyond mere religious activity and enter into true worship.

How incredible is the scene in the stable. This babe in a manger was so mute, yet His coming was so vocal—the Word himself, unable to speak a word. The One who formed all parts of speech was powerless to speak a single word. Yet this child was the Lord of all heaven and earth. He was not just a product of the womb—He was the producer of the universe!

Yes, this year will be different because of the gift of wonder. I will stand in awe at the birth of the Christ child. I will bow at the manger and worship with rapture and sing with new meaning:

> O come, let us adore Him,
> O come, let us adore Him,
> O come let us adore Him,
> Christ, the Lord.

Jesus, this Christmas I want to once again see through the eyes of a child and capture the gift of wonder, joy, and excitement as I kneel at the manger in reverence and awe of Your greatness and power.

December 21

Scripture: "I call to remembrance my song in the night" (Psalm 77:6, KJV).

An article I read several years ago revealed that some of the world's finest perfumes are produced from roses which grow in the Balkan Mountains. These flowers must be gathered during the darkest part of the night to obtain their lovely fragrance. Workers start shortly after midnight and conclude within two hours. This work period is brief because scientific tests have shown that during this time the rose blossoms give forth their most pleasing scent. When daybreak comes, 40 percent of the aroma fades.

This reminds me of a profound truth. Some of the darkest, most difficult times in my life were also times of spiritual growth. I remember when my mother called me to say, "Your dad had another stroke and is in the hospital again. The doctor will not know the extent of the damage for at least 48 hours."

Her voice sounded very tired and weary. The last few years had been extremely stressful for the entire family because of my father's illness, the repeated setbacks, his confinement to a wheelchair, and now hospitalization. He was such a kind and patient man. Throughout his long illness he seldom complained, but always expressed the hope that he would get well and walk again. This time he was hospitalized for more than four weeks when my mother suddenly began experiencing severe chest pains. She was placed on the cardiac floor across the hall from my father. Fortunately, she had not suffered a heart attack but was experiencing extreme anxiety and stress which would lead to more serious problems if not treated. She needed medication and time to rest and heal.

My father, unable to walk, was transferred to a nursing home for further treatment and therapy. My sister and I were troubled. There were no easy answers.

These are the times in a Christian's life when adversity has value. If we are willing, adversity can draw us closer to the Rose of Sharon, filling our life with the precious aroma of His presence. I remember asking God to supply the strength and grace needed for the moment. Suddenly, like a burst of light my mind was flooded with the comforting words of this familiar song:

> Great is thy faithfulness,
> Great is thy faithfulness,
> Morning by morning new mercies I see.

All I have needed thy hand hath provided,
Great is thy faithfulness, Lord unto me.

What a wonderful God who lifts our spirits through the words of songs inspired from Scripture! Few psychologists would deny the benefits of music to lighten the spirits of the depressed, lift the downhearted, and bring joy to our worship. Yes, I agree with the psalmist's words, "I call to remembrance my song in the night." If you are going through a dark time, try unwrapping the gift of song. Go ahead, burst into singing!

> Looking back it seems to me
> All the grief which had to be
> Left me, when the pain was o'er,
> Richer than I'd been before.
> —Anonymous

Thank You, God, for giving harmony and meaning to my life in difficult times. While sitting at Your feet, the song in my heart has been revived and my spirit renewed.

December 22

Scripture: "Those who sow in tears will reap with songs of joy" (Psalm 126:5).

Have you ever felt like a crybaby and wished you could control the fountain of tears? Do you find yourself crying at the drop of a hat, at weddings as well as funerals? When you sing the "Star-Spangled Banner" do you get a lump in your throat and become teary-eyed?

Regardless of what many husbands say, tears can be beneficial. Doctors tell us there is an antiseptic agent in our tears that fights eye infection. Some psychologists tell us tears have a purifying quality that cleanses and refreshes the spirit. Perhaps you have experienced that feeling after a good cry. But have you ever thought of tears as being a special gift from God?

Charles H. Spurgeon defined tears as liquid prayers. According to God's Word, tears play a vital role in spiritual warfare. When we plant seeds with a spirit of brokenness, the results will be a harvest with rejoicing. This truth became a reality at our first pastorate in Kincaid, Illinois. A group of women met faithfully each Tuesday morning for prayer. One morning I felt especially impressed to pray for one mother's son whose name had been on the list for salvation for a long time. That day a spirit of weeping and intercession filled the room, and great rejoicing followed. I knew beyond a shadow of doubt that the reaping of this harvest would be soon.

The following Sunday when the altar call was given, this young man, prompted by the Holy Spirit, walked down the center aisle and gave his heart to God. Today, he is still faithfully attending church and serving Christ.

God is moved with compassion when parents, through the gift of tears, weep for the salvation of their children. Jeremiah 31:16, 17 is a promise that He sees the tears, and we can claim this verse for our sons and daughters: "Refrain your voice from weeping, and your eyes from tears; for your work shall be rewarded, says the Lord, and they shall come back from the land of the enemy. There is hope in your future, says the Lord, that your children shall come back to their own borders" (*NKJV*).

In Bible times, the Jews had an unusual practice of storing their tears in a tear bottle, or cup. The bottle had a wide rim which was placed under the eye to catch tears. The bottle then was corked and stored. In Luke 7:38, 44, it tells us that a woman poured out her tears on Jesus' feet. There is a possibility she may have emptied her tear bottle, giving Him all her past grief and sorrow.

David said in Psalm 56:8, "You number my wanderings; put my tears into Your bottle; are they not in Your book?" (*NKJV*). If God cares enough about our tears to keep a record of each one that drops from our eyes and even to bottle them, what love and compassion He must have for each of us! Remember, when you unwrap the gift of tears, they are liquid prayers—a language God understands and rewards.

Father God, may our hearts be broken with the things that break the heart of God. And thank You for the promise that if we sow in tears, we will reap in joy.

December 23

Scripture: "Then He put out His hand and touched him, saying, 'I am willing, be cleansed.' And immediately the leprosy left him" (Luke 5:13, *NKJV*).

Ladies, how would you like to lower your husband's blood pressure this year? Or better still, how would you like to add two years to your own life? Actually, these findings in recent studies on the incredible power of meaningful touch are mentioned in the book *The Blessing*, by Gary Smalley and John Trent. The book goes on to say that a study at UCLA found that to maintain emotional and physical health, men as well as women need eight to 10 meaningful touches each day. Now, this doesn't mean reaching over and quickly patting your husband or wife on the arm eight times and counting it for an entire day.

The study concluded by saying if some Type A men would receive a kiss from their wives every morning before leaving for work, they would live longer. And if the husbands would hug their wives several times a day, it would increase their life span by almost two years! Sounds good to me.

Jesus certainly knew the value of a meaningful touch. He not only touched the children and blessed them, but He touched the unclean. In His day no one would think of touching a leper. They were banished from society. If they dared come close, the people would actually throw stones to keep them away. Luke records the incident of a leper who came to Jesus "covered with leprosy" (v. 5). What did Christ do? He touched him! Instead of being afraid of the contagious disease of leprosy, Jesus himself became contagious and touched lives with His infectious love—and they were never the same. Recognizing that the man's deepest need was to be loved and accepted, Jesus by His actions displayed total acceptance and love—before He spoke to him or healed him.

Cleta and Albert Childers, my aunt and uncle, also reached out in love, touching the lives of those no one else wanted, and made a difference for eternity. Once a call came to the parsonage: "Could you possibly help my husband and me, Reverend Childers? A man we didn't know left two little girls about 2 and 4 years of age at our home and has not returned. They are in great need, and we do not have the means to care for them. I have contacted 15 ministers in the area, and they have not been able to assist us. You are our only hope."

So the pastor and his wife of the Kannapolis, North Carolina, Elm Street Church of God took the girls, Annie and Ethel, into their home. They held them, hugged them, and loved them. The newspaper and radio spread the news, and soon money, food, and clothing came in. The Elm Street Church of God in one Sunday alone gave over $10,000 (a sizable sum in 1944). Even Mr. C.A. Cannon, president of Cannon Mills, called to ask if he could be of assistance. As the pastor related the events concerning the children, Mr. Cannon responded, "Maybe we need an orphanage here in Kannapolis." He proceeded to give seven acres of land for such a home, and the initial plans were made to build a cottage.

In the meantime, the Childers family grew by three more homeless children. One baby was left on the front porch of the parsonage by someone seen leaving in a taxi. For nine months Cleta and Albert Childers lived in a crowded parsonage with five children, plus three of their own while construction was being completed on the cottage.

Today after 50 years, Annie and Ethel, two lovely Christian women, are still thanking Mom and Dad Childers for their love and acceptance and for touching their lives when no one else wanted them.

This Christmas as well as in the days ahead, you hold within your hands the power to make the difference in the lives of many the world has discarded—the homeless, the AIDS victim, the prisoner, the forgotten elderly.

Just as our heavenly Father gave His Son to a desperate world in need of a Savior, let us unwarp and give the gift of a meaningful touch to those we come into contact with.

Let's hug the lonely and forgotten as well as our loved one. Let's learn to shake and squeeze hands more frequently. Let's tenderly touch arms and shoulders more often.

Jesus, with a soft touch You communicated love to those rejected and abandoned by society. Help me to give the gift of a meaningful touch this Christmas to someone that possibly no one else will reach.

December 24

Scripture: "Do not be afraid, I bring you good news of great joy that will be for all the people" (Luke 2:10).

The Gospel of Luke tells us the lowly shepherds were the first to learn of Jesus' birth. Even though the shepherds cared for the Temple flock (1,000 lambs were sacrificed each year), they were still considered outcasts. The shepherds were also considered ceremonially unclean because they had to be in the fields for many weeks, unable to attend the synagogue or Temple sacrifices. So it must have been thrilling to the shepherds when God chose them to share the news of the long-awaited Messiah. This was indeed good news—the gift of joy had come to all people.

The testimony of a shepherd was not acceptable in a court of law in Israel in Jesus' day. But we read this account in Luke 2:17, 18: "Now when they had seen Him, they made widely known the saying which was told to them concerning this Child. And all those who heard it marveled at those things which were told them by the shepherds" (*NKJV*).

Yes, God entrusted to lowly shepherds—those not considered to be influential or important—the good news of the birth of His Son. They became witnesses to this event for generations to come. That fact changed my life.

Today I recall myself at the age of 5 or 6, kneeling at the feet of my grandmother in the upstairs bedroom of the old farmhouse in Asheville, North Carolina. The same good news the shepherds heard almost 2,000 years ago brought the gift of joy to my heart. I'm so happy this news is for all people—even children who are often considered insignificant. Since that night that occurred when I was still a child, my life has never been the same. Tucking me into bed, my grandmother said, "God gave the baby Jesus so that He might die for your sins, and then you will be able to live with Him forever in heaven."

After praying and asking Christ into my heart that eventful evening, I looked outside. Even the stars seemed to rejoice. They were dancing in the sky and twinkling more brightly than I had ever seen before. How grateful I was that from the first hours of His birth, my Lord identified with the poor, rustic, outcast shepherds—the last people anyone would expect to be visited by God with good news and great joy! This message brings real encouragement to me personally and possibly to you as well. We all feel weak and unimportant at times. But when we recall that night long ago, we can celebrate the birth of Jesus Christ in our hearts.

The shepherds were excited! They ran to the manger to see Jesus, the spotless Lamb of God. When they left, they went glorifying the Father.

This year as you place the baby in the manger and share the shepherd's story, why not also explain to your children and grandchildren the simple plan of salvation. They need to hear the good news so they too can experience the gift of joy. What a way to spend Christmas Eve!

Lord, thank You for showing great mercy to all the people in the earth. Help me to share the wonderful news of Jesus' birth and the joy of my salvation with others.

December 25

Scripture: "Thanks be to God for his indescribable gift!" (2 Corinthians 9:15).

A story in the *Wolf Magazine of Letters* told about a woman who purchased 50 Christmas cards without ever reading the message inside. She quickly signed all but one and in the rush to get them in the mail still did not take time to read what the cards said. The verse on the inside was completely overlooked. Can you imagine her embarrassment when a few days later she glanced at the one unmailed card and read the following words:

> This card is just to say,
> A little gift is on the way.

Needless to say, that gift was never received by anyone. Forty-nine disappointed people must have wondered what happened to their presents.

My daughter Tanya also wondered what happened to her present one year. When my children were small, they became ecstatic when the Christmas catalogs arrived from Sears and J.C. Penney. They poured over the pages for days, changing their minds a dozen times. All you could hear was, "Mother, can I have this doll? No, I like this one better."

My son, Todd, declared, "I want a red bike. Well, maybe I'd rather have a blue and white one instead." This Santa got more and more confused as the days passed. To help ole Santa out, I came up with a great solution, or so I thought. "Make a list of four or five toys you want most for Christmas," I instructed. "You will get these if at all possible." Of course there were five on each list.

That Christmas I searched frantically for an item one of the children asked for. After a thorough search, I realized the stores had sold out of this item and it would be impossible to fulfill my promise. As much as we intend to keep our word as parents, sometimes it simply is not possible, and we have to break a promise.

How different our heavenly Father's promises are to us. He not only promised a gift—"Behold, a virgin shall conceive, and bear a son, and shall call his name Immanuel" (Isaiah 7:14)—but He also gave it: "when the fulness of time was come, God sent forth his Son" (Galatians 4:4, 5, KJV).

On this Christmas Day as we celebrate the birth of Jesus, I want to bow and give thanks to God the Father for giving His Son and fulfilling His Word. Our scripture for today says it best: "Thanks be to God for His indescribable gift!"

Why not start a new tradition today in your family. Gather all the children around and read the Christmas story. Conclude your worship time by singing "Happy Birthday" to Jesus and share a cake together.

Dear Father, help me to celebrate with joy and thanksgiving today the wonderful gift of Your Son, Jesus Christ. Thank You that You not only promised . . . You gave.

December 26

Scripture: "You will go out in joy and be led forth in peace" (Isaiah 55:12).

One cold, wintery morning after moving to North Dakota I was having my devotional time, sharing with the Lord just how difficult this adjustment period was for my family. We were hundreds of miles from our family, friends, and the warm, loving church people back in Warren, Michigan. It has been said, "Minot is not the end of the world, but you can see it from there." Well, that particular day I felt like it was the end of the world!

As I continued my devotions, my prayer went something like this: "Lord, I trust Your sovereignty . . . but Minot? Lord, surely You have made a mistake this time. I am desperate. I need to hear a word from You today. Please speak to my spirit and bring peace to my heart, I pray."

I opened my Bible to Isaiah 55 and my eyes fell on verses 8 and 9. The words seemed to leap off the page: "For my thoughts are not your thoughts, neither are your ways my ways, saith the Lord. For as the heavens are higher than the earth, so are my ways higher than your ways, and my thoughts than your thoughts" (KJV).

As the tears flowed down my cheeks, I thought, *You certainly speak direct, Lord.* I continued reading because I knew He had more to say to me that day. Verse 12 said, "You will go out in joy and be led forth in peace; the mountains and hills will burst into song before you, and all the trees of the field will clap their hands."

He had promised to give me joy and peace. I became excited wondering how this was going to come about in my life. I continued reading verse 13: "Instead of the thorn shall come up the cypress tree, and instead of the brier shall come up the myrtle tree" (*NKJV*). I had certainly experienced the thorn and brier, but I wanted to know what God was saying to me about the cypress and myrtle trees. So I quickly went to the encyclopedia and found these interesting facts.

Both are evergreens and stay alive, green and growing, regardless of their surrounding circumstances. The cypress tree is a tall tree which adapts readily to various climates and situations. The myrtle is an attractive evergreen with shining blue-green leaves and fragrant white flowers. Even the bark and berries are fragrant, and manufacturers use them in making perfume. Both are often used as ornamental greens in garden settings.

I was in awe! While sitting at His feet that day, the Word of God spoke so forcefully to my spirit. My heavenly Father had confirmed that we were in the Dakotas by His divine appointment. He had promised that He would give the gift of peace to my heart, and even bring joy in the midst of it all. And then He said, "You are to remain alive, green, and growing regardless of circumstances and be willing to adapt readily to various situations. Only then can you bear precious fruit and give forth My fragrance so that others may be drawn to Me."

What consolation. What joy. What peace! And living in the Dakotas? Those four years proved to be one of the most enjoyable experiences of our ministry. God is faithful.

Try unwrapping the gift of peace today by trusting God in all circumstances of your life.

Dear Father, thank You for giving peace in the midst of my storm. May I always remember in times of discouragement to sit at Your feet. You are only a prayer away.

December 27

Scripture: "One of them, when he saw he was healed, came back, praising God in a loud voice. He threw himself at Jesus' feet and thanked him" (Luke 17:15).

Long after the festivities had past, I kept hearing the tune over and over again in my mind:

> We are His heart. . . . Is His heart beating?
> We are His hands. . . . Is His hand reaching?

This was the theme song for the children's presentation on August 2, 1995, at the 75th Anniversary—Diamond Jubilee Celebration of the Home for Children in Sevierville, Tennessee. My husband and I joined other special guests in the anniversary observance.

Since 1920 the Home has been caring for homeless, neglected, abused, and troubled children. Operating under the auspices of the Church of God Department of Benevolence as a residential child care and placement agency, the Home has cared for thousands of needy children since its inception.

On this particular night live testimonials were given by several who grew up at the home and were now leading successful lives in various parts of the country. All the testimonials were moving. One, however, given by Bill and Sheila Barton especially touched my heart. I will never forget what they said.

Sheila spoke first.

> I was the oldest of six children, and I would often go to the neighbors' garbage cans to find food for my brothers and sisters. Once in a while a neighbor would put out a bucket of fried chicken so I could find it. I think she knew we were hungry. When we were taken out of our home by the state, it was difficult to place us because we didn't want to be separated. No foster home wanted six children. The Home for Children, however, opened its arms and welcomed my family. We arrived with the clothes on our backs and a small bag containing the rest of our belongings. They took all six of us to the clothing store at the Home, and let us pick out six outfits for school and dress clothes for church. I was so upset because I knew I couldn't pay for all those clothes. The lady in the store detected my concern and said, "Honey, don't worry. You don't have to pay for them. They are free." I just want to say thank you tonight to the Church of God for loving me and giving my brothers and sisters a home.

By this time everyone was reaching for a hankie. Her husband, Bill, began:

> As a young boy I also came to the Home for Children to live after my mother's terrible accident which took her life. (He paused, choking back tears.) I had a difficult time at first, but with love and understanding, I made it. I just want to say tonight that the Home for Children is the best second home a child could ever have. Sheila and I fell in love at the Home, and when we became of age we married and left to begin our lives in another state. For several years we worked and we were happy. One night, however, I had a vision. I saw Jesus and the 10 lepers He had healed. Only one returned to thank Him. That night the Lord spoke to me and said, "Bill, I have healed you too. And I want you to be the one who returns to the Home to thank Me for what I have done for you."

By now there was not a dry eye among us.

For 10 years Sheila and Bill Barton have been house parents in one of the residential cottages at the Home. They are touching the lives of others who need to be made whole. It's their way of unwrapping the gift of thanksgiving for what God has done for them. True gratitude, like love, must find expression in actions, not words alone! I can still hear that song . . .

> We are His heart. . . . Is His heart beating?
> We are His hands. . . . Is His hand reaching?

Jesus, may my heart and hands reach out today to others in thankfulness for what You have done in my life. Help me to be that one who returns often to give You praise.

December 28

Scripture: "Blessed are those who mourn, for they will be comforted" (Matthew 5:4).

As I prepared dinner for the family, the ringing of the phone called me from the kitchen. I stopped briefly to stir the vegetables and check the meat browning in the oven. The aroma filled the room. Everything was ready! The unwelcome sound of the phone was heard again. *I hope this is not one of those long telephone conversations my husband often gets just about the time we sit down to eat,* I thought. *This happens almost every evening. Why didn't I take the phone off the hook so we could eat in peace. I hate warmed-up food.*

By the time I lifted the receiver upstairs, my husband had answered from the state office, located in the lower level of the parsonage in Minot, North Dakota. It was September 1, 1977, a day that would change our lives forever. The call was from a brother-in-law. He was crying. Something was wrong! My husband asked, "Ben, what is the matter?"

"There has been an accident," he replied. "Your mother was hit by a car while crossing the street in downtown Gatlinburg."

"How bad is it?" my husband asked. There was a long pause. Then between sobs he said, "I'm sorry, she didn't make it."

I rushed downstairs and threw my arms around my husband. Crying together, we tried to absorb the shock of the terrible news. Death with its dark clouds hung heavy over the room. We were filled with disbelief and despair.

Silently I prayed, "O Father, please help us through this ordeal. Send the comfort of the Holy Spirit to my husband and his family during the difficult days ahead." And then I stopped for a moment. "And, Father, forgive me for getting so caught up in the dailiness of life that I complain about insignificant things—phone calls, interruptions, cold food." It all seemed so trivial now.

The following days were filled with questions: What possible good could come from all this grief and sadness? . . . Why had God allowed this to happen? . . . Why this terrible tragedy?

There were no answers. After my husband returned home from the funeral, a friend felt impressed to give him a beautiful poem inscribed on a brass plaque. The poem didn't answer the *whys* of it all. However, it did give added assurance that God was still in control.

In the ensuing days and years this poem became a gift of comfort to my husband. Perhaps it will be the gift that strengthens you today.

The Weaver

My life is but a weaving
   Between my Lord and me,
I cannot choose the colors,
   He worketh steadily.
Oft-times He weaveth sorrow
   And I in foolish pride
Forget He sees the upper
   And I, the underside.
Not till the loom is silent
   And the shuttles cease to fly
Shall God unroll the canvas
   And explain the reason why.
The dark threads are as needful
   In the Weaver's skillful hand
As the threads of gold and silver
   In the pattern He has planned.
     —Author Unknown

Father, thank You for the Holy Spirit's gift of comfort that brings solace and peace in the midst of sadness and grief. You said, "Blessed are those that mourn, for they shall be comforted." I claim that blessing today.

December 29

Scripture: "Her children rise up and call her blessed" (Proverbs 31:28, NKJV).

"Life can be beautiful—even in the parsonage. Go ahead and dare to believe it, and set about to fulfill your plans!" These are the words my mother wrote describing her philosophy of life. As a child I remember her attempting to do just that—make life beautiful for all of us in the parsonage.

When we moved to a new church, the physical condition of the parsonage would sometimes be less than desirable. She never allowed discouragement to linger. More than once she accepted the challenge and set about improving the situation. A coat of paint, a new pair of curtains, or maybe just a familiar picture—she knew exactly what was needed to create a comfortable atmosphere, one that made our family feel at home.

Like the woman in Proverbs, my mother placed more emphasis on the beauty of the inner person than on material things. Her life and teachings reflected a spirit that comes only from a daily relationship with Jesus Christ. At our house the discipline of family devotions, prayer, and Bible reading took top priority. We seldom went to a doctor, but we did pray. If there was a problem at school, we prayed. If there was a problem with finances, we prayed. So at a tender age, I learned from my mother's example that prayer was as vital to living as the air I breathed.

Her attitude about the ministry also influenced my life tremendously. She believed when you took up residence in the parsonage, you were to remember that God placed you there and you were important. She would say, "Don't ever forget what a joy it is to belong, to be loved, and to have the privilege of being called the pastor's children." Yes, somehow my sister and I felt we were a small part of the high calling God had placed upon the lives of our parents. It was not a burden but rather a joy and an honor to serve God and live in the parsonage.

It is interesting to note that in a survey several years ago conducted by Columbia University that over one quarter of a million dollars was spent to reaffirm the premise that the home helps to form and mold attitudes and habits in a child which will last a lifetime. Their conclusion was that there is no second competitive force in the life of a child that can compare with the home. It marks them forever!

So I'm grateful that God unwrapped the gift of a godly mother and placed me in her home. My mother not only gave verbal instructions, but she also displayed a beautiful attitude, modeling Christ in her living. Her example provided a basis for character building and internalization of the Christian values I live by today. I can truly say, "Her children rise up and call her blessed."

Will your footprints lead your children to Christ? The secret . . . sitting at His feet.

The Secret

I met God in the morning
When the day was at its best,
And his presence came like sunrise,
Like a glory in my breast.

All day long the Presence lingered,
All day long he stayed with me,
And we sailed in perfect calmness
O'er a very troubled sea.

Other ships were blown and battered,
Other ships were sore distressed;
But the wind that seemed to drive them
Brought to us a peace and rest.

Then I thought of other mornings,
With a keen remorse of mind,
When I too had loosed the moorings,
With the Presence left behind.

So I think I know the secret,
Learned from many a troubled way;
You must seek him in the morning
If you want him through the day!

—Ralph S. Cushman

Father, thank You for a home that placed preeminence on knowing Jesus Christ as Lord. Help me to live a life that will influence my children to follow You.

December 30

Scripture: "Call unto me, and I will answer thee, and shew thee great and mighty things, which thou knowest not" (Jeremiah 33:3, KJV).

All night long my husband, Delbert, paced the floor in excruciating pain. We prayed for a miracle, asking the heavenly Father to remove the pain and give us the gift of healing. But the pain persisted, growing increasingly worse.

The initial tests revealed a kidney stone. However, one of the doctors detected something on the X-ray that alarmed him. Three other doctors were consulted, but all three agreed there was nothing on the X-ray but kidney stones. Convinced there was more, the attending doctor ordered further tests. The diagnosis came with the alarming announcement: "Cancer. The left kidney must be removed immediately."

Dr. Paul Y. Cho from Korea was speaking at the Mount Paran Church of God in Atlanta. Arrangements were made for Delbert to be anointed with oil and prayed for by Dr. Cho, the elders, and Pastor Paul Walker. Confident that he had received a miracle, we went back to the doctor and requested another CAT scan. The doctor consented but replied, "You already have a miracle. It's a miracle we found the cancer this soon." Still believing for complete deliverance, we proceeded with the scan. We were shocked to again hear the report—cancer. The kidney had to be removed.

Waves of doubt, disbelief, and fear overcame me. Hadn't we obeyed His Word . . . claimed His promises . . . fasted . . . prayed . . . believed for a good report? Doesn't God still give us the gift of healing?

Suddenly, the Holy Spirit calmed my spirit with an indescribable peace that indeed "passes all understanding." God is always faithful to His Word . . ."a very present help in trouble." The Holy Spirit quickened my memory with words from Isaiah 53:8, 9: "For my thoughts are not your thoughts, neither are your ways my ways, declares the Lord. As the heavens are higher than the earth, so are my ways higher than your ways and my thoughts than your thoughts."

One evening before the surgery, Delbert sat alone in the den, not knowing if this was a life-and-death situation. Suddenly he felt compelled to get a Bible—*The Living Bible*—which he had placed on a shelf months before. This cherished book had belonged to his mother. It was given to him by Mrs. Randall Frashier upon his arrival in North Georgia as overseer. She and her husband were pastoring the Bremen Church of God where my father-in-law had pastored before the fatal accident my mother-in-law had on September 1, 1977. For more than 10 years Mrs. Frashier had preserved this Bible, hoping to find a family member to give it to.

Holding the Bible in his hands, Delbert read Psalm 91. When he came to the last two verses, the words leaped off the page: "When he calls on me I will answer; I will be with him in trouble, and rescue him and honor him. I will satisfy him with a full life and give him my salvation" (*TLB*).

I will satisfy him with a full life. This was his answer. He was going to live! The room was filled with praises, flowing from a heart of gratitude and thanksgiving. Depression and fear were replaced with hope and faith.

On November 16, 1991, a radical nephrectomy was performed,

removing Delbert's left kidney. A few days after surgery the doctor delivered more bad news: "The cancer has gone beyond the kidney wall. More treatment is necessary."

As I thanked the doctor and prepared to leave, he reminded me, "You know, we have already had one miracle."

I responded, "And I'm expecting another."

We did get a second miracle. An experimental drug called interferon was on the market for treating kidney-cancer patients with good results. However, doctors could not prescribe it. They could only submit my husband's name and medical data to the Emory University Medical Center where the selection for recipients was made by the experimental team which used a screening process based on information fed into a computer.

In a few weeks the answer came. Delbert was selected to receive this wonder drug, which would otherwise have cost thousands of dollars, absolutely free.

Oh, the providence and sovereignty of Almighty God! Man's reach, as extensive as it is, is limited. Prayer and the gift of miracles associated with prayer know no limits. They have no boundaries! Unwrap yours today.

Thank You, Father, for the gift of miracles. Thank You for skilled doctors and technicians who administer knowledge, medicine, and treatments.

December 31

Scripture: "A man has joy by the answer of his mouth, and a word spoken in due season, how good it is!" (Proverbs 15:23, *NKJV*).

It was Sunday. The weather was cold, gloomy, and dreary in Warren, Michigan. The pastor's family was preparing for church. Our children were small at the time and for some reason this day just didn't get off to a good start. They woke up cross and began arguing about the clothes they were to wear to Sunday school.

Breakfast was no better. The cereal was not right. The squabbling continued: "Mom, he is staring at me," Tanya yelled. "I am not," declared Todd vehemently.

Turmoil, strife, and confusion would best describe the morning. Because of all the distractions and hassle, we were running behind time. Since my husband would almost rather die than be late, we got into a disagreement in the car, and exchanged unkind words. However, when we pulled into the church parking lot, we adjusted our halos and went inside.

Immediately following the morning worship service, a young

woman who had recently accepted Christ, said to me, "It must be just wonderful being married to that man" (talking about my husband). "I was so blessed by what he had to say this morning. He always seems to know how to speak just the right words to encourage and lift me up."

As she turned and walked away she was saying, "It must be wonderful being married to him." *Well*, I thought. *I wish he would have spoken some of those kind words at home this morning and blessed me a little bit.* But I graciously accepted her comments, said "Thank you," and went on my way.

Later, as I pondered the events of the day, I read several passages of Scripture from one of my favorite books—Proverbs. "A gentle answer turns away wrath, but a harsh word stirs up anger" (15:1). "A man has joy by the answer of his mouth, and a word spoken in due season, how good it is" (15:23, *NKJV*). "Pleasant words are a honeycomb, sweet to the soul and healing to the bones" (16:24). "Let no corrupt communication proceed out of your mouth, but what is good for necessary edification, that it may impart grace to the hearers" (Ephesians 4:29, *NKJV*).

The Holy Spirit gently reminded me that my attitude had not been so great that morning, either. The words I had spoken certainly were not pleasant and gentle words that would bring healing, build up, or edify anyone. And grace—something you need but don't deserve—certainly wasn't evident. Asking the Father for forgiveness, I determined to daily unwrap the gift of kind words to give as presents to others—especially those I loved the most, members of my family.

Mark Twain was aware of the power of words. "I can live for two months on one good compliment," he once said. Since today is the last day of the old year and tomorrow is a new beginning, why not make a conscious effort to speak words of kindness to at least one person each day for the next 365 days, even if they don't deserve it. Make yourself accountable. While sitting at His feet, record in your prayer journal the lives you have touched. Remember, "Pleasant words are a honeycomb, sweet to the soul and healing to the bones." Also "a word spoken in due season, how good it is!"

> Kind words can be short and easy to speak,
> but their echoes are truly endless.

> —Mother Teresa

Father, may I learn to be obedient to Your Word in the days ahead and look to You for the right time to speak, and gently unwrap the gift of kind words. Then I will experience joy by the answer of my mouth.